THE MILITARY ENLIGHTENMENT

THE MILITARY ENLIGHTENMENT

WAR AND CULTURE IN THE FRENCH
EMPIRE FROM LOUIS XIV TO NAPOLEON

Christy Pichichero

CORNELL UNIVERSITY PRESS
Ithaca and London

Copyright © 2017 by Cornell University

All rights reserved. Except for brief quotations in a review, this book, or parts thereof, must not be reproduced in any form without permission in writing from the publisher. For information, address Cornell University Press, Sage House, 512 East State Street, Ithaca, New York 14850. Visit our website at cornellpress.cornell.edu.

First published 2017 by Cornell University Press
First paperback printing 2020

Library of Congress Cataloging-in-Publication Data

Names: Pichichero, Christy, 1976– author.
Title: The Military Enlightenment : war and culture in the French Empire from Louis XIV to Napoleon / Christy Pichichero.
Description: Ithaca : Cornell University Press, 2017. | Includes bibliographical references and index.
Identifiers: LCCN 2017006129 (print) | LCCN 2017008106 (ebook) | ISBN 9781501709296 (cloth) | ISBN 9781501712296 (ret) | ISBN 9781501709654 (pdf)
Subjects: LCSH: War and society—France—History—18th century. | Military art and science—France—History—18th century. | France—History, Military—18th century. | Enlightenment—France—Influence. | French literature—18th century—History and criticism. | Military art and science in literature.
Classification: LCC DC46.7 .P53 2017 (print) | LCC DC46.7 (ebook) | DDC 306.2/7094409033—dc23
LC record available at https://lccn.loc.gov/2017006129

ISBN 978-1-5017-5206-3 (paperback)

To my family

Contents

Acknowledgments ix

Introduction: What Is Military Enlightenment? 1

1. The French Military Enlightenment: Figures, Forces, and Forms 25

2. Before Fraternity: Martial Masculinity, Sociability, and Community 65

3. Humanity in War: Military Cultures of *Sensibilité* and Human Rights 110

4. A Nation of Warriors: The Democratization of Heroism 151

5. The Dialectic of Military Enlightenment: The Revolutionary and Napoleonic Eras 192

Epilogue: The Modern Heritage 230

Notes 241

Index 289

Acknowledgments

I am grateful to many people and institutions for their support in writing this book.

Under the benevolent sun of "the Farm," my dissertation advisors and mentors at Stanford were key advocates of this project. I owe a great debt to Hans Ulrich "Sepp" Gumbrecht, Dan Edelstein, and Keith Michael Baker for their incredible insights, encouragement, and guidance, from my doctoral research and early articles through the major expansion and transformation that became this book. Robert Harrison, Joshua Landy, John Bender, and Roland Greene were also fantastic interlocutors and supporters of my work, as were the staff, faculty, and postdoctoral fellows in Stanford's Introduction to the Humanities Program. Research, writing, and visiting scholar fellowships from the Georges Lurcy Foundation, the Stanford Humanities Center, King's College University of Cambridge, the École normale supérieur (rue d'Ulm), and Stanford's Gerald J. Lieberman Award were vital to the development of the project and to supporting my archival research in France. A Mathy Junior Faculty Award from George Mason University and a Tyree-Lamb Fellowship from the Society of the Cincinnati provided funding and time to complete a second phase of archival research that brought the book from a continental focus to a global one. Special thanks go to John Garrigus for his advice on archival sources on Saint-Dominigue and to staff members of the Service historique de la défense at the château de Vincennes, the Archives nationales (Pierrefitte and Paris), and the Bibliothèque national de France as well as Luc Forlivesi at the château de Chambord for facilitating my work. The participants in the 2015 Bloomington Workshop on the theme of care at Indiana University helped me to sharpen my arguments. Members of the Washington, DC region's Old Regime Group also provided excellent feedback on the project and on chapter three of the book.

A number of people read parts or the full manuscript of this book in draft form: Jack Censer, Jennifer Heuer, Howard Brown, Clifford Rogers, John Lynn, Alan Forrest, and Dan Edelstein. I am forever in their debt for their close scrutiny of the manuscript and comments that greatly enhanced the book in its final form. I am deeply grateful to Guy Rowlands, Rafe Blaufarb, and David A. Bell for their mentorship, support, and keen observations and suggestions regarding my work in the past years. I would also like to thank the two anonymous readers of the manuscript for their detailed and constructive critiques that helped me to improve the work in critical ways. Endless appreciation goes to Michael McGandy at Cornell University Press, who believed in this project from our first encounter at the AHA and whose insights have transformed this book into a work of scholarship far superior than it was at its inception. Thank you also to Bethany Wasik, Susan Barnett, Sara Ferguson, and the rest of the team at Cornell, Michelle Witkowski at Westchester Publishing Services, and indexer Kay Banning for their kindness and efficiency in the process of getting this book through press.

Parts of chapters 2 and 3 were previously published in article form in "Le Soldat Sensible: Military Psychology and Social Egalitarianism in the Enlightenment French Army," *French Historical Studies*, Volume 31, Number 4 (Fall 2008), 553–80; and "Moralizing War: Military Enlightenment in Eighteenth-Century France" in *France and Its Spaces of War: Experience, Memory, Image*, ed. Daniel Brewer and Patricia Lorcin (New York: Palgrave Macmillan, 2009).

Long before I imagined pursing graduate studies and joining the professoriate, the teachers at my public high school, Pittsford Sutherland, and my professors at Princeton University encouraged me to be hungry and think big in my academic work. I feel profound gratitude toward my advisors in comparative literature at Princeton—Robert Hollander, Sandra Berman, and April Alliston—for encouraging me to take on ambitious interdisciplinary projects. Words of camaraderie and incredible artistic opportunities offered to me by Cornel West and Toni Morrison helped me to find a voice, a sense of personal legitimacy, and a newfound courage to make a place for myself as a student, an artist, and later a professor.

My colleagues in Modern and Classical Languages, History and Art History, Women and Gender Studies, and the Center for History and New Media at George Mason, in addition to my wonderful students, have been unflinching supporters of my work and career. Through the years, my hometown of Rochester, NY and the places that I have inhabited—Princeton, the Eastman School of Music, Stanford, Cambridge, ENS, Paris, the San Francisco Bay Area and Washington, DC—provided me with a treasure trove of brilliant, creative, and generous friends who have blessed me with conversation, advice, music making, and good times that were the antidote to the stresses of writing my first book.

The greatest thanks of all goes to my family: my parents Angela Bly Pichichero and Michael Pichichero, my brother David Pichichero, my extended family in the US and in France, my husband Thomas Escourrou, and our two daughters. Thomas, you are my rock, my partner, and in all ways my better half. From stem to stern, I could not have written this book without you. Cléa, at the mere age of four, you have twice the spirit and tenacity that I ever had. I learn from you every day and cannot wait to see where you are going in life. Marion, you came into the world in the same year as this book. Thank you for being the sweetest baby—sleeping lots, complaining little, smiling often—which has made it *slightly* easier for your parents to juggle our careers and raising you and your big sister. Our little family brings me support, hope, joy, and meaning every day. Thank you. This book is for you.

THE MILITARY ENLIGHTENMENT

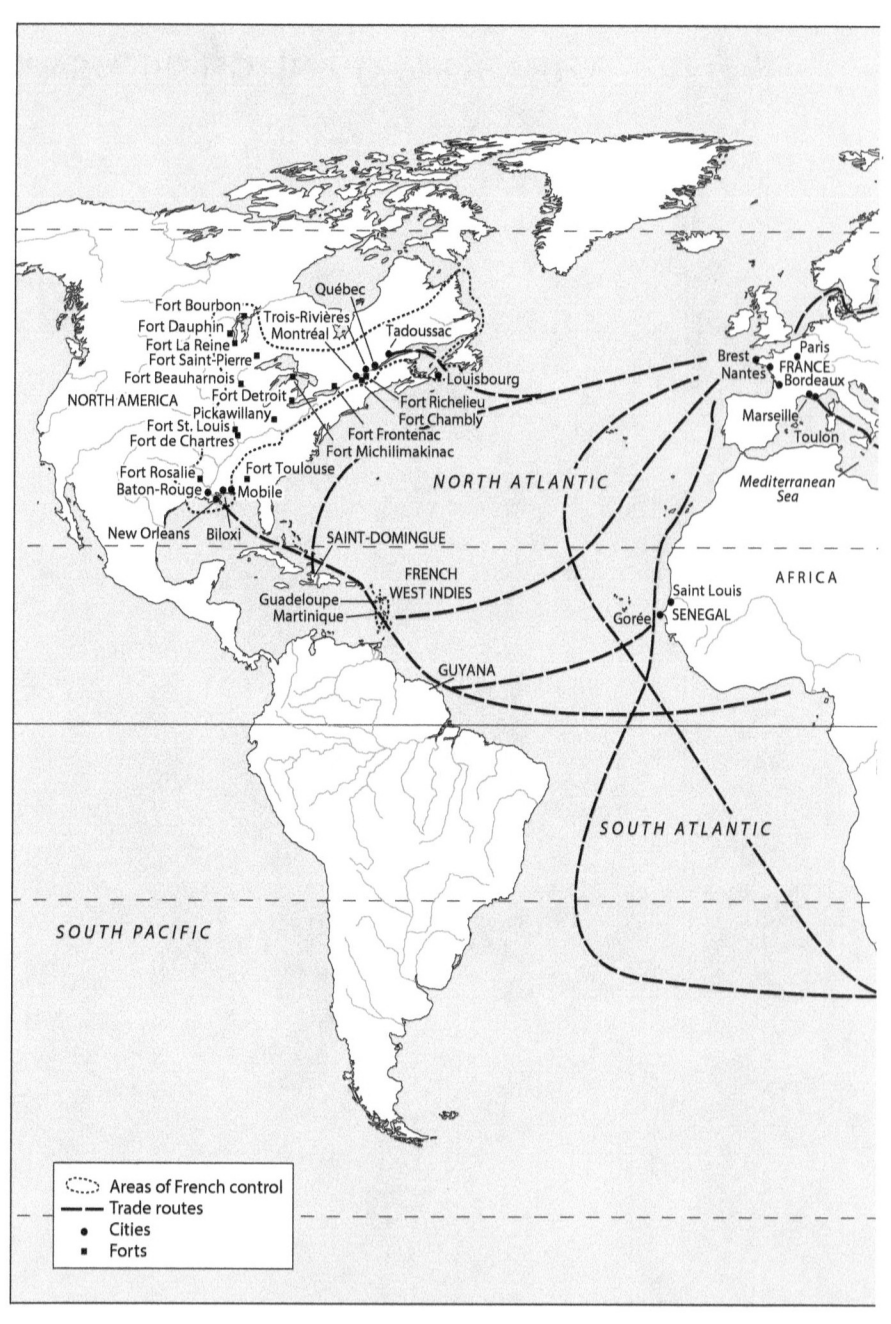

Map of French mercantile empire and overseas colonies, circa 1750. Courtesy of Bill Nelson Maps.

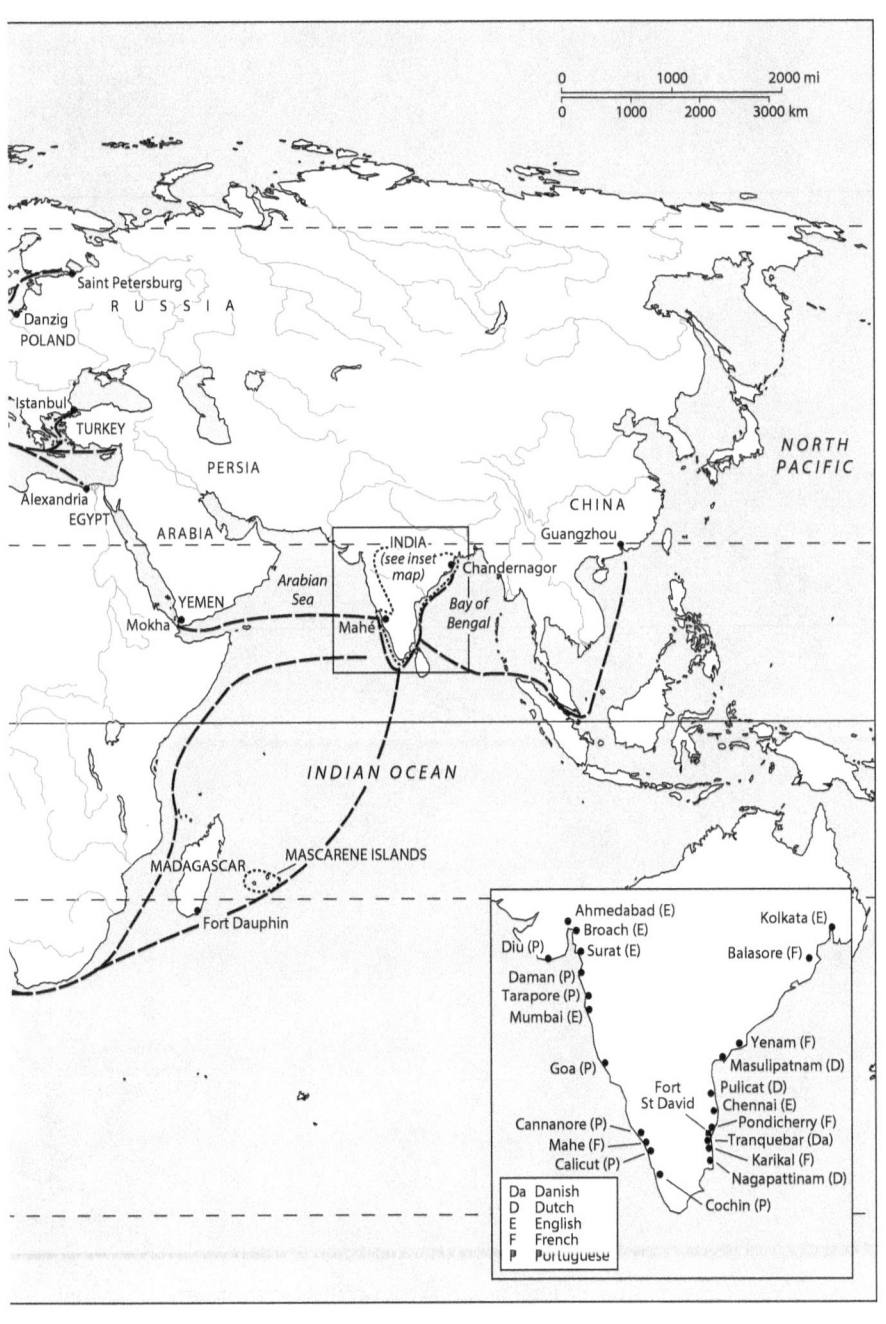

Introduction

What Is Military Enlightenment?

> *Philosophers! Moralists! Burn all your books . . . war is an inevitable scourge.*
>
> —Voltaire, "War," *Philosophical Dictionary* (1764)

No one in the eighteenth century needed Voltaire in order to know that war was destructive, horrific, tragic. Recognizing and lamenting the atrocities of war had become an expectation, even among members of the armed forces. Deviation from this perspective was frowned upon. At the battle of Fontenoy in 1745—one of the great victories of the eighteenth-century French army, but also one that counted nearly twenty thousand casualties—King Louis XV's sixteen-year-old son and heir, the dauphin (Louis Ferdinand de France, 1729–1765), was criticized for being insensitive to the carnage. René-Louis de Voyer de Paulmy, marquis d'Argenson (1694–1757), was serving as secretary of state for foreign affairs and remarked with opprobrium that the dauphin was "looking tranquilly out at the naked corpses, anguishing enemies, and smoking wounds." In a candid and heart-wrenching letter to Voltaire (nom de plume of François-Marie Arouet, 1694–1778), the marquis expressed his dismay in observing that a number of France's young heroes had not yet learned to disdain war's slaughter, what d'Argenson called an *inhumaine curée*, an inhuman scramble for spoils. For his own part, the marquis admitted that his "heart" failed him as he looked out at the grisly spectacle of the battlefield. Unable to hold back his emotion and horror, he turned away to vomit. "Triumph is the most beautiful thing in the world," he wrote. "The cries of 'Vive le Roi!' while waving hats in the air atop bayonets; the compliments of the king to his warriors; royal visits to the trenches, villages, and

1

redoubts that are still intact after battle; the joy, the glory, the tenderness. But the price of all of this is human blood and shreds of human flesh."[1]

D'Argenson's attitude toward war reflects "military enlightenment," an expression that seems an oxymoron at first.[2] Are not war and its agents—what Voltaire referred to as state-sponsored mass murder and brigandage enacted by organized bands of assassins—antithetical to the projects of enlightened pacifism, cosmopolitanism, humanitarianism, and progress in human civilization? The answer is unequivocally no. From the late seventeenth century through the eighteenth century, these seemingly antipodal phenomena were inextricably connected. War, military affairs, and enlightenment came together and constituted one of the greatest challenges, debates, and fights for progress of the century.

The notion of military enlightenment becomes intelligible in view of a historical definition of the Enlightenment.[3] Defining the Enlightenment, also known as Lumières, Aufklärung, Illuminismo, or Ilustración, is as contentious today as it was during the eighteenth century, although people of that time seemingly recognized it as a phenomenon that was French in origin.[4] The Enlightenment can be identified as a historically locatable phenomenon due to a number of developments that historians have pinpointed. First and foremost, as Dan Edelstein argues, the Enlightenment developed as a narrative by which people of the late seventeenth and early eighteenth centuries viewed themselves as "enlightened" compared to antiquity and other preceding historical times. According to this narrative, which grew out of the Quarrel of the Ancients and Moderns that took place in French academies, "the present age (*siècle*) was 'enlightened' (*éclairé*) because the 'philosophical spirit' of the Scientific Revolution had spread to the educated classes, institutions of learning, and even parts of the government."[5] Participants in the Military Enlightenment saw themselves as actors in a history of progress and they shared a conviction that the functioning of the armed forces and the conditions of warfare more generally needed to be improved. In the name of advancement in these areas, agents of the Military Enlightenment applied a critical philosophical spirit, or *esprit philosophique*, to acquire a deep understanding of war and the military, then proposed and implemented a myriad of reforms.

What is more, agents of the Military Enlightenment engaged in and generated what Clifford Siskin and William Warner consider to be another hallmark of the Enlightenment, mainly, "new, or newly important" forms of communication, protocol, and mediation that proliferated during the eighteenth century: newspapers, magazines, reference works, secret societies, learned academies, coffeehouses, the postal system, and more.[6] These media, along with the overarching narrative described above, helped to foster what J. G. A. Pocock, Dorinda Outram, and others see as the discursive context of the Enlightenment as "a series of interlocking, and sometimes warring problems and debates" or "flash-points where intellectual projects changed society and government on a world-wide basis."[7]

One of the most significant of these flash points—in scope, perceived importance during the eighteenth century, and legacy for modern society—pertained to war and the military. As Madeleine Dobie remarks, this period saw "the appearance of the first true metadiscourse on the aims and effects of war."[8] This metadiscourse was in part philosophical, contemplating the nature of war and its rightful conduct, ideal martial characteristics, the relationship between military service and citizenship, and the costs of war in economic, political, moral, physical, and emotional terms. The metadiscourse was also practical and technical—indeed military—aiming to effect palpable change in mentalities and practices pertaining to uniforms, weaponry, tactics, drill, and medicine. These dialogues and debates were not bounded by the monarch's chambers in Versailles, nor were they confined to the army, the navy, and their administrations. They engaged a far greater public: *philosophes* (public intellectuals of the day), literate elites, playwrights, poets, novelists, artists, political theorists, historians, doctors, mathematicians, and engineers. They were vital for members of the aristocratic *noblesse d'épée* (nobility of the sword), whose cultural identity and justification of socioeconomic privilege were tied to warfare.[9] They were also crucial for common folk of France who watched their sons march off to war, lodged soldiers in their homes, and shouldered the tax burdens that financed the many wars of the seventeenth and eighteenth centuries. War and the military were, in the most pervasive and profound sense, arenas of national concern.

This constitutes a new understanding of military enlightenment and of the French Enlightenment more broadly. Scholars of the latter have largely been unaware of or have not attributed sufficient importance to the centrality of war and the military in Enlightenment thought and reform. This is the case even in the *Cambridge Companion to the French Enlightenment*, an interdisciplinary edited volume published in 2014 in which each essay presents "a concise view of an important aspect of the French Enlightenment, discussing its defining characteristics, internal dynamics and historical transformations."[10] Despite its excellent intellectual rigor, the *Companion* nevertheless excludes any direct or sustained treatment of war. This omission is shocking given that the greatest philosophical, scientific, literary, economic, artistic, and political minds of the period dedicated considerable energies to this most topical subject. Similarly, military historians have underestimated the scope and culture of the Military Enlightenment. Some have imagined it to be a discussion among martial specialists of the time, and others have simply mentioned its existence as a given without further exploration. Cultural histories of war and the armed forces in early modern France have illuminated important themes such as Amerindian-French relations, citizen armies, discipline and soldierly honor, and the individual's relationship to war.[11] However, these studies do not explore the larger movement of which these themes were a part.

The Military Enlightenment was thus a part of the broader phenomenon of Enlightenment, following its general chronology, engaging in the same narrative and media, and embracing *esprit philosophique* in order to make war and military endeavors reflective of an enlightened age.[12] Philosophically and politically, participants brought a wide range of perspectives: some were atheists, others were deists; some promulgated Christian morality while others embraced concepts of secular moral philosophy; some championed a mechanistic *esprit de système* or *géomètre* and sought universal principles while others adopted an *esprit de finesse* that acknowledged human fallibility when confronting infinite contingencies; some advocated classical republicanism while others were unabashed royalists. Despite this diversity, an overarching project of the Military Enlightenment emerged, one that entailed a bipartite ambition. The first aim was to wage war only when necessary and to do so effectively and efficiently in order to achieve martial objectives while sparing costs and precious resources, especially manpower. The second goal was to wage war humanely and in a fashion that reflected the compassion, morality, rationality, and dignity of the human race.

This central project and the specific historical context in which it developed make it possible to refer to the movement explored in this book as "*the* Military Enlightenment." However, a transhistorical process that began during the long eighteenth century and continued on in the centuries that followed—a lowercase military enlightenment—was also at play. While agents of the Military Enlightenment aimed to effect immediate changes in behavior and policy in their own era, their theories, practices, and vocabulary set up paradigms for thought and action in the military sphere that persist until today. The Military Enlightenment therefore represents an important milestone in the history of what David A. Bell calls the "culture of war" and the military.[13]

Several aspects of the culture of war and the mentality toward it made the military sphere a main flash point of the French Enlightenment. These factors bear explaining. The first was a generalized belief that war was an inevitable part of human nature and society. The eighteenth century is famously bookended with plans for perpetual peace proposed by Charles-Irénée Castel, abbé de Saint-Pierre (1658–1743), in 1713 and by Immanuel Kant (1724–1804) in 1795. Their hopes were obliterated by the mass numbers and global scope that characterized war in the decades after they penned their treatises, from the War of Austrian Succession (1740–1748) and the Seven Years' War (1756–1764) to the Revolutionary and Napoleonic Wars (1792–1815). Apart from Saint-Pierre and Kant, however, the unlikelihood of perpetual peace came as no surprise to most denizens of the long eighteenth century. People believed, as Voltaire did, that war was not just a scourge, but an "inevitable scourge." As many primatologists of today still maintain, Voltaire thought that humankind was naturally aggressive, a trait we share with animals:

> All animals are perpetually at war; every species is born to devour another. There are none, even sheep and doves, who do not swallow a prodigious number of imperceptible animals. Males of the same species make war for the females, like Menelaus and Paris. Air, earth, and water are fields of destruction. It seems that God having given reason to men, this reason should teach them not to debase themselves by imitating animals, particularly when nature has given them neither arms to kill their fellow creatures nor instincts which lead them to suck their blood. Yet murderous war is so much the dreadful lot of man, that except for two or three nations, there are none whose ancient histories do not represent them as armed against one another.[14]

Historical and ethnographic writings of the era confirmed the conviction that war was inherent to human civilization in all places at all times in history.[15] Even Jean-Jacques Rousseau (1712–1778)—who countered Thomas Hobbes's (1588–1679) vision of humanity as "war of all against all"—acquiesced that men existing in society meant men at war.

In addition to being an inexorable part of human civilization, war was viewed as necessary for sovereign states during the long eighteenth century, which has been called the "Second Hundred Years' War" (c. 1689–c. 1815). From 1672 to 1783 alone, France was at war for 50 out of 110 years and engaged in six large-scale conflicts. During this period, questions of colonial power and dynastic *gloire* eclipsed religion as a principal motivation for international war. As the French foreign and military minister Étienne-François duc de Choiseul (1719–1785), remarked, "Colonies, commerce and the maritime power which accrues from them will decide the balance of power upon the continent."[16] James Whitman argues that in this balance of power, war was "a kind of formal legal procedure used exclusively by sovereigns to claim rights through victory."[17] Lawyers working within the framework of *jus victoriae*, the law of victory in battle, sought to answer critical questions: *"How do we know who won?"* and *"What rights can the victor claim by virtue of this victory?"*[18] The stakes of *jus victoriae* were high, and the demands on globally oriented fiscal-military states were extreme. By the epoch of the War of Spanish Succession (1701–1714), French annual military expenditures were double those of the Dutch War (1672–1678). Military expenditures skyrocketed across Europe as states were increasingly responsible for the recruitment and maintenance of troops as well as for funding continued naval expansion, army barracks, more extensive fortifications, and other military equipment whose prices had risen significantly.[19] Under crushing financial pressure due to massive war-related deficits, a pattern emerged in which intermittent phases of intensified conflict (1688–1714, 1739–1763, 1787–1815) were followed by periods of peace during which states attempted to recuperate their domestic finances and prepared for future war.[20]

Many believed that war, in addition to being necessary in a mercantilist and colonialist age, was beneficial for the reputations of sovereigns and their states. The historians Joël Félix and Frank Tallett assert that "governments and the ruling elite, together with a significant, if unknowable, section of public opinion, accepted that France's prestige demanded both pre-emptive and reactive military action. This was certainly the case for Louis XIV [(1638–1715)] and Napoleon Bonaparte [(1769–1821)], but it was also the case during the reigns of Louis XV [(1710–1774)] and Louis XVI [(1754–1793)] . . . War ultimately provided the most telling verdict on national worthiness and the ruler's qualities of leadership."[21] As John A. Lynn shows, the kingly dynastic and aristocratic culture of *gloire*—the desire for glory and esteem—was a fiery force that consumed Louis XIV and blazed on through the eighteenth century.[22] Geopolitics and the paradigm of *gloire* conspired to fuel a belief that war was, perhaps justifiably, here to stay.

The metadiscourse on war was increasingly urgent as unprecedented numbers of combatants fought on warfronts that spanned the globe. During this era, most European states maintained forces four to five times larger than those of two centuries earlier.[23] In France, military forces went from 50,000 to 80,000 under the Valois kings and Louis XIII (1601–1643), then doubled to 253,000 during the Dutch War and to 360,000 during the Nine Years' War (1688–1697) under Louis XIV.[24] The Sun King's minister of finance, Jean-Baptiste Colbert (1619–1683), mounted a formidable French battle fleet—ninety-three battleships larger than 1,000 tons by 1695—that rivaled the English and Dutch fleets in quality if not quantity.[25] In the long eighteenth century, then, humankind's belligerence engaged a greater number of people in a greater number of places and at a far greater cost than in previous times. Given these high stakes, it is not surprising that the arena of warfare attracted the zealous attention of Enlightenment thinkers and reformers.

Making "Good War"

The disheartening sense of war's inevitability, necessity, and overwhelming scale did not breed resignation or apathy. The armed forces, the intelligentsia, and an engaged public took an active, even optimistic, approach that was also grounded in their understanding of war. Dictionary and encyclopedic definitions of war from the period are revealing in this regard. The entry on war, "Guerre," in the first edition of the *Dictionnaire de l'Académie française* (1694) defined it as a quarrel between princes or sovereign states whose outcome is determined by arms. Among the usages of the term cited near the beginning of the entry is "faire bonne guerre," to "make good war": to maintain in warfare "all of the humanity and civility [*honnesteté*] that the laws of war permit." War, as described in the *Dictionnaire*, could be an activity that reflected humankind's dignity and morality or, conversely, it could liken humans to ferocious beasts of prey. The entry for war in the *Encyclopédie, ou dictionnaire raisonné des sciences, des arts et des métiers*, published in France between 1751 and 1772 and edited by the *philosophes* Denis Diderot (1713–1784) and Jean-Baptiste le Rond d'Alembert (1717–1783), replicates this definition.[26]

These characterizations underscore central tenets of the Military Enlightenment. First, they communicate an ontology of war as a phenomenon whose principles, terms, and conduct are subject to human agency and inquiry. As the crusades and religious warfare faded from view, so did the concept of divinely ordained and determined "just war."[27] War became an activity whose justifications, processes, and outcomes were of human devising. This humanist approach was inherited from the Renaissance. The historian Hervé Drévillon theorizes that "military humanism" of the Renaissance "not only postulated the human character of war, but also man's capacity to define its principles and to explore its rationality."[28]

The call to bring rationality to warfare is a second foundational characteristic born of previous centuries and further developed by agents of the Military Enlightenment. In the context of Renaissance and early seventeenth-century thought, military theorists believed that a rational approach would beget desirable martial and moral outcomes. Humans could employ the faculty of reason to discern universal principles of war, thereby rendering it a science whose end point was strategic and tactical "perfection"—a science of martial victory. Armed forces could sculpt the contours of warfare so as to foster human dignity and elevate the human spirit toward the divine. Rationalism in this context meant a neo-Stoic doctrine of restraint in warfare, which displayed human worth and constituted logical solutions to the horrors of civil war that racked France during the Wars of Religion (1562–1629) and the disorderly and violent hordes of soldiers of the Thirty Years' War (1618–1648).[29]

Making "good war" in the eighteenth century, however, required surpassing the rationalism and science of Renaissance-style military humanism. A new "enlightened" approach was necessary. As the 1694 *Dictionnaire*'s definition of war conveys, making war in a just and "good" manner meant "humanity" and "civility." These terms and their lexical sisters of sensibility, sociability, and society are of capital importance: they irreversibly transformed and indeed modernized perspectives on war and military constitution. These terms were newly interconnected through sensationalist moral philosophy that invented words and altered the meaning of existing terms. "Humanity," which had previously indicated human nature, evolved to signify a more specific moral stance and capacity. According to the *Dictionnaire* of 1694, "humanity" meant "gentleness, civility, goodness, and sensitivity to the misfortunes of others" ("douceur, honnesteté, bonté, et sensibilité pour les malheurs d'autrui"). "Civility" or *honnesteté* continued to designate courtesy in manners and conversation, but its meaning took on a new valence as being constitutive of genuine human bonds.

The cult of sentiment implied by the word *sensibilité* (sensibility, sensitivity, or feeling) was also a key component of military and elite culture of the period.[30] Based on sensationalist philosophy advanced by John Locke (1632–1704), David Hume (1711–1776), and Étienne Bonnot de Condillac (1714–1780), the concept of *sensibilité* came to be viewed as the quintessential human trait. For physicians, it was the foundation for human knowledge and identity; for moral philosophers like Rousseau, Diderot, and Adam Smith (1723–1790) it was responsible for creating fellow feeling between human beings.[31] Being a man or woman of feeling—an *âme sensible* (sensitive soul)—who cared for others became a sign of superior physical and moral makeup and represented a new type of social capital. As Dan Edelstein has argued, noblemen and bourgeois elites sought to be a part of the *noblesse du coeur* (nobility of the heart).[32]

Moral sentiment and its lexicon—*sensibilité, humanité, bienfaisance* (benevolence), *sociabilité*, and *social* (the latter two being neologisms dating to the eighteenth century)—represented a departure from traditional themes of military humanism and were an authentic development of the period. An epistemic shift from the rational toward the sentimental was under way in what Joan DeJean has called an "affective revolution."[33] This revolution is reflected in the values of the Military Enlightenment. The chivalric code—which, as understood by medieval chevaliers, was far more ferocious than nonmedievalists appreciate—was replaced by the notion of being gentle, respectful, sociable, benevolent, and compassionate *while waging war*.[34] These ideas saw their first full and deliberate articulation during the Enlightenment age.

The moral sentiments in question were not solely ideals. They had far-reaching implications for military medicine in its physical and psychological aspects and for the treatment of civilians, soldiers and sailors on campaign, prisoners of war, and veterans. Certain foundations for these practices were laid earlier in the seventeenth century before blossoming, transforming through the cult of sentiment, and becoming normalized in the eighteenth.[35] The neo-Stoic Dutch jurist Hugo Grotius (1583–1645) wrote *De jure belli ac pacis* (*On the Law of War and Peace*, 1625), which formed the backbone of the Treaty of Westphalia as the "first general peace settlement of modern times."[36] He maintained that there must be moral guidelines for restraint, since the law of nations permitted indiscriminate devastation, pillage and capture of property, enslaving of captives, and killing of subjects regardless of age, sex, or status as noncombatant (book 3, 3–9). He addressed *temperamenta belli* (book 3, 10–16), or moderation in the conduct of war, arguing that if the laws of war were permissive, there were natural laws (those of humanity) and moral laws (those of Christianity) that should make combatants choose restraint. The Swiss jurist Emer de Vattel (1714–1767) rearticulated *temperamenta belli* in secular terms in his 1758 work *The Law of Nations or the Principles of Natural Law Applied to the Conduct and to the Affairs of Nations and of Sovereigns* (*Droit des gens; ou, Principes de la loi naturelle appliqués à la conduite et aux affaires des nations et des souverains*), championing *humanité* as an impetus for restraint.

Grotius and Vattel recognized that the international laws of war would always be insufficient. The imperfections of international law were perfectible, however, through human choice and action. This meant that the "legal-political" dimension of the metadiscourse of war gave way to scientific discourse and, most importantly, a "humanitarian-philanthropic" framework based on the moral philosophy of sentiment.[37] This reframing shifted the nexus of change away from states and toward individuals. Noble military officers could demonstrate their moral sentiments through ad hoc "gentlemanly cartels" or conventions that contained specifications on the handling and exchange of prisoners as well as the treatment of the wounded and medical personnel. These cartels were not new in the eighteenth century; however, they became increasingly widespread, detailed, and public as military officers had their cartels published in order to publicize their good deeds. The cartels and those who enacted them referred directly to the sentiment of humanity. Actions at the individual level in the "humanitarian-philanthropic" dimension then influenced the "legal-political." By the end of the century, cartels went from being ad hoc individual arrangements to being codified into state policies that prefigured institutions such as the Geneva Conventions and the International Red Cross.

The culture of moral sentiment also had important implications for relationships between men serving together in the armed forces. War was a privileged circumstance in which men, and a few women, discovered and defined their relationship to self and other. Military and moral philosophers believed in humankind's natural capacity for being sociable and forming relationships. Whereas honor, traditionally construed, led to social competition among nobles and disparaging of soldiers of the common classes, sociability unified men. *Humanité, sensibilité,* and *honnêteté* joined with sociability and natural law to cultivate familiarity, camaraderie, community, respect, and the recognition of merit throughout the ranks.[38] Forming humane social bonds within the armed forces, it was believed, supported combat effectiveness, recruitment, and retention. As internal discord faded, esprit de corps and primary group cohesion would rise, and military men could shift their focus toward a shared *esprit de métier* (professional spirit) augmented by improved training and educational opportunities. Such bonds also bolstered physical and psychological health, which were recognized and theorized in the military space for the first time. The rise of interiority—the study of self, identity, and affect in relation to physicality—bloomed in seventeenth-century sensationalist philosophy, medicine, and literature, animating the first modern psychological novel, *La Princesse de Clèves* (1678), by Marie-Madeleine Pioche de La Vergne, comtesse de La Fayette (1634–1693). These developments were seen to be distinctly modern. As the writer Charles Perrault (1628–1703), a partisan of the moderns in the Quarrel of the Ancients and Moderns, remarked, "Just as anatomy has discovered in the heart ducts, valves, fibers, movements, and symptoms of which the Ancients had no knowledge, in the same manner moral philosophy has discovered attractions, aversions, desires, and repulsions which the Ancients never knew."[39] These perspectives undergirded the rising awareness of the cost of war on human bodies, minds, and hearts.

The dynamics and practical applications of moral sentiment, therefore, were not mere niceties. They were seen as strategic to the armed forces and as holding broad implications for society. They could win wars, improve international standing, forge national identity, and issue forth new heroes endowed with human benevolence *and* the willingness to die for their homeland. They aided officers in forming martial alliances with cultural, linguistic, and ethnic "Others" in colonial and mercantile outposts, at once facilitating empire and in some way diminishing its hegemonic, Eurocentric character. What is more, making "good war" in this enlightened mold could also, to some extent, make war less destructive and devastating for present generations and those to come. For members of the armed forces, government administrators, and nonmilitary intellectuals alike, this was a worthy purpose.

The Military Enlightenment engaged these human values, but at the same time was practical, technical, and impactful. "Enlightening" war meant adopting the *esprit philosophique* of the times: studying, questioning, challenging, and trying new things. In these experimental efforts, often the result of their own wills rather than royal injunction, military thinkers and actors moved into the realm of what Kant called the "private" use of reason, "that which one may make of it in a particular civil post or office which is entrusted to him." Kant was wary of this type of enlightening process and made direct reference to the military sphere in claiming that "it would be ruinous for an officer in service to debate about the suitability or utility of a command given to him by his superior; he must obey. But the right to make remarks on errors in the military service and to lay them before the public for judgment cannot equitably be refused him as a scholar." Subordination and obedience were, and continue to be, essential to military functioning, thus Kant's hesitation was clearly justified. However, eighteenth-century sources evince that members of the armed forces throughout the military hierarchy called into question their orders or regulations from Versailles in their quest to make "good war." Embarking on an experimental and "philosophical ethos that could be described as a permanent critique of [its] historical era," these martial actors embodied Michel Foucault's interpretation of enlightenment as "a process in which men participate collectively and as an act of courage to be accomplished personally. Men are at once elements and agents of a single process. They may be actors in the process to the extent that they participate in it; and the process occurs to the extent that men decide to be its voluntary actors."[40] These reformers in effect "operationalized" Enlightenment thought within the armed forces, turning theories into realities as spaces of war on the continent and abroad became laboratories or ateliers in which newfangled theories were put to the test.

While Drévillon views military humanism as enduring from the Renaissance until the fall of Napoleon, when military romanticism began, it is clear that another unique phenomenon occurred in between: military enlightenment, a flash point that defined the Enlightenment, from war-torn border towns and port cities overseas to intellectual hubs in Parisian salons and the government's seat in the gilded corridors of Versailles.

The processes and value systems discussed so far can be seen as pan-European and perhaps even global phenomena.[41] This is not surprising given the transnational movement of people and material culture during this era. Military men were often among the most mobile of their countries, traveling to regions across Europe and to continents that were oceans away as they moved to extend and defend the political ambitions, mercantile strongholds, and territorial claims of their countries. While soldiers may not always have rubbed elbows with their foreign counterparts, officers came into frequent contact. In France and countries across Europe, officers were gentlemen who shared a transnational culture of nobility. When their own kingdoms were not at war, many officers sought commissions in foreign armies, into which they integrated. As a result, officers of enemy forces dined together on the eve of great battles, displayed civility to one another, socialized, joined the same Masonic lodges, lent one another money and supplies, and demonstrated a general social and cultural solidarity. Medical personnel did the same due to their professional bond and mutual commitment to science. Battle and life on campaign were therefore not conditions that necessarily led to animosity and obstacles to interrelation. On the contrary, they fostered connection and exchange across borders, making real the notions of cosmopolitanism and social bonding through humanity and civility.

This supranational context is indisputable; however, national versions of military enlightenment had their own particularities due to local conditions, constraints, and cultures. The Germanic Military Enlightenment did not develop until a generation after the French one and was largely fueled by the Revolutionary and Napoleonic Wars, which elicited a public debate on war, heroism, and military culture.[42] Military Enlightenment in Austria had an even slower start and did not take form until the turn of the century with the writings of Archduke Charles (1771–1847).[43] Countries had their own military needs based on the natural borders of their territories, making the island-dwelling British invest the vast majority of military expenditures in their navy, whereas France, with its numerous miles of land and coastline borders, had greater need for ground forces in addition to a navy. France also faced specific problems because of the fiscal system in place.[44] What is more, just as universalism and cosmopolitanism were on the rise, so too were national sentiment and nationalism. France and other countries all sought to distinguish their own national identities and to elucidate a military establishment best suited to their nation's *génie*, or natural talents. For this reason, military enlightenment must be considered not only as a transhistorical and transnational phenomenon but also as a national one. Constructing a series of deep national histories is a necessary step toward formulating an empirically sound transnational history of military enlightenment.

Contributing Factors

In France, the rise of the Military Enlightenment related to the structures of its fiscal-military state, to the generalized sense of military crisis, and to a perceived degeneracy of military leadership. It also linked to cultural trends pertaining to the political and military spheres, such as vitriolic critiques of war and warriors by *philosophes*, the growing schism between the Bourbon monarchs and military activity, and a concomitant rise of what David Bell calls a "cult of the nation" that centered on notions of patriotism and citizenship.[45] These factors furnish an important backdrop for understanding the Military Enlightenment in France.

France's fiscal-military state developed slowly from the late medieval era through the eighteenth century. A standing army and a system of permanent taxation had existed in France since the (first) Hundred Years' War (1337–1453), and the last kings in the Valois line levied a military tax (the *taillon*) and commissioned intendants to help supervise the military effort against the Hapsburgs.[46] In the seventeenth century, the government succeeded in paying for a large part of its military expenditures through ordinary revenues composed of direct and indirect taxes such as customs and income from state-owned landed estates. Louis XIII's minister Armand Jean du Plessis, cardinal-duc de Richelieu et de Fronsac (1585–1642), expanded earlier initiatives and grew ordinary revenues from 25 million livres in the 1620s to 60 million livres in the 1640s. Louis XIV and his ministers surpassed this accomplishment.[47] Colbert's reforms easily raised the 58 to 68 million livres per annum (70 percent of the crown's ordinary annual revenues) required by the Dutch War of the 1670s. Despite the strains of long-term warfare and crop failures in the latter part of the seventeenth century, the Sun King was able to raise over 100 million livres per annum during the Nine Years' War, with a peak at 113 million per annum.[48] Louis XIII and Louis XIV thus oversaw critical—and increasingly problematic—developments in the financing of France's wars, including supplementing ordinary revenues with extraordinary revenues. The latter came from direct taxes such as the *capitation* (1695) and the *dixième* (1710), currency devaluations, and, most characteristically, the sale of offices and privileges, forced loans and gifts, and the extensive use of credit from financiers, bankers, corporate bodies, and the public.

Despite the exorbitant costs of war, France was Europe's leading economic power for much of the seventeenth and eighteenth centuries. The French population was the largest on the continent, almost three times that of archrival Britain. In what has been called the "demographic revolution," the French population rose from twenty-one million to twenty-eight million between 1715 and 1789. France also had a flourishing economy with a vibrant agrarian base and rapidly developing commercial and manufacturing sectors.[49] It was able to produce more revenues than any rivals (Britain included), its tax earnings producing a high of 285 million livres compared to 229 million in England, 140 million in the United Provinces and Spain, 92 million for the Hapsburgs, and 48.6 million for Prussia.[50] However, as the historian Hamish Scott explains, "International power rested on the ability to extract resources, rather than the level of resources per se."[51] Louis XIII and XIV had been relatively successful in extracting resources during the first three-quarters of the seventeenth century, a testament to the organization of their growing fiscal-military states. This was decreasingly the case by the eighteenth century, when the crown was forced to arrange financial deals with "dangerous and dishonest men," as Guy Rowlands describes them, and embark on less advantageous fiscal tools such as high-interest and self-amortizing loans.[52] This meant debt, debt, and more debt. In the 1760s, France's debt was estimated to be at least 2 billion livres, six times the crown's annual revenue. By that time, 60 percent of the crown's per annum revenues went to repaying charges. In 1788, costs of paying down France's debt were almost 62 percent of the crown's tax revenues and constituted half of its expenditures.[53]

Two important aspects of this Bourbon fiscal-military state had a direct relationship to fueling France's Military Enlightenment. The first had to do with the crown's fiscal dependence on the commodification of ennoblement and the problems this created within the officer corps. As the historian David D. Bien conveys, the French state could not rely on English constitutionalist or eastern European feudal mechanisms to levy high taxes or accrue low-interest loans to finance seventeenth- and especially eighteenth-century wars. As time went on, the crown could no longer afford to borrow from creditors who charged extortionate rates. Instead, it found the unique, if flawed, solution of drawing revenue from French subjects via selling venal offices, then imposing loans on its *officiers*, who in turn took out loans that were backed by corps of *officiers* and by their offices themselves. This financial dependence on the sale of offices and on the corps caused the crown to create and defend special privileges, or *privilèges*.[54]

In the military sphere, the system of *privilèges* translated to producing a top-heavy officer corps filled with *anoblis* (recently ennobled) or wealthy court nobles. These individuals could afford to pay for an officer's commission and sought it as social capital, but often lacked formal military experience, physical fitness, martial culture, and any semblance of professionalism. Maréchal Victor François, duc de Broglie (1718–1804), lamented the "total ignorance, from the sous-lieutenant to the lieutenant general, of the duties of their post and all the details that concern it."⁵⁵ The quantity and incompetence of these officers, particularly in the army, were catastrophic. By 1750, there were as many pensioned officers as on active commission, and the pay for the sixty thousand officers in the Seven Years' War totaled more than the expenses of the rest of the army put together (47 million livres versus 44 million livres). Reformers viewed the crisis in leadership that pervaded the French armed forces—a crisis that was the direct result of royal favor and the mechanisms of the fiscal-military state—as the essential force driving France's inglorious military record during much of the eighteenth century.

The extraordinary costs of military conflict and the dangerously high debts accrued by the French crown made "limited war" the order of the day.⁵⁶ Preserving France's precious military resources, especially manpower, became imperative. Casualties and deaths related to combat and disease represented a devastating loss on investment. Even more disastrous was the epidemic of desertion. Desertion represented a perennial problem for all warring countries, and European states undertook a variety of measures to fight it, largely to no avail. The historian André Corvisier estimates that nearly a quarter of all soldiers in the French army deserted during the War of Spanish Succession.⁵⁷ The eighteenth-century sieur Garrigues de Froment averred that there were over ten thousand deserters each year during the War of Austrian Succession, totaling sixty to seventy thousand men. Le sieur la Balme, lieutenant of the Senlis constabulary, counted eight to nine thousand deserters in 1761 during the Seven Years' War.⁵⁸

According to French reformers, these problems could be blamed on a backward military system, a nonexistent motivational system, and, most especially, faulty leadership. The result was martial failure. Between the latter wars of Louis XIV and the wars of the French Revolution, France experienced a dramatic military decline that stunned not just the armed forces but the entire nation. During the War of Spanish Succession, important political aims were met; however, France suffered military defeats all over west-central Europe as John Churchill, Duke of Marlborough (1650–1722), and Prince Eugene of Savoy (1663–1736) marched their armies toward Paris, successfully defeating the French at Oudenarde, Lille, Malplaquet, and Mons.⁵⁹ Save for a handful of victories, bungling and ineffectiveness also severely hampered French military performance in the War of Austrian Succession. During the Seven Years' War, French naval power was virtually annihilated, and the armed forces endured tremendous losses in Europe, India, Africa, and the Americas, succumbing to the tiny state of Prussia on the continent and losing nearly all strongholds overseas. For the largest, wealthiest, and most populous country in western Europe, one that had achieved great military glory in its far-removed and more recent past, these losses were seen as no less than "a national disaster."[60]

Losing this war was not just an exacerbating force but a critical motivator for both the critiques and the reforms of the Military Enlightenment. The spectacular defeats of the Seven Years' War, along with the generalized military crisis and failure in leadership, sharpened the tongues of critics. Needless militarism, martial insolvency, and botched diplomacy had caused France's entry into the war, military misconduct, and the disadvantageous terms of the Treaty of Paris. "The state lost its most flourishing youth, more than half the money in circulation in the kingdom, its navy, its commerce, its credit," wrote Voltaire. Associating the Seven Years' War with that of Austrian Succession, he sneered that "a few ambitious men, who wanted to make themselves valued and indispensable, precipitated France into this fatal war. It was exactly the same in 1741. The pride [*amour propre*] of two or three people was enough to destroy all of Europe."[61]

Relentless critiques of war and warriors flowed from the mouths, pens, and printing presses of *philosophes*, journalists, and other voices of the public sphere, heightening those that had appeared before 1763. Louis XV struggled to control public opinion, and aristocratic reactionaries loudly insisted on their continued supremacy in martial pursuits and their generosity in paying the *impôt du sang* (blood tax) that justified their privileges.[62] Meanwhile, the discourse of patriotism and the process that the historian Jay M. Smith has called the "nationalization of honor" further transformed the intellectual and political landscape.[63] Nationalizing honor meant democratizing it socially and contending that perhaps true heroes of war were not wealthy and famed officers who stood to benefit financially, socially, and politically from war. Perhaps it was rather common soldiers and subaltern officers, who so loved their country and king that they sacrificed their lives without hope of public recognition, advancement through the ranks due to merit, or meaningful monetary recompense. As condemnations of war and the loss of faith in kingly and aristocratic leaders spread, new ideas about heroism, citizenship, and martial agency coalesced, thereby giving a specific tenor to the French Military Enlightenment in the decades before the French Revolution.

In addition to these cultural forces, science and mathematics drove efforts to improve martial efficacy on land and at sea. During the long eighteenth century, the crown moved to professionalize the armed forces by creating royal and local military academies whose curricula centered on scientific and mathematical knowledge. In 1748 the crown founded the royal military engineering academy, the École royale du génie de Mézières. Louis XIV pioneered the first artillery school in 1679, and by 1789 there were seven of them, located in

La Fère, Douai, Valence, Auxonne, Metz, Besançon, and Strasbourg. The Académie de marine, located in Brest, was founded in 1752 and gained the status of royal academy in 1769. The École royale militaire was founded in 1750 (though its doors did not open until several years later), and numerous regional and feeder schools were also created. While military academies were founded across the English Channel and on the European continent during the century, France saw the proliferation of these specialized military schools well before most other countries. For example, the British Royal Naval Academy at Portsmouth Dockyard was founded in 1733, but the Royal Military College was not founded until 1801 and the School of Naval Architecture until 1811, and the Royal School of Artillery (formerly the School of Instruction for Royal Horse and Field Artillery) was not established until 1915.

Specialized French academies grew to supply maritime and land expertise, but they also aimed to overhaul the professionalization of the officer corps. To do so, they articulated new criteria for martial professionalism, which was to become based on formal vocational and scientific skills. David Bien has shown the centrality of science and mathematics in military education, with specific reference to the curriculum of the École royale militaire.[64] Entrance to the elite naval academy, which was the gateway to a commission as an *officier rouge* of the Grand Corps (as opposed to the reserve corps of *officiers bleus*), was notoriously difficult. Admission was based on a competitive examination in which candidates had to demonstrate competence in sophisticated mathematics. French authorities recognized that in addition to theoretical knowledge, practical experience was key to martial success. The crown therefore put science into action in training camps, enacting several new suites of drill in the army and an *escadre d'évolution* (training squadron) in which naval officers could gain invaluable practical experience during peacetime.

The influence of science and mathematics in the French armed forces of the period went beyond military education. Robert Quimby examines geometric tactical systems and the related debate between the battle formation of the *ordre mince* (maximizing firepower) and the *ordre profond* (optimizing for shock power).[65] John Lynn charts the prevalence of science and engineering in military articles of the *Encyclopédie*.[66] Azar Gat studies the influence of and faith in science and mathematics as the basis for establishing "universal principles of war."[67] Other scholars such as J. B. Schank, Ken Alder, and Alain Berbouche investigate the ways in which Newtonianism and other scientific perspectives influenced naval practice, military engineering, and artillery, including the highly influential Gribeauvalist system.[68] Medical science, examined in this book, also flourished and made important strides in hygiene, preventive, and curative medicine for military bodies and emotions. These studies document the remarkable extent and variety of mathematical and scientific pursuits associated with the Military Enlightenment and the technological arms race of the eighteenth century, particularly in the navy.

Complementing these scientific approaches advanced by specialists, a much broader spectrum of thinkers made cultural contributions to the Military Enlightenment in France. The vogue of philosophizing encouraged many people to engage in the process of "perfecting" war and military functioning from all perspectives: strategic, tactical, logistical, cultural, and moral. *Encyclopédistes* worked to record the most up-to-date knowledge on warfare; women in Parisian salons advocated abolishing the death penalty for deserters from the army; war ministers instituted new policies; and military men wrote treatises, memoirs, travel narratives, novels, and essays on war and civilization at home and abroad. As the home of pervasive military problems and as an epicenter for intellectual foment associated with *esprit philosophique*, France had all of the ingredients for its own process of military enlightenment, which unfolded on the continent and around the world.

Military Enlightenment and Overseas Empire

During the long eighteenth century, the French state largely prioritized martial success on the European continent and was only just conceptualizing empire and "colonial machines."[69] However, in the context of the Military Enlightenment, global perspectives represented a critical domain of interest. This is no surprise given that exploration and cross-cultural contact also constituted a flash point of the Enlightenment. Expeditions around the world aimed increasingly to gather information about nature and humankind. Scientific institutions of individual countries joined in international cooperation to identify and solve medical and geophysical challenges.[70] Travel literature, ethnography, and comparative history were important and popular genres during a century of remarkable geographical discovery.[71] Readers in France and beyond avidly consumed travel narratives like the *Voyage around the World* (1771) by military officer–turned–navigator Louis Antoine de Bougainville (1729–1811) and Diderot's literary response in the *Supplement to Bougainville's Voyage* (1772). Histories, ethnographies, and encyclopedias like the abbé Guillaume-Thomas Raynal's (1713–1796) *History of the Two Indies* (*L'histoire philosophique et politique des établissements et du commerce des européens dans les deux Indes*, 1770) were also widely read. In France, *L'histoire des deux Indes* saw over thirty different editions between 1770 and 1787; over fifty editions were published abroad, plus a number of abridged versions.[72] Napoleon Bonaparte brought the book with him on the Egypt campaign.

By the late eighteenth century, France had navigated, dispatched missionaries and scientific teams, established trade posts, or colonized lands on six of the seven continents (excluding Antarctica) and had sailed in three of five of the world oceans (ice in the Arctic and Antarctic Oceans prevented extensive exploration). Merchants were active in slave trade posts in West Africa, sugar plantations and penal colonies in the Caribbean, fisheries and fur trade posts in North American colonies, *comptoirs* on the Indian subcontinent and in China, naval outposts in Madagascar and the Mascarene Islands, and economic hubs throughout the Mediterranean Sea.[73] In this era of mercantilism, the French crown invested in and sanctioned monopolies for private companies such as the Compagnie des Indes and worked to secure France's first-tier position in the world of global trade. France's colony of Saint-Domingue, today Haiti, was the premier producer of sugar in the world. Louis XV, Louis XVI, and their ministers were therefore keenly focused on colonizing and controlling the French part of the island, on populating plantations with slaves, and on protecting the precious human and material cargo transported on ships going to and from the island. Naval sea and land units called the *compagnies franches de la marine*, as well as metropolitan regular army units, were deployed throughout the colonial and mercantile diaspora. Their task was to patrol and protect French interests, settle as colonists (a practice referred to a "military colonization"), and aid the private militaries hired by mercantile companies, especially in wartime, when trade routes and posts became the pathways and locales of warfare.

Global theaters of war were vital for European powers aiming to maintain and expand their interests. Competition between France and Great Britain was particularly fierce, and under the leadership of William Pitt (1708–1778) the British adopted the aggressive grand strategy of commandeering or debilitating the entire French Empire. The close of the Seven Years' War would mark a definitive success for the English. The French ceded Louisiana (west of the Mississippi) to Spain, along with the rest of Nouvelle France, except for the tiny islands of Saint-Pierre and Miquelon. In India, French trading posts that had been seized were returned, but all fortifications were destroyed so that no strong military presence could exist there, opening the way to British domination of the subcontinent. The Royal Navy captured all French establishments in West Africa, returning only the island of Gorée in the Treaty of Paris of 1763. France retained Guadeloupe, Martinique, and Saint Lucia, which had been captured by the British in 1759 and 1762, respectively, but relinquished

Dominica, Grenada, St. Vincent and the Grenadines, and Tobago to England. The American Revolutionary War (1775–1783) dealt a major blow to Great Britain and brought Senegal and Tobago back under French control, and Napoleon's victories later brought territorial gains to France, at least for a time. Bonaparte's final defeat at Waterloo on June 15, 1815, however, marked an end point to more than twenty years of coalition war and brought a close to what is referred to as "the first French colonial empire."

Empire and diaspora shaped the careers of military men in multiple ways. Some, like Charles-Hector, comte d'Estaing (1729–1794), held commissions in both the army and the navy and participated in battles across the globe, from the European continent during the War of Austrian Succession, to India during the Seven Years' War, to the Caribbean and North America during the American Revolutionary War. In these experiences, military officers occupied a number of important positions in addition to their martial roles. They were governors general, diplomats, explorers, cartographers, and pseudo-ethnographers who relayed invaluable information about foreign lands, leaders, cultures, and militaries. They wrote travel narratives, navigational logs, ethnographies, and memoirs (essays on learned subjects as opposed to biographical narratives) on cultures, politics, and commerce of different indigenous groups. In addition to published works, innumerable reports, journals, and proposals fill the archives of the Service historique de la défense (SHD), the Archives nationales, and the Archives nationales d'outre-mer, as well as local and national archives in Canada, Britain, and other countries around the world. Tattered and torn, stained with saltwater, sweat, and mold, these documents tell the story of a Military Enlightenment that traversed the center-periphery, *métropole*-colony divide.

French military men had an ambiguous and largely unarticulated relationship to empire. On one hand, they were by definition supporters of empire, since they were sent abroad to explore and secure territories, commerce, and alliances. On the other hand, many pushed back against European cultural and colonial hegemony in ways that revealed them to be part of a movement that was disinterested in and sometimes critical of empire.[74] Their writings evince both of these perspectives. While some military men who served across the globe remained mired in Eurocentric stereotypes that degraded cultural and ethnic "Others," many *militaires philosophes* insisted that cultural awareness and compromise were crucial from strategic and ethical, human standpoints. These men tested and adapted continental frameworks of the Military Enlightenment, but also developed new understandings and themes as they engaged with indigenous authorities and peoples. For this group, French military men around the world were not there to "enlighten" others; they were responsible for enlightening themselves by a relativist understanding and acceptance of local geographies and norms of civilization.

This latter viewpoint is predominant in the manuscript sources that inform this book. They reveal the linguistic, cultural, and martial intermingling that took place as French nationals made negotiations, allegiances, and wars with different indigenous populations. These archival findings corroborate the revisionist narrative of early modern European colonialism. In this, scholars increasingly recognize that the triumphalist "Spanish model" of overwhelming conquest by guns, germs, and steel, popularized by the Spanish themselves and more recently by Jared Diamond, has dominated the historical imaginary of colonialism, but is largely inaccurate for all but the conquistadors.[75] It "was not always, or even mostly, a story of direct 'conquest' but, rather, a story of convincing, cajoling, and coercing indigenous agents to harness their own resources and to project power, either at the imperial behest or at least in the imperial interest," writes Wayne Lee.[76] Documents in the French military archive affirm that

> local peoples proved to be essential determinants of imperial success or failure. Far from being mere victims, these peoples found ways to profit from imperial maneuverings: they could find employment and profit as allies, or they might direct the interests and energies of imperial powers against their traditional enemies. Indeed, imperial "expansion" was very often illusory, and Europeans' ability to project power actually depended entirely on local cooperation. In turn, that cooperative process shaped and reshaped the warfare and diplomatic practices designed to define and establish sovereignty and control, whether local or European. New cultures of power and cultures of war were born in the many crucibles of encounter around the globe.[77]

By and large, these eighteenth-century encounters cannot be understood as acculturation of a Eurocentric, imperialist sort: a superior European "us" versus an indigenous "them" or "Other" that justified the civilizing mission or "white man's burden." Instead of adhering to such structuralist binaries, revisionist scholars emphasize strong interconnectedness and cross-culturation in an ever-changing world of mutual need. This hermeneutic perspective highlights encounters in which no party, be it French, Amerindian, Indian, and so on, had sufficient power to force the other's hand completely. Firsthand accounts written by French military men serving in North America and India support this interpretation and relay the presence of what Richard White, in his classic work, called a "middle ground": a space in between where "indianization" and "frenchization" happened concomitantly and were attended with considerable misunderstanding and misinterpretation that represented both the fibers and fissures of alliances.[78]

In interpreting these environments, it is essential to understand the different political stakes that undergirded questions related to the Military Enlightenment. In North America (Canada and Louisiana), India, and Africa, for example, there was never a question of indigenous peoples becoming French nationals. India and Africa were never colonies per se, and in North American settlements, alliances (or slavery) and indigenous martial merit never elicited debates on military service and citizenship. Saint-Domingue was completely different. There, military and police service were embroiled with questions of race, economic status, and citizenship.[79] Inhabitants of Saint-Domingue and continental officers who served on the island developed competing definitions of Military Enlightenment themes, such as *sensibilité*, in order to influence crown policies and public opinion.

Methods, Sources, and Motivations

This book aims to sketch a vision of the Military Enlightenment and a methodology for studying it, creating fertile ground for continued exploration of the subject in France and beyond.

The Military Enlightenment was an extensive and eclectic phenomenon. This eclecticism demands an equally diverse methodology that goes beyond the confines of "war and society" to combine the analytical and evidentiary paradigms of several disciplines: literature (philosophical tale, poetry, novel) and the performing arts (theater and opéra comique); visual arts (painting); philosophy (sensationalism, moral philosophy); history (military, intellectual, cultural, gender, race, medical, colonial).[80] It is necessary to read a myriad of primary sources in parallel, such as military treatises, memoirs, and correspondence (archival and published); crown regulations and edicts; works of moral philosophy and political theory; newspapers; paintings; popular plays; and songs. Literary close reading techniques are essential to discovering the interconnectedness of language and themes across these different media, especially manuscript memoirs and correspondence preserved in the war archives of the SHD.[81]

Investigations in this book examine military thought and mandates sent from Versailles, but also practices that took place on the ground resulting from personal initiatives, experimentation, and disregard for policy. There are many individuals and groups—female soldiers, free men of color who served in the *chasseurs d'Amérique* of Saint-Domingue, thousands and thousands of soldiers—

who were "voiceless" and in certain cases "invisible" in the hierarchical society of the *ancien régime*. Capturing their experiences is at once a challenge and a priority of this book. Every effort has been made to reach them through the intermediaries that relayed some version of their voices and made them visible to the crown, the public, and posterity. For those whose names and biographical data are known, this information has been included in the narrative.

The chronological and geographical scope of this book prevents an exhaustive treatment of all aspects of the Military Enlightenment across the entire French diaspora and to transhistorical process of military enlightenment across space and time. Detailed inquiries into West African outposts, those in the Mascarene Islands, and other locales are not included in this study. In-depth analyses of reform culture in the cavalry and the artillery have also been excluded, and other historians have illuminated the tenor and results of naval reform. Writings focused on religion in the armed forces were scarce in the archive, so this fertile theme is not developed. While sources are scarce and of varying quality—some read as dry chronicles, whereas others relay details of conversations and opinions—indigenous writings about and experiences with the French are included in investigations of India and North America. Writings by French officers serving abroad, especially in India and Saint-Domingue, are also rare and of varying quality. A small number of documents from that corpus form the backbone of the observations and arguments about experiences and ideas that came from service in these geographies. In an effort to escape the anecdotal, such documents have been analyzed alongside other primary and secondary sources in order to shed greater light on their significance.

Certain archival series, primary sources, and historiographical works have been crucial to knitting together the idea of the Military Enlightenment in France that this book presents. From the SHD at the chateau de Vincennes, the series 1M, A1, Xi, Xk, Xb, and 1YD form the bulk of archival findings. For research on Saint-Domingue, two series at the Archives nationales in Pierrefitte and Paris were particularly important: the Fonds amiral d'Estaing (562AP/1–562AP/55) and the Collection Moreau de Saint-Méry (sous-série F^3 [1492/1818]-MCOL/F/3/1-297). Also at the Archives nationales, the Fonds Rostaing (100AP/1–100AP/5) and the Fonds d'Éprémesnil (158AP/1–158AP/82) supplied key sources on India.

Many primary sources by the best-known military thinkers of the eighteenth century, such as Maurice, Count of Saxony (Hermann Moritz Graf von Sachsen, referred to as Maurice de Saxe in France, 1696–1750), and Jacques-Antoine-Hippolyte, comte de Guibert (1743–1790), are published and easily accessible, as are the journals of men who served in the American Revolution and a plethora of medical publications. In addition to these more specialized works, dictionaries, encyclopedias, political essays, poems, songs, plays, paintings, and engravings by *philosophes*, writers, and artists are widely available and were sources vital to this book. The extensive engagement in the Military Enlightenment in France necessitated examining a wide range of primary sources and an equally wide range of secondary ones, at times bringing a different perspective to them. This book draws on the rich historiography of the French army of the long eighteenth century, especially works by R. Blaufarb, J. Chagniot, A. Corvisier, A. Guinier, M. Hughes, J. Lynn, B. Martin, J. Osman, and C. Tozzi. A. Gat's work on military thought, J.-L. Quoi-Bodin's research on military Freemasonry, works on patriotism by E. Dziembowski, D. A. Bell, and J. M. Smith were key sources. J. Garrigus's work on Haiti, R. White and C. Crouch on Canada, and S. Steinberg's research on women and gender were also main references. These and all other sources are cited in endnotes and a full bibliography can be accessed on my website: www.christypichichero.com. Except where otherwise noted, all translations from French to English were made by the author. The original French for many of the songs and literary works can be found side by side with translations on my website as well.

Overall, this book aims to bring war and military thought to their proper place in our understanding of the Enlightenment. It advances evidence to overturn, or at least complicate, the classical Western civilization narrative that posits the Enlightenment as a culture of pacifism, cosmopolitanism, and universalism that was largely opposed to and separate from war and the military sphere. The Military Enlightenment shows that far from being incompatible, war, military thought, and policy were central theaters in which the Enlightenment unfolded. This narrative at once illuminates important facets of the eighteenth century and also a much longer genealogy. It contributes to a *longue durée* history of war, society, and individuals and the culture of war, touching on human rights, the trauma of battle, and the importance of camaraderie and humanitarian sentiments, whether in the laws of war or as espoused by individual combatants. The complex legacy of the Military Enlightenment is discussed in the epilogue of this volume, and one of its key takeaways is also a fundamental motivation for writing this book: if war is to persist in human society, an understanding of the multifarious costs of war and the impetus to imbue it with as much humanity as possible should remain worthy elements of our consciousness and actions.

CHAPTER 1

The French Military Enlightenment
Figures, Forces, and Forms

The images did not seem inflammatory at first, but there was something provocative, even subversive, about the color engravings crafted by Antoine Louis François Sergent (1751–1847) for his work *Portraits of Great Men, Illustrious Women, and Memorable Subjects* (*Portraits des grands hommes, femmes illustres, et sujets mémorables*, 1786–1792). Sergent created this volume, which depicted great men and women of French history, to kindle patriotic sentiment in his fellow countrymen and women. He seemed to follow long-standing tradition by selecting a rather predictable range of French men and women for his portrait gallery: kings, queens, clerics, ministers, and *many* military men.

Despite the apparent predictability, Sergent carefully constructed his portraits of the latter—army and navy officers—to carry important messages about the changing face of war, warriors, and heroism. Sergent made sure that the focus of these portraits was not the celebration of courage and tenacity in combat. Instead he praised his martial protagonists for other, more humanist and humane actions both on and off of the battlefield. He glorified the chevalier de Folard not merely for his service in Louis XIV's army, but also for his role as a military thinker and teacher. He chose to represent Jean-Charles, chevalier de Folard (1669–1752), seated at a table instructing marshal Maurice de Saxe, France's premier general during the War of Austrian Succession, on the principles of war. Sergent lauded the chevalier Bayard (1473–1524) for his continence toward a female prisoner on whom he took pity and spared her the expected treatment of rape or death. Similarly, his engraving of the comte d'Harcourt (1601–1666), known as the *cadet à la perle* (pearl cadet), depicted d'Harcourt's actions *after* the victorious siege of Turin (1640) when he ignored the harsh terms of the capitulation and brought wine and victuals to the sick and hungry Italian victims of the besieged city. D'Harcourt was a hero because he had disobeyed orders (see figure 1).

The portrait of Abraham Fabert d'Esternay (1599–1662), featured on the cover of this book, seemed to fall perfectly in line with this schema of praise, as Sergent celebrated the marshal for his humanity in sparing the lives of wounded enemy soldiers. Yet, the engraving went further than all of the others in spurring a profound reflection on war and peace. On the right, the enemy army retreats from the still-smoking battlefield, while in the foreground two French soldiers are poised to kill two enemy soldiers who lie on the ground writhing in pain from their injuries. On the left, Fabert is mounted on a white steed; at the moment one of his soldiers raises his sword to strike the fatal blow to the fallen enemy, Fabert thrusts his sword forward to block the murderous blade from crashing down. The cavalrymen to the far left and the soldier to the far right look on in bewilderment as time and the violence of battle suddenly stop. His sword stayed by that of Fabert, the soldier in blue is suspended in a pose that incites both thought and emotion: instead of killing his enemy, he holds his enemy's hand.

For Sergent, a liberal who had grown up in Chartres with soon-to-be revolutionaries Jacques Brissot de Warville (1754–1793) and Jérôme Pétion de Villeneuve (1756–1794), these military men were heroes because their actions were in keeping with the values of the Military Enlightenment. They were men of letters and philosophy, men of professional dedication and camaraderie, men of humanity and sentiment toward other warriors and civilians. They took personal initiative to educate others and to treat them with dignity, even if such actions meant breaking official policies. Sergent's portraits did not hide that "the ultimate fact of military history is combat, actual fighting with all its danger and its heavy costs."[1] No matter how decisive or indecisive, battles and sieges were brutal, and these men fought to win. Yet Sergent's engravings also relay that during the eighteenth century, the fundamental goal of victory was problematized with a new set of ethical and ideological concerns about warfare. Could war, despite its violence and devastations, and the military, despite its belligerent mandate, be spaces in which humanity and human dignity could prevail?

Agents of the Military Enlightenment did not regard this question as paradoxical. They wholeheartedly believed that the answer was yes. This chapter

FIGURE 1. "Stroke of Humanity by the comte d'Harcourt," in Antoine Sergent, *Portraits des grands hommes, femmes illustres et sujets mémorables de France* (1786–1792). Courtesy of the Bibliothèque nationale de France.

examines the personalities, spaces, and means of the French Military Enlightenment. It shows the broad engagement in thinking about the processes, manifestations, and meanings of war in the history of human civilization and in the eighteenth century. Different agents brought their perspectives to bear on this subject. Kings, royal mistresses, and war ministers explored pathways to improving martial efficacy, efficiency, and education, establishing new policies and institutions. Military officers, largely of noble birth but varying widely in socioeconomic, political, and geographical identity, took on the role of the *philosophe*, applying critical thinking to their martial experience. Some offered calculations for proper marching and drill, while others imagined means of moral and social reinvigoration in the army officer corps or served as cartographers and explorers charting far-off lands and waterways. These men knew that they were key conduits of valuable information, be it on military matters or on interacting with foreign peoples in foreign lands. They proposed policy changes, enforced those mandated by Versailles, or rebelled against them by refusing to implement punishments or practices that they deemed unjust. They shared their experiences and opinions with others through conversations, letters, manuscript memoirs (understood here to mean essays on a learned subject), and published works of literature, history, pseudo-ethnography, philosophy, and military science. These *militaires philosophes* became prominent figures in spheres of enlightened discourse. At the same time, nonmilitary thinkers, writers, scientists, physicians, artists, and members of the reading public were highly informed and engaged in contemplating, discussing, and representing war and warriors. They openly condemned injustices of the military system, but at the same time helped to develop and spread military knowledge, be it shipbuilding, ballistics, tropical medicine, or tactics best suited to the French national character. Like Sergent, they commented on and spread the new military values through works of art and questioned war's pervasive influences through encyclopedias, novels, and plays. All of these agents of the Military Enlightenment embraced an *esprit philosophique*, or critical, philosophical spirit, as they made war and military matters into one of the great public debates and nexuses of change in France and the French empire during the eighteenth century.

Mistresses, Ministers, and Reform Absolutists

Louis XV and his grandson Louis XVI are usually excluded from the list of enlightened absolutists (or enlightened despots), which includes Frederick the Great of Prussia (1712–1786), Hapsburg Holy Roman Emperors Joseph II (1741–1790) and Leopold II (1747–1792), Catherine the Great of Russia (1729–1796), King Gustav III of Sweden (1746–1792), King Charles III of Spain (1716–1788), and several German princes. Eighteenth-century monarchs of England and France are usually discounted, since Britain's constitutional system and powerful Parliament rendered it not "absolutist" enough to fit the category, and, conversely, the French monarchy was "too absolutist" and traditionalist to merit the qualifier "enlightened." "The fact that both Louis XV and Louis XVI held on to the idea of the divine right of kings typifies French conditions . . . On the whole, the French monarchy trended towards ossification," claims the historian Martin Fitzpatrick. "While there was an enlightened milieu which conducted a critical and intensive debate on political, social, legal and religious issues, its influence on matters of state was limited. Attempts at reform took place only sporadically; and, in most cases, they failed."[2]

This conclusion is simply untrue in the case of the French armed forces. From the close of the War of Spanish Succession until the Revolution itself, the French state attempted to reform its military constantly. Though Louis XV may have had a stronger penchant for women than for war, and Louis XVI preferred hunting and locksmithing to affairs of state, both monarchs undertook a diversity of ambitious reform programs, including the abolition of serfdom, efforts to buttress religious tolerance, and a total overhaul of the naval fleet and system. This period saw notable reform efforts and progress in military system organization, education, medicine, and technology thanks to royal support.[3] Louis XV and Louis XVI did not necessarily spearhead these reforms, but they did endorse them. With this in mind, both kings can be described as reform absolutists, if not enlightened absolutists.

Military reforms often originated from high-ranking crown administrators, especially ministers of war, as well as from royal mistresses. Following the transformation of "Richelieu's Army" into the "giant of the Grand Siècle" under Louis XIV, reforms to military education and the national police force (*la maréchaussée*) began under the ministry of Claude Le Blanc (1669–1728) after the War of Spanish Succession.[4] However, the first of a new generation of "enlightened" administrators did not take office until the middle of the eighteenth century. Marc-Pierre de Voyer de Paulmy, comte d'Argenson (1696–1764), minister of war from January 1743 to February 1757, was the most exemplary of this type. He was a consummate politician from a well-connected family, and his amicability and chameleonic talents allowed him to ally himself with cabals as diverse as that of Queen Maria Leszczyńska (1703–1768) and her *dévots* and that of Louis XV's mistress the marquise de Pompadour (née Jeanne-Antoinette Poisson, 1721–1764). During his fourteen-year term, d'Argenson undertook a vast military reform program that was as much influenced by martial needs as it was by currents of "enlightened" thought.

D'Argenson was a friend and protector of the greatest *philosophes* of France. Before becoming minister of war, he had served as the director of the royal library and developed into a historian, archivist, and *philosophe* interested in the preservation and spread of knowledge. Denis Diderot and Jean le Rond d'Alembert dedicated their *Encyclopédie ou Dictionnaire raisonné des sciences, des arts et des métiers* to him. Voltaire, who served as royal historiographer, recognized his indebtedness to d'Argenson in procuring documents and information vital to his histories of Louis XIV and XV. D'Argenson applied his encyclopedic spirit and his practical experience as an archivist to reform the Dépôt de Guerre, created by the Sun King's war minister François-Michel le Tellier, marquis de Louvois (1641–1691) in 1688 to collect and preserve a historical archive of military memoranda (referred to as "mémoires) and maps. D'Argenson was named an honorary member of the Académie des sciences in 1726 and of the Académie des inscriptions et belles-lettres in 1748.[5]

Upon taking office, he brought his enlightened sensibilities and academic expertise to the domain of war. He aimed to preserve knowledge for posterity and to improve military service and efficacy from scientific and humanistic perspectives. He was a friend and close correspondent of marshal Maurice de Saxe, and at the latter's behest he implemented a suite of reforms based on recent scientific findings, most notably to the artillery. These changes played an important role in the French victories of 1745 during the War of Austrian Succession. Following the war, d'Argenson continued his efforts and made further ameliorations to fortifications, artillery, and drill practice (influenced by Prussian methods), and established the Royal Grenadiers, a system of military camps, and several royal military academies, including the engineering school (École royale du génie de Mézières, 1748) and the royal military academy (École royale militaire, 1750).

D'Argenson was also keenly interested in questions of human interest and instituted improvements aimed to better the lives of those who served the state in arms. He pioneered reforms to military hospitals and created a ministerial environment that was open to input from military men themselves. He also worked to bring justice, social cohesion, and professionalism to the army's officer corps through the creation of the *noblesse militaire* (military nobility, 1750) and the École royale militaire. The edict regarding military nobility buttressed meritocracy and mandated that all *roturiers* (commoners) who had reached the rank of *maréchal de camp* (field marshal) or higher would be ennobled. Their ennoblement was hereditary by their legitimate heirs and granted them all privileges of the Second Estate, including exemption from the *taille* land tax. Nonnoble officers in inferior ranks who had served for thirty years (of which twenty were at the rank of captain or above) and those who had been honored as *chevalier de l'ordre royal et militaire de Saint-Louis* were also exempted from paying the *taille*. This edict reaffirmed the age-old French definition of nobility as a social category earned by merit through courage and self-sacrifice in armed service to the monarch.[6]

According to Jean-Baptiste Pâris de Meyzieu (1718–1778), second intendant of the École royale militaire and author of the article "École militaire" in the *Encyclopédie*, the king founded the school at the request of his favorite, Madame de Pompadour. The monarch's motivation was reportedly not only to offer a state curriculum to educate officers, but also to give poorer provincial nobles a financial hand in their military careers. In order to qualify for admission, students had to have insufficient means to pay for an education or officer commission, be sons of long-serving military fathers, and prove four generations of nobility. The *philosophe* César Chesneau Dumarsais (1676–1756) stated in his encyclopedia article "Éducation," published in 1755, that "we have in the military school a model of education, which all persons who are in charge of bringing up young people should try to emulate; either with regard to health, food, cleanliness, decency, etc. or with regard to what concerns the cultivation of the mind."[7] The historian Marie Jacob confirms Dumarsais's shining assessment of the school and places the institution at the forefront of Enlightenment education.[8]

D'Argenson was a key player in founding the École royale militaire; however, as Pâris de Meyzieu and the official website on the history of the École relay, Louis XV's mistress, the marquise de Pompadour, was "the veritable soul of the project."[9] The future marquise was born of a noble mother, Louise-Madeleine de la Motte (1699–1745), and a *roturier* father, François Poisson (1684–1754). She was given an excellent education at the Ursuline convent in Poissy and came of age participating in some of the most famed hubs of Enlightenment debate, the Club de l'Entresol and the salon of Madame de Tencin (1682–1749). There, Poisson interacted with many of the great thinkers of the time, such as Charles-Louis de Secondat, baron de la Brède et de Montesquieu (1689–1755), Claude-Adrien Helvétius (1715–1771), and the famed Freemason Andrew Michael Ramsay (1686–1743). In 1745 she became official mistress or *favorite* of Louis XV, who gave her the title marquise de Pompadour. Intelligent and refined, Pompadour quickly adapted to life at court in Versailles and exercised considerable influence over the king, much to the chagrin of other courtiers who considered themselves of higher social rank and therefore more worthy of the king's attention (figure 2).

Scholars have attempted to discern exactly what role Pompadour played in domestic and international affairs. This is a challenge, since Pompadour was highly effective in self-publicity and tended to give herself and Louis XV credit for ideas that were not their own. This was certainly the case with the École royale militaire. Writing to her friend the comtesse de Lützelbourg, Pompadour bragged about the project of the military school, claiming that "his Majesty has been working on it for a year and his ministers have played no role and did not even know of it until he had already arranged everything to his liking."[10] This representation is exaggerated, if not fallacious. The proposal to establish the École royale militaire was written by the school's founder and first intendant, the financier Joseph Pâris Duverney (1684–1770). Nor was Pâris Duverney the originator of this idea, since he drafted his proposal to establish the school based on a reformulation of a plan designed by his eldest brother twenty-five years earlier. It is also indisputable that Pompadour herself played a crucial role in founding the École. She served as a mediator among Louis XV, d'Argenson, and Pâris Duverney and took on advocacy for the project with zeal, as she did that of the edict of military nobility and other projects that related to social justice.

FIGURE 2. Portrait of Madame de Pompadour by Maurice Quentin de la Tour. Musée du Louvre. Photo credit: Scala/Art Resource, NY.

The "think tank" and power arrangement behind this edict and the École combined the efforts of several "enlightened" figures—an intellectual-financier, a minister, and a mistress—followed by approval by the monarch himself. Though he acted as a "reform absolutist" in these endeavors, Louis XV was just as likely to take actions that were harmful to military effectiveness and budgets. He cheerfully distributed military posts to all of the favorites of his future mistress Madame du Barry (1743–1793) regardless of their merit and the cost of doing so. D'Argenson's successors in the Ministry of War inherited this game of tug-of-war between reform and tradition. They faltered between pursuing d'Argenson's legacy of technical and social reforms, on the one hand, and preserving the status quo by favoring the wealth, social status, and privileges of the *haute noblesse*, on the other.

Ministers Charles Louis Auguste Fouquet, duc de Belle-Isle (1684–1761), and the duc de Choiseul both leaned toward reform. They encouraged military men to send their observations and proposals to the war ministry and took measures to reduce the financial difficulties that plagued subaltern and junior officers. Belle-Isle increased their pay, and Choiseul instated a controversial policy by which the state took control of financing and administering captaincies. This helped shatter the "glass ceiling" that prevented deserving but poorer nobles from ascending to that rank. Simultaneously, though, this reform foisted the financial burden onto an already indebted state treasury and infuriated wealthier and more traditionally minded nobles who felt that their power and culture were being usurped by the state. Louis Nicolas Victor de Félix d'Ollières, comte du Muy (1711–1775), installed a system of seniority that bolstered merit-based advancement through the ranks, and Claude-Louis, comte de Saint-Germain (1707–1778), drastically cut back venal posts and high-cost ceremonial units (the *maison militaire*, musketeers, and grenadiers) while fostering professionalism through his system of *cadet-gentilhommes* (a one-year unpaid military internship for nobles).

Leaning toward tradition, ministers Louis François, marquis de Monteynard (1713–1791), and Emmanuel-Armand de Vignerot du Plessis de Richelieu, duc d'Aiguillon (1720–1788), both caved in to the vociferous backlash against Choiseul's reforms. They either repealed them or persisted in granting senior officer commissions for powerful nobles and court favorites despite the lack of public funds or military merit. Alexandre Marie Eleonor of Saint-Mauris, count of Montbarrey, then prince of Montbarrey (1732–1796), did not manage to effect change, but his successor, Philippe Henri, marquis de Ségur (1724–1801), later took what seemed a decisively anti-egalitarian stance in his regulation of 1781 that stipulated furnishing proof of four generations of patrilineal nobility in order to attain an officer post. The cycle of reform attempts and reversals continued until the eve of the French Revolution.

The archives of the Secrétaire d'état de la marine et des colonies (Secretary of State of the Navy and Colonies) also show remarkable reform efforts in areas of technological, medical, and humanistic innovation.[11] This was the case despite great odds, since the naval ministry was often strapped for cash and less influential than that of war, notwithstanding its enormous responsibilities. Not only did the naval ministry direct French maritime war forces; it was also charged with overseeing metropolitan ports and arsenals, managing colonial governments and militaries, administering consulates, regulating and surveying overseas markets and fisheries, charting forest routes, tracing canals, and more. The ministry's structure as a catchall and its chronically overworked and underfunded condition were signs of its inferior status compared to the Ministry of War. The crown and its ministers prioritized continental dominance and thus the army, whose means and results during wartime were somehow more tangible. This general opinion was best articulated by Jean-Frédéric Phélypeaux, comte de Maurepas (1701–1781), who was France's most longstanding *secrétaire de la marine* of the eighteenth century, serving for twenty-six years: "What is a naval battle? We cannon one another, we separate from one another, and the sea remains as salty as it was before."[12]

Excepting the period running up to and through the American Revolutionary War, the naval ministry was incapable of overcoming major hurdles, including maintaining its fleet and recruiting manpower. Effectives stagnated at sixty thousand sailors for most of the eighteenth century, compared to one hundred thousand in the British navy. There were around one thousand permanent officers of the grand corps (*officiers rouges*) and a variable number of supplementary officers (*officers bleus*) who were demobilized in peacetime. This number limited the quantity and size of vessels the navy could maintain knowing that a seventy-four-cannon vessel required 750 sailors and a one-hundred-cannon *trois ponts* needed at least 1,000 men.[13] The annihilation of entire crews by battle, shipwreck, and, most often, disease were nothing less than devastating.

Despite these constraints, the eighteenth century was a great age of naval experimentation in France, for both war and commerce. Successive ministers received innumerable tactical and technical memoirs, on subjects such as navigational tools and techniques, naval artillery, and new ship designs optimized for speed, maneuverability, cargo, and firepower. During the Regency, the naval ministry pioneered the first school of naval medicine at Rochefort in 1722. The following year, Maurepas took office and throughout his term undertook efforts to improve efficiency and professionalize the navy through a program of test ships (*navires d'essai*), a clearer system of ranks, and the École des ingenieurs-constructeurs de la marine, founded in 1740. Minister Antoine-Louis Rouillé, comte de Jouy (1689–1761), who served from 1749 to 1754, followed suit and founded the French naval academy at Brest (Académie de marine, 1752; made royal academy in 1769).

A broader public participated in naval development in different ways. Private shipbuilders and mercantile enterprises offered to construct model ships, and Choiseul, who took over the ministries of the navy and war during the early 1760s, famously asked the (wealthy) French public to raise money to construct eighteen ships in 1761. France was therefore able to participate in the unfolding naval technology arms race in which the century's cosmopolitan tendencies gave way to competition and industrial espionage. Between the Seven Years' War and the American Revolution, ministers reconstructed the French navy to take on the British, and important changes were made to the Colbertian code that had been in place since 1669. Charles Eugène Gabriel de La Croix, marquis de Castries (1727–1801), maréchal de France, and *ministre de la marine et des colonies* from 1780 to 1787, instituted a final series of reforms in the decade preceding the French Revolution. Along with the aforementioned reforms targeting science and professionalization, Castries enacted a number of humanitarian reforms. These measures, discussed in chapter 3, aimed to improve conditions of recruitment and service in the navy and to support the families of sailors, who often fell into destitution when the breadwinners of their households were forcefully conscripted.

While the decade of the 1780s was one of victory for the French naval ministry, the opposite was true for the war ministry. Contemporaries expressed resignation, frustration, or even disgust at the swinging pendulum of reforms and counterreforms coming from the Ministry of War, policies that seemed to knit and then unravel the fabric of the French army. Such inconsistency thwarted a linear narrative of progress, but the constant movement and effort to effect change are notable and relate the lived experiences of different war minsters. Louis XV and XVI did not as a general policy obstruct initiatives proposed by their martial ministers (though the naval ministers had a more difficult time of it), but rather gave them a certain leeway as experts in martial affairs to make many changes to the military system, drill, and so on. Though Pompadour exaggerated the king's role in founding the École royale militaire, Louis XV's and Louis XVI's openness to instituting military reforms is clear. From the perspective of the army and navy, then, the stereotype of their reigns as backward-looking compared to those of "enlightened despots" is not tenable. These monarchs, as well as their mistresses, their ministers, and, as the following section details, their military officers, were critical voices in the debates and reforms that constituted the Military Enlightenment.

Militaires Philosophes

In 1768 a scandalous critique of religion was published: *Le militaire philosophe ou difficultés sur la religion proposées au Reverend Père Malebranche* (*The Military Philosopher or Difficulties on Religion Proposed to Reverend Father Malebranche*). The anonymous author claimed to be a veteran officer, and despite declaring a lack of education or any contact with philosophers, he revealed: "I read the Scriptures with reflection: I have a little experience in history, am something of a physicist, I have some knowledge of mathematics such that I understand all that is conceptually solid no matter how abstract."[14] He was not just a veteran, but an intellectual; not just a *militaire*, but a *philosophe*.

In fact, this incendiary treatise was not penned by a military man at all. Rather, it was the creation of Jacques-André Naigeon (1738–1810), artist and atheist philosopher, and Paul-Henri Thiry, Baron d'Holbach (1723–1789), fellow atheist philosopher and author of a materialist worldview in *Système de nature* (1770). Choosing a veteran officer as the fictitious author and narrative voice lent certain advantages to the ideas expressed by Naigeon and d'Holbach. By the year in which *Le militaire philosophe* was published, it was imaginable, if not expected, for a veteran officer to possess knowledge in a multitude of areas: history, physics, math, and religion. This diverse education, most likely acquired at a military academy and in personal study, was understood to impart a perspective imbued with honesty, reason, thoughtfulness, intelligence, and realism. In addition to being the perfect authorial voice for a treatise aiming to decry religious dogma, Naigeon and d'Holbach's choice of faux author and title for the work reveals the plausibility and normalization of a primary figure of the Military Enlightenment: the *militaire philosophe*.

In previous centuries, and particularly before Louis XIV's personal reign, members of the *noblesse d'épée* were notoriously ill mannered and uneducated. Until recently, historians have perpetuated this stereotype and largely disregarded intellectual life in the military sphere of eighteenth-century Europe and America. Christopher Duffy, Armstrong Starkey, and others have claimed that the Prussian army was an exception to the norm of military anti-intellectualism in that it had "a dynamic intellectual center in the person of the king, who encouraged his officers to read professionally and challenged them by setting forth tactical problems for them to solve."[15] In the British, French, American, and other armed forces of the period, however, only small "pockets of intellectual curiosity flourished amidst a sea of Philistines."[16]

While it remains difficult to define and quantify, scholars have increasingly shed light on military intellectualism in armies and navies of the eighteenth century. Ira Gruber's study of the libraries maintained by British officers during the eighteenth century offers strong insights into their intellectual engagements and reading habits, which concerned a wide array of military and nonmilitary topics. Officers studied the art of war through foundational texts of antiquity by Vegetius, Julius Caesar, and Polybius as well as more recent treatises such as Saxe's *Mes rêveries* and the *Essai sur l'art de la guerre* (1754) by Lancelot Turpin, comte de Crissé et de Sanzay (1716–1793). Alongside these books were literary works by Homer, Racine, Milton, Sterne, and Rousseau as well as some "lighter" reading in the form of pornographic libertine novels.[17] Charles Royster and Sarah Knott illuminate the influence of the cult of *sensibilité* in the American army. Christopher Duffy notes that some Prussian officers adopted a withering, melancholic affect emulating characters like Saint-Preux in Rousseau's *Julie ou la Nouvelle Héloïse* (1761), one of the bestsellers of the century.[18]

Napoleon Bonaparte, who went to military school at the École militaire de Brienne and later the École royale militaire, was an avid reader of and commentator on military and nonmilitary texts during his early years in France. His collected early writings evince his enthusiasm for reading broadly and his personal initiative to process his contemplations through writing. Among many subjects, his notes include reflections on his specialty of artillery, on the politics and ways of war of the ancients, on the history of Corsica, and on philosophical debates of the day regarding glory, nobility, or the relative merits of republics and monarchies.[19] Ever inhabited with literary sensibility, Napoleon also tried his hand at writing literature, penning a "dialogue on love."

Yet much more must be said of military intellectualism during the eighteenth century, particularly in the French armed forces. Louis XIV had already introduced a higher level of cultivation in the officer corps, especially in the senior ranks. Whether at Versailles, in Parisian salons, or on campaign, these gentlemen engaged in fine dining, musical and theatrical performances, and lively conversations about war and other subjects. They were expected to be fluent in the language and gestures of *politesse* as much as any other courtier and to don the finery that exhibited their status and civility as well as those of the Sun King, himself an accomplished dancer. Influenced by Cartesian rationalism and Newtonian science, military culture under Louis XIV and ministers Sébastien le Prestre, marquis de Vauban (1633–1707), and François Michel Le Tellier, marquis de Louvois, also gave greater emphasis to siege and field warfare as processes that were calculable, predictable, and refined in a way that reflected the louisquatorzian aristocratic code of war.[20] The belief that war was knowable and controllable by humankind (as opposed to being arbitrary or ruled over by God) led to both the system of cabinet war (*guerre de cabinet*) and to a rising belief that professional training was necessary for military men. One of Louis XIV's generals, Antoine de Pas de Feuquières (1648–1711), published his *Memoirs on War* (*Mémoires sur la guerre où l'on a rassemblé les maximes les plus nécessaires dans les opérations de l'art militaire*), the first French military work to detail all of the roles and responsibilities of each rank and position in the newly rationalized standing army. Officers were to understand their duties and prepare for them in financial, physical, and intellectual terms.

The code of civility and *mondanité* (worldliness) as well as that of learned professionalism persisted into the eighteenth century and transformed under the influences of fiscal, military, and cultural pressures. As France's military crises became increasingly evident, ministers of the army and navy solicited critical observations or proposals for reforms.[21] Yet the vogue of philosophizing that Dumarsais complained about in his encyclopedia article "Philosophe" flourished in the military sphere. Military officers of different ranks recorded minute observations as they implemented new policies, made comparisons with previous ones, and proposed reforms pertaining to continental and overseas warfare. In peacetime, they were particularly active. As an anonymous writer of a memoir entitled "Projet d'un militaire," or "Project of a Military Man," wrote, "Without the opportunity to spill my blood for the good of [the king's] service, I offer these reform projects."[22]

Officers read a spectrum of works, translated texts, commented on them, and drew up their own theories both about the art of war and about ameliorating the military and cultural crises that plagued the French armed forces. Military thinkers participated actively in the "rational-critical debate" that Jürgen Habermas associated with the "structural transformation of the public sphere."[23] They, like other elites, frequented salons, Freemason lodges, clubs, and cafés, as well as the halls of Versailles in certain cases. They corresponded with other French officers and foreign military allies, with ministers of the crown, and with members of the nonmilitary intelligentsia.

Most especially, *militaires philosophes* dedicated themselves to writing. Azar Gat tracks the "revolutionary growth in military publications" across Europe and especially in France during the eighteenth century. Referring to Jean Pöhler's *Bibliotheca historica-militaris*, Gat quantifies this growth in the category of works (general and theoretical) on the art of war and finds that more than seventy items were published in a steady stream in the seventeenth century and that a similar rate of publication characterized the period between 1700 and 1748, roughly thirty works over a fifty-year period. In a sudden spike, the rate of publication jumped fourfold in the years 1748–1756 between the Treaty of Aix-la-Chapelle and the outbreak of the Seven Years' War, with twenty-five works published in that period alone. This rate was maintained up until the

French Revolution, totaling more than one hundred publications on the art of war.[24] From great military theorists who wrote multiple erudite tomes, to lower-ranking officers who wrote a single memoir on army drill, these authors were the backbone of the Military Enlightenment. They were engaged in the era's *esprit philosophique* and merit recognition as bona fide *philosophes* possessed of the characteristics that Dumarsais attributed to the name.

By surveying the corpus of published and manuscript works as well as their authors, two categories of *militaires philosophes* can be discerned. The first group concerned itself primarily with martial matters and intended to influence that sphere alone, while the second group engaged in matters outside of the military domain, from authoring literature, ethnographies, plays, and essays on cultural debates to patronizing arts and men of letters.

The first group of martially focused *militaires philosophes* shared the goal of improving military functioning, though they brought vastly different approaches and ontological perspectives on war to their studies. Thinkers such as the chevalier de Folard, Jacques-François de Chastenet, marquis de Puységur (1656–1743), Paul-Gédéon Joly de Maïzeroy (1719–1780), and François Jean de Graindorge d'Orgeville, baron de Mesnil-Durand (1729–1799) were influenced by the Cartesian concept of clear and distinct ideas and believed that rational and universal principles of war existed. Due to their systematic methods and beliefs, these *militaires philosophes* were dubbed *faiseurs de systèmes*, or makers of systems, by their peers. Folard, who grew up in Avignon and ran away to enlist in the army while a student at a Jesuit collège, is often seen as an exemplar of this type of *militaire philosophe*. His opus includes four extensive volumes and an abridged version, all of which demonstrated his learnedness as a classical historian of military arts, a scientist of war theorizing on rational and universal principles, and a modernist seeking to navigate human, psychological elements at play in strategy and tactics.[25] Folard's dissertations on military history and science, as well as his preference for battle formations that favored shock tactics rather than firearms, were provocative and widely debated in the international military community.[26] King Frederick the Great even wrote a tome on Folard, published in 1761.[27]

Puységur, like Folard, turned to antiquity in search of principles that would allow him to establish a universal theory of war. He combined the study of ancients (Herodotus, Homer, Socrates, Xenophon, Thucydides, Polybius, Arrian, Plutarch, Vegetius) with that of moderns (Turenne, Montecuccoli) in order to make field warfare as mathematical and systematic as siegecraft had become by Vaubanian principles. Turpin de Crissé, a military thinker and *mondain* who opined on nonmilitary subjects, also held that "the principles of war among all nations and in all times have been the same."[28] Like Puységur, he championed Vaubanian siegecraft, literally transposing lines of circumvallation to field warfare (troops advance, build fortifications and depots akin to the first parallel, troops advance again, make another parallel, and so on). His *Essai sur l'art de la guerre* (1754, 1757) was translated into German (1756, 1785), Russian (1758), and English (1761).

Maïzeroy, who enlisted at age fifteen and fought in Maurice de Saxe's campaigns in Bohemia and Flanders with Karl Theophilus Guichard (an officer and *militaire philosophe* also known as Quintus Icilius, 1724–1775), was similarly an accomplished classical historian and a military mathematician. Known to be one of the most expert Hellenists of his time, particularly in military affairs, Maïzeroy is credited with having coined the word "strategy" in its modern understanding. He became a member of the French Royal Academy of Inscriptions and Belles Lettres in 1776, thanks to his 1770 translation of the *Tactica* or *Military Institutions* by Byzantine emperor Leo VI the Wise (866–912), a work that itself was based on the *Strategicon* by Emperor Maurice (539–602). He applied Pythagorean philosophy to war and believed that numbers underlay all phenomena in the universe. He drew a fundamental distinction between tactics and strategy, judging that successful military tactics had to be based on correct choice of universal numbers, while strategy engaged what he called "military dialectic" and was "dependent on innumerable circumstances—physical, political, and moral—which are never the same and which are entirely the domain of genius."[29] Maïzeroy's universalist theories brought together historical, mathematical, and global inputs. The third part of his major work, the *Cours de tactique théorique, pratique et historique*, examined warfare of the Turks and of Asian populations. Along with others among his nine major works, the *Cours de tactique* was highly influential, first published in 1766, with two complementary volumes printed in 1767 and 1773, reprints in 1776 and 1785, and translations into German (1767, 1773) and English (1781).[30]

If the methods espoused by these *faiseurs de systèmes* were similar, their calculations and conclusions were not. This led to multiple doctrinal controversies, the most famous of which involved a heated face-off between proponents of the *ordre profond* (column battle formation optimized for shock weapons or *armes blanches*) and the *ordre mince* (battle formation of long, shallow lines of soldiers optimized for maximum firepower or *armes à feu*). These conflicts, however, did not take place in a bubble of theory alone. Universalists meant for their systems to have practical applications, and this in effect led to experimentation in training camps and in battle. Mesnil-Durand's system of shock-based tactics, advanced in *Fragments de tactique* (1774) and his earlier tactical work published in 1755, was extensively tested at the camp of Vaussieux in 1778 by the maréchal de Broglie.

Yet for many other *militaires philosophes*, the universalist theories proposed by *faiseurs de systèmes* proved excessively fallible and unrealistic, since they were based more on a priori calculation than on experience. Universalism was simply not possible in warfare due to countless contingencies that even Maïzeroy had recognized in his conception of strategy. Military empiricists such as Pierre Joseph de Bourcet (1700–1780) and Maurice de Saxe were more particularistic and anthropocentric in their approaches to both tactics and strategy. Bourcet began his military life as a nine-year-old boy when he followed his *roturier* father, a captain in the Alpes dauphinoises, during the War of Spanish Succession. He served in multiple branches of the armed forces (infantry, artillery, then later the engineering *corps de génie*) to become an expert in mountain war. He advocated for a concept of organized dispersion or a "plan with branches" (having a large army march in separate columns along parallel roads and form three columns within each column). This "plan" not only confused the enemy as to one's destination and forced him to divide his own forces in preparation for defending multiple locations, but also allowed rapid battlefield deployment and the combination of all branches into a single powerful force. Bourcet was a prolific writer and circulated numerous manuscripts and published works that won him recognition from the military community and from the crown.[31] He was ennobled in 1756 when he became *maréchal de camp* thanks to d'Argenson, Pompadour, and Louis XV's edict of military nobility and was later assigned by the king to oversee fortifications along the borders between France and Piedmont. He founded the first general officer training school at Grenoble under Choiseul, an institution that focused on alpine warfare and that would inspire Napoleon's establishment of military education.

Maurice de Saxe was also given to particularism in his military thought. His essay *Mes rêveries* was a work of enormous influence that was reprinted three times (1757, 1761, 1763) and widely circulated in German (1757, 1767) and English (1757, 1759, 1776). Saxe divided his study into "sublime" aspects of war adapted to particular topographic exigencies (grand tactics for open field warfare, mountain and rough terrain, sieges, and field fortifications) and into what he referred to as "details" (army organization, battle formation, armament, uniforms, and so on). A global thinker, Saxe penned an essay, "Mémoire militaire sur les Tartares et les Chinois," in his collections of miscellany written before his death; it was published posthumously under the Montesquieu-inspired title *Esprit de lois de la tactique* in 1762. Most importantly, Saxe emphasized the "human factor": the unpredictability of men (as opposed to the predictability of numbers on which *faiseurs de systèmes* relied) and the need to understand their physiology, psychology, and *coeurs*, or hearts, when engaged in battle and other military operations.

The second group of *militaires philosophes* was highly skilled in the culture of worldliness and became celebrities in their time not only as military thinkers, but also as patrons *philosophes*, and men of letters (figure 3).[32] No man is more strongly associated with this group than Jacques Antoine Hippolyte, comte de Guibert. Well-read and given to literary aspirations, Guibert composed a tragedy in verse at age twenty-six (*Le connétable de Bourbon*, 1769), the same year he reached the rank of colonel after fighting in campaigns of the Seven Years' War and in Corsica (1768). His scintillating charisma, eloquence, and patriotic fervor have led historians to be nearly as enamored with Guibert as were the intellectual elite of Paris and his love, Julie de Lespinasse (1732–1776). He reached "meteoric renown" with his *Essai général de tactique*, which had four editions in five years (1770, 1772, 1773, 1775) with translations into German (1774) and English (1781). "Guibert wrote the *Essai* with a pronounced and conscious intention to create an immortal masterpiece; this is apparent in every line of his work," comments Gat. "His intellectual environment clearly determined not only the nature and strength of his desire, but also the attitudes and themes required for its realization. The ambitious and enthusiastic young man appeared to have incorporated into his military treatise as many ideas of the Enlightenment as possible and touched upon most of its major concerns."[33]

A true child of the Enlightenment, Guibert was influenced by great thinkers of the early modern era and his own time, such as Newton, Leibniz, d'Alembert, Montesquieu, Voltaire, Frederick the Great, Saxe, and Rousseau. He distilled popular discourses in his work: *sensibilité*, classical republicanism, antiluxury, prussophilia, patriotism, and freedom. This influence is most visible in the preliminary discourse of the *Essai* with its defense of the *philosophes* and its daringly critical "Review of Modern Politics," which assessed the degradation of the military, social, and political systems of absolutist Europe. In a well-known passage, Guibert derided contemporary politics as characterized by "tyrannical ignorance" and "weak administrations," a corrupt and dysfunctional system that could be transformed only by people following the model of ancient republics, whose patriotism, vigor, and moral uprightness he admired. Discussions of the *Essai* spread across Parisian salons and intellectual circles like wildfire and made Guibert the darling of the European intelligentsia. His ideas left their mark, in terms of his poetic political commentary and especially his military recommendations that in some way crystallized reflections made by other *militaires philosophes*: greater flexibility, mobility, speed, and bold, divisive maneuvering bolstered by divisional column formations and living off the land. These ideas would mold French ways of warfare during the Revolutionary and Napoleonic eras.[34]

Guibert showed how *militaires philosophes* could be expert not only in military matters and history but also in political analysis and thought. Others transformed their military experiences to a new medium, that of literature, becoming famed writers in their time and stalwarts of the European canon to this day. Pierre Ambroise François Choderlos de Laclos (1741–1803), a twenty-two-year-old noble officer who had been trained at the École royale d'artillerie de La Fère, was filled with professional ambition after his promotion to second lieutenant before the close of the Seven Years' War. However, peacetime and a series of noncombat deployments squelched his hopes of military glory and transformed the young lieutenant into an *auteur*. After some unfortunate attempts at lyric poetry and writing for the stage, he turned toward the ever-proliferating and more experimental genre of the novel.[35] He aimed to create something exceptional, to "make a work that departs from the ordinary path, that will make noise and still resound on this earth when I will have passed." Thus, in 1778, Laclos began to compose his most celebrated work, *Les liaisons dangereuses*, published to enormous acclaim in 1782. In this epistolary novel Laclos employed an explicitly tactical, beyond metaphorical, usage of war, his protagonists la marquise de Mertueil and the vicomte de Valmont literally utilizing contemporary military strategy to succeed in their schemes of seduction and ultimately declaring war on one another.[36] Laclos did not limit his writing to literature. He wrote a treatise on the education of women (1783), political works in the first years of the French Revolution, and a treatise entitled *De la guerre et de la paix* (*On War and Peace*, 1795).

Similar in his military-turned-literary penchants, Donatien Alphonse François, marquis de Sade (1740–1814), first made his career in the army and took inspiration from his service. Sade wrote detailed accounts of military engagements, his own actions, and his belligerent penchants during his participation in the German campaigns of the Seven Years' War. This led him to varied war-related philosophical reflections: on the contrast between bravura and ferocity, on women warriors, and on man's natural inclination to destroy. "Let us not doubt, there are epochs when men need to destroy one another; moved by the elements that cooperate in this, they want to lead by example in helping along this pull toward disorganization, which itself is nothing but a regeneration to which we submit despite ourselves because the nature that constrains us to it would be necessarily outraged by the stagnation of apathy."[37] War was both an inevitable part of nature and a space of human agency in which the

FIGURE 3. Engraving by François-Bernard Lépicié (1698–1755) after Antoine Watteau (1684–1721), *Portrait of Antoine de La Roque* (engraving 1733, original artwork lost). Courtesy of the Bibliothèque de France. Antoine de La Roque (1672–1744) was a *militaire philosophe* who served as a constable of the Royal Guard and lost one of his legs at the battle of Malplaquet (1709) during the War of Spanish Succession. He retired from the service following his convalescence and received the Croix de Saint-Louis from King Louis XIV. He dedicated the rest of his life to the humanities, journalism, and art collecting. He composed an opera (*Thésée*, 1715), took over the privilege of the *Mercure de France* in 1721, and collected over three hundred pieces of fine art, including paintings by Rubens, Veronese, Poussin, Wouwerman, and Watteau, with whom he was friends. This portrait by the latter shows La Roque to be a *militaire philosophe*: he reclines in the foreground, the cuirass and cane indicating his military career and injuries, while musical instruments, sheet music, and the muses in the background display his status as an artist.

injustices of hierarchical society could be avenged and perhaps overturned. Since "society is composed but of the weak and the strong," Sade explained, "the state of war, which existed before, must have been infinitely more preferable because it gave each person the free exercise of his strength and his industriousness of which he found himself deprived due to the unjust pact of society that always takes too much away from one and never gives enough to the other."[38] War was a foundational element of both his materialism and his moral philosophy, however repugnant.

Pierre-Jean-Paul Berny de Nogent (1722–1779), another military officer and well-known man of letters, wrote a hybrid military-cultural work, *La guerre dans tout ce qu'elle a de plus général tant offensive que défensive avec des réflexions précises sur l'étude et l'exercice militaire* (War: Everything General, Offensive and Defensive with Precise Reflections on Military Study and Exercise) of 1773. Turpin de Crissé dabbled in martial cultural questions as well as those of moral philosophy and literature. He jumped into several hot debates of the mid-eighteenth century and boldly addressed some of the century's greatest minds. In 1754, he published *Amusemens philosophiques et littéraires de deux amis* (Philosophical and Literary Amusements of Two Friends), written in collaboration with his writer-journalist friend Jean Castilhon (1720–1799), who would later found the *Spectateur français, ou journal des moeurs*, in 1776. The *Amusemens* included poetry and literary criticism as well as essays on philosophical and cultural subjects, several of which had significance for the military sphere, such as essays on honor versus virtue, on emulation, and on the "great man" (*le grand homme*) versus the "hero." The first item in the collection was a "friendly" letter to Jean-Jacques Rousseau. Written in ten-syllable verse, the letter criticized Rousseau's misanthropy and self-imposed isolation and offered the beleaguered *philosophe* advice on how to better deal with people:

> See, without regret, from the same root,
> The rose that shines and the thorns that grow.
> In the early morning see the adroit butterfly
> Suckle the flower and brave the needles:
> Do as it does: simply choose such that your hate
> Does not include the entire human race.[39]

Rousseau issued a brief reply to Turpin de Crissé, one that communicates the same haughty "friendliness" conveyed in the original letter: "Your collection is not bad enough for me to reject you for the work, nor it is good enough to discourage you from the hope of writing something better."[40]

Turpin de Crissé and Castilhon's *Amusemens* as well as Guibert's and Berny's work are examples of how *militaires philosophes* connected martial issues with broader philosophical and cultural questions and then brought these meditations to a larger public.

Global War and *Esprit Philosophique*

Living and fighting abroad in wars around the globe was a source of inspiration and challenge for *militaires philosophes* of the eighteenth century. In North America, these individuals were adopted by Amerindian tribes, learned "forest diplomacy," and embraced local ways of war. They coupled with native women, depended on native medical practices, and traded their rations for moccasins. They scalped enemies and were scalped themselves. Oceans away on the Indian subcontinent, they trained and led forces of sepoys (or *cipayes*, Indian mercenaries) and struck up tenuous alliances with sultans such as Hyder Ali Khan (1720–1782) and other local authorities. They collaborated with African princes in Senegal to assure a supply of slaves and the security of French slave-trading posts and ships. Such experiences could not but transform these men, confirming or debunking stereotypes about ethnic "Others" and also about the alleged superiority of European culture and society. Like their counterparts who never left Europe, *militaires philosophes* at sea, in the colonies, and at mercantile *comptoirs* recorded their observations, wrote reports and recommendations for the naval and war ministries, and authored treatises on the places and peoples with whom they interacted. While a plethora of cultural misunderstandings and misgivings took place, published works and manuscripts convey the deep interest, cultural adaptability, and epistemological legitimacy they exercised as explorers and inhabitants, albeit at times temporary, of these worlds.

By the mid-eighteenth century, officers going abroad had access to a growing canon of travel narratives, geographical, and proto-ethnographic works that they could study in preparation for their deployment. Those traveling to North America, for example, could examine the Jesuit relations of the seventeenth century, the *New Voyages to North America* (*Nouveaux voyages dans l'Amérique septentrionale*, 1703) by fellow army officer Louis Lom d'Arce, baron de Lahontan (1666–1716), the *History of North America* (*Histoire de l'Amérique septentrionale*, written in 1702, published in 1722) by Claude-Charles Le Roy Bacqueville de La Potherie (1663–1736), and especially the *History and Descriptions of New France* (*Histoire et description générale de la Nouvelle France*, 1744) by Pierre-François-Xavier de Charlevoix (1682–1761).[41] Opting for a more geographically and culturally anachronistic route, Louis-Joseph de Montcalm (1712–1759), who led the French metropolitan regular army forces sent to fight in North America during the Seven Years' War, read Homer's *Iliad* and *Odyssey* and Virgil's *Aeneid* with his officers and those of the naval ground troops (*compagnies franches de la marine*), channeling these epic narratives as useful lenses through which to understand battle experience in North America.[42] Raynal's *L'histoire des deux Indes* of 1770 was a popular and controversial work that army and naval officers read avidly.

While officers of the army, navy, and marines certainly undertook study to prepare for the places and populations they would encounter, they also viewed themselves as privileged producers of knowledge. They did not hesitate to critique widely held assumptions spread by intellectuals on the European continent, many of whom, like Rousseau and later François-René, vicomte de Chateaubriand (1768–1848), had never traveled to the places about which they wrote. *Militaires philosophes* asserted that their knowledge and experience should take precedence over ideas spread by mainstream *philosophes* and natural philosophers like George-Louis Leclerc, comte de Buffon (1707–1788) and the Dutch ethnographer Cornelius de Pauw (1739–1799). The case of de Pauw and military reactions to his stereotypes about Amerindians is a telling example. De Pauw was thought to be the foremost authority on Amerindians. His work, the *Recherches philosophiques sur les Américains, ou Mémoires intéressants pour servir à l'histoire de l'espèce humaine. Avec une dissertation sur l'Amérique & les Américains* (*Philosophical Research on the Americans, or Interesting Memoirs in the Service of the History of the Human Species. With a Dissertation on America and Americans*) was published in several editions in the late 1760s and early 1770s. It promulgated a monolithic, deeply unflattering, racist view of Amerindians:

> The American, strictly speaking, is neither virtuous nor vicious. What motive has he to be either? The timidity of his soul, the weakness of his intellect, the necessity of providing for his subsistence, the powers of superstition, the influence of climate, all lead him far wide of the possibility of improvement; but he perceives it not; his happiness is: not to think; to remain in perfect inaction; to sleep a great deal; to wish for nothing, when his hunger is appeased . . . In his understanding there is no gradation, he continues an infant to the last hour of his life. By his nature sluggish in the extreme, he is revengeful through weakness, and atrocious in his vengeance.[43]

De Pauw believed that Europeans who spent time in America slowly degenerated.

De Pauw's characterizations incensed people in Europe and across the Atlantic. Thomas Jefferson (1743–1826) and James Madison (1751–1836) refuted his claims, as did a number of French officers such as Zacharie de Pazzi de Bonneville (ca. 1710–ca.1771). Bonneville published a commentary of Maurice de Saxe's writings on war and also penned a treatise entitled *On America and Americans* (the full and slightly sarcastic French title was *De l'Amérique et des Américains: ou Observations curieuses du philosophe La Douceur, qui a parcouru cet hémisphere pendant la dernière guerre, en faisant le noble métier de tuer des hommes sans les manger*, 1771). Bonneville challenged the legitimacy of de Pauw's work, beginning in the preface, in which he denounced the broad generalizations and lack of sufficient on-the-ground experience that formed the foundations of *Recherches philosophiques*. Bonneville declared that he would not honor de Pauw's ideas by refuting them one by one, but rather that he would simply speak the truth and convey only that which he had witnessed with his own eyes.[44] His most important and culturally modern message concerned the diversity of Amerindian peoples, the many different nations, subcultures, and national characters that existed among them, and each Amerindian person's status as an autonomous individual possessed of his or her own personality.[45] He tried to help European readers understand that the infantilized "objects" of de Pauw's essay were individual thinking, breathing, meritorious human beings. They were subjects, not objects.

Animated by *esprit philosophique*, officers in the *compagnies franches de la marine* and those of French regular forces like Bougainville who traveled to Nouvelle France in the Seven Years' War were eager to measure stereotypes and "book knowledge" about America and its inhabitants against their own observations and experiences. Some encountered Amerindians while preparing for campaigns, while others first interacted with different tribespeople and French Canadians in the great melting pot of Montreal, where "Mohawk women traveled 'to visit French chapels, Nipissing men brought deer meat to the market square, Oneida families visited French friends, enslaved Apache girls carried water to the garden.'"[46] Though some officers, like the chevalier Le Duchat, found that their own observations confirmed negative stereotypes, Jean Baptiste d'Aleyrac (1737–1796) and others, such as Anne Joseph Hippolyte de Maurès, comte de Malartic (1730–1800), contested continental judgments. They noted the many positive qualities different tribesmen possessed: fortitude in the face of pain and adversity, athleticism, and dancing, hunting, and fishing skills. They also disputed banal assertions that could have the pernicious effect of dehumanizing Amerindians, such as the claim that the latter were extraordinarily hairy, like beasts. "The Savages of Canada are very different from the idea commonly held of them in France," wrote d'Aleyrac rather wryly; "far from being hairy, as is believed, they are much less covered with hair than we are."[47]

These experiences turned many officers into amateur ethnologists of India, Africa, the Mascarenes, the Antilles, and other geographies. They sent letters, personal memoirs, travel narratives, and "scientific" memoirs back to the continent, sharing their impressions of the environs, people, and cultures they encountered. Some officers inevitably offered racist, Eurocentric commentary. In his *Mémoires* of his time serving in the Mascarenes and in India, chevalier Jean Jacques de Cotignon (b. 1761) deployed racial bias against peoples of African descent in order to relay his complete disrespect for Indian sepoys, whom he called "the country's negroes" and constantly disparaged as weak, cowardly, incapable of discipline, and militarily ineffective, such that "fifty thousand Frenchmen could rout six hundred thousand" of them.[48]

Conversely, many military men serving abroad became enthusiasts of the foreign geographies, cultures, and leaders they came to know. Some even became cultural ambassadors, especially of the country that would become the United States of America. Gilbert du Motier, marquis de Lafayette (1757–1834), was one such officer who transformed himself from a tragically awkward (but wealthy and well-connected) fish out of water at Versailles to a hero and champion of the American Revolution.[49] A darling of George Washington and perhaps the first great Americanophile, Lafayette and his wife, Marie Adrienne Françoise de Noailles (1759–1807), purchased a home on the Left Bank of Paris referred to as the Hôtel Turgot and made it a hub of American culture in the city. Lafayette decorated the abode with American keepsakes and hosted many of the most important American dignitaries for meals in his sumptuous mirrored salon. French elites rubbed elbows with the likes of the Jeffersons, the Adamses, and the Jays at Lafayette's "American dinners," where English was the language of choice for conversation and for evening entertainment often offered by Lafayette's own children, Anastasie and George Washington Lafayette. Even the invitations to these soirées were on billets printed in English. The American dinners were meant to be culturally authentic and apparently succeeded, since several Americans, even the puritanical Abigail Adams, purportedly felt very much at ease at the Lafayettes' home.

Not all military men were interested (or could afford) to bring America to France in this literal fashion, so they simply recorded their experiences and observations to send them home to their families. Of the 492 officers who traveled with marshal Jean-Baptiste Donatien de Vimeur, comte de Rochambeau (1725–1807) to aid the American cause, war journals and other personal accounts from over forty men are extant, notably those of Jean-François-Louis, comte de Clermont-Crèvecoeur (1752–1824), Marie-François-Joseph-Maxime Cromot du Bourg (1756–1736), baron Gaspard de Gallatin (1758–1838), Jean-Baptiste-Antoine de Verger (1762–1851), and baron Ludwig von Closen (also known as Louis-Jean-Christophe de Closen, 1755–1830). Collections of memoirs and letters have also been assembled for Rochambeau himself as well as for Armand Louis de Gontaut, duc de Lauzun (later known as the duc de Biron, 1747–1793), and others. These documents not only reveal military details of Rochambeau's campaigns and collaboration with the Americans but also show how these French warrior-authors engaged in cultural analyses and communicated their ideas back to their homeland.[50]

Officers debated on the appearance, mores, and fighting capacities of their Amerindian allies and took positions on the practice of slavery: some condemned it based on humanitarian arguments, while others purchased slaves to use as domestic servants. Von Closen noted critically that "a dog often leads a happier life and is better nourished than the poor negro slaves and mulattos."[51] Yet paradoxically, von Closen judged slaves as either "thieves like magpies or as faithful as gold" and acquired a slave named Peter whom he put into the latter category. Officers were most interested, however, in Americans of European descent, though they tended to snub their American counterparts due to the latters' difference in social standing. The former were aristocrats, while many American officers were of the humble artisan class of blacksmiths, bakers, cobblers, and innkeepers. For this reason, French officers often preferred to keep company with English and German officers and frequently shared meals with them, although they passed judgment on the behavior of these foreign gentlemen as well. Verger was appalled at British atrocities perpetrated against Americans in Jamestown, Virginia. He recounted with horror the vision of a young, pregnant American woman whose body had been mutilated and eviscerated, then hung on a door, with her defunct fetus hanging from her hollow womb with a sign that read, "Damned Rebel! No longer shall you give birth."[52]

Kinder hospitality and mores could be found between enemy generals and also in the *haute bourgeoisie* of American society whom French officers met in cities like Philadelphia, Williamsburg, Boston, and Newport. However, there were some American mores that French officers simply could not fathom. A number of officers marveled at the practice of *bondelage* or "bundling," which allowed young couples—engaged to be married or unengaged—to spend hours and even entire nights together alone in a bedroom. There they were to remain completely clothed, but could kiss and, and as Clermont-Crèvecoeur put it, "devote themselves to tender caresses . . . excepting those that only marriage has the right to permit." A show of incredible trust, self-control, and respect, "bundling," Clermont-Crèvecoeur concluded, "is really only for Americans."[53]

With somewhat informed ethnographically inclined imaginations, military officers such as Clermont-Crèvecoeur, Laurent-François Lenoir, marquis de Rouvray (1743–1798, army; served in Saint-Domingue), and lieutenant colonel Russel (artillery; served in India) functioned as unofficial cultural and political diplomats who deepened and spread knowledge of peoples and cultures from around the world. The *militaires philosophes* of the colonies and the continent discussed above and the scores of other authors of both manuscript memoirs and published treatises were intellectuals of the military sphere who influenced knowledge, public opinion, and policy during their lifetimes and beyond. They popularized military matters to become a domain in which mainstream nonmilitary *philosophes*, literary, performing and fine arts, and the public engaged.

A Military-Minded Intelligentsia and Public

Voltaire opened chapter 23 of *Candide* (1759) with a multifaceted critique of war. The eponymous protagonist and his fellow traveler Martin, a Dutch Manichean philosopher, arrive in England. First comes the famous line in which Martin says that the English and French are equally foolish, as evidenced by their being at war over "a few acres of snow in Canada" (quelques arpents de neige vers le Canada). "They spend much more on this beautiful war than the whole of Canada is worth." Having set the stage, Voltaire launched into a frontal attack of a more pointed subject, that of the harsh and often arbitrary naval penal code:

> The coast was lined with crowds of people attentively watching a big man kneeling, his eyes bandaged, on the upper deck of a warship in the harbor. Four soldiers were positioned opposite to this man; each of them fired three bullets point-blank into his skull with all the tranquility in the world; and the whole assembly disbursed feeling perfectly satisfied.
>
> "What is all this?" said Candide; "and what demon exercises his powers in these parts?"
>
> He then asked who was that big man just killed with so much ceremony. "He was an Admiral," they responded.
>
> "And why kill this Admiral?"
>
> "It is because he did not kill a sufficient number of people. He gave battle to a French Admiral; and it was found that he was not near enough to him."
>
> "But," said Candide, "the French Admiral was just as far from the English Admiral as the latter was from him."
>
> "That is indisputable," they replied, "but in this country it is seen as good to kill an Admiral from time to time in order to encourage the others."
>
> Candide was so overwhelmed and shocked by what he saw and heard that he did not want to set foot on shore, and made a bargain with the Dutch skipper (were he even to rob him like the Surinam captain) to conduct him to Venice without delay.[54]

This episode was based on a shocking true story. Just two years before *Candide* was published, British naval officer John Byng (1704–1757) was sentenced to a public execution by firing squad on the upper deck of his ship, the HMS *Monarch*. This disproportionately cruel punishment was meted out by court-martial to penalize Byng for losing the battle of Minorca against Roland Michel Barin, marquis de La Galissonnière (1693–1756), in 1756. It was decided that Byng had exercised an excess of caution and shown an inability to adapt his traditionalist tactics to changing circumstances as his first line of battleships was battered by the French and his second line was unable to advance within cannon range of the heavily armed French fleet. With substantial damages to his fleet and none to the French, Byng retreated to Gibraltar, judging as a failure his mission to debilitate the French fleet and relieve the last standing British garrison on the island at Port Mahon. The naval victory and the taking of Minorca were trumpeted near and far by the French crown and press. It was a triumph of symbolic importance as one of the opening battles of the Seven Years' War, and it also held strategic value, especially when the Treaty of Paris was devised and Minorca was exchanged for the return of the French Antilles and Belle-Île off the coast of Brittany. As this occurrence and Voltaire's narrative evince, the cruelty and cost of war extended far beyond battles themselves. Crimes were perpetrated not only by enemies but also by the very state for which a military man had been willing to lay down his life in combat.

Philosophes like Voltaire slung vitriolic aspersions against warfare and warriors. These writers carried on a tradition of antiwar and antimilitary critique that had burgeoned in the seventeenth century. As had Pierre Corneille (1606–1684) in his theatrical retelling of the story of the Horatii, the Jansenist Blaise Pascal (1623–1662) decried the fact that killing citizens of a neighboring country was wholly acceptable and even virtuous, while killing one's neighbor and countrymen were considered criminal. In fragment 47 of the chapter "Vanité" in his *Pensées*, published posthumously in 1670, Pascal demonstrated this irony:

> Why do you kill me?—What? Don't you live on the other side of the water? My friend, if you lived on this side, I would be an assassin and it would be unjust to kill you in this way. However, since you live on the other side, I am courageous man and this is just.
>
> *Pourquoi me tuez-vous?—Et quoi? Ne demeurez-vous pas de l'autre côté de l'eau? Mon ami, si vous demeurez de ce côté je serais un assassin, et cela serait injuste de vous tuer de la sorte. Mais puisque vous demeurez de l'autre côté je suis un brave et cela est juste.*"[55]

In the chapter "Misères," Pascal commented on the abhorrent and odd way that war transpired: one man, a prince, declaring war on another prince, both of whom sit comfortably on their thrones waging cabinet war while thousands of men between whom there is no quarrel must murder one another out in the fields. He made this point while reiterating the irony that horrendous acts against humanity were often viewed as virtuous when perpetrated against an enemy during a time of war. In sarcastic words that Voltaire would echo multiple times in his writing, Pascal remarked that "larceny, incest, the murder of children and fathers—all have their place among 'virtuous actions'."[56]

The moralist Jean de la Bruyère (1645–1696) was even more scathing in his appraisal of war in *Les caractères* (1666), prefiguring Voltairian vitriol.[57] The Catholic pacifist François de Salignac de la Mothe-Fénelon (1651–1715), tutor of Louis XIV's grandson, the Dauphin, taught his pupil the tenets of Christian humility, fairness, pacifism, and restraint—traits that the warmongering Louis XIV did not always exhibit.[58] He imparted these lessons in a series of moralistic fables and fairy tales as well as a celebrated novel, *Les aventures de Télémaque* (1699), in which time and time again the protagonist, Ulysses's son Telemachus, learns from his guide Mentor that "all of humankind is but a single family dispersed across the face of the earth. All people are brothers and must love themselves as such. Misfortune to those impious men who search for a cruel glory in the blood of their brothers, which is their own blood. War is sometimes necessary, it is true; but it is the shame of humankind even if it is inevitable on certain occasions."[59]

The pacifism, Christian and secular humanism, and cosmopolitanism expressed in these works of the seventeenth century fueled literary and philosophical critiques of war in the century to follow. Yet eighteenth-century French writers and intellectuals did more than articulate generalized criticism. They demonstrated a greater awareness of the French military system, of historical and current warriors, battles, and tactics than their predecessors. This more specialized knowledge, gained from the press and publications like the *Encyclopédie*, public spaces, and private relations, allowed intellectuals to engage in specific issues, as did Voltaire in his condemnation of the naval penal code in England. This knowledge permeated libertine literature and novels of worldliness (*mondanité*), which not only depicted war as a metaphor for seduction and sex as well as for elite social relations as a whole, but also showed a literal use of military tactical thinking as seducers tried to infiltrate a woman's bedchamber or aristocrats aimed to defeat rivals in elite social circles.[60] The painter Jean-Antoine Watteau (1684–1721), born and raised in the war-torn town of Valenciennes on the northeastern border of France, likewise painted a series of military scenes during the War of Spanish Succession that relayed an insider's knowledge about contemporary problems of violently coerced conscription, incompetent officers, and the troublesome results of social inequality in the army.⁶¹

It is worth remarking that many of these writers and *philosophes* brought as much ardor to exalting warfare and warriors as they had to criticizing them. Voltaire himself celebrated martial prowess on numerous occasions in his histories, in the epic *La Henriade* (1723), and in poetry like the "Poème de Fontenoy" (1745). Rousseau, likewise, criticized equally the brutality and injustices of perpetrators of war and the illusions of peace embraced by pacifists, all the while lauding the austere military culture of the Spartans. Finding a type of *juste milieu* in his typical anti-Hobbesian perspective, Rousseau insisted that "the human species was not created uniquely to destroy itself." Rather, war, "a mutual disposition, constant and manifest, to destroy the enemy state or at least to weaken it by all means that one can," was born of society and was thus "natural" to states as the pure product of collective human art.⁶²

Other *philosophes* approached war as military men did: as something that was not going to disappear, and thus something that must be understood. Rousseau did this to some extent, as did Montesquieu, Gabriel Bonnot de Mably (1709–1785), Charles Rollin (1661–1741), the *Encyclopédistes*, and others. Ancient warriors and warfare were subjects of scrutiny and historical learning for these *philosophes* just as they were for *militaires philosophes* such as Folard, Maïzeroy, and Turpin de Crissé. In his *Considérations sur les causes de la grandeur des romains et de leur décadence* (1734), a veiled critique of eighteenth-century French society, Montesquieu extolled the courage and physical strength of the Roman soldiers as well as the spirit of obedience that prevailed and made a strict system of martial law unnecessary.⁶³ Montesquieu also theorized on honor in *De l'esprit des lois* (1748), a key sentiment thought to animate subjects of monarchies and in particular military men.⁶⁴ In several of Mably's works, including the *Observations on the Romans* (1751) and the *Entretiens de Phocion sur le rapport de la morale avec la politique* (1763), he opined on the moral advantages of a patriotic citizen army, as did Joseph Servan de Gerbey (1741–1808), Guibert, Saxe, and many others. "With a love for their country, for their honor, and their fellow citizens," wrote Rollin in his seven-volume *Ancient History of the Egyptians, Carthaginians, Assyrians, Babylonians, Medes and Persians, Macedonians, and Grecians* (1730–1738), military discipline and effectiveness would come effortlessly.⁶⁵

Military subjects constituted a major part of Diderot and d'Alembert's *Encyclopédie*, a compendium that sold roughly twenty thousand copies and included seventeen volumes published between 1751 and 1765, eleven volumes of plates published between 1762 and 1772, and four supplementary volumes plus one of plates in 1776 and 1777 (after Diderot stepped down as editor).⁶⁶

In his oft-cited article "Guerre," written during the Seven Years' War, Louis de Jaucourt (1704–1799) condemned war but accepted it as an inevitable part of human civilization. "War smothers the voice of nature, of justice, of religion, and of humanity." Nevertheless, he conceded, "we inherited it from our first ancestors; from the infancy of the world, they were making war."[67] Jaucourt and other *Encyclopédistes* discussed current polemics on honor, glory, and heroism, as well as detailed technical and historical knowledge in the many articles concerning military art.

John Lynn estimates that of the 74,044 entries in the *Encyclopédie*, about 1,250 were categorized by editors under "art militaire," a figure that does not capture articles on naval warfare or many other moral and political articles such as Diderot's "Hostilité," Jaucourt's "Conquête," "Transfuge," and "Patriotisme," Jean-François de Saint-Lambert's (1716–1803) "Honneur" Rousseau's "Economie," and other articles drafted by Voltaire, d'Holbach, Nicolas-Antoine Boulanger (1722–1759), and Antoine-Gaspard Boucher d'Argis (1708–1780) that had military elements and implications.[68] Lynn painstakingly compiled a list of these entries, creating a useful index of articles on land-based military art; he also surveyed the writers who contributed most in this category. The mathematician and military scientist Guillaume le Blond (1704–1781) leads this group with 65 percent of the entries; next come Jaucourt with 9 percent and Diderot with 2.2 percent, followed by other writers such as d'Alembert, Jean-Baptiste Luton Durival (1725–1810), Edmé-François Mallet (1713–1755), Charles-Louis d'Authville des Amourettes (1716–1762), and Jacques-François Blondel (1705–1774).[69]

Encyclopédistes worked to record all pertinent military knowledge, from military history and *jus ad bellum* to the manufacture and use of weaponry, fortifications, drill, field and siege tactics, discipline, recruitment, and military armor and dress. Inspired by the movement to render warfare more scientific, *Encyclopédistes* placed military tactics and architecture under the rubrics "Science of Nature" and "Elementary Geometry" in the "Detailed System of Human Knowledge."[70] In addition to critical and scientific approaches, certain authors openly praised military men. Louis-Elisabeth de la Vergne, comte de Tressan (1705–1783) lauded the moral fiber of men of war in his article "Homme de guerre," amalgamating medieval chivalric and modern bourgeois values. Jean-François Marmontel (1723–1799), in his article "Gloire," declared that "there is no glory comparable to that of warriors, for that of legislators might demand more talent, but much less sacrifice . . . Supposing that the plague of war is inevitable for humanity, the profession of arms should be the most honorable since it is the most perilous." Marmontel lamented that French authors did not honor these warriors as much as ancient historians had their own. "The

French military man has a thousand traits of this beauty that Plutarch and Tacitus would have taken great care to collect. We relegate them to individual memoirs as if insufficiently dignified for the majesty of history. One must hope that an *historien philosophe* will liberate himself from this prejudice."[71]

Medical professionals comprised another part of the intellectual public seeking to spread military knowledge. *Médecins philosophes*, or doctor-philosophers, discussed in chapter 3, formed a cosmopolitan community with surgeons and hospital intendants working to improve military medicine. They created a dynamic exchange of ideas on hygiene and preventive medicine, infectious diseases, surgical tools and techniques, and the maintenance of hospitals. Discourse on diseases in armies and navies of the eighteenth century was a collaborative, multinational endeavor, as historians David Vess, Laurence Brockliss, Colin Jones, and Erica Charters have established.[72] In the *république des lettres* of military medicine, physicians and surgeons from across Europe and the colonies traveled to study under one another; read one another's works in translation and original languages; shared their findings and experiences at various battlefronts; and were invited to sit as foreign members in scientific societies such as the Académie royale des sciences in Paris and London's Royal Academy.[73] John Pringle's (1707–1782) *Observations on the Diseases of the Army* (1752), Richard Brockleby's (1722–1797) *Oeconomical and Medical Observations* (1764), and Gerard van Swieten's (1700–1772) *Diseases Incident to Armies* (1776) were among the most significant and widely read works of the century on disease in the military. Colonial wars fostered what the historian Michael Osborne calls the "emergence of tropical medicine," which grew out of naval medicine in works such as Antoine Poissonnier-Desperrières's (1722–1793) *Traité des fièvres de l'isle de S. Domingue* (1763) and *Traité sur les maladies des gens de mer* (1767) as well as the Scottish physician James Lind's (1716–1794) *Essay on the Most Effectual Means of Preserving the Health of Seamen* (1762) and *An Essay on Diseases Incidental to Europeans in Hot Climates* (1768).[74]

An active medical periodical press grew out of this cosmopolitan dialogue. Whereas there had been a total of six medical journals in England and France during the seventeenth century, their number grew to twenty-six and over fifty, respectively, during the latter eighteenth century.[75] In France during the last decades of the *ancien régime*, seven periodicals, including the *Journal de médecine militaire* (first issue 1782), discussed in the following section, and the *Receuil d'observations de médecine des hôpitaux militaires* (two volumes, 1766 and 1772), targeted a military medical readership and published first-rate studies.[76]

In addition to these thinkers who earned the monikers of military, medical, or simple *philosophe*, a broader public engaged and influenced authorities in military affairs. Readers discussed what Voltaire meant with the war between the Abares and Bulgares in *Candide* and debated his Hobbesian assessment that all of society, especially in "civilized" Paris, is in a state of perpetual war. Prussophiles enumerated the qualities of Frederick the Great and his victorious army, Anglophiles worshipped the British patriotism believed to have won them the Seven Years' War, and fans of the new American republic glorified the virtue and martial stalwartness of these free people. Women and men of salons and social circles venerated or railed at Guibert's *Essai*. They also deliberated on the military penal code and joined together in chorus to reject the death penalty for deserters and corporal punishment for offenders of certain petty crimes.

In unprecedented measure, war and military affairs became an active element of discussion and advocacy in the nonmilitary public sphere. This was in part due to the means by which and the spaces in which the Military Enlightenment unfolded.

Means and Spaces of the Military Enlightenment

In terms of means, as we have seen, writing and reading played a central role in disseminating innovative thought, debates, and reforms concerning the military. Many print media—treatises, encyclopedias, periodicals—were intended to be read by members of the military and nonmilitary alike. Manuscript treatises and memoirs as well as epistolary correspondence also constituted essential means of developing and communicating reform-minded thinking, although they targeted individuals and small groups, as opposed to a large, more diverse public. Similarly, in this period that literary critic Benedetta Craveri calls "the age of conversation," discussion was a common and thus essential means of sharing and spreading ideas. Public and private reading as well as conversation took place in a multiplicity of venues: salons, private suppers, clubs, cafés, Freemason lodges, academies, and of course the court at Versailles. Military officers inhabited all of these locations when not at garrison, on campaign, or back at their own private residences. Active duty also encouraged writing, reading, conversing, and experimenting with novel attitudes and practices. Camps, barracks, and theaters of war were crucial laboratories in which military officers and soldiers engaged with and fostered the Military Enlightenment.

Expanding literacy rates and the growing market of printed publications made books, encyclopedias, and periodicals primary conduits for spreading new theories. Publication records including reprints and translations of works like Saxe's *Mes rêveries* and Guibert's *Essai général de tactique* evince their popularity and potential influence on military affairs. Likewise, the military content and publication record of Diderot and d'Alembert's *Encyclopédie* helped to make it a pillar of learning. Other reference works, such as the *Encyclopédie méthodique* (1782–1832) and different dictionaries such as Voltaire's polemical *Dictionnaire philosophique* (1764) distilled historical and technical information as well as opinions and judgments on warfare. Yet these items, especially multivolume works like the *Encyclopédie*, were luxuries that came at a steep cost in financial and logistical terms (lugging around thirty-three volumes of text and plates was impractical, to say the least). Cheaper print items, chiefly periodicals, therefore, also held particular importance as a means of the Military Enlightenment.

Newspapers like the *Gazette de France*, the official mouthpiece of the crown established in 1631 by Théophraste Renaudot (1586–1653) and printed in Paris, and the *Gazette de Leyde*, printed in the Netherlands, were key vehicles spreading propaganda and news of current events, including war-related subjects such as major battles and diplomatic agreements.[77] Historian Jeremy Popkin's study of the French press during the age of revolution shows that these papers enjoyed wide readership. Drawing on subscriptions, he calculates that during the American Revolutionary War the papers together sold nearly 30,000 copies a week (14,560 twice a week).[78] Many subscribers were officers in the French armed forces who kept informed about battles and events on the other side of the Atlantic and also learned a rather mythologized version of American martial and civic culture.[79] These and other newspapers played a similar role during the War of Austrian Succession and the Seven Years' War, relaying narratives that varied in accuracy and political bias about battles in far-flung places from the Ohio River valley to the Bay of Bengal.[80]

In addition to the growing quantity and circulation of newspapers in France, this period saw the rise of military periodicals that targeted learned officers of the armed forces and the reading public. France was a pioneer in this regard since it was the first country in the Atlantic world to produce military journals. England, Prussia, Austria, America, and other countries would not do so until the late eighteenth century or the early nineteenth century.[81] Bulletins, almanacs, calendars, and *états* of the royal army were precursors to the military periodical press. Publications like the *Almanach royal* of 1700 and later the *État de la France*, as well as Roussel's *État militaire de la France* (1748), contained information about military ordinances as well as specific units, their deployment, and their officers. They often showcased the latter, functioning in a vein similar to the popular genre of the noble genealogy.[82]

The first military journal, the *Encyclopédie militaire*, was more technical than journalistic and focused on military science with some battle narrative and noble genealogy. A monthly review whose first issue was dated January 1, 1770, the *Encyclopédie militaire* was printed in Paris and was written by "a society of veteran officers and men of letters." The primary writer was a former cavalry captain, Adrien-Marie-François de Verdy Du Vernois (1738–1814), who was known for writing genealogies and panegyrics of military men. The first issue was dedicated to Choiseul, who supported the project in order to foster martial professionalism, which made it semiofficial in character. The *Encyclopédie militaire* referred to itself as "the school of young warriors" and called for military men to become dutiful scientists and *philosophes*, declaring that "we are no longer in times of ignorance; the military man must be learned by profession."[83] "From its first issue," the historian Marc Martin explains, "the journal proposed in effect to reexamine military art with the same *esprit critique* that animated the philosophical movement; later, it promised to deliver to its readers the same reflections contained in the articles on the art of war in the great *Encyclopédie* [of Diderot and d'Alembert] which would be lost on many military men 'who cannot . . . drag behind them this immense work, better suited to libraries than garrison and camps.' "[84] As such, the *Encyclopédie militaire* relayed information from the *Encyclopédie* and also featured all of the great tactical debates (*ordre mince* versus *ordre profond*; guerrilla war or *petite guerre*; sieges versus field battle; the role of artillery, and so on).

The *Encyclopédie militaire*'s list of subscribers included members of the Bourbon court, military and nonmilitary individuals, bookstores, and, importantly, army regiments. Choiseul intended each regiment to have at least one subscription to the journal, and while his hopes were not fulfilled, nearly half of all army regiments had subscriptions (75 out of 165 regiments). Five out of eight artillery regiments subscribed to the *Encyclopédie militaire*, since their work was decidedly technical, whereas cavalry and hussar units were the lowest subscribers and least technical forces, though sixteen out of forty regiments held subscriptions.[85] These numbers illustrate that numerous military officers accepted the charge of becoming learned and regularly increased their arsenal of military knowledge.

A number of other military journals fed this trend. The *Journal militaire et politique* was first published in Paris in April 1778 with bimonthly issues through June 1779. It was promulgated by Charles Gravier, comte de Vergennes (1719–1787), who served as foreign minister from 1774 to 1787, in order to spread professional knowledge and cultivate support of French involvement in the American Revolution.[86] The *Journal de la marine* had its first issue in August 1778. Proposals to establish the journal were submitted two years before this date in order to aid French seamen who were covertly helping the Americans, but these solicitations were rejected by Antoine de Sartine (1729–1801), naval minister under Louis XVI, since he was afraid the appearance of the journal would tip off the English that the French were getting involved in America. The journal primarily concentrated on technical communications on maritime subjects and then secondarily on administrative topics, mainly ordinances from the naval ministry. The *Journal de la marine* was thus scrupulously censored by Sartine: no information on ships or squadrons or naval news on America could be released, and if such content were approved, it was only after similar content had been printed in newspapers like the *Gazette de France* and the *Mercure*. As French naval engagements in America drew to a close, so did the journal, printing its final issues in 1781.[87]

The *Journal de la médecine militaire* was also a notable example.[88] Written by military doctors for military doctors, the journal was published by order of the king and completely funded by the Ministry of War. Issues rolled off the presses of the *imprimerie royale* every three months between 1782 and 1789, making it the most stable of the military periodicals thanks to the crown's continued support. The journal represented a culmination of several royal initiatives: the reorganization and centralization of the *corps de santé* and hospitals between 1758 and 1781; the state appointment of military doctors and surgeons in 1759; and the mandating of medical reports by military medical staff in 1763. These reports were collected and published by Pancoucke in 1766 and 1772 under the title *Recueil d'observations de médecine des hôpitaux militaires* (Collection of Medical Observations from Military Hospitals). Minister of War Ségur furthered these in 1781 when he mandated the reorganization of the military medical academies and the founding of the *Journal de la médecine militaire*, which would make public the many interesting letters and memoirs addressed to the ministry by medical personnel and administrators. It united deep explorations and experiments in infectious diseases, hygiene, tropical medicine, local epidemiology, and the physical as well as mental, or moral, causes of illness. The journal was printed in runs of eight hundred to a thousand copies and was distributed free of charge to some six hundred medical professionals. The *Journal de la médecine militaire* prioritized knowledge and progress over politics and professional dogma; it was a shining emblem of the influence that French reform absolutism had in the medical and military arenas.

Military administrators, officers, and medical personnel read these published documents and responded with their own manuscript memoirs and an extremely active correspondence with colleagues, as collections at the Service historique de la défense show (military correspondence in sous-série A^1, officers' private letters in sous-série 1K, officers' dossiers in sous-série Yd, 1Yb, 1Yf). A military *république des lettres* flourished in which writers shared their knowledge of current and historical campaigns and battles, scholarly works, and new regulations and also discussed their own challenges, methods, and experiments. In addition to circulating manuscript letters, others were printed and published for broad consumption.

Epistolary communication was not only a practical professional activity; it was also an essential form of elite sociability and therefore of noble identity during the eighteenth century.[89] This correspondence had many different genres, from official letters to personal, familiar ones, but in no instance were such letters considered private by default. Guibert was an avid correspondent whose letters were "events" in and of themselves. When members of his entourage received a letter, they immediately informed other members of the group, who would get together, read the letter out loud, and lend it to one another for further public or private reading.[90] Similar occurrences took place in barracks and camps, where letters of fellow officers or administrators were read aloud, both for the purposes of sharing professional information and for sociability, since letter writers often asked their correspondents to greet others whom they realized would be present when the letter was received and read. Friends, family, and powerful women of the intellectual milieu also had a significant hand in publicizing military-related ideas and the reputation of reformers. Julie de Lespinasse hoped to convince the influential marquise du Deffand (1697–1780) to write a letter to the king of Poland telling of the young colonel's brilliance.[91]

Discussion was also a principal medium of the Military Enlightenment.[92] Incalculable numbers of conversations took place while military officers were on active duty, in places like barracks, camps, and military Freemason lodges. Correspondence, treatises, and memoirs give only a glimpse into these conversations when they are mentioned in passing, such as that between Saxe and the maréchal Claude-Louis-Hector de Villars (1653–1734) referenced in *Mes rêveries* (discussed in chapter 3). These military spaces were ideal not only for exchanging information and ideas but also for testing them by putting them into practice.

Other conversations took place in nonmilitary spaces that were often created specifically to foster discussion: salons, clubs, cafés, and Freemason lodges. Many military men hosted salons in various locations. Ministers of war and other senior administrators were charged with hosting high-visibility salons and meals at Versailles. Choiseul, for example, held a *table ouverte*, or open table, for select courtiers and foreigners. The lunchtime meal was served at 2 p.m., and place settings were automatically prepared for thirty-five people with an option to add more. Upon his disgrace, Choiseul continued this same practice in the courtly political salon in exile at Chanteloup. As Madame du

Deffand described it, "going to Chanteloup is going to the court [of Versailles], it is to look for the world of grandees." Ministerial salons at Versailles or in exile were rife with political intrigue and were at the same time ideal places to discuss ideas with the powers that be.

Similar to the Choiseuls, military officers and their wives also hosted well-frequented salons of political and cultural import and were regulars at other notable salons and social circles. Not all salons held by military men were reputed for the brilliance of the host, company, or topics of discussion. That of the maréchal Charles de Rohan, prince de Soubise (1715–1787), who was known to have been a rather untalented general, allowed him to redeem his reputation by being an expert *mondain* who hosted some of the best gourmet meals in the city.[93]

As noted, topics of the Military Enlightenment were also discussed in other urban social spaces, such as cafés and Freemason lodges. "Maisons de café," or coffeehouses, came into fashion along with the caffeinated drink in the latter seventeenth century and spread through France like wildfire in the century that followed.[94] In 1762, a military café was erected on rue Saint-Honoré and was designated for use by officers of the armed forces. The neoclassical architect Claude-Nicolas Ledoux (1736–1806) took on the commission and worked to create a space meant to resemble "a well-ordered military encampment in which officers could rest after a victorious combat." Twelve columns carved in the shape of lances bundled together by laurel leaves and topped with plumed battle helmets separated panels of decorative mirrors or ornate mounted sculptures of shields with screaming Medusa heads, standards, and laurel-leaf crowns. The décor of this six-by-ten-meter space (now in the Musée Carnavalet) made the military café an environment that encouraged conversation and evoked the masculine martial culture of antiquity. "In this capital there is a café with noble new decorative details that are causing quite a stir," wrote Elie Fréron (1718–1776) in his *Année littéraire* (The Literary Year) of 1762. "This is the Café militaire, rue Saint-Honoré . . . Everyone goes there to admire . . . Everything there is rich, grand and simple, and exudes an air of antiquity . . . It is extraordinary that a café shows the imprint of real taste and offers us a model for this."[95] Military cafés became customary in all garrison towns, offering a special venue for discussing military life, events, theories, and practices.

Masonic lodges were also hotbeds of the Military Enlightenment, as we shall see in the following chapter. Military men were among the first to join foreign lodges in France, thereby incarnating the era's cosmopolitan ideals. Military men were also among the first to form bona fide French lodges, later spreading Masonic culture throughout France and beyond as they formed military lodges in garrison towns and mobile lodges attached to specific regiments. Masonic lodges offered the opportunity to practice polite masculine sociability and to form friendships based on shared professional and ideological interests.[96] Legend has it that becoming a Freemason contributed to Lafayette's fervor for the American cause, exciting his chivalric and Masonic imagination as he envisioned Americans as "people fighting for liberty."[97]

Masonic lodges were also spaces that spread military culture into a broader nonmilitary society of elite men and women. Officer-turned-diplomat and man of society Marc-Marie, marquis de Bombelles (1744–1822), wrote numerous anecdotes revealing how military culture was featured in salons, societies, and Masonic lodges. He reported a particular soirée hosted by the lodge La Candeur (Candor), which functioned from 1775 to 1785 and included elite women and men, *philosophes* like Voltaire, and multiple military officers including Turpin de Crissé fils in its membership.[98] On the evening of March 9, 1784, La Candeur invited the lodge La Fidélité along with other visiting Masonic men and women to a grand evening meeting that included a lecture, a banquet, theatrical performances, and a ball. Following the lecture and before dining, a moving military ceremony took place to honor a dewy nineteen-year-old injured veteran soldier who had lost his arm at just seventeen years of age during the taking of the Île Saint Christophe, a naval battle in Saint Kitts during the American Revolutionary War. Bombelles relayed with some emotion the arrival of the soldier with four of his comrades at the soirée, marching into the hall to music and the beating of drums. A panegyric oration then told of the soldier's derring-do. During the battle, the soldier and a comrade had been tasked with carrying an explosive attached to a pole to a specific spot. The two boys were struggling to move this weapon when a cannonball struck the soldier's right arm and left it hanging by threads of flesh. In an astounding show of persistence and courage, the soldier insisted on continuing with his mission; he moved the weapon to his other shoulder, and when he realized that his dangling arm was impeding his movement, he took a knife and cut it off. At this point, his comrade fled the scene, but the soldier continued and heroically accomplished his orders. The speech made in this soldier's honor left him incredulous. He apparently turned to his comrades and said, "I didn't realize that what I did was so beautiful." The soldier was awarded a medal that would "preserve the memory of his intrepid courage for centuries to come," received a monetary reward of one hundred *écus*, and was promoted to sergeant-major.

This episode reveals the polyvalent ways in which the Military Enlightenment unfolded in Masonic lodges. The soirée mixed both military and nonmilitary attendees, allowing them to socialize and to focus on a military topic.

The ceremony relayed detailed information about a tactical operation in a battle in the Caribbean, bringing far-off military events of recent history to light. It also brought justice to an unsung "subaltern" hero who merited public recognition. Acknowledging his heroism translated to policy on a small scale, as the veteran soldier not only received symbolic and monetary rewards, but also a promotion to a higher rank. In the soirée hosted by La Candeur on March 9, 1784, military knowledge became public knowledge that engaged a wider group of people—military and nonmilitary, men and women—which in turn resulted in a kind of vigilante-style Masonic justice for a subaltern hero as well as "official" justice through a real promotion.

The institutions and practices of the public sphere and the world of polite society played a central role in the Military Enlightenment. Many more people became aware of and engaged in military issues. Monarchs, mistresses, bureaucrats, and military officers connected "enlightened" thinking with the military realm fostering innovative policies and experimentation. However, military thinkers and actors did not welcome all influences from *le monde*, as chapter 2 shows. The positive and negative effects of worldliness and sociability were debated in the military sphere and became an early focus of reform efforts that pointed to people, instead of tactics or universal theories of war, as the key to rehabilitating metropolitan forces and to solidifying France's status as a global power.

CHAPTER 2

Before Fraternity
Martial Masculinity, Sociability, and Community

"My life, what a novel!" On the island of Saint Helena in 1816, Napoleon famously bellowed this dramatic characterization of his life during a conversation with his memorialist Emmanuel-Augustin-Dieudonné-Joseph, comte de Las Casas (1766–1842). Yet when it came to waxing poetic about the days and deeds of the Corsican emperor-warrior, no one was as effusive as Napoleon's soldiers and officers. The veritable onslaught of personal memoirs penned by Bonaparte's veterans upheld their leader not only as a formidable conqueror, but as a kind and equitable commander. He even appeared to them, in some ways, to be a friend. Napoleon himself likened the military to Freemasonry, since "there is a certain understanding between all of them that makes them recognize one another anywhere and unmistakably; it makes them search for one another and get along well, and I am the Grand Master of their lodge."[1] Elzéar Blaze (1786–1848), a captain in the Grande Armée, told of Napoleon's intimate relations with his men, whose merit he honored regardless of their social origins:

> One often saw the Emperor detach his own cross of the Legion of Honor to fasten it himself on the chest of a brave soldier. Louis XIV would have asked first if the brave man were noble. Napoleon asked if a noble were brave. A sergeant who had shown prodigious valor during a battle was brought before Louis XIV.

"I grant you a pension of 1,200 livres," said the King.

"Sire, I would rather have the cross of St. Louis."

"I can believe that, but you won't get it."

Napoleon would have hugged the sergeant; Louis XIV turned his back on him.

Blaze remarked in conclusion to this anecdote: "That is an example of the sharp difference between the two periods."[2]

Historians have generally agreed with Captain Blaze's assessment. Brian Martin writes that Napoleon's "insistence on group solidarity represented a radical departure from the more recent past in France, where rigid class division during the eighteenth century presented enormous obstacles to mutual respect and cooperation among soldiers." According to Martin, the Revolutionary concept of *fraternité* was the source of "a growing belief—or emerging military theory—in nineteenth-century France that friendship between soldiers could be an effective strategy for regimental unity" and that "success in combat depended on greater trust and intimacy between soldiers in the Grande Armée or what can more broadly be called Napoleonic friendship."[3] Martin and Michael Hughes explore the mechanisms of this solidarity, from Napoleon's own behavior to his nationalist and militarist propaganda system, which encouraged male social bonding and a shared masculine identity based on sexual and martial prowess.[4]

While rigid social divisions persisted during the *ancien régime*, military officers and administrators of the eighteenth century were not blind to the notion that collective identity and group solidarity were important forces in military success. Before fraternity and Napoleonic friendship, there were enlightened martial sociability, masculine identity, and *société militaire* (military society or community).

Large-scale dysfunction in the armed forces evidenced by a number of humiliating defeats, most notably at Dettingen (1743) and Rossbach (1757), brought sharper focus to the flaws of Louis XIV's aristocratic culture of war and to problems in the military and tactical systems in place.[5] Reformers believed that venality, favoritism, and *guerre de cabinet* had curtailed heroism in the officer corps, engendering indiscipline, corrupt and effeminate morals, and an eroded sense of individual and collective martial identity. The lack of *société* was visible in the petty, destructive relationships between officers as well as in the officers' abusive treatment of soldiers. Poor material conditions and social abasement were held to be principal causes of disease and desertion among the troops, as well as contributors to homesickness or *nostalgie*, which was thought to be deadly.[6]

Agents of the Military Enlightenment sought to repair these moral and social problems through sociability. This human faculty could encourage social bonding, foster *société militaire*, and revitalize martial identity. As opposed to looking to mathematics and Greco-Roman antiquity for archetypes of stalwart martial identity and discipline, certain military writers of the 1720s to 1760s espoused "enlightened" moral philosophy and social institutions such as the salon and the Masonic lodge as ideal cultural models. Reformers focused on values associated with natural sociability and social etiquette—humanity, friendship, benevolence, and collective spirit (esprit de corps)—that could promote respect through the ranks and with allies around the French mercantile and colonial empire. Maurice de Saxe experimented with warfront comic theater, which he believed would cultivate community, masculine martial identity, and ultimately victory in continental warfare. In French theaters of war around the globe, sociability had equally high stakes. Antifraternization was a sign of European cultural superiority and racial purity for many military men. However, from North America and the Antilles to the Indian subcontinent, *militaires philosophes* argued for throwing off the yoke of Eurocentric stereotypes, cultural rigidity, exoticism, and racism. They advocated for learning indigenous cultures and languages, befriending local peoples, seeking points of commonality in culture or national character, and acknowledging merit. These practices were key to forming international, multicultural military communities.

Military thinkers were convinced of the manifold benefits that sociable practices would bring to the armed forces. Adopting enlightened moral philosophies of sociability, reinvigorating military identity, igniting a sense of solidarity in multiple forms, and demonstrating cultural acumen and respect while abroad could alleviate the social and cultural causes of military crisis. Equally important, this new *mentalité* and unofficial martial code could restore the reputation of warriors as virtuous moral agents worthy of praise rather than blame in the eyes of *philosophes* and the public. What they did not know is that they were fashioning philosophical, social, and emotional dynamics that set the stage for Revolutionary fraternity, Napoleonic friendship, and the military "band of brothers" of the modern day.[7]

From Gentlemen's War to Military Society

Captain Blaze was right on one count: Louis XIV cared about nobility. On March 21, 1691, the Sun King, cloaked in his military garb of brilliant white and gold, emerged from his royal carriage to behold the battlefront at the great siege of Mons in Flanders. No siege had ever seen the likes of the forces that Louis collected at Mons—ninety-two thousand men were sent to overwhelm a mere six thousand men in the enemy garrison. Louvois, the Sun King's minister of war, had prepared for this siege for nearly a year and had spared no detail in his planning for when the trenches of the lines of circumvallation opened on the night of March 24, 1691. Two batteries of twelve mortars each bombarded Mons, setting the city ablaze. By the time the garrison surrendered on April 8, artillery and trench fighting had killed one-fourth of enemy forces. Louis XIV himself had dodged a cannonball, narrowly escaping an untimely death that fortune instead bestowed upon the soldier standing beside him.

Despite the unavoidable bloodiness of such a battle, the siege of Mons was conducted with a gentlemanly flare representative of the glory and gallantry of the Sun King and his noble officer corps. In addition to decadent rations, including a special order of some 220,000 aged red-skinned Dutch cheeses, the French accented their assault with a grandiose courtly gesture. On the morning of March 26, Louis XIV called for a general cease-fire—not to end the siege, but rather to offer the women of Mons a musical serenade played by the orchestra of the Régiment du Roi. As cannon ceased to boom, music soared into the air, and the women of the besieged town, along with men of both armies, enjoyed a magnificent springtime concert worthy of the court at Versailles.[8]

Just as chivalric codes ostensibly guided military conduct and values in the days of medieval knights, so an aristocratic ethos pervaded the ideals of military conduct and value systems of the last centuries of the *ancien régime*.[9] In France, as across Europe, the nature and structures of early modern war were dominated by the aristocratic life form. Noble values of honor, virtue, and *gloire* were expressed on a large scale through what Carl von Clausewitz (1780–1831) later characterized as duel-like warfare of aristocrats and monarchs.[10] Military documents from the seventeenth and eighteenth centuries exhibit the penchant and even pressure to show gestures of total refinement and civility that permeated the aristocratic officer corps in the French army and navy.[11] Officers held sumptuous dinner parties, hosting fellow officers and local nobility for delectable meals served on silver platters and porcelain china that officers brought with them to war. Paying great attention to self-presentation, officers donned the most elegant and up-to-date fashions of embroidered coats with gold buttons and buckles, silk stockings, powdered wigs, and full makeup, even in combat. Joseph Sevin, comte de Quincy (1677–1749), recalled in his *Mémoires*, written between 1738 and 1742, that at the siege of Turin in 1706 during the War of Spanish Succession, commander Louis d'Aubusson de la Feuillade, duc de Roannais (1673–1725), was "bedecked as if he were going to

FIGURE 4. Almanach image of 1706 entitled "Ville Franche assiégée par M. le duc de la Feuillade et rendue par capitulation à l'obéissance du Roy le 2 avril 1705." Courtesy of the Bibliothèque nationale de France. Louis d'Aubusson, duc de La Feuillade (1673–1725) is featured in the top half of the image, seated demurely in his finery and surrounded by high-ranking aristocratic officers as he signs the terms of the capitulations.

a ball: he had a scarlet frock with gold embroidery on all of the stitching, his hair was finely powdered, and he mounted a handsome gray horse" (figure 4).[12]

In order to sustain such luxury on campaign, army officers brought teams of valets, horses, cooks, and servants (or took a few soldiers out of their companies) who transported and monitored great baggage trains of weaponry, clothing, books, dinnerware, toilette accessories, and other supplies. Naval officers on tightly packed ships could not bring to sea an equipage quite as elaborate as their counterparts in the army, though they maintained sufficient trappings associated with their status.[13]

This aristocratic ethos and its practices were exclusive by design and held a particular social significance in distinguishing nobles from commoners. In Louis XIV's army, as in noble society, it was "by their way of living, of speaking, of acting, of amusing themselves, of enjoying each other's company that the noble elite would persuade themselves of the unshakeable certainty of their own superiority."[14] On the battlefield, as on ships of the line, physical grace and technical ability as well as gentlemanly conduct "implied a special sort of valor and superiority in arms that placed one above the ordinary soldier."[15] This aristocratic ethos and code fostered a certain seventeenth-century sense of sociability among elites. Sociable behavior made manifest one's nobility and one's belonging to a transnational European caste of officers. Exchanging courtesies, sharing meals, and battling in a controlled, rationalized manner exemplified aristocratic ideals that European officers held in common.

Soldiers and sailors had no seat at this high table. Commoners of the Third Estate filled the rank and file of the armed forces, and their noble officers typically saw them as "beneath contempt" and "usually failed to credit their social inferiors with the same values," be it physical grace and address or moral pursuits of personal or family honor, glory, and merit.[16] The soldier, his individual identity, his values, and his humanity were invisible. Despite social prejudices, there was a loose expectation that aristocratic officers would be concerned over their soldiers' welfare, if not out of a Christian or aristocratic paternalism, at least for sheer self-interest, knowing that officers paid to recruit, arm, and maintain soldiers and would lose on their investments if soldiers deserted or died. There was no real notion that soldiers could be heroes, or that the hardships of their lives at war were any different than those of their poor, disenfranchised nonmilitary lives. Socializing with them, let alone respecting them, was out of the question. Sociability was not seen as something of tactical value, and a unified military society was unthinkable.

All of this changed in the wake of the War of Spanish Succession. When Louis XIV died on September 1, 1715, he left behind a military in crisis. The officer corps had degenerated from multiple perspectives. Favoritism and money dominated recruitment, retention, and promotion. Court nobles (*présentés* in the army or *petits marquis* in the navy) who had connections to Versailles easily attained officer commissions, rewards, and promotions. Poorer provincial nobles had no access to such opportunities, which stunted their careers and created growing resentment. Venal officer commissions, an important source of income for the state, dictated that positions in the military could be purchased by anyone who could afford the hefty price. This ensured an influx of rich nonnobles (*roturiers*) and newly ennobled (*anoblis*) into the officer corps.[17] Court nobles, *roturiers*, and *anoblis* were seen to lack military experience and to be wholly disconnected from the aristocratic culture of war. These flaws of Louis XIV's military system, it was believed, were to blame for martial ineffectiveness and for social and ideological divisiveness in the noble Second Estate, which had fancied itself a corporate group based on equality among its members.

What is more, Louis XIV's *guerre de cabinet* was thought to have greatly eroded officers' military skills, agency, and cultural pride. Vauban's system of siege craft, along with the influence of Jules Louis Bolé de Chamlay (1650–1719) and other proponents of conducting warfare by a priori rationalization, convinced Louis XIV that "all things related to war could be decided at Versailles." They therefore contended that "it was only necessary to have obedient generals punctually executing orders received."[18] As if this were not humiliating enough, Louis XIV's disastrous fiscal-military state at times left even its greatest generals in a shocking state of privation while on campaign. After the hard-won French victory at Cassano in 1705, an officer recounted the misery of Maréchal Louis-Joseph, duc de Vendôme (1654–1712), whom he found "at the table eating with his brother the Grand Prieur. All that they had for their feast was a ration of bread and a small piece of cheese."[19]

Peacetime following the War of Spanish Succession added to the military crisis and irreversibly altered the aristocratic culture of war. Disenchanted with Louis XIV's wars, and enjoying several years of peace after the Treaty of Rastatt (1714), French military officers grew increasingly invested in their lives as courtiers and members of *le monde*, the social elite of Paris and Versailles. It is no surprise that novels of worldliness or *mondanité* by Crébillon fils (Claude Prosper Jolyot de Crébillon, 1707–1777) and others that rose to popularity during the 1720s and 1730s featured noble male protagonists who utilized their military prowess not for real warfare but for devising campaigns and tactics to compete with their rivals and to seduce women.[20] The elite, urban society of *le monde* at Versailles and in Paris had corrupted the *noblesse d'épée*, particularly the younger generation. In a memoir dated 1712, M. de Saint-Hilaire, who was an army officer and a member of the Conseil de Guerre in place from

September 1715 to October 1718, complained: "We've settled for teaching them some Latin and Humanities and then we thrust them into the corrupt *monde* at the tender age of fourteen or fifteen without having given them the time to arm themselves with proper protection. Their fathers are already corrupted themselves, driven by the glitter of false vanity, and have, from the moment their sons enter *le monde*, already procured important positions for them through credit, intrigues, and money."[21]

The dangers of *le monde* became a subject of inquiry throughout the eighteenth century. The Swiss physician Samuel-Auguste Tissot (1728–1797) later posited that those who inhabited *le monde* were literally sick people: physically, morally, and socially. Tissot's etiology of modern maladies was based on a polarization between urban and rural cultures and communities, not dissimilar to the dualism adopted by the Physiocrats.[22] While country folk who led simple, more "natural" lifestyles exhibited robustness, city dwellers—especially those who participated in the elite society of *le monde*—were excessively delicate and denatured by pathological environmental influences. "The urban/worldly mode of life lies at the point on Tissot's scale that is farthest removed from man's natural state, and is therefore antithetical to sound physical and moral health," explains Anne Vila. "Worldliness, he insists, saps the strength of those born to it and of those who aspire to it, for it has unleashed an epidemic of false pleasures, perverted moral values, and bad physical habits that has spread throughout society."[23]

A great number of military thinkers agreed with Tissot's analysis. Life in Paris and Versailles was believed to cause a catastrophic degradation of the aristocratic martial code that had moral, physical, and social dimensions. This abasement was presented in highly gendered terms and cast "worldly" officers as lacking in masculinity. Military and nonmilitary intellectuals purported that *mondanité*, whose codes emphasized superficial forms of sociability and politeness accompanied by frivolous gaiety (*légèreté*), was dominated by the tastes, attitudes, and actions of women. In period writings on gender and French mores (*moeurs*), women were thought to have held a strong influence over this realm because frivolity, gaiety, and a penchant toward luxury were believed to be innate to the female sex.[24] François Ignace d'Espiard de la Borde's (1707–1777) *L'esprit des nations* of 1752 conveyed the ambivalence of many male intellectuals regarding the powerful influence that women were seen to hold over men of *le monde* and French mores more generally. On the one hand, he declared that "the Frenchman owes the amiable qualities which distinguish him from the other peoples to interchange with women," while he later admitted bitterly, "Foreigners say that in France, men are not men enough."[25]

It was not just foreigners who thought French men were not "men enough." Eighteenth-century intellectuals and military thinkers also believed that French men—particularly those of the army—had fallen prey to the cultural influence of women to the detriment of their military science and masculine belligerence. They had grown overly effeminate in their mores, polite to the point of ridicule, and decadent in their taste for sensual and material pleasures. Later in the century, in his *Tableau de Paris* (1781–1788), Louis-Sébastien Mercier (1740–1814) rearticulated a decades-old accusation that "the luxury of the capital kills not just courage, but the bellicose spirit of our officers. The delights of an effeminate and sensual life are incompatible with the hard work and fatigues of war: soldiers have no need for the pleasures suited for rich merchants, citizens living on unearned income, or amateurs of the arts. I believe that I recognize a real weakening in our military virtue."[26] Treatises, memoirs, and letters dating to the early eighteenth century—from the comte de Quincy's *Mémoires* to manuscripts submitted to the Ministry of War—had long before addressed this cultural conundrum and its dangerous consequences in the space of war. Military thinkers wrote of linguistic and social problems that they saw to be directly related to the "civilian" lives of noble officers. Ethically and linguistically, the system of values and the language of aristocratic service were tainted by those of *le monde*, creating semantic corruptions of key concepts of the traditional noble warrior ethos: *gloire, honneur, vertu, mérite.*[27] These "signifiers" came to house nefarious "signifieds" such as unabated hubris, vanity, unprofessionalism, and moral bankruptcy.

These misguided priorities were seen to manifest themselves in a growing lack of aristocratic sociability that compromised military effectiveness. Officers, it was claimed, had become absorbed by the superficial culture of gossip and petty competition prevalent in *le monde*. The naval officer corps was the most contentious of all of the armed forces. Disdain was rampant between *officiers rouges* of the Grand Corps, *officiers bleus* of the reserve, those of the commercial marine, and *intrus* (intruders) from the army such as Bougainville and d'Estaing, to whom the crown had awarded high-level naval commissions despite their lacking a maritime background. Ship-based military personnel clashed with land-based civil administrators who ran ports and arsenals. Officers and sailors attached to different naval ports viewed one another with condescension and even hatred. Armand Louis de Gontaut, duc de Lauzun (later became duc de Biron), was shocked to see that in naval units detached from Brest and Provence (north and south), "between themselves, the officers hated one another: those from Brest called those from the Mediterranean 'freshwater mariners.' Was this impertinence justified by any veritable science? In absolutely no way."[28]

In the army, Minister of War Marc-Pierre de Voyer de Paulmy, comte d'Argenson, rebuked those who sowed vicious competition between men of the same unit. He decried those "who are delighted when officers of their unit are officially reprimanded, people who, instead of taking care to hide such dishonor, take great pleasure in spreading word of it, not only within their regiment but also to the public. Is it not shameful that a unit composed of allegedly honest people desire to destroy one another? . . . Every day we see entire regiments behave as if they were enemies. Where do such ideas come from? Whence does such a lack of *société* emerge?"[29] According to d'Argenson, officers and whole regiments were more concerned with destroying one another's reputations than with destroying enemy armies. Proof of this assertion abounded in the eighteenth-century armed forces. A violent quarrel between the regiments of Auvergne and of the Maine in April 1776 offered a salient example. While both regiments were stationed at the garrison in Lille, graffiti was scribbled in chalk onto a sentry box at the garrison's edge: "Vive l'Auvergne et Merde pour du Maine" (Long live the Auvergne and Shit for the Maine). This declaration seems more sophomoric than sinister, yet it quickly escalated into a dangerous affair when a corporal of the Maine burned an Auvergne uniform to display his regiment's collective outrage. Competitiveness exploded into violence as the two regiments tacitly declared war on one another, exchanging insults, blows, and gunfire.[30]

D'Argenson's move to consider "entire regiments" is significant. Rather than concentrating solely on high-ranking officers, d'Argenson cast a wider net to think about the culture and behavior of subaltern officers and soldiers. Reformers criticized officers' poor treatment of their troops and connected social abuse to martial failings. In *La morale universelle*, d'Holbach denounced "the revolting spectacle" of "commanders who, by their luxury, liberality, and sumptuous meals, starve the camp," allowing "a mob of do-nothing servants to swim in abundance while the exhausted soldier lacks even the most basic necessities."[31] Another writer remarked that "the troops have nothing left but courage. Their officers are without dedication to their jobs and without emulation . . . They neglect to take care of their troops, nor do they apply themselves to the daily tasks of military service. They have forgotten the significance of obedience and do not bother to make sure that they are obeyed. What is more, often they do not deserve to be obeyed because of the lack of care they have for their troops."[32] Soldiers often fled the battlefield in fright, deserted from the army, or died of sickness, isolation, boredom, or unhappiness, all of which was only further exacerbated by degrading treatment by their officers. Officers often held such poor opinions of their soldiers that they refused to care for them. An anonymous writer told of the detrimental psychological effects of this social prejudice, relaying that, for soldiers, "the incertitude of their future, the contempt heaped upon them, plunge them into a despair that breaks them down in sickness or forces them to desert the army. Such bad treatment destroys the little good will that they could have had. What service can we expect from such soldiers?"[33]

Soldiers and subalterns were no longer invisible. D'Argenson and likeminded thinkers examined discrete relationships among officers, between officers and their soldiers, and between soldiers. Henri-François, comte de Bombelles (1681–1760), similarly observed that regional differences posed a challenge to group cohesion in the army. Soldiers from different provinces of France "live together with great difficulty," Bombelles wrote. "A Gascon has no reason to make himself feel fondness towards a Norman nor to give him the helping hand that he would need, not even just advice."[34] In both the officer and soldier corps, tensions between veterans, new recruits, and recent appointments from court ran high, the veterans proud and war-hardened and the latter groups naïve at best, and at worst exhibiting the effeminate worldly character and behaviors that certain military men despised.

D'Argenson and Bombelles advanced the idea that every regiment, and indeed the entire French army, should function as a mutualistic, caring, and amicable *société*. In this period of growing cosmopolitan consciousness, "society"—a word that had long existed—took on new dimensions, great and small. It went beyond the here and now to evoke the whole of human civilization across history. It included, at least in theory, all of the different peoples living across the globe concurrently. "Society" also meant particular communities, from national community to neighborhood to a group of friends. François Furet has remarked on "the appropriation of ontology by society" during this period, indicating "a link between the emancipation of society from transcendent justification and the eventual substitution of society for transcendency as a principle of thought."[35] This view of society led to a nascent body of neologisms, such as "sociability," "social," and "civilization." These terms became central principles of a new moral philosophy that naturalized the capacity to form bonds and communities. This philosophy held that society was less the result of religious or political identity or supervision and more the result of human nature, the faculty of reason, and compassionate feelings of *sensibilité* and *humanité* that ineluctably brought people together.

The French laid claim to being the most sociable of peoples. "Most of our writers brag about our nation's spirit of society [*esprit de société*] and indeed, most foreigners see us as the most sociable," wrote Jaques-Henri Bernardin de Saint-Pierre (1737–1814).[36] Diderot claimed hyperbolically that extreme sociability was a part of French national character and that there is no nation that is more like a single family. A Frenchman swarms about in his town more than ten Englishmen, fifty Dutchmen, or a hundred Muslims do in theirs. The same man in the same day will be at court, in the center of town, in the countryside, at an academy, a salon, a banker's, a notary's, a barrister's, a solicitor's, a great seigneur's, a merchant's, a workman's, at church, at the theatre, and with the call girls. Everywhere he is equally free and familiar. One would say that he had never left his home and that he had simply changed rooms.[37]

The moral philosophy of society and sociability were of keen interest to thinkers participating in the Military Enlightenment. It seemed fertile ground for innovations that could aid the social and cultural dysfunctions that plagued the armed forces. If properly nurtured, French natural sociability could render military life more livable, if not pleasurable, and could form the basis for martial identity and community building. If thinkers were sure that *société militaire* could not but improve military efficacy, it was also clear that questions of sociability and military community were deeply fraught: Could aristocrats of different ranks and regions be considered friends or "brothers"? Even more provocative, could commoner soldiers and noble officers ever imagine themselves to be "brothers"? What would this mean for subordination? Where did the forming of social bonds end? Could it traverse the battlefield to unite enemies and therefore put an end to war?

Ideas and institutions related to this type of thinking blossomed in the eighteenth-century French armed forces. Officers turned to Freemasonry and the ideal of male friendship to form moral and social communities. Ironically, others turned to *mondanité*, salon etiquette, and the theater as means to bolster social ties. The moral philosophy that championed *commerce* (reciprocal communication) and *société* formed the bedrock of a new "enlightened" military identity on individual and collective levels.

Freemasonry and Military Friendship

Freemasonry in France had foreign and military origins. The first lodge was called La Parfaite Égalité and was allegedly founded in 1688 during the Nine Years' War in Saint-Germain-en-Laye by the Royal Irish Regiment that served under the exiled King James II of England (1633–1701). The first lodge in France to receive an official patent from the Grand Lodge of London in 1732 was called Saint-Thomas, dubbed Louis d'Argent. Officers of the French armed forces soon clamored to take part in this cultural import from across the

Channel. The first high-ranking French military officer to be initiated into a lodge was Maréchal Victor-Marie d'Estrées (1660–1737) in 1737, followed by Maurice de Saxe, who joined the Louis d'Argent lodge. While the first Grand Maître of the Masonic Lodges in France was English (Philip, first Duke of Wharton [1698–1731], recognized in 1728), military members of grandee rank took over this role a decade later. Louis-Antoine Pardaillan de Gondrin, duc d'Antin et d'Epernon (1707–1743), was "Grand-Maître général et perpetual des Maçons dans le royaume de France," and upon his death in 1743 Louis de Bourbon-Condé, comte de Clermont (1709–1771), took the reins. Frederick the Great established the first military lodge in a German-speaking country in 1739, and the first French-founded military lodges date to 1744 during the War of Austrian Succession.

The army and navy played a central role in eighteenth-century Freemasonry in France. The military represented the single largest social group in the Freemason community and was essential to the growth and diffusion of Freemasonry. Officers established ambulatory military lodges attached to specific regiments and set up mixed civilian and military ateliers. Typically, a lodge was founded by a military unit stationed in a city somewhere in France, and then, when the unit departed, the directing officer transferred leadership to a local civilian who carried on the lodge's activities.

In 1789 there were sixty-nine military lodges with official patents, but there were probably more than one hundred military lodges in operation, considering that not all lodges were under the auspices of the Grand Orient de Paris.[38] In addition to ambulatory lodges or field lodges, which were the most numerous type, there were lodges unattached to a specific unit and that grouped officers from different units and armed services (artillery, cavalry, and so on) as well as lodges that did not have an official military title but whose membership was military in majority.[39] The historian Jean-Luc Quoi-Bodin locates Masonic lodges affiliated with the following units across the armed forces, on the continent and abroad:[40]

1. Maison du Roi
   - Gardes du corps
   - Gardes françaises
   - Gardes suisses
   - Mousquetaires
2. Maison des Princes
3. Line Infantry
4. Light Infantry
5. Cavalry

6. Hussards
7. Dragoons
8. Chasseurs
9. Artillery
10. Génie (military engineering)
11. Gendarmerie
12. Navy
13. Colonial Regiments
    - Regiment of Guadeloupe
    - Regiment of Pondichéry
    - Regiments in Saint-Domingue

In the line infantry, 23 percent of all officers were Masons (690 out of 3,000), with the maximum percentage of effectives in the Penthièvre-Infanterie, 53.2 percent of whose officers were Masons.[41] In the navy, certain ships formed their own vessel-based lodges, such as those on the frigates *La Cybèle*, *La Vestale*, and *L'Union*.[42] Following the reforms of 1775, almost the entirety of units in the Maison du Roi were *maçonnisées*.[43] Three of the five units that formed Rochambeau's expeditionary corps during the American Revolution had lodges involving at least one hundred officer-Masons (initiated at different times), including many of the most notable figures: Lafayette, Louis-Philippe, comte de Ségur (1753–1830, son of war minister Ségur), and Louis-Marie, Marc Antoine vicomte de Noailles (1756–1804), all of whom participated in lodges before crossing the Atlantic.[44] In military administration, between 1773 and 1789 at least twenty high-level functionaries in different offices of the Ministry of War were members of Parisian lodges.[45] Similarly, in naval administration, Masons served in several top civil servant positions, from commissioners of the Admiralty to attorney generals. Military men were also at the center of Masonic administration.

Given the deep connection between the armed forces and Freemasonry during the eighteenth century, it is clear that numerous noble officers placed sociability between military men at the center of their identities and activities. What is more, Pierre-Yves Beaurepaire explains, "taking into account the very strong presence of the *noblesse d'épée* in the central direction of the Grand Orient, military men often serve[d] as intermediaries between Paris and provincial lodges, guaranteeing the moral and social qualities of the lodges that they accepted to sponsor or visit."[46] These moral and social qualities were several. First, the ideal of equality looms large, as the names of different Masonic lodges clearly evince, such as the Irish La Parfaite Égalité and the Parisian L'Égalité Parfaite et Sincère Amitié. Official Masonic dogma dictated that all men are created equal in the eyes of Nature. However, historians have rightly warned about the limits of such equality as practiced in lodges and the ways that the concept of equality was interpreted in order to justify inequality or exclusion. As a Mason of the elite aristocratic military lodge Trois Frères Unis at Versailles wrote:

> The system of Masonic equality, as revered as it is, is not sufficiently imposing to bring together at the same level men whose characters, souls, minds, fortunes, or stations are not well matched . . . These differences, it is true, are foreign to masonry according to its dogma, but they are important in its practice. A failing in the matching of station is therefore an evil and perhaps the origin of other evils. This is what we are experiencing in our lodge. Military men founded it and if they had made a law for themselves to only accept military men, they would in all likelihood have conserved unaltered peace [in the lodge].[47]

The practical interpretation of Masonic equality exercised at the Trois Frères Unis was a justification for social reactionism and exclusion. Furthermore, it seems that there is little or no record of soldiers who were brothers in military lodges, and it is unclear whether common sailors were invited to participate in lodges formed at sea.

Despite these tendencies, competing evidence suggests that Masonic equality was taken more literally in certain lodges. Membership rosters attest to this, showing that men of different levels of social standing and officers throughout the chain of command intermixed in military and nonmilitary lodges. The cost of membership seems to have been the main prohibiting factor for subaltern officers, who still joined lodges in the status of "frère-servant" (brother-servant). However, the diverse leadership (the Vénérables) of the lodges indicates a support of a certain equality in membership. In 1788 the Vénérables of lodges in the line infantry were as follows: one colonel, three lieutenant colonels, one major, fifteen captains, nine lieutenants, three sous-lieutenants, one adjutant-major, two surgeon-majors, one chaplain, and one master hatter of the État-Major.[48]

As this elastic notion of equality relays, equality and hierarchy or subordination were not necessarily seen as incompatible during this period. The article "Société" (moral classification) in the *Encyclopédie* is revealing in this regard. The anonymous author claimed that "men were made to live in society" and that society is necessary for human beings.[49] As such, humans must abide by four principles or rules in order to foster society. The first rule stipulates that the common good must always take priority over one's personal interests. Second, "the spirit of sociability must be universal; human society embraces all men with whom we can have commerce."⁵⁰ Third, and importantly for this discussion, "the equality of nature between men is a principle of which we must never lose sight. In society, it is a principle established by philosophy and religion; whatever inequality the difference in conditions seems to put between us, it was only introduced to make people better succeed in their common end, according to their present station."⁵¹ Accepting natural equality and functional social hierarchy engendered community, public service and good, as well as collective happiness that permitted men of different ranks and stations to socialize and form friendships. Lastly, the fourth and final rule established guidelines for reestablishing society when it has been broken. If an individual violates the bond of society through a crime or injustice, the offended party can pursue justice and act in self-defense, but must not hold a grudge or take vengeance. Friendship and goodwill should return as soon as justice has been served and there is nothing more to fear from the offending individual. The faculty of sociability and the principle of society remain undamaged.

In addition to equality, ideals of friendship, social and moral responsibility, and happiness were fundamental to French Freemasons of the eighteenth century. This was especially the case in military lodges, where "the masonic group was not only perceived as a support for military effectiveness. Even over the course of the Napoleonic Wars, the fraternal cell remained a place of stability, and in compensation for the fury of war, an outlet for collective sensibility."⁵² Louis-Narcisse Baudry des Lozières (1761–1841), colonel inspector general of the Royal Dragoons in Saint-Domingue, founded a lodge on the island and described his ecstasy in returning to the lodge after a long absence. "After more than ten years of being alone in the universe, what exquisite pleasure [*volupté*] did I not experience in letting my soul soar in this majestic temple and in feeling this charming worry about which one of you I should love more."⁵³ Kenneth Loiselle has analyzed a similar rhetoric of love, hearts, souls, and friendship in the correspondence of members of the Bussy-Aumont lodge. Like many other Masons who were influenced by Fénelonian and Rousseauian morality and *sensibilité*, military and nonmilitary members communicated that sentiments and relations of friendship and love with their fellow brothers were essential to their being and well-being.⁵⁴ In an 1803 document of the Masonic lodge of the 64th of the Line, a writer exclaimed: "Friendship! Divinity that truly multiplies our being by associating our tastes, our inclinations, our needs with those of our Brothers through whom we think, we act, we suffer as they do for us." Among certain Freemasons in the military, the modern "band of brothers" concept was already a reality.

Like their nonmilitary counterparts, military lodges maintained moral ideals that pursued serving the public good, as expressed by the encyclopedia article on society. They conducted charitable activities for people in need, both within the military and without. Chevalier de Pawlet de Caumartin (1737–1809), who was a Mason and had served in the regiment of the Reine-Cavalerie, left the army in 1763 and gave himself over to charitable enterprise. After allegedly taking in an orphaned boy who was the son of a deceased veteran dragoon, Pawlet began work to establish a school for orphans of defunct soldiers and subaltern officers. With the crown's support, Pawlet established the school, which was first located on the rue de Sèvres and then was moved to the old barracks of the Gardes françaises in 1789. His theory of *éducation mutuelle* implemented at the school was inspired by the same principles expressed in Masonic culture and in the *Encyclopédie* about *société*—consent, mutualism, natural equality, and functional hierarchy.

In 1777 a Société des Philanthropes of fifty-four members of a predominantly military lodge in Strasbourg proposed to sponsor another program for educating the poor and caring for the ill and elderly. A similar proposal was issued four years later in the Île Bourbon (La Réunion) where an aide-major who also served as a Vénérable in La Parfaite Harmonie called for his brothers to create a public school to educate local children whom he referred to as "creoles." Military Masons were also enthusiastic proponents of the abolitionist group La Société des Amis des Noirs and the celebrated Société (or Maison) philanthropique. In the latter group of 358 members, rosters show that 111 were military men (31 percent) and that of those, 30 percent were Masons.[55] This means that both in and outside of the Masonic community, military officers were interested in engaging in charitable activity and valued the moral stance of *bienfaisance*.

An important characteristic united many of the Masonic proposals for charitable organizations: that of modesty. Combatting self-interest—in the name of the brotherly community, of aiding those less fortunate, of contributing to society, and of embodying Masonic moral ideals—was a way to refurbish social relations and moral rectitude. *Société* was a cornerstone of military Masonic culture and soon became a theme concerning the armed forces at large.

Imagining *Société Militaire*

In his *Réflexions diverses* of 1665, army officer and moralist François de La Rochefoucauld (1613–1680), dedicated his second meditation to society. "It would be useless to say how necessary society is to mankind," he declared, defining society as "the particular commerce that honest people [*honnêtes gens*] must have together."[56] He detailed the personal attributes that were constitutive of society—an open mind, kindness, politeness, humanity, confidence, and the ability to speak sincerely.[57] He also stipulated that each person in such a society should be free and that although certain inequalities in birth or personal qualities between these persons might exist, inequalities should not be palpable and certainly not demonstrated in any abusive manner. La Rochefoucauld's idea of society, one that military thinkers of the eighteenth century would emulate, implied a moral and social code that was largely developed in the space and discourses of the seventeenth-century salon milieu in France. "The ideology of the salons rested on [the] substitution of behavior for birth," writes Carolyn Lougee Chappell. "The quality perennially cited as the earmark of *belles gens* was *esprit*: wit, urbanity, the ability to converse and participate in all the pleasures of society."[58] The salon was a place of cultural and social assimilation, in which it was thought that women served as catalysts to men's learning to become "honnêtes hommes." As the seventeenth-century "feminist" scholar of manners Poulain de la Barre observed about men of his age, "If they wish to center in *le monde* and play well their role in it, they are obliged to go to the school of ladies in order to learn there the politeness, affability, and all the exterior graces which today make up the essence of *honnêtes gens*."[59]

Salon sociability took form in five principal modes, according to Daniel Gordon. Three of these are particularly useful for understanding the military's adoption of its terminology and moral and behavioral tenets. First, sociability took the form of socialization and education, initiating people into the cultural norms of a specific space. Martial reforms also focused on such processes in the form of indoctrination. Second, sociability was seen as the love of exchange that held pleasure as its principle rather than utility alone. In the case of military sociability, exchange was suggested to be both pleasurable and useful.[60] Third, it was seen to be constitutive of bonds among strangers in spaces of *mixité* (social mixing) that included men and women, nobles and bourgeois alike.[61] Given the diversity of the armed forces and the tensions it brought, forming bonds among strangers became a priority. The language of sociability, which included such words and concepts as society, humanity, reciprocity, mutualism (*mutualité*), politeness, honesty, and *esprit*, was as practical as it was philosophical, which attracted military thinkers.

Military reformers of the eighteenth century integrated and expanded on this vocabulary and set of ideals. References to the salon and the influence of women were largely implicit, but nevertheless quite discernible, especially for the bureaucratic, noble, or royal reader to whom eighteenth-century military treatises were directed. Reformers spoke of the primacy of polite behavior and "noble" morals, emphasizing that one's upright inner qualities were to be privileged over gracefulness and good looks. As M. de Lamée, a noble lieutenant in the army, averred: "The substance of an officer is in his *esprit*, his heart, and his sentiments. A pleasing countenance, charm, and graces are supplements to these other perfections. The first ones keep him from committing errors; the second ones make him commit new ones every day." Open-mindedness, moral uprightness, and sociability linked up with military professionalism to form the essential qualities of the ideal officer: "Having an *esprit* that is flexible, sociable, and even a bit ingratiating; being polite and obliging without insipidness; loving virtue; savoring one's job [*faire son métier par goût*] without inhibition; the desire to instruct; these are the qualities that form an officer. Possessing these qualities is what we call having *l'esprit du métier*."[62] Having *esprit du métier*—spirit of the profession—meant being an *honnête homme* and, as an officer named Lagarrigue argued, being a *philosophe* in pursuit of truth. He insisted, "We could not form a good officer without forming an *honnête homme*. The lieutenant-colonels must then apply themselves to inspiring the officers they command with the love of truth, horror for even the least artifice, and a taste for honor and virtue."[63] Lagarrigue's words actually prefigured the *Encyclopédie*'s definition of the *philosophe* as an "*honnête homme* who acts through reason, conjoining a spirit of reflection and justice with sociable qualities and mores."[64] The ideal French army, according to Lamée, was not to be composed of "courtier-warriors," but rather of *militaires philosophes*.

The comte d'Argenson likewise suggested that embracing such philosophical, sociable ways could be highly productive in improving military service at large. "Be polite, generous, compassionate," offered d'Argenson, "the well-being of military service, the pleasure of society, and tranquility of the soul—all of this will be found in this happy way of thinking."[65] D'Argenson believed that a generous and compassionate politeness was vital to eliminating gossip and competition within the army because it would help reflect the deeper importance of social unity among human beings. "For the betterment of military service," he argued, "it is of utmost importance to establish a perfect union within a unit. The foundation of this union is humanity." Humanity in this context indicated not only shared human nature but also a compassion-born sentiment of benevolence for all men.

D'Argenson's vocabulary of military improvement united politeness with moral philosophy, a tie further iterated through his usage of the term *société*.[66] "People must be reasonable, establish social bonds, and live together as friends and as comrades according to the tenets of good society [*la bonne société*]." In the tradition of Samuel von Pufendorf's (1632–1694) theory of natural law developed in *De Jure Naturae et Gentium* (1672), a work translated into French by jurist Jean Barbeyrac (1674–1744) and published in five editions between 1706 and 1734, d'Argenson posited that rational choice would beget social bonds.[67]

D'Argenson specified that these social bonds of friendship and camaraderie were to function according to the tenets of "good society," which indicated "the ensemble of salons and those who frequent them."[68] D'Argenson proposed that men of the French army apply their faculty of reason, thereby realizing their common humanity and natural mutual benevolence, which in turn would permit them to form social bonds that should function according to the precepts of salon etiquette.

Lamée iterated a similar framework for social bonding in the military based on principles of moral philosophy and salon-style sociability. "The military profession calls men forth from the farthest provinces of the Kingdom," Lamée explained; "the faces, mores, sentiments, and even the names of those with whom we are going to live are unfamiliar to us. This idea alone is surprising at first; it is too difficult to grasp. Our *esprit* brings this idea closer to us, familiarizes us with it, teaching us that humanity submits all men to the same laws and that men cannot remain strangers amongst themselves."[69] For Lamée, society was an inexorable human inclination: "Man was created to think, to have ideas, to communicate ideas and to receive the impressions of the ideas that others create. *L'esprit* is the link of society, and all men are brought together in society." Accordingly, and again intermingling discourses of natural law and sociability in Pufendorfian fashion, "the power of personal interest and the love of pleasure make necessary what we call life's commerce between men . . . It is a mutual deference that unites men and that serves as a foundation for society. Man must be useful to man, and the reciprocal communication of our ideas is as necessary to us in rendering our existence useful as the regular movement of the planets is indispensable to conserve the harmony of the world."[70]

Mutual deference and need, as well as the desire to be useful to one another, were to be found in the heart and mind of every man. What is more, as in a salon, reciprocal communication was a prime goal of coming together, as were the pleasures of companionship and the building of knowledge through discussion and collective reason. Such natural forces and practices of communication were useful for the betterment of military service and learning, said d'Argenson, since it was "through such society [that] one finds opportunities to discuss the military profession and, during these little conversations, discover things about it of which one was quite unaware."[71]

Trust, emulation, and subordination would ensue. Lamée argued that when human equality is the basis on which military society is founded, men feel more inclined to see the functional utility of subordination. Being aware of their status as essentially equal to all other men in the army and then witnessing those around them—inferiors, equals, and superiors—agreeing to fall into the hierarchy of subordination would depersonalize and thus mitigate the initially unpleasant feeling of submitting oneself to orders.[72]

The moral code of the army was to become one of modern politeness, marked by profound human bonds and natural equality. In the minds of these military thinkers, establishing this kind of social unity would finally optimize the army's functioning, sweeping away the cultural crisis marked by semantic errors, intra-army competition, social abuses, and general lack of dedication to the service. The French army's combat effectiveness would reach its pinnacle and rehabilitate France's martial glory to the heights it had attained in its past. "It would be of infinite benefit," proclaimed d'Argenson, "if all of the King's troops could live together in perfect union. If we could just get to that state, we would be invincible."

Forging Social Bonds

Establishing a "perfect union" among troops was a daunting, if not impossible, task. Nevertheless, living together and establishing increased familiarity were feasible, especially given the crown's policies regarding officers' leave, garrisoning, and personnel recordkeeping.[73]

Throughout the eighteenth century, the crown built more and larger garrisons. By 1775, barracks could house up to two hundred thousand men. At the same time, regulations aimed to better codify and enforce the periods during which officers and soldiers were to remain in garrison.[74] Following Choiseul's reforms of 1763, soldiers stayed in garrisons for two years before being transferred, though certain units, such as the Gardes françaises and cavalry corps, were more or less permanently garrisoned in specific locations. In order to save the cost of moving men between garrisons and also in the name of integrating military men into local populations, the Conseil de Guerre passed a permanent garrison law in 1788. While soldiers and officers were always accounted for by garrison administration, they were not trapped at the barracks, and left military premises for work in the town, for fun, and also during their leave.[75]

Alongside and in support of these efforts, the state worked more assiduously to identify military personnel. While the process of identifying military servicemen began with Louis XIII, it was not until the 1716 ordinance on desertion that the crown established unit registers called *contrôles des troupes*. André Corvisier has compiled and studied these *contrôles* exhaustively, allowing historians to trace the transformation "from identification to individuation."[76] Per the 1716 ordinance, *contrôles* listed the name, birthplace, age, height, and any distinctive mark that would aid in identifying every serviceman in every regiment. After the Seven Years' War, the crown mandated that *contrôles* become increasingly detailed, including more in-depth descriptors of individual facial features, eye and hair color, and notes on personality. Each man was issued a certificate of identity, and efforts were made to render these documents difficult to falsify. Men also wore marks of honor and service on their clothing, such as the veteran's chevron, which allowed one to immediately glean information about an individual's rank and potential trustworthiness.

These policies reduced (although they did not eliminate) officer absenteeism and desertion and decreased hostilities between soldiers and local populations. The evolution of troop registers and garrisoning also furnished means to cultivate familiarity, communication, and collective culture among military men. Military administration remained somewhat wary of such social bonding, however, especially esprit de corps. As in the case of the conflict between the regiments of Auvergne and the Maine stationed at Lille, esprit de corps spawned tensions between different units, thereby feeding into the misdirected competitiveness and lack of *société* that the crown knew to be destructive in the armed forces. It could facilitate regional culture or personal relations taking precedence over state authority. Choiseul attempted to curtail this possibility by making sure that majors and lieutenant colonels were not of the same geography and culture as their regiment. This could help prevent a situation of dueling authorities in which esprit de corps and personal adherence to a regiment's culture and value system formed a justification for breaking state law.[77]

Despite these administrative concerns, service members continued to champion esprit de corps. "Why is it," inquired an anonymous writer, "that a soldier from Navarre, from Champagne, or from any other regional unit . . . of good reputation or accredited with certain actions should be more valiant than another soldier from another unit that lacks such a reputation if it is not that esprit de corps has made him undergo a total metamorphosis?"[78] *Militaires philosophes* sought to uncover the mechanisms of esprit de corps, which they saw as essential for combat effectiveness and the ability to withstand the privations of military life. They delved into philosophical questions regarding identity and what we now call psychology. They understood that esprit de corps necessitated associating personal identity and honor with those of the unit. Reformers theorized that neither officers nor soldiers could be expected to take on a collective identity naturally. There had to be a meeting halfway. This could come in the form of numbering units as opposed to naming them after their noble commander, which blocked self-identification for all other men in the unit. Distinctive flags could also foster esprit de corps, being at once objects that inspired collective pride and that made the actions of a regiment visible to all others on a battlefield, evoking praise and emulation of a regiment that fought courageously, or conversely, shame and condemnation for a regiment that cowered or fled from combat.[79] Seeking peer male approval was, according to the chevalier de Folard, "this common interest that animates us, that makes each person take part in the common glory and shame, which is certainly the truest motivator of men of war."[80] Collective identity and emulation would follow from this drive.[81]

By the late eighteenth century, reflections on esprit de corps led to a new taxonomy of martial collective identity. Jean-Girard Lacuée, comte de Cessac's (1752–1841) definition of the expression in the *Encyclopédie méthodique* attributed four declensions to esprit de corps: *esprit de classe*, which united all men of the French military; *esprit général de corps* for each different branch of the armed forces; *esprit de corps* uniting members of a regiment; and *esprit de groupe* for smaller units, from battalions to companies or squadrons.[82] The resolution of the Auvergne-Maine debacle discussed earlier in this chapter was at once a visualization of this taxonomy and also a spectacle of military prowess and male sociability. The officers of both regiments pooled money so that their men could come together for an alcoholic libation, like an enormous drinking circle. They then formed their regiments for a musical parade through Lille that symbolized their martial discipline, their regimental pride (esprit de corps), and their collective union or société under the French flag (*esprit de classe*).

Yet these symbolic processes and objects would always be insufficient, some reformers upheld. The truest and most infallible means of reaping the benefits of esprit de corps was to establish real social bonds between members of a regiment. Lacuée de Cessac went so far as to say that regiments should be composed of family members, while other thinkers investigated primary group cohesion for the first time in French military thought.[83] "Never underestimate the importance of roommates [*les chambrés*]," suggested the chevalier de Montaut, or the support that comes from "the friendship that bonds those who share the same bed and eat at the same table ... that brings them joy as they share the sorrows, the hard work, and the misery" of military life.[84] Ordinances of the eighteenth century increasingly regulated the daily tasks of men in companies who ate together, shared rooms, and completed chores in small groups, such as fetching water and preparing meals.[85] Men were grouped into sections (fourteen to sixteen men, roughly a half-company) that formed the infantry *ordinaire* or mess/lodging group, which, according to John Lynn, represented the basic unit of primary group cohesion from the mid-eighteenth century onward.[86] The intimacy of family and close friendship was seen as a true asset, and these structures of military life fostered such relations.

Moving from identification and individuation to relationship also meant communication and an earnest impulse to get to know others. Officers across the armed forces took it upon themselves to open lines of communication between themselves, subaltern officers, and soldiers in order to garner information about the experiences, grievances, and desires of those with whom they served. Cavalry officer Louis Drummond, comte de Melfort (1722–1788), related such an effort in a memoir to Choiseul of 1762.[87] His narrative recounts a conversation he initiated in his dragoon unit about Choiseul's reforms, his men's experiences, and the reasons that so many men refused to reenlist. Rather than accept the status quo and ponder his soldiers' lives from afar in the officers' quarters, Melfort took an empirical, empathetic approach and opened a direct line of communication to his troops. He avoided making decisions on their behalf based on his own assumptions in a paternalist fashion. Instead, he came to his men with a sense of curiosity about why no one was reenlisting and hoped that there was sufficient trust between them that the men would answer honestly.

After arranging the men in a layered semicircle and announcing to the troops that he had proof of the king's goodwill and of the war minister's attentions, he invited anyone in the regiment to step forward to form an inner circle of discussants. Not one man stepped forward. Melfort then singled out several sergeants, engineers (*fourriers*), brigadiers, and other officers, asking them if they wanted to reenlist. None did. At that point, Melfort dismissed the officers in order to speak directly with his dragoons. He exhorted them to trust him and to tell him how they felt about their service and their superior officers. They responded laconically that their officers were good to them and that they could not complain. Then silence.

Melfort knew that these men did not trust him and were afraid to speak their minds. In order to prove that they could have confidence in him, Melfort showed them a tactical memoir that he had sent to Choiseul, the contents of which demonstrated that he was truly interested in their well-being. Their suspicions and doubts then seemed to dissipate, and, one by one, Melfort's men began to speak openly with their commander. Many wanted to discuss specific points of Choiseul's recent reforms. Older soldiers feared that they would not get the full salary they were due. They had been told upon enlisting that they would receive it after sixteen or twenty-four years of service, but they felt sure that they would not touch their payoff until after thirty years of service. Another dragoon spoke up and divulged that many men never received their due leave and were basically being kept in the service by force. He also revealed that a number of men were never paid after their first term of enlistment. If they were paid properly, the dragoons told him, "it would prove to us that the King doesn't demand that we serve him for nothing."

This statement resonated with a great number of Melfort's men, so much so that he reported that all of them started to speak at once. Their conversation went in many directions, and Melfort probed further to gain a deeper understanding of these individuals, their mentalities, and the realities of their lives. Ultimately, he relayed, despite his best efforts to guarantee a change in the dragoons' circumstances, the abundance of proof to the contrary easily conquered his strongest reassurances. In their eyes and in his own,

> the calamity of circumstances did not permit taking care of their needs. I have seen regiments that were almost naked and although the minister's orders indicated that all the regiments that I inspected were to be given new clothing, it is no less prevalent to find those who have been wearing the same tattered clothing for one year and who have been deeply afflicted and humiliated by this. I can even say on this subject that I saw soldiers and dragoons refuse to take leave of the army because they would have been too embarrassed to appear in their hometowns looking like beggars [*gueux*]. These were their own words, which greatly affected me and which I cannot forget.[88]

Melfort's efforts to learn about his men, his willingness to listen to them and converse with them at length, and to take in their individual experiences exemplify a type of "caring curiosity" that departed from the power framework of paternalism. It came from a desire for military effectiveness, but also from respect for his men as warriors and human beings. He expressed a genuine concern for their lives and well-being in and outside of the military. Melfort's genuine care is crystallized in his vocabulary, which at once evinces his grasp of the emotions of his men ("deeply afflicted," "humiliated," "embarrassed") and communicates his strong empathetic response ("greatly affected me," "I cannot forget").

This conversation between Melfort and his dragoons exemplifies d'Argenson's idea of establishing a "perfect union" in a unit based on humanity. As the hesitant, doubtful, and surprised reactions of his men illustrate, Melfort and like-minded officers were pioneers in reaching out to their troops and taking their experiences into account. Not only did Melfort's actions give insight into why men did not want to reenlist, but they created a sense of community, of common purpose, and of real caring. Familiarity, intimacy, communication, and caring were modes of relating that could bring military men together across regional and class divides. These relationships could not only build increased trust through the ranks and encourage all levels of esprit de corps; they could also form the basis for justice in the military system. Martial community could constitute a step forward out of dysfunction and toward the type of unity that d'Argenson believed made an army "invincible."

Maurice de Saxe also espoused these priorities, though he took a more lighthearted approach. Saxe embraced a cultural institution of *le monde*—the theater—which he deployed as an emotional technology of war designed to achieve military effectiveness as well as more humane goals.

Theater, Masculinity, and Emotional Community

In early January 1746, Charles-Simon Favart (1710–1717), famed comedic playwright and director at the Opéra-Comique in Paris, received a letter with a surprising proposal from an unexpected correspondent. Maréchal Maurice de Saxe invited him to come to the warfront at Brussels the following April to become the director of his *théâtre de guerre* (war theater). "Do not believe that I view this as a simple object of amusement," Saxe wrote; "[the comedy] figures into my political views and the plans for my military operations."[89] Saxe was a theater enthusiast and already had a troupe of thespians attached to his army, which was engaged in the Low Countries at that time during the War of Austrian Succession. However, Saxe was not satisfied with his current troupe under the direction of André Parmentier, and, in light of recent decisions made at Versailles, he wanted to bring a superior and more specific type of talent to his *théâtre de guerre*.

First, on the strategic front, the marquis d'Argenson, secrétaire d'état aux affaires étrangères and brother of the comte d'Argenson, balked at a militarily aggressive agenda following the victory at Fontenoy for fear that it would strengthen German and English ties to Vienna. As a result, rather than invading the Dutch Republic or probing into the Rhineland, Saxe and his army of one hundred thousand troops in Flanders were ordered to embark on a dreary campaign of sieges. The prospect of several years of the slow pace and tedious work of siege war troubled Saxe. He believed, as many others did, that boredom was one of the most dangerous emotional states for the French, whose national character and *genie* (spirit) comprised impatience, frivolity, and strong natural passions such as ardor and the love of freedom.[90] This emotional disposition made the French more suited for attack, for shock column versus line tactics, and for hand-to-hand combat as opposed to slow and methodical siege craft. Ennui, a chagrined lassitude that involved the dulling of the body's sensible fibers, was seen to be a veritable illness that provoked desertion and could even lead to death for the vivacious Frenchman.[91]

Second, machinations in Bourbon family politics also posed a serious challenge to Saxe's military leadership and effectiveness. In early 1746, Versailles appeased the ambitions of several *princes du sang* (princes of the blood) who claimed their hereditary right to lead military units. Louis-François de Bourbon, prince de Conti (1717–1776), a declared enemy of Saxe, was given command of an independent army formed in part by some of Saxe's own troops. The comte de Clermont (1709–1771) agreed to serve under Saxe, but on the condition that he be given control of a large army corps. The Louis-Philippe d'Orléans, duc de Chartres (1725–1785), Louis-Auguste de Bourbon, prince de Dombes (1700–1775), and Louis-Jean-Marie de Bourbon, duc de Penthièvre (1725–1793) all came to the front. The arrival of these princes, followed by that of the king and some of his minsters, delayed the 1746 campaign season and set a different tone for the forces at Flanders. As Frederick the Great of Prussia remarked in his *Histoire de mon temps*: "The courtiers filled the camp with intrigues and foiled the general's plans. The general and the numerous court demanded ten thousand rations for their horses and crews alone."[92] Saxe himself complained bitterly to the chevalier de Folard, "I don't know if you realize what it is to have a court-army [*armée de cour*] and all of the inconveniences that it carries with it."[93] The *armée de cour* in the Low Countries represented all the evils of the dysfunctional French army: a top-heavy, extravagant, insubordinate, and often inexperienced officer corps serving alongside disgruntled subaltern officers and soldiers.[94]

Saxe recruited Favart as part of a broader effort to cope with these problems. The theater was to become a technique to optimize emotional health, build community, and sculpt martial identity in the *armée de cour* in the Low Countries. To achieve these goals, Saxe did not seek an epic poet, a tragedian, or a panegyrist. Rather, he chose Favart, a well-known comedian of the opéra comique genre whose talent lay in simple yet witty, lighthearted comedy, at times irreverently parodic and burlesque. Opéra comique had originated in 1678 and developed through the first half of the eighteenth century in the fairs or *foires* of Saint-Laurent and Saint-Germain at which puppeteers, pantomimes, tightrope walkers, animal trainers, and other street performers entertained fairgoers.[95] The *théâtre de la foire* was so popular that the Comédie française and the Académie royale de musique both took turns attempting to squelch it and to reassert their privileges, claiming exclusive rights to "performances with dialogue" in the first case and to "performances with singing, dancing, and musical accompaniment" in the second. Both of these efforts were brilliantly subverted by ruses of *foire* theater troupes. Mischievously abiding by the new rules, they switched dialogues into monologues, dialogued with interlocutors off stage, and used signs or large rolls of paper showing the words of the play. They also invited the audience to recite or sing the lines. It was precisely this type of ingenuity, irreverence, and playful humor that Saxe sought for his theater with the intent to bring gaiety to his army.

Saxe's strategy to elicit happy sentiments through opéra comique is reflective of philosophical medical discourse of the period. In 1753 the physician Antoine Le Camus (1722–1772) published an immensely popular work, *La médicine de l'esprit*, that recorded many popular medical beliefs and practices circulating during the previous decade. His book discussed achieving holistic wellness through a pseudo-Hippocratic monitoring of the six nonnaturals (air, motion and rest, sleeping and waking, food and drink, excretion, and the passions or emotions). In particular, it focused on the importance and methods of stimulating gaiety in the French. Le Camus pinpointed opéra comique and vaudeville as authentically French creations that reflected national character and that could be used to produce or resuscitate joy in that population:

> It is this gaiety that distinguishes French character from that of other nations. It is [gaiety] that inspires the genres of poems in which [the French] excel. It is in France that vaudeville and *opéra-comique* were born ... If deep in ourselves we no longer find this gaiety whose sweet influence spreads a graceful polish over our most serious writing and our most interesting conversations, we have an easy means to get to the state in which the free spirit, cheerful and more entrepreneurial, presents things in a humorous light.[96]

Le Camus claimed that the particular type of humor of vaudeville and opéra comique—an intelligent humor that is light and a bit sensual (*voluptueux*)—found its precedents in ancient times as well as in French writers of the sixteenth and seventeenth centuries: François Rabelais (1494–1553), Michel de Montaigne (1533–1592), Paul Scarron (1610–1660). Compared to prose and theatrical works by those authors, however, eighteenth-century inventions of vaudeville and opéra comique had the added virtue of including song, which expressed and fostered healthy laughter and happiness, according to Le Camus. "Where is this gaiety better expressed than in the songs of the French?" he wrote. "One has hardly sung a few couplets before one becomes disposed to laughter and finds oneself at ease in good company where this tone makes it clear from the get-go that liberty will reign."[97]

Le Camus argued that the "moderate joy" (*joie modérée*) occasioned by vaudeville and opéra comique offered a manifold sense of freedom: social freedom, intellectual freedom, and freedom "to taste the full extent of one's happiness."⁹⁸ Moderate joy also fought off the opposing humors of Saturn, those of *ennui* and *dégout*, and was thought to cure sickness, alleviate discomfort, chagrin, and anxiety, and prolong life by years.⁹⁹ Moderate joy, Le Camus explained through the example of the Greek lyric poet Anacreon (582–485 BCE), was particularly important for those close to death and was contagious, like "a zephyr that spreads serenity in the air, dissipates clouds from the imagination, animates the charms of conversation, sows cheerfulness everywhere, and ushers back the laughs and games that seemed to have been banished."¹⁰⁰

Saxe's commitment to martial happiness and his vision of his opéra comique as a mechanism to achieve it is evidenced in the frontispiece of the two collections of plays he had published in 1748 under the title *Théâtre du Maréchal de Saxe à Bruxelles*. The frontispiece, designed by François Boucher (1703–1770) and engraved by Pierre Quentin Chedel (1705–1763), showed five Cupid figures surrounding Saxe's blazon with the motto *ludunt in armis*— "they play in arms" (figures 5 and 6). Favart witnessed Saxe's desire to deliver such levity on several occasions. For example, on the eve of the battle of Rocoux, Saxe surprised his men with news of the battle at the end of a performance by Favart's troupe. The announcement was sung by an actress in vaudeville to the tune of "De tous les Capucins du monde":

We fulfilled our task,
Tomorrow we shall be on break,
Warriors, Mars will guide your steps;
Will that your ardor renews itself:
To intrepid soldiers
Victory is always faithful.

Tomorrow battle, day of glory;
Will that in the golden days of history
The name of the French triumph again,
Worthy of eternal memory!
Return after your success,
To enjoy [*jouir*] the fruits of victory.

Favart's relation of how this announcement was received reveals the success of Saxe's enterprise in using theater to ignite excitement, joy, and eagerness for battle. "My couplets caused a universal surprise," Favart wrote. "The crowd ran to the general's lodge, believing that this was temerity on my part. He confirmed what had just been announced. The room reverberated with doubled applause and the only words one could hear were 'Tomorrow battle! Tomorrow battle!' The euphoria passed in a single moment from officers to soldiers and became the portent of victory."[101] The French were indeed victorious at Rocoux on October 11, 1746.

This incident illustrates Saxe's beliefs regarding the power of theater as a political and military tool capable of enhancing happiness, courage, and community. It also distracted officers from more nefarious behaviors (gambling, prostitutes, court intrigues, and so on). As Favart explained, "The comedy was a meeting point for all of the officers. Their predilection for the theater stopped them from abandoning themselves to gambling or to other equally dangerous excesses. This was the maréchal's goal and one of his primary political objectives."[102]

Favart's couplets announcing Rocoux also show the way in which his theater and other forms of entertainment constructed military identity. The above lines mythologize the French army and its valor, deploying tropes that portrayed the French as legends in their own time and as favored by the gods of war and victory. Favart's creations aimed to spark a quixotic impulse in his warrior audience, not only in terms of martial feats but also in that other arena of pursuit distilled in the Ovidian phrase printed on copies of the plays: *Militat omnis amans, et habet sua castra Cupido* (Every lover is a soldier, and Cupid hath his camp). Favart portrayed military men as romantic heroes and adapted his earlier plays to foster identification in a martial audience, changing characters into different military personnel and usual suspects at camp such as doctors and sutlers.[103] When selecting works by other playwrights to stage for Saxe's army, he chose ones like the anonymously penned *La Brabançonne généreuse* of 1746, in which a high-born Flemish girl is engaged to an important figure in Holland, but is in love with a young French captain.[104] Similarly, popular songs sung by troops communicated the romantic desirability of military men.[105] In the song "Auprès de ma blonde" ("By My Fair One's Side"), a woman sings of her handsome husband who has been captured at war and is being held prisoner in Holland. When the woman is asked what she would give to get her husband back, she shows utter dedication, replying, "I would give Versailles, Paris, and St. Denis." Other songs communicated that military men were considered to be the best lovers and husbands. In fact, as the "Chanson d'un capitaine" relayed, men must enlist if they have any hope of attracting a good woman.

The themes of seduction and romantic love were staples of such popular songs and of Favart's wartime theater. What is more, in the game of love, the actresses themselves represented objects of pursuit, as Favart and Saxe were both well aware.[106] When the "attractive young actress" sang the words

FIGURE 5. Frontispiece of the Théâtre du Maréchal de Saxe à Bruxelles, designed by François Boucher and engraved by Pierre Quentin Chedel (1748). Courtesy of the Bibliothèque nationale de France.

Figure 6. Pastel portrait of Maurice de Saxe by Maurice Quentin de la Tour (ca. 1748). Photo: Hans-Peter Kint. Gemaeldegalerie Alte Meister, Staatliche Kunstsammlungen, Dres.Photo Credit: bpk Bildagentur / Gemaeldegalerie Alte Meister, Staatliche Kunstsammlungen, Dres / Hans-Peter Kint / Art Resource, NY.

"Return after your success / To enjoy the fruits of victory," Favart stoked the soldiers' and officers' sexual imaginations knowing full well that the verb *jouir* meant both to enjoy and to have an orgasm. The battle announcement for Rocoux was a bald sexual provocation concocted by Favart to incite a desire to win not one, but two battles. Favart unabashedly fostered this virile military heroism in various ways and on many occasions. In July 1747, Favart staged a mock military evolution called the *Ordre de bataille de l'armée feminine en Flandres* ("Battle Order of the Feminine Army in Flanders"). In it, actresses and prostitutes lined up in battle formation. The *état major* and *généralissime* were played by principal actresses (at least two of whom were Saxe's lovers), while other actresses commanded "reserve troops" and a "detachment." Commingling love of country with love of a woman, *la mort* and *la petite mort* in their respective battles, Favart made real both the image and the promise of *militat omnis amans*. Saxe's antics and Favart's performances, such as the *Armée feminine en Flandres*, not only provided comic relief but fostered a light-hearted way for the troops to distance themselves from the warring enterprise.

Though Saxe and Favart did not invent wartime entertainment, they were trailblazers in their military application of new medical ideas and practices relating to theater. Philosophical medical writings, such as Antoine le Camus's *La médecine de l'esprit* and Pierre Fabre's (1716–1793) *Essai sur les facultés de l'âme, considérées dans leur rapport avec la sensibilité et l'irritabilité de nos organes*, in which they examined the psycho-physiological effect of drama, were published later, in 1753 and 1785, respectively. This innovation had both a utilitarian motive and a humane impetus to create "emotional community" formed of the hardships of war and to acknowledge community as a healing force against these hardships. Saxe's and Favart's *théâtre de guerre* is reflective of the broader eighteenth-century movement "to create space for happiness on earth," even in the most unlikely of places.[107]

Martial Sociability around the World

While it may have been possible for the *théâtre de guerre* to unite men of Saxe's army, no such easy solution existed for military men and their allies in Canada, India, the Antilles, or the soon-to-be United States of America. Political and cultural philosophers of the eighteenth century made the possibility of forming social bonds with these "Others" seem unattainable. Environmentalist theories correlated different cultures and national character with external conditions such as local diet and climate. If place determined identity, then being born and raised oceans apart created ineluctable intrinsic differences between people. Natural philosophers such as Georges-Louis Leclerc, comte de Buffon (1707–1788), developed theories of race that pinpointed environmental factors responsible for producing varied physical and moral traits. Often racist and sexist, these theories openly or tacitly portrayed Africans, Asians, Jews, mixed-race women, and other groups as inferior and dangerous to European white men.

Officers of the French armed forces on assignment around the globe grappled with these theories, stereotypes, and prejudices. This process cannot be romanticized, since it is clear that a great many officers never bothered to challenge *idées reçues* about "the Amerindian race," Marathas in India, or free men of color from the sugar colonies. They instead did everything they could to reinforce notions of European superiority. On the other hand, it is also clear that many were intent on maintaining an open mind and a malleable stance during their service abroad. Necessity drove this cooperative disposition, as did notions of sociability and the *esprit philosophique* that propelled reform in the metropole.

Over 70 percent of French ambassadors and plenipotentiary ministers came from the military.[108] These men knew that their role required surmounting closed-mindedness and cultural assumptions. French warriors and administrators recognized that sociability was one of the primary catalysts of diplomacy, a term that first entered French dictionaries at the end of the eighteenth century.[109] The fifth edition of the *Dictionnaire de l'Académie française* defined diplomacy as a science, that of "relations and interests between powers." Sociability, described as "the aptitude for living in society" in the same edition of the *Dictionnaire*, was essential for diplomacy and gained another facet as military men exercised their aptitude for living in *different* societies while abroad. During this period of their infancy, as today, the terms "sociability" and "diplomacy" were inextricably tied.

These military diplomats and *militaires philosophes* displayed an empiricist, ethnographic, and multicultural awareness. They observed, adapted, learned local languages and customs, and ultimately formed what Richard White calls a "middle ground" fabricated by their experiences and cultural imaginary. While these men still ultimately supported the projects of French empire in their work abroad, they made conscious efforts to discern points of similarity between peoples and cultures and to respect other nations and ways of being. Some became advocates for compromise, allegiance, and friendship. They also aimed to overthrow erroneous prejudices, becoming cultural ambassadors of populations and individuals alongside whom they served on continents around the world. Yet the problematic of equality—human, military, social, civil—

infused these writings and demarcated the limits of sociability in North America, the Antilles, and India.

Sociability was key to relations among Amerindians, colonial settlers, *compagnies franches de la marine*, and French regular army forces in Nouvelle France (figure 7).[110] Forest diplomacy, battle, trade, festivities, friendship, marriage, miscegenation, and adoption of French military men into different Amerindian tribes constituted a complex network of bonds.[111] Leaders of French naval troops were at the center of negotiating intercultural social relations. By the eighteenth century, the majority of marine officers had been born in Canada, some of miscegenated heritage, like Charles-Michel de Langlade (1729–1801), son of Augustin de Langlade, a French Canadian fur trader, and Domitilde, a preeminent daughter of a war chief and sister of the Ottawan chief Nissowaquet. Langlade was schooled in both cultures of his heritage. He was given a French education by Jesuit missionaries at Fort Michilimackinac, located near present-day Mackinaw City in Michigan. At the same time, Ottawan was Langlade's first language, and he grew up practicing all of the traditions of his mother's people. This translingual/transcultural competence permitted Langlade to pass relatively seamlessly between Canadian and native populations and to translate between the two groups, anchoring alliances for trade and military pursuits which were beneficial for him personally as well as for the Canadians, French, and Ottawas. "Langlade would not have achieved his position without demonstrating talent for the demands of cross-cultural etiquette," asserts the historian Christian Crouch. "But unlike most marine officers, his *métissage* and consistent connection to his mother's family gave the Ottawas a direct voice in official French imperial military action not only by sustaining French territorial claims but also by determining the parameters of acceptable conduct by the colonial military elite."[112]

French officers without family connections to indigenous tribes took a scientific approach to observing and intermingling with Amerindians, who were often referred to as *sauvages*, meaning "wild men." While French military men recognized that the Amerindians were not civilized *à la française*, many relativized this difference (as had Montaigne) and were adamant that the tribes with which they came into contact were far from existing "without civilization." Antoine Le Moyne de Châteauguay (1683–1747), Jean-François-Benjamin Dumont de Montigny (1696–1760), Jean Bernard Bossu (1720–1792), and others who served in Louisiana and the Pays d'en Haut were "adopted" by an Amerindian nation, took on indigenous names, battled along with their tribes, participated in rites and rituals, and were honored as tribal warriors by a series of painfully administered tattoos. Bossu, a captain of the *troupes de la marine* who had been adopted by the Arkansas (les Akanças), got a tattoo of a deer on his

Figure 7. "Military commission granted to Chief Okana-Stoté of the Cherokee by Governor Louis Billouart, chevalier de Kerlérec" (1761). Courtesy of the National Archives at College Park.

thigh. A contraposition to the Bougainville, who was adopted by the Iroquois, Bossu did not view his interactions with the Akanças and the tattooed mark of honor as exotic curios, nor did he want the French back in the metropole to perceive them that way. He instead applied hermeneutics that could more faithfully translate his experiences for a European audience. He likened the ceremonial tattooing of warriors to the culture of chivalry, which also had rituals of initiation following a period of trials that proved a warrior's worthiness. Bossu articulated the meaningfulness of his warrior tattoo and said that the honor was similar to the one that Louis-François-Armand de Vignerot du Plessis, marshal and third duc de Richelieu (1696–1788) received when his name was inscribed in the Genovese *livre d'or* (*annuario*) in which the names of local noble families and stories of heroic feats were recorded.[113]

Bossu and like-minded *militaires philosophes* concluded that the French and the Amerindians were not so dissimilar. The men of both societies were ambitious and sought the recognition of their peers. Zacharie de Pazzi de Bonneville concurred, claiming that young Amerindian and French men had many points of connection in their national characters. According to his observations, the former are "lively, playful, and live for dancing, especially those who frequent the French, whom of all Europeans relish [dancing] the most because of their light and playful temperament that meshes so well with that of the *sauvages*."[114] Amerindian accounts also suggest that these assessments of similarity were mutual, and not merely unilateral assumptions by the French. The respect for solemn ritual and ceremony was considered an important point of cultural and spiritual resemblance that made the French intelligible and respectable to indigenous tribes.[115] These alleged similarities in character and culture, along with quotidian interactions between Amerindians and Frenchmen, especially in what Arnaud Balvay calls "sociétés des forts" (fort societies), fostered solidarity, intermarriage, and friendship.

Misunderstandings and projections were clearly a part of establishing this "middle ground"; however, these *militaires philosophes* were clear that the greatest evil was a lack of sociability. Those who displayed this lack were agents of calamity for the French on the North American continent. Some authors wrote with disgust of their peers who abused social bonds and trust by trying to manipulate Amerindian warriors through falsifying spiritual omens. Dumont de Montigny and others condemned one Captain de Chépart (sometimes spelled d'Echéparre, Chopart, Chepare), commander of Fort Rosalie in Louisiana, blaming his antisocial and abusive behavior as the primary cause of the infamous Natchez massacre of 1729 in which nearly a third of the local French population (250 out of 700) were murdered.

Failures in these arenas and those of sociability during the Seven Years' War played no small role in the loss of Canada. French army regulars under and including Montcalm struggled in their encounters with the Iroquois Confederacy, in which women were the central decision-making power, particularly with regard to war, diplomacy, and the needs of the community. Montcalm expressed wonder at the diplomatic process by which matrons bestowed honor on him by giving wampum belts, after which he was expected to offer such "necklaces" in return and to sing songs of war with them. Others noted their surprise at receiving female ambassadors.[116] While French Canadians and marine officers had long adapted to these modes of sociability and diplomacy, officers from the Metropole often found, as Montcalm did, that interacting with Native American matrons took "an angel's patience." In the end, their disrespectful, unsociable behavior and disregard for honoring commitments to indigenous tribes—in particular promises regarding the spoils of war—were at the heart of the military disasters that led to the fall of French imperial claims in North America.[117]

On the Indian subcontinent, the stakes of sociability were equally high. French military officers and governors socialized with one another, with other European presences, and with Indian princes, sultans, and other local powers.[118] Official crown policy and that of various incarnations of the Compagnies des Indes indicated neutrality and noninterference in Indian politics. However, Pierre-Benoît Dumas (1668–1745) and Joseph-François Dupleix (1697–1763), who served as governors of Pondicherry from 1735 to 1741 and 1742 to 1754, respectively, both aimed to transform French mercantile trade posts into a veritable French-Indian colony. The trading post at Pondicherry was granted self-governance by Mughal and later Mysorian sovereigns in a pseudo-feudal fashion, in the knowledge that European trade buttressed the economy. As the Mughal Empire disintegrated between 1707 and the 1730s, Dumas and Dupleix seized the opportunity to gain territorial possessions from local principalities in exchange for military assistance in their conflicts. This imperial and interventionist policy, which was never endorsed by Versailles or the Compagnie, drove both governors to seek a much deeper knowledge of regional politics and customs.

Earning respect through military effectiveness, sociability, and a representation of power that was culturally legible to Indian leaders constituted the foundation of French survival and potential expansion on the subcontinent. Dumas's success in these arenas occasioned a momentous political event: the Grand Mughal (Padishah) bestowed a patent of nawab, meaning Indian governor, on the position of the governor of Pondicherry in perpetuity. The governor was no longer a foreign presence representing France and the Compagnie; he was a local authority whose office was in essence that of an Indian prince. Dumas invested exorbitant sums of time and money in hosting Indian authorities in order to demonstrate his rightful place among the region's governors and princes. One military officer wrote that "not a week goes by without [hosting] embassies of Moorish and Gentile princes or visits from lords of the land whom the governor insists upon receiving with ever more pomp so as to give them the most advantageous idea of the nation."[119] Dupleix reportedly traveled to diplomatic visits with a dazzling and ornate entourage, including a procession of twelve elephants.

Dupleix did not rely on spectacle alone. He wisely constructed a team of family, friends, intermediaries, and advisers in order to carry on Dumas's legacy of power. He married Jeanne Vincens (or Jeanne Begum, 1706–1756), a woman of mixed Indian-European heritage who spoke multiple Indian languages and who had strong knowledge of different local customs. Madame Dupleix was a constant presence, serving as a translator and cultural mediator for her husband. Dupleix also attained information and effected diplomacy through Jesuit missionaries, but most important, he depended on French military men serving Indian leaders. Charles Joseph Patissier de Bussy, marquis de Castelnau (ca. 1718–1785), was Dupleix's foremost officer and ambassador. A *militaire philosophe*, Bussy applied himself to learning local languages and cultural mores and prided himself on his capacity to function within the norms of various "Asian" (*en Asiatique*) comportments. Other memoirs written by military men offered notes on negotiating with local nawabs, on the impressive accomplishments of the Marathas (contrasting their image as deplorable raiders that had been promulgated by the *Encyclopédie*), and on the personalities of Mysore sultan Hyder Ali Khan and his son Tipu Sultan (1750–1799)[120] (figure 8).

In 1781 cavalry lieutenant colonel Russel had served in India for twelve years when he wrote a memoir to Naval Secretary de Castries about Hyder Ali and Tipu Sultan, with whom he had lived and battled as allies. He argued that friendship and intercultural understanding were the primary vehicles for continued French presence in India. Russel gave details of the exchanges and the deep friendship he had developed with the crown prince while serving together:

> When I was with him, which happened twice a day during sieges, we waited for his father to arrive at the trenches and he questioned me about our customs, our mores, our military forces, our ways of making war. He consulted me on what type of conduct he should embrace when he became the master of his people and made me envisage the epoch of his reign as being advantageous for France. "I want," he said to me, "to chase them [the English] from India. I want to be a friend of the French for all of my life."[121]

The governor general and officers must have perfect knowledge of Indian politics, claimed Russel, for "it is above all in India that one gains better advantage through negotiation than by force of arms." In support of this, Russel wrote a detailed account of the cultural and social "politics to observe" when interacting with Hyder Ali. Tipu Sultan told Russel exactly what gifts to bestow upon his father during a first encounter in order to establish respect, bonds, and alliance: different colored taffetas to make coats, as well as binoculars, money, and other items. Following this initiatory sequence, Russel implored French officials to "fulfill our engagements" and to extend the dynamics of friendship to all of Hyder Ali's people, who should be treated with "humanity, goodness, and gentleness."

The rhetoric of friendship pervades both Indian and French sources of the period. The memoirs of Hyder Ali Khan and Tipu Sultan establish friendship as a primary mode of political, social, and economic engagement; however, they relay little detail about its processes. On the other hand, the memoirs of Ananda Ranga Pillai (1709–1761), originally written in Tamil, provide rich particulars regarding Franco-Indian relations.[122] Pillai was born into a wealthy

Figure 8. Meeting of Pierre Andre de Suffren de Saint Tropez (1729–1788) and Hyder Ali (1728–1782), in Antoine Sergent, *Portraits des grands hommes, femmes illustres et sujets mémorables de France* (1786–1792). Courtesy of the Bibliothèque national de France.

merchant family in Madras and immigrated to Pondicherry, where in 1747 he became the chief *dubash*, a merchant in the service of the Compagnie who translated, facilitated, and oversaw Franco-Indian trade relations. Pillai became one of Dupleix's favorites, and they formed a deep and complex friendship that combined trust and emotional connection, bribery, and pressure to perform in cultural, political, economic, and military arenas.[123]

Mishaps and misunderstandings that characterize the "middle ground" occurred no matter how diligent, objective, and faithful agents like Pillai and *militaires philosophes* such as Russel aimed to be. One document told of an abortive diplomatic gesture between the French and the Marathas in 1741. Dumas had lent his forces to Chanda-Sahib (d. 1752), governor of the fortress of Trichinopoly and relative of the nawab Dost Ali Khan (d. 1740), to take the city of Karikal from the king of Tanjore (now Thanjavur). Chanda-Sahib offered Dumas the city in exchange for this blow to his enemy. In retaliation, the king of Tanjore allied with the Marathas, who attacked Dost Ali Khan's territories and killed him, besieged Trichinopoly, and then did the same to Pondicherry, where the defunct nawab's family were taken in as refugees. Waging war on multiple fronts proved overwhelming for the Marathas, who withdrew from Pondicherry. The Marathas marked their withdrawal from the region and cessation of conflict by sending the French governor a *serpeau*—"an Indian piece of clothing that is the greatest mark of honor and recognition." Dumas, following what he believed was necessary for social *bienséance* (propriety) and for solidifying their peaceful bond, sent a gift back to the Marathas valued at 2,400 pagodas. The Marathas, who considered themselves an invading third party, did not expect a gift in return and did not wait around to receive one. The French ambassadorial detachment searched far and wide, believing in the urgency of their mission, but the Marathas were long gone.[124]

As was the case in North America, Russel and other officers viewed asocial behaviors and cultural ignorance as the greatest evils. The loss of French strongholds in India during the Seven Years' War was a case in point. During the first rumblings of the war, it was clear that the French in India would need reinforcements and should prepare for sea and land battle. Bussy—talented, knowledgeable, and experienced in Indian terrain and culture—seemed the obvious choice to lead the French forces. However, politics in Versailles dictated the choice, and Naval Minister Jean-Baptiste de Machault, comte d'Arnouville (1701–1794), gave the appointment to Thomas Arthur, baron de Tollendal, comte de Lally (1702–1766), an Irishman who had long served in the French army and was one of the marquise de Pompadour's protégés. Lally had never set foot in India, knew nothing of local languages, politics, leaders, or customs, and was known to lack social and diplomatic skills. After initial successes in the Carnactic, French forces grew thin and were outnumbered by those of the British, especially when the small fleet commanded by Anne Antoine, comte d'Aché (1701–1780), was forced to retreat due to a monsoon. A number of officers, including Bussy, who remained in India to serve under Lally, encouraged the latter to forge alliances with local nawabs in order to attain military support. Lally refused and expressed, according to sources, his incapacity to understand "the Indians," whom he saw as wild savages, and his scorn for sepoys, whom he viewed in abusive racist and classist terms as "the country's negroes."[125]

Meanwhile, the British received strong reinforcements, struck numerous alliances with nawabs, then took back lost territory and opened an amphibious siege on the only remaining French stronghold at Pondicherry. After an arduous ten-month battle during which Lally's own officers and men mutinied due to lack of food, munitions, and pay, Lally capitulated on January 14, 1761. Lally was captured by the British, sent home to France, where he was imprisoned in the Bastille, and sentenced to death by public beheading for his "multiple crimes." Lally was a convenient scapegoat, and his case became a cause célèbre, due in part to his brutally botched decapitation; the executioner misjudged what was to be a fatal blow to Lally's neck, instead hacking off his jawbone and sending his teeth flying from the scaffold. Voltaire and others took up Lally's defense (albeit too late), but most military men who had served under him in India shunned him for his unwillingness to learn, adapt to, and respect Indian leaders, customs, and politics.[126]

If race, class, and culture influenced Lally's disregard for nawabs and sepoys, such judgments were even more prevalent in the French Antilles. In Saint-Domingue, social tensions were increasingly racialized, especially following the Seven Years' War, when an influx of poor whites (*petits blancs*) arrived on the island to make their fortunes. They banded together with white planters, and together they advanced a rhetoric of white racial purity and superiority. Pseudo-scientific writings advanced the belief in the inferiority of people of color in biological and gendered terms. Pierre Barrère's (1690–1755) *Dissertation sur la cause physique de la couleur des Nègres* (*Dissertation on the Physical Cause of the Color of Negroes*, 1741) argued that black skin color was the result of "humoral imbalance" in the form of an excess of black bile. In the *Déscription de la partie française de Saint-Domingue* (1789), Martiniquan chronicler Médéric Moreau de Saint-Méry (1750–1819) would later expound on the effeminacy and excessive sensuality of mixed-race "mulatto" people, especially the women, whom he believed were responsible for corrupting white male colonists and culture. Just as in the metropole, discourse in the colony denounced effeminacy and the dangers of female passions that would weaken colonists morally and physically. However, the threat of emasculation and a morally bankrupt colony was racialized in Saint-Domingue: people of color were clearly to blame. This discourse on white racial superiority had specific effects in the military life of the colony, since it was deployed to exempt white settlers from socializing with people of color or from engaging in activities considered beneath them, such as military service in local militias or in the *maréchaussée* (constabulary police force). The history of these institutions shows the increasing racial divide and the specifically asocial and nonfraternal character of both the militias and the constabulary.[127]

What is more, racial tensions and injustices were so rampant in Saint-Domingue that they were used as a motivator by metropolitan officers attempting to recruit free men of color for the Chasseurs volontaires d'Amérique unit that d'Estaing brought to fight in the American Revolutionary Wars. Lenoir de Rouvray told his recruits to say to themselves: "I have a better physique than the white soldier; I will support the fatigues of war four times better; I have the honor to serve the king just like he does; every difference between us in our way of doing things is to my advantage; I have all sorts of motives that engage me to be more worthy than him. I must make the whites blush from the scorn that they heap upon me in my civil status and the injustices of tyrants that they continually exercise on me with impunity. I must prove to them in my status as a soldier that I am capable of at least as much honor and courage and of more fidelity."[128] Military service in Saint-Domingue, according to the above historical evidence, was structured on difference and was animated by prejudice and even a spirit of vengeance.

Yet these and other sources also uncover the transformative force of military social ties for free people of color. Bonds formed with comrades during military service created what Stewart King calls a middle-class "military leadership group." Individuals such as Capitaine Vincent Olivier (d. 1780), Sergeant Jean-Baptiste Magny (known as Malic or Mali), and Pierre Augustin solidified wartime relationships through "family" notarial acts and through a myriad of other roles and actions: becoming godparents at baptisms or witnesses at marriages and burials, and offering financial assistance and, in some cases, manumissions. Military friendships formed the foundation for the blossoming of an entire community.

Metropolitan officers like Lenoir de Rouvray also acted to fight stereotypes about free people of color and to promulgate military equality. Forgoing any gendered framework, Lenoir de Rouvray spoke of the physical superiority, courage, and selflessness of free men of color, all of which were martial virtues sought for in the metropolitan army. They "can become excellent soldiers if not given [the] impression that [the] profession of soldier is lower than that of a slave," he wrote. In this regard, it was imperative that they be spared all "humiliating and oppressive distinctions" and that "as soon as they enroll they must be treated like other soldiers." Lenoir de Rouvray was emphatic in saying: "I will never cease to insist on the necessity of giving these *chasseurs* the same status and the same existence as white soldiers. Let us not profess a prejudice regarding a difference in color. Some may say that a difference exists in their civil status, that is, between [the rights of] a *chasseur* and [those of] a citizen, but between *chasseur* soldier and white soldier it does not exist. I maintain that any such proposition is absurd and contrary to all military principles."[129] As *militaires philosophes*, officers were to hold themselves to a higher moral standard, and military principles could right the wrongs of civil society, if only within the armed forces.

From the standpoint of white colonists, such military sociability was a direct political threat. France's American allies in their fight for independence from England also represented a potential political danger. While many were enthusiastic about the Americans' fight for freedom, the crown and high-ranking military officials were nervous about whether the fires of violent revolutionary fervor might jump from American troops to French ones. Strict antifraternization laws were implemented in order to keep American and French soldiers from socializing.[130] Officers seemingly avoided one another. The comte de Clermont-Crèvecoeur remarked that "one never sees a French officer with an American one. We had a strong understanding between us, but we did not at all live together. This, I think, was the best thing that could have happened to us. Their character being so different from ours, quarrels would surely have broken out quickly."[131] On the French side, "hardly five of every hundred were not noble and outside of sharing in military service, they had very little in common with their American homologues who were often cobblers, butchers, and most often, innkeepers" whom the European aristocrats quietly or demonstratively snubbed.[132] French officers felt far more affinity for enemy British officers. Rochambeau and Lauzun invited high-ranking British and German officers to dine with them in their camp. Rochambeau even lent money to Lord Charles Cornwallis (1738–1805) so that he could cover his immediate expenses, which the British general promptly reimbursed along with a friendly gift of Cheshire cheese and one hundred bottles of wine. Journal writers within the French forces noted the grandiose sociable gestures made by the French toward British and Hessian officers at Yorktown, which made American officers quite jealous.[133]

Policies and prejudices that fueled antifraternization would not be the lasting character of social relations between French and American officers. When the American War of Independence drew to a close in 1783, American major general Henry Knox suggested the formation of a society that would permit the officers of the Revolution to remain in contact, to care for the widows of fallen compatriots, and to preserve the ideals of the Revolution in family and public memory. The society was founded in May 1783 and was named for Lucius Quinctius Cincinnatus (c. 519–430 BCE), who left his farm to become Roman consul and then wartime dictator (*magister populi*); however, once peace had been settled, he returned lawful power to the Senate and went home again to plow his fields alongside his family. George Washington (1732–1799) became the society's first president. Initially, membership in the Society of the Cincinnati, which had a chapter in each former colony, was limited to American army and navy officers who had served a minimum of three years. Still, society members sought to make a gesture of gratitude and to forge an enduring bond of friendship with their French counterparts and therefore invited high-ranking officers to join the society as well. Rochambeau, Lafayette, and Alexandre-Théodore-Victor, comte de Lameth (1760–1829) were among fourteen French founding members of the society. A French branch was founded in

December 1783.¹³⁴ While friendship between French and American officers had not been common during the war itself, they promulgated it as a fictional memory of Franco-American sociability during the war.

From Sociability to *Sensibilité*

The significance of sociability as a sub–flash point of the Military Enlightenment relates to the history of moral philosophy, race, and gender. Echoing theories by Pufendorf, which took a more radical expression in works by d'Holbach, Diderot, and the *Encyclopédistes*, metropolitan martial philosophies of sociability combined natural law and the rules of salon etiquette to give a particular account of human nature and society. Recognizing common human traits and needs, they argued, would lead men to join together in partnership, subordination, and polite comportment. In North America, India, and Saint-Domingue, race, mores, and social stature challenged and in many ways tempered martial visions of sociability. Yet officers such as Bossu, Russel, and Lenoir de Rouvray contended that it was the responsibility of a *militaire philosophe* to recognize merit, to search for commonalities in culture and national character, and to recognize as autonomous "Selves" those whom they had formerly viewed as "Others."

In terms of gender, this strain of military thought offers a counterpoint to misogynistic perspectives by which certain reformers upheld that martial and political decay could be remedied only by annihilating female cultural influence and replacing it with a classical republicanism that was strictly male in character.¹³⁵ For Lamée, d'Argenson, Saxe, and others, the "effeminate" civilized society of *mondanité* was not a wholly evil influence. On the contrary, it could offer solutions to military dysfunction and furnish models for leadership, communication, and community. At the same time, Saxe and Favart's *théâtre de guerre* created masculine identity and community at the expense of women, whose sexual objectification was a foundation for male self-image and homosocial bonding.

Despite the increasing focus on sociability in military thought of the eighteenth century, most men of the French armed forces did not view their comrades in arms as "brothers." This was certainly the case between noble officers and soldiers. Yet cross-corporate bonds and an evolution in the perspective of officer-soldier relations were under way. These trends were furthered through martial contemplations of *sensibilité*. As the following chapter elucidates, the medicine and moral culture of *sensibilité* became an innovative framework for military progress, ushering in a new focus on compassion and humanitarianism in the space of war.

CHAPTER 3

Humanity in War
Military Cultures of *Sensibilité* and Human Rights

Dettingen was paradoxically one of the most humiliating defeats of the century for the French army and at the same time a shining victory for humanity in war.[1] In late June 1743, Adrien Maurice, duc de Noailles (1678–1766), marshal of France and commander of French forces in the Rhine-Main country, was poised to inflict an easy defeat on the weak and retreating Pragmatic Army stationed along the north bank of the river Main outside of Dettingen (now Karlstein am Main in Bavaria). Noailles had conceived of a tactical disposition that he dubbed *la souricière*, or the mousetrap. It was to snare the combined British, Hanoverian, Austrian, Hessian, and Dutch forces under King George II of England (1683–1760) on all four sides, thereby cutting off their retreat toward Hanau. With the Spessart Heights to the north and the waters of the Main to the south offering natural obstacles, Noailles marched some twelve thousand French troops to Aschaffenburg to the rear of the Pragmatic Army while his nephew, Louis, duc de Gramont (1689–1745), and his twenty-three thousand troops waited outside of Dettingen to block the allied line of retreat. Noailles's mousetrap offered ample opportunity to thwart King George's army. The enemy's left flank was completely exposed to French cannon firing from across the Main, and King George's troops would long be bottlenecked as thirty-five thousand beleaguered men attempted to cross a single bridge above a shallow ravine and bog outside of the town (figure 9).

HUMANITY IN WAR 111

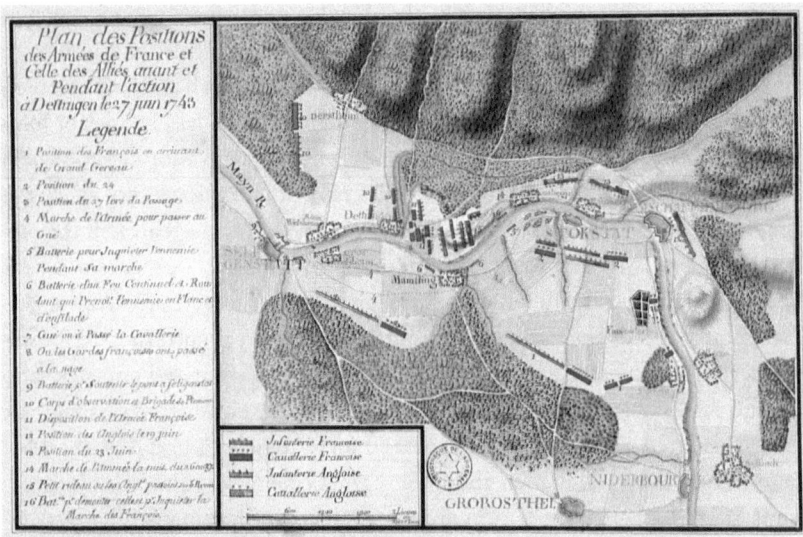

FIGURE 9. Map of French and allied positions before and after the battle of Dettingen, June 27, 1743. Courtesy of the Bibliothèque nationale de France.

Noailles's *souricière* backfired, catching the trapper rather than the mouse. The impatient duc de Gramont, without having received orders to do so, advanced his troops over the tiny bridge to engage the allied army on the other side of the marsh. Leading with the elite Gardes françaises of the Maison du Roi and then following with French infantry, Gramont led an attack that was initially successful, with three charges that broke through the British line. However, with their own troops suddenly in the line of fire, the French artillery across the river were forced to desist and watch as Gramont's exhausted troops fell to a forceful counterattack that sent even the highly trained Gardes françaises fleeing back over the bridge or into the ravine in a scene of utter panic and carnage.[2]

This failure was a lasting embarrassment. It eliminated the chance to make the British monarch Louis XV's prisoner and cost the French what had been an easy opportunity to win the war by forcing the Pragmatic Army to surrender or starve. The cost of the defeat at Dettingen did not end there. What had been imagined as a relatively leisurely and bloodless victory for Noailles in reality resulted in heavy losses. Gramont's insubordination and tactical misjudgment at Dettingen led to more than four thousand French casualties and prisoners, among them many of France's finest warriors. This was a devastating blow, one that would later influence Choiseul's military policy.[3] The allied army sustained more than two thousand casualties on its side.

Considering that other battles of the War of Austrian Succession, such as those at Mollwitz, Chotusitz, and Camposanto, were far more sanguinary, some scholars have concluded that the battle of Dettingen has been attributed too much importance.[4] This was not so, however, for either Noailles or John Dalrymple, second Earl of Stair (1673–1747), who served as King George's field marshal and commander-in-chief at Dettingen. For them, it was not solely the number of casualties and prisoners, but rather the humane treatment they received, that was of extraordinary importance. Marking a precursor to the Geneva Conventions, the enemy marshals signed a treaty, or cartel, in Aschaffenburg before the battle. It guaranteed to protect their respective hospitals, which were viewed as sanctuaries, and that the wounded and sick who fell into enemy hands would be cared for rather than considered prisoners of war. These two resolutions would indeed form Articles 1 and 6 of the 1864 convention.[5] Both the French and the Pragmatic armies respected this agreement, such that when the latter continued its retreat, leaving behind their injured, the French indeed took care of the enemy's wounded.

Commenting on the mentality behind the Dettingen cartel, Marshal Stair wrote to Noailles, "My sentiments are and always will be to make war with all the generosity and all the humanity possible."[6] He articulated his motivation in the language of sentimental moral philosophy. The term "humanity" is of capital importance, as it took on new meaning in the context of the epistemic shift toward sentiment.[7] Dictionaries of the seventeenth century, such as Robert Crawdrey's dictionary (1604) and the first edition of the *Dictionnaire de l'Académie française* (1694), equated humanity with gentleness (*douceur*), courteousness (*honnêteté*), goodness, and, in the French case, sensitivity to the misfortune of others. According to Diderot's article in the *Encyclopédie*, humanity "hardly enflames itself but in a great and sensitive soul [*une âme grande et sensible*]." Sensibility, "a tender and delicate disposition of the soul that renders it easily moved and touched," was the mother of humanity, according to Louis de Jaucourt.[8] In the eighteenth century, the benevolent disposition that defined humanity changed from a passive to an active principle. Diderot's article on humanity in the *Encyclopédie* explains that "this noble and sublime enthusiasm torments itself for the pain of others and with the need to relieve them; it would traverse the world to abolish slavery, vice, superstition, and misfortune."[9]

Diderot's "humanity" was not only a sentiment of tenderness. According to him, it also brought with it explosive violence that was at once emotional, moral, and physical. "It makes us severe in the treatment of crimes. It tears [*il arrache*] from the hands of the criminal the weapon that would be deadly to the good man."[10] Such ferocity in justice seeking was not equally possessed by all. Diderot reproached, "I have seen this virtue, which is the source of so many others, in many heads and in very few hearts." Only an elite few had sufficient sensibility to feel humanity. As Dan Edelstein suggests, "Not everyone could be an *âme sensible*: There was a *noblesse du coeur* just as there was a *noblesse de cour*."[11]

Following the largely rational, sociability-based thought examined in chapter 2, *militaires philosophes* turned to emotion as a new foundation for military identity and reform. By the middle of the eighteenth century, being a part of the moral elite of the *noblesse du coeur* was becoming just as important as being a member of the *noblesse d'épée* for many officers in the French armed forces. Military officers were proud to be a part of this moral elite as agents of *sensibilité* and humanity in war. This is surely one of the reasons for which the handwritten or verbal cartels such as that of Dettingen were quickly printed and circulated, like the Convention of Brandebourg ratified by maréchal des camps et armées Pierre-François, marquis de Rougé (1702–1761), for the French and by Major General Johann Heinrich, baron of Buddenbrock (1707–1781), for the Prussians on September 7, 1759. The marquis de Rougé himself had already benefited from this type of convention when he was taken prisoner and then exchanged following the battle of Rossbach in 1757 (figure 10).

Enthusiasm regarding the cult of *sensibilité* and the chance to enact it in the military sphere was a transnational phenomenon. Surveys of libraries by Ira Gruber and research by Christopher Duffy, Armstrong Starkey, Charles Royster, and Sarah Knott illustrate that military officers across Europe and the Atlantic avidly consumed literature of *sensibilité*.[12] They were enthralled with works like Rousseau's *Julie, ou La Nouvelle Héloïse* (1761) and *Émile* (1762), which were imbued with a secular, materialist notion of morality that Jean-Jacques termed *la morale sensitive*, sensitive morality.[13] Reading the literature of *sensibilité*—novels such as Marivaux's *The Life of Marianne* (1731–1745) and Richardson's *Pamela* (1740), along with those by Rousseau and others—was imagined to impart many benefits befitting an enlightened military man. Not only did such novels supply models for virtuous emulation, as Diderot proclaimed in the "Éloge de Richardson" (1761), but reading them and identifying with characters also allowed one to exercise and improve one's sensibility, as Anne Vila and Lynn Hunt argue.[14] Cultivating humanity and sensibility in this way fostered a capacity to look at other humans empathetically and to become the type of warrior for justice that Diderot described in the *Encyclopédie*.

The military culture of *sensibilité* and humanity represents an important counternarrative to Michel Foucault's notions of "discipline" and "docile bodies." *Militaires philosophes* such as Maurice de Saxe integrated attitudes of humanity and sensibility into the space of war by advancing ethics and practices

TRAITÉ,
ET
CONVENTIONS,
Pour les Malades, Blessés & Prisonniers de guerre des Troupes de Sa Majesté Très-Chrétienne & de Sa Majesté le Roi de Prusse.

NOUS,

PIERRE - FRANÇOIS, Marquis DE ROUGÉ, Maréchal des camps & armées du Roi;

JEAN-HENRI-GUILLAUME, Baron DE BUDDENBROCK, Général-Major de Sa Majesté le Roi de Prusse, & Chevalier de l'Ordre de Saint Jean de Jérusalem.

Au nom de Sa Majesté Très-Chrétienne;

Au nom de Sa Majesté le Roi de Prusse;

SAVOIR FAISONS, qu'en vertu des pleins-pouvoirs qui nous ont été donnés, & que nous nous sommes communiqués, nous avons fait le présent Cartel, pour avoir lieu, par échange & par rançon, entre les Troupes de Leurs Majestés Très-Chrétienne & Prussienne; & que nous sommes convenus que les Articles ci-après énoncés, auroient leur pleine valeur & entière exécution, tant pour les Prisonniers qui ont été faits

ci-devant, que pour ceux qui pourroient être faits de part & d'autre par la suite.

ARTICLE PREMIER.

TOUS les Prisonniers de guerre, de quelque qualité, espèce ou condition qu'ils puissent être, sans aucune réserve, qui ont été faits depuis la présente guerre entre les troupes des deux Puissances, & dans quelque pays que ce soit, seront échangés ou rançonnés aussi-tôt après la ratification du présent Cartel, le plus diligemment que faire se pourra, ainsi qu'il sera plus amplement expliqué dans l'article XXV du présent Traité, & M.rs les Généraux respectifs, commandant les armées belligérantes & auxiliaires, conviendront entre eux à l'avenir des endroits où se feront réciproquement les échanges ou rançons des prisonniers qu'on se rendra de part & d'autre.

II.

TOUS les Prisonniers de guerre desdites Troupes, sans aucune réserve, qui seront faits de part & d'autre après le premier échange ou rançon, seront rendus de bonne foi quinze jours après leur détention, ou, aussi-tôt que faire se pourra, par échange de Prisonniers de pareille charge ou équivalente, ou autre, en faisant compensation du plus au moins, ou payeront leurs rançons sur le pied qu'elles seront ci-après marquées, savoir, en florins d'Allemagne à compter de soixante creutzers de part & d'autre, faisant deux livres dix sols argent de France.

III.

LE présent Cartel ne dispose en aucune façon de l'échange ou rançon des prisonniers faits ou à faire pour les Troupes Prussiennes qui se trouvent ou pourroient se trouver à l'avenir à l'armée alliée commandée par Son Altesse Monseigneur le Duc Ferdinand de Brunswick; c'est en vertu de la convention de l'Écluse, que leur échange ou rançon doit avoir lieu: & par conséquent les prisonniers faits ou à faire par les armées de France sur lesdites troupes de Sa Majesté le Roi de Prusse, sont à échanger ou rançonner le plus tôt que faire se pourra, vis-à-vis des prisonniers François faits ou à faire par ladite armée alliée.

IV.

IL sera tenu un livre des prisonniers faits dans les armées belligérantes & auxiliaires, dans lequel il sera marqué le nombre qui sera renvoyé de part & d'autre dans chaque mois, afin qu'au premier du suivant il soit envoyé de chaque côté un état de ce qui aura été reçu & rendu, pour que huit jours après il soit payé exactement & sans difficulté le nombre excédant qu'un parti devra à l'autre; son compte aussi des avances qui auront été faites auxdits Prisonniers, pour qu'elles soient remboursées en même temps, & que tous les comptes soient arrêtés, sans qu'ils puissent être portés au mois suivant; & au premier échange ou rançon desdits prisonniers de part & d'autre, on se liquidera de toutes les avances qui leur auront été faites, sur des états valables qui seront produits.

V.

TOUTES les fois qu'il sera renvoyé des prisonniers d'une part ou d'autre, on y joindra un état qui sera remis au Commandant du lieu où ils auront été conduits, lequel donnera un reçu de la quantité & qualité qu'il recevra, pour être compté chaque mois, ainsi qu'il est dit ci-dessus.

VI.

ET afin qu'il n'arrive aucune contestation ni difficulté, tant par rapport aux postes & qualités des Officiers de part & d'autre, que des rançons qui devront être payées pour chacun d'eux, il a été estimé à propos de spécifier ci-après les postes & charges qui sont dans ces armées belligérantes & auxiliaires, & marquer le prix d'icelles.

VII.

Charges & Officiers servant dans les Armées & Garnisons de Sa Majesté Très-Chrétienne.		Charges & Officiers servant dans les Armées & Garnisons de Sa Majesté le Roi de Prusse.	
Général d'Armée ou Maréchal de France	Florins d'Allemagne. 25000.	Feld-Maréchal	Florins d'Allemagne. 25000.
		Général de Cavalerie, d'Infanterie ou d'Artillerie . .	10000.
Lieutenant général	5000.	Lieutenant général	5000.
Grand-Maître d'Artillerie . .	6000.	Grand-Maître d'Artillerie . .	6000.

	Florins d'Allemagne.		Florins d'Allemagne.
Maréchal-de-camp	1500.	Général-major	1500.
Colonel général de la Cavalerie	2000.		
Colonel général des Dragons	1500.		
Mestre-de-camp général de la Cavalerie	1500.		
Mestre-de-camp général des Dragons	1000.		
Commissaire général de la Cavalerie	1000.		
Brigadier de Cavalerie ou de Dragon	900.		
Brigadier d'Infanterie . . .	700.		
Major général d'Infanterie .	500.		
Maréchal général des logis de l'armée	500.		
Maréchal général des logis de la Cavalerie	100.		
Majors de brigade, tant de Cavalerie, Dragons qu'Infanterie	150.	Major de brigade	150.
Inspecteurs d'Infanterie, Cavalerie & Dragons . . .	150.		
Les Aides-de-camp payeront suivant le grade ou le brevet qu'ils auront dans l'armée.		Les Aides-de-camp payeront suivant le grade ou le brevet qu'ils auront dans l'armée.	
Intendant d'armée ou des provinces	650.	Conseiller privé des finances.	650.
Subdélégué ou Ordonnateur de la guerre	250.	Conseiller de guerre ou de Cour	250.
Commissaires des guerres .	150.		
Le Général des vivres . . .	300.	Commissaire général des vivres	300.
Trésorier de l'extraordinaire des guerres	250.	Trésorier de campagne ou Kriegs-zahl-meister . .	250.
Principal Commis de l'extraordinaire des guerres de chaque armée	150.	Le Commissaire des guerres, les autres Commissaires, le Maître général de la boulangerie, le Maîtres de boulangerie, le premier Valet de boulangerie, & les autres Valets de boulangerie payeront un mois de leurs gages.	
Les autres Commis de l'extraordinaire des guerres . .	50.		

FIGURE 10. Treaty and Conventions of Brandebourg (Traité et Conventions de Brandebourg) pertaining to "the Sick, Injured, Prisoners of war among the Troops of His Very Christian Majesty and His Majesty the King of Prussia" signed by the marquis de Rougé (1702–1761) and baron de Buddenbrock (1707–1781). Printed by the royal press in 1759. Like other such cartels, this one establishes the exact ransom to be paid for prisoners of war of differing military ranks. Courtesy of Count Aymeric de Rougé.

of care, particularly for soldiers. Far from viewing them as automata, military thinkers viewed them as *soldats sensibles*—sensitive soldiers—whose minds, bodies, and hearts required and deserved care.[15] Saxe centered his reforms on the concept of *le coeur humain*, the human heart, which he claimed to be the most crucial yet understudied part of the military enterprise. He modeled his understanding of the human heart on holistic conceptions of the human body burgeoning in the medical world of the time. *Médecins philosophes*—doctor-philosophers—such as Théophile de Bordeu (1722–1776) and Antoine Le Camus understood the human organism as a "sensible body" in which physiological, passional, and moral life were interwoven. They believed that each of these elements could be studied and cared for in order to foster health and happiness in individuals and society at large. This medicine of sensibility offered a road map to caring for the *soldat sensible*. United with the optimism of the era and the moral imperative associated with *humanité* and the *noblesse du coeur*, it also gave impetus to officers and the military medical community to make progress in specific areas: disease control and treatment, surgical procedures, the hospital system, and practices of hygiene. The conceptualization and objectives of the latter were ambitious, as military thinkers aimed to develop hygienic *régimes de vivre*, regimes of life, that would care for the soldier's physical and emotional being. This led to groundbreaking contemplations on emotional reactions to war and military life that founded what we now call military psychology.

These ideas coalesced into what Jean Chagniot refers to as a *révolution humanitaire*, a humanitarian campaign arising from and targeting the military that proliferated in the 1760s. The campaign involved a joint effort of military reformers, *philosophes*, and the public to effect change. Reform-minded thinkers were frustrated with the war ministry's and the crown's refusal to act, so they turned to nonmilitary intellectuals and the public in order to create a cause célèbre condemning capital and corporal punishment for deserters and military men guilty of petty crimes. The campaign is also historically momentous because it participated in the process of "inventing" human rights that Lynn Hunt examines. The eighteenth century in France, as Dan Edelstein argues, is an important yet overlooked point in the history of *les droits de l'homme*, the rights of man.[16] The military partook of and contributed to this history as the instigator and beneficiary of one of the first great victories of the proto–human rights movement in France.

Far from the metropole, the rhetoric of *humanité* and *sensibilité* was deployed to two ends: first, in order to buttress alliances, cultural understanding, and racial acceptance of indigenous peoples and free men of color; and second, to reaffirm ethnic stereotypes and cement them into racially and politically hegemonic policies. Humanity and sensibility could cut both ways.

Docile Bodies?

In *Discipline and Punish: The Birth of the Prison* (1975 in French, 1977 in English), Foucault formulates a case study of the soldier's body and the "military dream of society" in early modern France. In the seventeenth century, he argues, one could recognize the natural courage, strength, pride, and valor of a soldier through a "bodily rhetoric of honor." Honor had a physical semiotics by which these inherent martial qualities were made manifest through corporal signifiers of posture, mannerism, and physiology. Foucault claims that this conception of the military body changed in the latter half of the eighteenth century when the soldier became "something that can be made; out of a formless clay, an inapt body." "The fundamental reference was not to the state of nature, but to the meticulously subordinated cogs of a machine, not to the primal social contract, but to permanent coercions, not to fundamental rights, but to indefinitely progressive forms of training, not to the general will, but to automatic docility."[17] While conceding that in every society the body is subject to power, he contends that the eighteenth century was a watershed moment in defining and controlling the "docile body" through multiple "disciplines" that targeted even the most minute movements of the body.[18]

Foucault illustrated the military "disciplinary" stance and its emphasis on detail by quoting from the introduction to Maurice de Saxe's *Rêveries*: "Although those who concern themselves with details are regarded as folk of limited intelligence, it seems to me that this part is essential, because it is the foundation, and it is impossible to erect any building or establish any method without understanding its principles. It is not enough to have a liking for architecture. One must also know stone-cutting."[19] Foucault found support for his interpretation in ordinances such as that of January 1, 1766, regulating infantry exercise: "'The ordinary step will be executed forwards, holding the head up high and the body erect, holding oneself in balance successively on a single leg, and bringing the other forwards, the ham taut, the point of the foot a little turned outwards and low . . . etc.'"[20] His visions of the docile soldierly body and disciplinary power are corroborated by a number of sources from the period.[21]

While Foucault's schema was grounded in solid evidence, it has been contested with particular attention to the French army.[22] Alongside the "Foucauldian" method of creating and controlling docile bodies, less "disciplinary" or consciously "undisciplinary" accounts also flourished throughout the century. Saxe, whom Foucault cast as a proponent of a military-political anatomy of detail, was in fact one such case. Saxe did argue for increased attention to the study of details in war as opposed to "sublime" subjects like grand tactics that received far more attention from theorists. However, in the very same paragraph from which Foucault culled the above quote, Saxe declared his "undisciplinary" stance with regard to detailed knowledge of military bodies. "It is easier to take people as they are than to form them into what they should be," he asserted. "We do not command [*l'on ne dispose pas*] people's opinions, prejudices, or wills, and my goal is not to lay down rules [*donner des règles*]."[23]

If the larger framework of service in the military is in its essence the subjugation of bodies to political ends, Saxe's approach to details was not that of a Foucauldian "disciplined man." Saxe openly eschewed such dictates from both epistemological and practical standpoints. Applying deductive methodology to warfare and drawing logical conclusions based on a priori rationalizations, as did the Chevalier de Folard, was commendable as an effort to combat the ignorance and prejudices that characterized the art of war. However, it did not constitute a viable method for knowing, predicting, or controlling war and its agents. The Chevalier de Folard, Saxe explained, "goes too far; he advances an opinion and determines its success without considering that the success depends on an infinity of circumstances that human prudence could never predict. He supposes that men will always be brave without considering that troops' valor changes daily, that nothing is so variable, and that the general's task is to know how to guarantee his troops through positions, dispositions, and the enlightened traits that characterize the great captains."[24] Saxe defined what he considered to be "enlightened traits." Advocating for a humane and empirical approach to this "infinity of circumstances," especially the troops themselves, Saxe advanced a new framework for military leadership that centered on two concepts: compassion and the human heart.

Saxe subtly expressed his compassionate posture in his rhetoric throughout *Mes rêveries*. Writing in the 1730s, he did not have access to the diverse lexicon of sensibility that was just beginning to develop in medicine and in novels such as Prévost's *Manon Lescaut* (1731). He therefore distilled his sympathetic viewpoint in a single sensitive term: *pauvre*, or poor. The *Dictionnaire de l'Académie française* of 1694 identified *pauvre* as a word conveying compassion, tenderness, familiarity, concern, and lament for the misfortune of others. Beginning in the second article of *Mes rêveries*, on soldiers' uniforms, Saxe critiqued the excessive attention that military thinkers gave to contemplating skills such as the *coup d'oeil* instead of examining questions of soldierly health. He bemoaned the pitiful state of soldiers' uniforms, complaining that their tattered clothing and rotting shoes were not only uncomfortable, expensive, and useless, but also unhealthy. Once the rainy season began, the soldier's "head is never dry," and he has no change of clothing.

His "pants, shoes, and feet rot together" such that "this poor soldier is soon sent off to hospital."[25] Saxe evoked compassion in discussions of tactics, urging fellow officers not to deploy combat formations that staggered small groups of infantry within cavalry units. "This is worthless," he decried; "the weakness of this order intimidates your infantry troops because these poor miserable men [*pauvres misérables*] feel that they are lost if the cavalry is beaten."[26]

Through his usage of the word *pauvre*, Saxe signaled the importance of compassion in military functioning and designated to whom it needed to be directed. In fact, maintaining a compassionate perspective was a methodological cornerstone of Saxe's innovative military thinking. It led him to focus on "details" and on the second key conceptual pillar of his approach, the human heart.[27] Saxe opened up this field of inquiry in the preface to *Mes rêveries* and contended that "no one has addressed this subject, which is the most considerable, the most learned, and the most profound in the profession of war."[28] Adhering to his empirical principles, he gave an example of an almost comical episode in which Villars's French troops fled after winning the battle of Friedlingen in 1702:

> At the Battle of Friedlingen, the French infantry, having pushed back that of the Imperial forces with incomparable valor, after breaking their lines several times and chasing them through some woods and into a neighboring field, received news that its forces had been separated. At that moment, two squadrons appeared (quite possibly French) and the entirety of this victorious infantry fled in horrible disorder, without anyone attacking or following them, ran back through the woods and didn't stop until they had run well beyond the battlefield. The maréchal de Villars and the generals made efforts in vain to bring the troops back. The battle had been won, so there wasn't a single enemy in sight. It was these same men, these same troops that had just defeated the Imperial infantry, whose senses had been so disturbed by a panicked terror that they lost their countenance to a point of no return . . . Whoever would like to look for similar examples will find a great number of them in armies of all nations. This is sufficient proof of the changeable quality of the human heart and the case that must be made for it.[29]

Saxe did not offer a precise definition of the human heart that incited Villars's army to react in this manner. Instead, he proffered examples to serve as data points that mapped the influence of the human heart at war. Why is it that troops who are hopelessly defeated when defending trenches would have been victorious had they been attacking? Why is it that men are more apprehensive when imagining danger than in confronting it when it arrives?

Why is it that when something unexpected occurs, men automatically stop what they are doing and ogle or flee in haste? Why is it that a massive column of troops attacking an entrenchment can be sent into a panicked flight if a mere handful of enemy soldiers were to appear at the edge of the trench? The response, Saxe proclaimed, "is in the human heart and we must search for it there."[30]

Different from a seventeenth-century military understanding of *coeur* as a synonym for courage, Saxe's notion of the heart was far more scientific. His examples created a definition of the human heart not as an organ, but as a mind-body complex amalgamating emotion, psychology, physical reflexes, and instincts. Saxe's new military thinking aimed to illuminate the shadowy nexus of the physical, mental, and passional to offer a holistic account of human nature, which was the same project that *médecins philosophes* in France and across Europe embarked on in the science of *sensibilité*. Saxe was precocious in this endeavor. He wrote his memoir in the early 1730s and was a generation older than the most famed practitioners of philosophical medicine. Yet, many of the central tenets of philosophical medicine were already present in his work on human nature and war, so that not only did *Mes rêveries* participate in what would later be called the "science of man"; it was also a pioneering text that has not been recognized as such.

As the century progressed, *médecins philosophes*, surgeons, apothecaries, and military leaders alike worked to bring humanitarianism and sensibility-born medical and moral practices to the military sphere. Like Saxe, later proponents of the new military thinking exhibited a caring stance toward sensible bodies at war as opposed to a disciplinary and coercive stance toward docile bodies.[31] They followed Saxe's model of giving increased attention to "details" pertaining to hygiene, military psychology, and the human heart.

Sensible Bodies at War

The roots of Saxe's concept of the human heart dated to the work of seventeenth-century physicians like Guillaume Lamy (1644–1683) and Étienne-Simon de Gamaches (1672–1756).[32] They grounded their analyses of anatomy, movement, and the human heart in a medical science of sensibility.[33] In France, this science sprouted from post-Fronde physicalist theories of emotionality and sensationalist concepts of the body, knowledge, and identity advanced by John Locke, who was later popularized by Voltaire, David Hume, and Étienne Bonnot de Condillac.[34] These philosophers posited the body as a "sensible" organism due to its receptivity to impressions from within and without. Sensibility-based medicine had developed in opposition to iatromechanistic views of the body made famous by the Dutch botanist-anatomist Herman Boerhaave (1668–1738). Rather than seeing the body as a hydraulic machine, the Swiss physiologists Albrecht von Haller (1708–1777) and Charles Bonnet (1720–1793) advanced a vitalist account of a "sensible" and "irritable" body endowed with reactive nerves and fibers.[35] In medical schools across western Europe, and particularly in the celebrated faculties in Montpellier and Edinburgh, sensibility was thought to be the most fundamental function of the human body, unifying all of the individual parts of the body into an operative whole. Montpellier professor Théophile de Bordeu claimed that the body could be likened to a beehive, an *animal in animali* of many discrete parts working together to form a whole. Sensibility was the unifying force of the "beehive," establishing internal links between molecules, body parts, and the body and mind, as well as external connections between the body and its surrounding world.[36]

The doctrine of sensibility ambitiously and optimistically aimed at wellness writ large, from individuals to communities and society as a whole, all of whom could achieve balance and happiness through properly attuning sensibility. For *médecins philosophes*, the quest to improve humanity in health, virtue, and intelligence was so dependent on their analyses and treatments of sensibility that they considered the process of enlightenment itself to be a medical matter.[37] Physicians such as Antoine Le Camus and Charles Augustin Vandermonde (1727–1762) joined pseudo-medical and nonmedical *philosophes* like Helvétius, Anne Robert Jacques Turgot (1727–1781), and Nicolas de Condorcet (1743–1794) in their theorizing of human perfectibility. "This was an age that saw significant extensions to the concept of the medicable, a far greater emphasis on prophylaxis or hygiene, and a novel optimism about the future therapeutic potential of medical science."[38] Fueling this medical optimism were changes "in the meanings ascribed to death and disease, and the relationship between the two," write Brockliss and Jones.

> With more secular attitudes on the rise, and with death dethroned from its position as keystone of triumphant post-Tridentine evangelism, the focus had shifted from the moment of death to eternity's prelude, namely prior experience of life—and disease. The philosophes' expectations of medicine and health in producing societal happiness must be seen in the context of the transformation occurring within the epidemiological landscape and the changing cultural climate. Attention was now less fixed on the trauma-laden and putrescent corpse which had dominated representations of disease in an epidemiological landscape in which

bubonic plague held pride of place. The decline in mortality triggered a discursive explosion to do with disease, as the focus now passed onto the morbid body.[39]

In the expansion of commercialism and consumerism that marked the elite classes during the eighteenth century, health itself was "becoming a commodity like a racehorse or an umbrella, and medical practitioners were transmuting into technicians of the morbid body."[40]

The aspiration of individual and collective mind-body health met one of its greatest challenges in eighteenth-century armies and navies. Army encampments and naval vessels were unhygienic in the extreme and veritable hotbeds of infectious disease. Soldiers and poorer officers often suffered from malnutrition and scurvy, which left them even more susceptible to yellow fever, typhus, typhoid fever, measles, and whooping cough. "All of Europe had its eyes on Prague," Voltaire said of the siege in 1742 during which over one-third of the seventy thousand Austrians and twenty-five thousand French died of typhus.[41] In the *Recherches sur l'histoire de la médicine* (1764), Bordeu dedicated three out of four sections of his chapter on military medicine to inoculation against and treatment of smallpox and venereal disease, the two scourges of armies and navies. Frequently exposed to the elements—cold nights, rain, sleet, snow—troops also fell prey to pneumonia, pleurisy, rheumatic fever, and tuberculosis, all of which could be fatal. Latrines were set up in camps and on ship bows, but were not always used or respected, such that human excrement, along with that of animals, polluted camps, waters, and ship decks. Cholera and dysentery ripped through encampments, leading to high mortality rates. Nuisances such as frostbite, chilblains, lice, and skin conditions that were not typically fatal easily became so if aggravated, resulting in gangrene, impetigo, and amputations. On ships, tight, unsanitary quarters spread contamination, while the lack of potable water and vitamin-rich fresh fruit, vegetables, and meats decimated crews left susceptible to disease. A typhus outbreak in 1757–1758 crippled the French navy, taking ten thousand seamen out of service in the critical opening years of the Seven Years' War. What is more, epidemics jumped from sea to land as commercial and naval vessels brought diseases into ports. This was the case with the last epidemic of the bubonic plague, which killed over one hundred thousand people in and around Marseilles in 1720.

Ironically, mortality rates often increased for military men admitted to hospital, fueling the *légende noire*, the "Black Legend": the (at times deserved) reputation of hospitals as more likely to kill than heal.[42] Diderot's 1765 article on the Parisian Hôtel-Dieu hospital and Jacques Tenon's hospital death rate statistics published in 1788 supported this legend:

> Picture a long row of contiguous rooms where they assemble all types of sick people and where they often cram three, four, five, and even six into the same bed; the living next to the dead and dying; the air infected by the exhalations of this multitude of unhealthy bodies, giving one another pestilential germs from their infirmities, and the spectacle of pain and agony given and received from all sides. That is the Hôtel-Dieu. Also these miserable people leave the hospital carrying diseases they didn't bring with them to the hospital and often they pass them on outside of the hospital to those with whom they live.[43]

Tenon reported death rates of one in four at the Paris Hôtel-Dieu, one in six at Paris Saint-Sulpice, one in seven at Paris Charité, and one in eight in Versailles.[44] Across the Atlantic, where French troops joined in the American Revolutionary War, Pennsylvanian physician Benjamin Rush (1746–1813) complained that "hospitals are the sinks of human life in the army; they robbed the United States of more citizens than the sword."[45] This was no exaggeration. Estimates showed varyingly dour statistics that reflected badly on the control of disease and on the effectiveness of hospital treatment in America during the war: six out of seven soldiers' deaths were caused by camp illness, one in nine soldiers died from battle wounds compared to disease, and a soldier had a 2 percent chance of dying in combat compared to a 25 percent chance once admitted to a military hospital.[46]

If war on the European continent posed considerable medical challenges, colonial warfare and the global conflict of the Seven Years' War indeed heightened these challenges exponentially. Fighting in theaters in North America, the Caribbean, Africa, and the Indian subcontinent exposed armed forces to a host of new diseases and climates:

> When British troops arrived in French-held Martinique and Guadeloupe in January 1759, it took only two months for almost half of the five thousand troops—including their commander, General Hopson—to fall ill or die from sickness. Similarly, it took only three months for the British garrison in Quebec to be decimated by disease during the autumn of 1759 . . . In India, during the rainy season, European regiments—French and British alike—regularly suffered sickness rates reaching 50 to 60 per cent. Until the twentieth century, disease always killed and demobilized far more men than did combat. This was long recognized by military leaders; as the marquis de Bussy recorded in India, the climate and the unhealthy season were "the biggest enemy that we have to fight."[47]

Disease was also one of the biggest enemies for indigenous populations, whether allies or foes of European colonizers and mercantilists. Lacking immunity to European infectious diseases, native peoples were victims of unintended transmission as well as purposeful biological warfare. British field marshal Jeffrey Amherst (1717–1797) infamously used smallpox as a weapon against Amerindian tribes allied with the French by "gifting" them blankets infected with the virus: "You will do well to try to inoculate the Indians, by means of blankets, as well as to try every other method that can serve to extirpate this execrable race."[48]

In response to the devastations that disease caused in armies and navies, European powers allocated significant resources to military medicine.[49] Though not without corporate quibble, medical personnel and bureaucrats worked together to confront disease, injuries, and accidents as efficiently and effectively as possible on the continent and across the oceans.[50] This military medical community transcended national borders and formed a cosmopolitan *république des lettres* of military medicine.[51] Practicing medicine under extreme wartime conditions was at times exceedingly difficult due to mass numbers of acute injuries and illnesses as well as shortages of supplies and personnel. However, these conditions also provided a unique opportunity for bold experiment and improvisation not readily available in everyday civilian medical circumstances. David Vess argues that innovations generated in the sphere of military medicine during the latter part of the eighteenth century were an engine for broader medical progress such that this period constituted a "Medical Revolution."[52] Participants in the military medical *république* from the War of Spanish Succession to the Revolution were well aware that advancements in caring for the sensible body through therapeutics (surgery, hospital care, treatment of disease) and physical and mental hygiene would have implications far beyond their origins at the warfront. These efforts, briefly surveyed here, were animated by sentiments of enlightened *humanité* and a Saxian moral imperative to care for the military man.

The Military "Medical Revolution"

A *république des lettres* of military medicine flourished during the eighteenth century. Surgeons, doctors, and hygienists consulted with one another at the battlefront, traveled to study under one another or to join foreign scientific societies, and wrote of their theories, treatments, and encounters with disease and surgical conundrums in correspondence, journals, and treatises that were read and translated into multiple languages.

During the 1720s, Paris became the European capital of surgery and would remain so for more than a century.[53] Anatomy courses at the Invalides debuted in 1727, and the Académie de chirurgie was founded the following year, serving as a harbinger for the Société royale de médecine and the Collège royal de pharmacie, created later, in 1776 and 1777, respectively. Those who spearheaded this movement—Jean-Louis Petit (1674–1750), Sauveur-François Morand (1697–1773), and Henri-François Le Dran (1685–1770), a professor of Albrecht von Haller—were all celebrated military surgeons. In both military and civilian spheres, they offered more accessible training environments that ushered in a second generation of surgeons like Antoine Louis (1723–1792), who also served in military medical units. While the greatest contribution of these surgeons may have been consolidating and improving on surgical techniques of the past so that operations could be performed more efficiently and effectively, they were also innovators who utilized their military practice to develop new equipment and techniques. Military surgeons such as Petit, Louis, Hugues Ravaton, and Jean-Jacques Perret (1730–1784) designed improved tools including forceps, tourniquets, scissors, amputation knives, and devices for resetting broken bones. Pierre Desault (1738–1795) invented a bandage and a method of wrapping an arm to protect a broken collarbone that still bear his name today. At warfronts, there was no shortage of cadavers that could be used for autopsy. Citing a quote by the Italian anatomist Giovanni Morgagni (1682–1771), Bordeu put it dryly: "Hic locus est ubi mors gaudet succurrere vitae": "this is the place where death delights to help the living."[54]

In addition to the above-mentioned innovations in surgery and treatment of acute wounds, an ordinance of August 4, 1772, created an ambulatory hospital service staffed with 134 men: a surgeon-major, twelve surgeon aides-major, thirty surgical students, thirty medical attendants, plus several physicians, a war commissioner, a director, an assistant director, a cook, a baker, priests, and other helpers. Each army of twenty thousand men was assigned such an ambulance, (purportedly) equipped to care for two thousand wounded.[55] These ambulances were stationed "more or less within reach of the place where an engagement occurs," explained surgeon Jacques Bagieu, and served as "the first depot where wounded are collected, from whence they are carried to cities farther removed as these become crowded. It is rare that surgical operations are performed in the field proper."[56] In order to protect medical personnel and those under the ambulatory hospital's care, regulations stipulated that the ambulance remain at least one league (around four kilometers) from a place of combat. As a result, many critically injured died on the field of their injuries while lying in wait for medical staff to collect them. Also, the injured were treated according to military rank rather than by the gravity of the injury, so that an officer with a broken arm would receive treatment before a soldier with a severed limb.

The frustrations and injustices of the initial ambulance system later motivated Dominique Larrey (1766–1842) to design the more agile *ambulance volante*, a smaller, horse-drawn "flying ambulance" that traversed the battlefield to treat the wounded. He also instituted a more socially egalitarian system of triage in 1797.[57] "The best plan that can be adopted in such emergencies, to prevent the evil consequences of leaving soldiers who are severely wounded without assistance," Larrey contended, "is to place the ambulances as near as possible to the line of the battle, and to establish headquarters, to which all the wounded, who require delicate operations, shall be collected to be operated upon by the surgeon-general. Those who are dangerously wounded should receive the first attention, without regard to rank or distinction. They who are injured in a less degree may wait until their brethren-in-arms, who are badly mutilated, have been operated on and dressed, otherwise the latter would not survive many hours; rarely until the succeeding day."[58]

The ethic of solicitude and benevolence that motivated Larrey's creation of the flying ambulance is evident in narratives of the state military hospital system. The April 1674 edict that established the veterans' hospital of the Hôtel des Invalides was steeped in such rhetoric, and the Sun King went on to prepare and enact important advancements in military medicine.[59] A January 1708 edict issued during the War of Spanish Succession established several important precedents. It founded fifty-one military hospitals in cities across France, mandated that sick and wounded military men be cared for by qualified doctors, and established a bureaucratic hierarchy of military medical personnel presided over by the First Physician, the First Surgeon, and the minister of war. Edicts issued in the years following the War of Spanish Succession and Louis XIV's death continued to change the face of military medicine. In 1716 the crown abolished the purchase of medical positions and instituted a surgical training program in military hospitals. In 1718 the first exhaustive code of military hospital regulations was issued. It dictated roles and duties of medical personnel and administrators and detailed methods of hygiene and treating disease. These groundbreaking developments not only set state policy regarding the military health establishment but also exhibited the crown's care for the men of France's armed forces.

Later, in the preliminary discourse of his *Code de médecine militaire pour le service de terre* of 1772, Jean Colombier (1736–1789) emphasized the particular attention and respect that the French monarchy exhibited toward its military men as evidenced by the Invalides, military hospitals, the École royale militaire, and numerous monuments.[60] "It is a constant that we have always seen more soldiers perish by disease . . . than by arms and if we made progress in this regard during the last two wars [Austrian Succession and Seven Years' War], the losses are still too great for the government not to pay them great attention and to redouble the zeal of those who, by their care and *lumières*, race to diminish [such losses]."[61] The military hospital was one of the most important and successful of such ventures. While the imbrication of religious ideology and state policy hindered medical innovation and education in civilian hospitals, which numbered roughly two thousand by the end of the *ancien régime*, their military counterparts provided a much more favorable environment for meaningful advancements. Foucault and other historians credit the 1790s with having seen "the birth of the clinic"; however, the major elements of that setting—sanitary environments monitored by inspection procedures; the collection of medical statistics; teaching and research; and a focus on bedside medicine—already existed within the French military hospital establishment.[62] The crown created the position of war commissioner in the penultimate year of the War of Austrian Succession, an office charged with inspecting military hospitals, among other tasks. War commissioners and hospital inspectors such as Pierre-Isaac Poissonnier (1720–1798), appointed inspector of naval hospitals in 1769, his brother Antoine Poissonnier-Desperrières, and Colombier all advanced hygiene and hospital care in ways that contributed to the well-being of military men and subsequently the nation more broadly. A French commentator reviewing Richard de Hautesierck's *Recueil d'observations de médecine des hôpitaux militaires* in the June 1767 issue of the *Journal des Sçavans* declared that advancements in the system of French military hospitals would form the basis for a "national medicine."[63]

Contemporaries attributed the impetus for these projects to the call of humanity and compassion. In the report of the Académie des sciences printed at the beginning of Poissonnier-Desperrières's *Traité sur les maladies des gens de mer*, the academicians opined that "it would be a service to humanity to put into the hands of naval surgeons a clear and methodical treatise that could guide them with assurance in the treatments that they must administer, . . . which is what M. Desperrières has undertaken."[64] After pandemics of the flu in 1767 and smallpox in 1770 (the latter claiming Louis XV's life in 1774), it was clear that prophylactic, palliative, and curative medicine for fevers and diseases in naval personnel would be of service to society at large. Poissonnier-Desperrières underscored this point in his preliminary discourse and spoke of the humanity and royal benevolence that were at the heart of the disease-fighting medical enterprise. "Only humanity is necessary to conceive of such a plan; and if there were ever to be favorable circumstances for its execution, it is when one sees beneficence from the Throne, when a King, who is the true father of his subjects, ensures their security and happiness and finds the same sentiments [of humanity] in his soul as those whom he assigns the exercise of the supreme [medical] Administration."[65]

Invoking terms of sentiment and humanity, as had Maurice de Saxe, Poissonnier-Desperrières designated fellow-feeling as the origin and key to success of medical progress. This rhetoric and moral ideology were nowhere more evident than in works treating physical and mental hygiene. Here, medical and military thinkers alike theorized on how to achieve and maintain wellness of body and soul for every member of France's armed forces, from the marshal down to the foot soldier. What is more, the latter deserved even more attention and care, since the rank and file did not have access to funds, equipment, or personnel that aristocratic officers regularly called upon. In their efforts to prevent and alleviate suffering in the sensible human being, these thinkers advanced new standards of wellness and happiness in the space of war, and in doing so planted the seeds of a military culture of human rights.

Le Soldat Sensible

The word "hygiene" had a much broader and deeper significance during the eighteenth century than it does today. The term was relatively new at the time, its first usage dating to 1671 and its appearance in any major French dictionary dating to the fourth edition of the *Dictionnnaire de l'Académie française* of 1762. The anonymous author of the article on hygiene in the *Encyclopédie* (first edition, vol. 8) wrote more than 3,400 words and trumpeted its importance: "Thus the part of medicinal science that can have the most beneficial effect on humankind is without question hygiene since it has as its object the duration of a healthy life, [which is] the worldly gift [*le bien de ce monde*] that it tries to conserve, that is the easiest to lose and the most difficult to recover."[66]

Definitions in the *Encyclopédie* and the 1762 edition of the *Dictionnaire* convey that contemporary notions of hygiene were based on a highly individualized vision of health. It could be managed by a medical practice of sensibility built on Hippocratic categories of the six "nonnaturals" that were considered to be regulators—or deregulators—for all functions of the human body. The proper calibration of the six nonnaturals was completely personal. As Jaucourt explained in the article "Health" in the *Encyclopédie*, "The perfection of health does not assume therefore a same way of being in different individuals who enjoy it . . . It follows that there no longer exists a state of health which can suit everyone; each has his/her way to be well, because this state depends on a certain proportion in solids and fluids, in their actions and their movements, which is peculiar to each individual."⁶⁷ With this in mind, the task of the hygienist working to conserve an individual's health was threefold: (1) to maintain a healthy state in conformance with the person's complexion, temperament, age, sex, climate, profession, and state; (2) to fend off all causes of sickness, correct the effects of those that cannot be avoided, and change a person's disposition to being infected by them; and (3) to render life as durable as possible through a *régime de vivre*, or regimen of living, that included all necessary conditions for maintaining good health.⁶⁸

The profession of arms necessitated specific physical and mental qualities: strength, vigor, address, and valor. These characteristics were thought to occur naturally in certain men; thus, military thinkers agreed that attention to the selection of good recruits was capital. However, if men were less endowed with physical, mental, and moral constitutions best suited for war, the desirable dispositions could be hygienically cultivated and perfected through the nonnaturals and the social influence of others. Le Camus paid particular attention to attuning the *corps-esprit* complex for war in *La médecine de l'esprit*, first published in 1753 and then edited for a second and definitive edition of 1769. Employing the narrative and historical methodology of philosophical medicine, Le Camus furnished examples of great warriors from antiquity to his own day, relating their capacities to their hygiene. Strength, whose synonyms were valor, courage, magnanimity, intrepidity, heroism, and greatness of soul (*grandeur d'âme*), was a virtue exhibited by Julius Caesar (100–44 BCE), Kings François I (1494–1547) and Henri IV (1553–1610), Henri de la Tour d'Auvergne, vicomte de Turenne (1611–1675), and le grand Condé (1621–1686), along with countless other heroes. For Le Camus, physical and psychological strength went hand in hand.⁶⁹ "One can reach this by study, reflection, a regimen of living, and above all the change of climate, which can often metamorphose a coward and a poltroon into a brave and intrepid man."⁷⁰ Achilles ate the bone marrow of lions and wild boars in order to absorb the natural ferocity of these animals so accustomed to blood, carnage, and eating other animals.⁷¹ Jeanne d'Arc (1412–1431) allegedly carried mandrake, a hallucinogenic root, as a courage-inducing drug.⁷² As others during the century argued, Le Camus upheld that the moderate consumption of wine and other alcoholic liquors could chase away the miseries of war and that music could be used selectively to either stimulate courage or calm martial ferociousness, as Ovid (43 BCE–17 CE) claimed had been done with Achilles.⁷³

Colombier's work *Préceptes sur la santé des gens de guerre, ou Hygiène militaire* of 1775 was one of the most influential of the time. Reflecting the individualized practice of sensibility-based medicine, he described specific hygienic regimes based on three military grades and their corresponding social composition: high-ranking officers (generals and colonels, who were usually wealthy grandees and court nobles), middling and subaltern officers (poorer, provincial nobles), and soldiers (commoners). "This distinction," he explained, "while perhaps insufficiently methodical for a treatise on military art, is appropriate relative to the health of military men. It is even indispensable for proving that the same causes of illness have relative effects that are more or less grave in individuals who are essentially different with regard to physical constitution, diet, mores, and habits."[74]

Colombier's ideas on physical constitution, education, and hygiene were not particularly innovative for the time; rather, they were consolidations of preexisting discourse and practices. This was particularly the case in his comments on high-ranking officers.[75] More historically significant is Colombier's treatment of hygiene for soldiers, which represented the vast majority of the treatise (six out of the seven chapters), yielding evidence that the "details" that largely had been viewed as petty and ancillary at the time Saxe penned his *Rêveries* had gone mainstream forty years later. Citing Saxe, John Monro (1716–1791), and others, in chapter 2 of the *Préceptes*, Colombier theorized on appropriate clothing, food, air and physical positioning, discipline, mores, and the manner of recruitment for the *soldat sensible*.[76] While Colombier did not discount the critical role played by good leadership in the army, he attributed greater importance to the role of, and care for, foot soldiers. "Their service is punishing, their pay more modest, and they are less properly outfitted. What is more, they are almost always shut away in garrisons or barracks, more exposed to the torments of the weather, to the influence of bad air, and to the illnesses caused by fatigue ... In a word, it is the species of the soldier that demands the greatest care [*soins*] in all respects."[77]

With this in mind, Colombier pored over how to offer such comprehensive care. He complained that the only infantrymen who were properly dressed in protective uniforms were the elite Gardes françaises of the Maison du Roi, whose long jackets better shielded them from the elements. He posited that every soldier should have such jackets and matching culottes, both preferably made of buffalo hide, that would be worn over tightly knit burlap (hessian) shirts and undergarments. The latter would be changed twice a week and stockings once a week for cleanliness and should be replaced when worn through. Referencing Monro, he argued that soldiers should not be asked to sport tight collars and neckties or garters (*jarretières*) that were uncomfortable and cut off circulation. They should be given gaiters for their boots and have different types of head protection to wear over hair cut short—helmets or leather hoods that would be worn depending on the weather and the season.[78] In article 2 as well as in the final chapter of the treatise, Colombier advanced a multitiered plan for how to nourish troops properly, especially in circumstances when it was not possible to procure bread or meat. Quality should trump quantity, he argued, and social eating was preferable to eating alone, since the former helped troops be more measured in their consumption of food and alcohol, while a soldier taking meals alone was more likely to drink away his meager pay than to use it to purchase food.[79] Such social bonding could also help to curb the psychological and physical disease of nostalgia, also referred to as melancholia, homesickness, or *mal du pays*, which Colombier previously discussed in his *Code de médecine militaire pour le service de terre* of 1772 and which he thought claimed the lives of at least one-quarter all new recruits.

From this hygienic perspective, military thinkers focused on the physical, psychological, and moral repercussions of certain tactical practices, from devastating towns to deploying specific battle formations. Saxe worked to preserve the health and happiness of his men through eliminating futile, tiresome activity that would waste troops' physical and emotional resources. He remarked on the needless harm caused by the tactic of having men in the trenches stay up all night shooting their muskets toward an enemy fortress in the early stages of a siege. Not only did this musket-fire do little or no damage to the besieged enemy, but it also destroyed men's guns as well as their health as they damaged their shoulders from excessive shooting and grew physically and emotionally ill: "We fatigue the troops to the point where they are overwhelmed [*l'on fatigue les troupes de façon qu'on les excède*]. The soldier, whom we make shoot all night, grows bored [*s'ennuie*], his rifle gets filthy, breaks down and he must spend a good part of the following day cleaning and readjusting it as well as making more cartridges. Finally, this activity robs him of the rest that he should have, which is something of infinite consequence and which, if one does not pay great attention, causes disease and disgust [*dégoût*] that no amount of good will could resist."[80]

Similarly, Saxe insisted that officers be aware of combat emotion (*l'émotion que cause le combat*) and take it into account in the choice of weapons and battle formations.[81] Such emotion caused men to forget to rip open their cartridges of gunpowder, making their weapons useless. Following Raimondo, count of Montecuccolli's (1609–1680) principle of mutual support during battle between cavalry and infantry, Saxe offered the adage that in the heat of combat, "any troop that is not supported is a troop defeated."[82] The common practice of positioning the cavalry on the flanks of the infantry was not efficacious and elicited fear in both. "This position alone intimidates your troops without knowing why because every man who sees nothing behind him to which he can draw back or find support is already half beaten, which is why often times the second line breaks while the first is in combat. I have seen this more than once and I think many others have, too, but no one has seemingly searched for an explanation: it is again, the human heart."[83]

The interlacing of mind and body of Saxe's *coeur humain* and the holistic, sensibility-based notion of hygiene led to more pointed contemplations of emotional health, with particular attention to the *soldat sensible*, establishing a discourse on military psychology.

The Birth of Military Psychology

Psychological reactions to camp life and combat were an increasingly pervasive subject of discussion in eighteenth-century military writing.[84] This development of early modern military "emotionology" was a watershed moment in the history of military psychology, one that could only come about through the confluence of the two forces examined in this chapter: first, the moral imperative to care for soldiers and military men, with the priority of improving their health and happiness; and second, the expanded vocabulary and understanding of psychosomatics and emotional life rooted in philosophical medicine of sensibility.[85] Previous writings that theorized combat motivation, such as Honoré Bonet's *Tree of Battles*, written between 1386 and 1390, were rare and only briefly mention such elements as the effects of good leadership, the support of comrades in battle, and proper armor. Conversely, *militaires philosophes* of the eighteenth century contemplated such issues in great number and depth, laying the foundation for military psychology as a field of study.

Memoirs reveal that the French military typology, lexicon, and standards of feeling possess certain distinguishing qualities. Outside of Saxe's single reference, the word *émotion* was seldom used in military writings of the period, since "at no time [in history] has the word been the primary affective term" in the French language.[86] Rather, thinkers employed other general terms of emotionality—*passion*, *affection*, or *sentiment*—and addressed specific emotions in particular contexts. They wrote of simpler feelings such as happiness and fear and also broached more complex, multilayered emotions such as languor, disgust, worry, mortification, hope, and humanity.

This wide array of phenomena reflects the heterogeneous understanding of emotion during the eighteenth century. As William Reddy, David Denby, and Daniel Gross have shown, for early moderns, emotion was not understood as mere feeling or passion that could be differentiated from, or indeed exist in opposition to, processes of thought.[87] Emotion could be deliberative, involving feeling and judgment. This perspective relates to epistemological foundations of human understanding articulated in works like Hobbes's *Leviathan* (1651) and Condillac's *Essay on the Origin of Human Knowledge* (1756). "To consider all the workings of the intellect," Condillac stated, "it is not sufficient to have analyzed the operations of the understanding, for it would still be necessary to do the same for the passions and to observe how all these things combine and blend in one single cause. The influence of the passions is so great that without it the understanding is virtually at a standstill, so much so that for lack of passions there is barely any intellect left."[88] Condillac included this statement in the subsection entitled "On reason and on intellect and its different aspects," demonstrating how much emotion was constitutive of cognitive operations associated with reason. Through this epistemological connection, emotion existed in the same functional plane and semantic field as terms such as *sentiment, opinion,* and *avis*.[89]

Emotion also pointed to a movement, as did the word "passion" itself.[90] The Latin etymology of "emotion" indicates a movement (*movere*) out (*ex*) that military thinkers took quite literally. This motion away from centeredness could take two trajectories. On the one hand, it could take a destructive path in the Cartesian tradition of emotion, signifying tumultuous suffering due to a painful move away from what is a stable or normal state for a person.[91] On the other hand, this movement had constructive manifestations as a move toward a higher self through self-confidence or a move toward other people through sympathy, empathy, and the more active compassion of humanity. Characterizing the possible trajectories and affects of these movements was of prime interest to *militaires philosophes*, who approached the subject from pragmatic and humanitarian perspectives. Pragmatically, they sought ways in which knowledge of human passions could be applied to optimize aspects of waging war, from recruitment, retention, reenlistment, and promotion to combat effectiveness and the general capacity to withstand the hardships of life on campaign.

From this technological standpoint, and also that of Foucauldian discipline, there were officers who embraced a neo-Stoic philosophy and contended that all emotion should be extinguished in men of war. "It is the essence of hard discipline to stifle [*étouffer*] the voice of passion," an officer wrote in a memoir of 1770.[92] "The soldier who is submitted to it [discipline], stripped of sentiment, is solely susceptible to purely mechanical organization." Alongside and opposing this approach was a humanitarian strain of thought. Here, thinkers again promulgated a moral imperative to recognize and care for the emotional lives of men of war. Inquiries focused on a series of questions: What, then, were the passions that were most operative in the space of war, whether constructive or destructive? What were their origins and enabling conditions? How could they be addressed in the context of varied experiences of military life?

Military thinkers targeted two distinct categories of emotions. The first comprised emotions associated with stereotypes of national character. Most discussion of this category focused on essentialized notions of *génie*—natural talents, inclinations, and dispositions belonging to their spirit. The *génie* of the French included strong emotions, such as their natural ardor, impatience, and love of freedom, which were seen to cause indiscipline, a hatred of subordination, and, in the worst case, flight from battle like that at Friedlingen or Dettingen. At the same time, these emotions were believed to make the French more suitable for attack, for column versus line tactics, and for man-to-man combat.[93] Honor was also recognized as a key motivator for military men. It animated monarchy, according to Montesquieu, and had become deeply ingrained in French culture and identity, especially in the nobility. Reformers argued that honor needed to be resuscitated in the officer corps and that soldiers, too, were susceptible to honor. As the eighteenth century progressed, being French meant being driven by honor, and military leadership took this notion very seriously in their ideas for reform. Honor, ardor, and other sentiments of French *génie* were not seen as manipulable, suppressible, or imitable. Rather, members of the military had to work around or with these emotions, implementing, for example, tactics that allowed French ardor and impatience to function as assets.

While it was commonplace to discuss such clichés of national character, a small number of more daring thinkers delved into the controversial subject of trauma-related emotions: those that had a traceable cause in what was happening to men in the army. Since emotions triggered by these experiences could be avoided or provoked to differing degrees, it was essential to understand their enabling conditions. Aristotle's work in the *Rhetoric* on the mechanics of emotion is useful in uncovering what military thinkers relayed about feelings brought on by the experience of war.[94] Having identified who is feeling an emotion, Aristotle claimed that in order to understand and manipulate any single emotion, one must be able to pinpoint three things: (1) the state of mind of the person feeling the emotion; (2) toward whom (or what) the person feels the emotion; and (3) on what grounds people feel the emotion in question. Applying Aristotle's analytical methodology to military sources, it is clear that emotions, positive and negative, were elicited in officers and soldiers because of three main causes: first, due to the functioning (or dysfunction) of the military system (methods of recruitment, retention, promotion, and reenlistment); second, due to the quality of conditions of camp life (availability of shelter, clothing, and food); and third, the way that men of the army treated one another in words and actions.

Regarding the military system, officers and soldiers alike suffered from inconsistent pay, retirement, rewards, or advancement for merit. A 1764 memoir on the state of the French infantry following the Seven Years' War lamented that "most [poor] officers are despondent, discouraged, uncertain [*abbatus, découragés, incertains*] of their destiny and fearful for the future; those who, through the help of friends, can obtain an honest retirement or who possess some property or goods at home leave the service; the others without any resources or protection stay and vegetate without zeal and without hope; the remarks they make at inns and cafés mark their insouciance and the disgust that they feel for the state they are in."[95] Disenfranchisement in a military system moved by money and favoritism had caused in these poorer noble officers a litany of negative emotions and then finally disgust and apathy, a most unnatural state for the ardent Frenchman.

The duc de Choiseul's reforms had aimed at alleviating this type of disparity by having the state take on the administration of captaincies; however, this, too, was suffered as an emotional blow by many subaltern officers. The comte de Melfort wrote of a "general unhappiness" (*mécontentement général*) in the subaltern ranks and remarked upon the same disgust and indifference born of an excess of negative emotions related to the military system. "In taking away from captains the administration of their companies," he argued, "one took from them a confidence that one had in them and to which they were accustomed. The more honored they had been by this confidence, the more they are mortified at having lost it, and this loss, which they view as a humiliation, shrivels their soul and discourages their zeal."[96] Other memoirs attested that low-ranking officers and those hailing from the poorer nobility experienced emotions associated with victimization and debasement communicated in the terms "mortified," "humiliated," and "despondent [*abattu*]."

Enforcing this crooked military system was also a terrible burden that affected officers emotionally, especially those who self-identified as members of the *noblesse du coeur*. A recruiting officer named Boucher wrote to the minister of war in 1747 toward the end of the War of Austrian Succession to share his true sentiments regarding his position. Given the unsavory methods used to conscript men and the unfortunate destiny that awaited them, Boucher relayed the cruelty of his job and the toll it was taking on him: "I take the liberty, Monsieur, of admitting to you that [my job] is one of the most *sensible* catastrophes of my life. I am not at all made for such work; after all of the goodwill that you have had for me until present, I owed you at least to accomplish this humiliating job; you asked me to and I did it willingly. [Yet] permit me to tell you that if my meager fortune has obliged me to take up the profession of recruiting sergeant, my feelings are repulsed by this work."[97]

Soldiers fared even worse in this victimization by the military system, enduring infrequent or nonexistent pay and retirement benefits, but also being subject to forced enlistment and detention in the army. Many military reformers spoke of the injustice of the latter and its emotional effects on the soldiers, as well as its role in that other "epidemic" of the army, desertion. The chevalier de la Rochelambert explained that "it is the greatest injustice possible that a man who enlists for a certain period of service on the promise of being released and in the end he finds himself not only deceived, but sometimes trapped as a soldier for 15 to 20 years. This brings them to despair [*désespoir*] and makes them desert the army or disgusts them out of the desire that all young people have to do five or six campaigns."[98] An anonymous writer claimed that having no fixed term of service (or violating the fixed term that had been agreed upon) caused soldiers to fall ill, contracting the sicknesses of abasement, such as chagrined lassitude (*ennui*) and languor (*langueur*).[99] The inaccessibility of the Invalides, even to soldiers with a long history of service, caused them emotional distress. "Today, surprised by their situation, the soldiers are no longer happy, they believe themselves to be without support or resource, they fear the future and one can discern the disgust [*dégoût*] that overcomes them."[100]

Guibert brought emotion-related critiques of the military system to an apex through his bold condemnation of the political regime in the *Essai général de tactique* (1770). Due to morally bankrupt monarchical culture, the fearful French state did not foster constructive emotions in the military sphere, but rather a nefarious weakness that made

> our military constitution so imperfect and ruinous. It is this weakness that, not able to make citizen armies, must compensate by making large armies. It is this weakness that, not knowing how to award its armies with honor, pays them with gold. It is this weakness that, not able to count on the courage and fidelity of its people because the people are angry and unhappy, must buy mercenary militias . . . It is this weakness, finally, that is busy extinguishing martial virtues in nations, not even developing them in their troops, because she fears that such virtues would spread to all citizens who would rise up in arms one day against the abuses that oppress them.[101]

In lieu of a political revolution or the institution of universal military service, for which Guibert and Saxe both advocated, reformers proposed changes to the military system that could foster a more positive psychology. Saxe hypothesized about the role of hope in combat morale and the capacity to withstand military life. "Hope [*l'espérance*] makes men capable of undertaking and enduring anything; if you take hope away from them or if it seems too far off, you take away their soul."[102] In 1748 an anonymous writer urged officers to encourage hopeful thoughts in the imagination of the military man. "All is but opinion for man," he averred. "It is the principle of his happiness or of his misfortune, as well as his courage or his weakness. Put noble and agreeable ideas into his mind that flatter his hopes, and he will produce wonders of all kinds; one cannot, then, do enough to avoid blackening his imagination by the fear of an unhappy future that already troubles his reason too much."[103]

Reformers argued that a primary means of fostering hope, confidence, and motivation was to establish concrete opportunities for recognition, reward, and advancement in the ranks based on noteworthy actions and services. Saxe believed that hope would result from institutionalizing proper pay and a merit-based system of promotion. He asserted that a man must feel that he can "get ahead [*parvenir*] by his actions and services." The chevalier de Montaut proposed a system of rewarding common soldiers, something quite novel in the French army, which had important honoraria and awards only for officers.[104] He suggested that when presented with grand ceremony, the symbolic value of such awards would be high even if the objects themselves were of little monetary value, such as a small gold ring, a ribbon, or a paper certificate with the soldier's name on it.[105] With high rates of desertion plaguing the army during the eighteenth century, such a system would give simple soldiers, who were the most likely to desert, the chance to feel pride and honor, which until then only officers could claim through institutionalized rewards.

The injustices of the military system that denied soldiers hope, pride, or honor might have been less onerous had the conditions of life at camp been more tolerable. According to many reformers, however, the conditions in which poor noble officers and soldiers existed at the front could only be described as miserable. Indeed, *misère*, misery, was the most frequent descriptor. While the wealthiest aristocratic officers enjoyed sumptuous multicourse meals served on ornate silver dishes, the "poor nobility cannot sustain itself when living on what the king gives it; it is a fact that most officers of this kind do not have enough to pay a valet and many in certain garrisons only have a meal at the inn at lunchtime and do not eat dinner at all, though not because their stomachs are not in need."[106]

Yet if officers of the lesser nobility suffered this kind of privation, one can only imagine the conditions weathered by soldiers. It is well known that soldiers faced starvation, lacked clothing and shoes, and were often forced to sleep outdoors, regardless of the weather, on meager, insect-infested straw mats. Many of them barely survived for a month due to the deplorable conditions of their recruitment that so distressed the sergeant Boucher cited above. Charles de Mattei, marquis de Valfons (1710–1786), wrote in his *Souvenirs* that "we recruit in the depths of the provinces; in February and March, we assemble twenty thousand young men from all over the kingdom; poorly dressed, overwhelmed [*accablés*] by the long route, we send them to the army where without caution we give them the uniforms of dead soldiers . . . ; the most robust of them hold out until April or May when the still-frigid nights soon cause them to follow their deceased comrades."[107]

The comte de Melfort's heart-wrenching memoir, examined in chapter 2, told one tragic tale of the dehumanizing humiliation suffered by such soldiers.[108] He also signaled an erosion of social bonds between officers and their soldiers, designating, as other reformers did, that wartime emotions had a direct relationship to how one was treated by military men. In such memoirs, the discussion of emotion at war functioned to unfurl a powerful indictment of the social abuses and prejudices of the French society of orders as manifested in the armed forces. An anonymous writer described the situation of soldiers and their struggles with the contempt expressed toward them by their military (and social) superiors: "The incertitude of their future, the contempt heaped upon them, plunge them into a despair that breaks them down in sickness or forces them to desert the army. . . . Such bad treatment destroys the little good will that they could have had. What service can we expect from such soldiers?"[109]

In a memoir of 1771, M. de Fauville made a similar accusation of social abuse and called for a wholesale revaluation of the French soldier in the name of humanity and the *patrie*:

> Let us humanely decide the fate of these unhappy soldiers. Let us choose: is he a being that is useful to the interests of the *patrie*, respectable for his humanity, defender of the state and supporter of the prince; or is he but a being created for our caprices [*menus plaisirs*], ambition, trials and tribulations as well as the skeleton for anatomy experiments? If this soldierly being is truly useful for the interests of the state, for the honor of the *patrie*, and the honor of humanity, is it possible for us to have too much care for him? It would be impossible to work too much for or pay too much attention to everything that contributes to his conservation, his health, and his happiness. He is a man often more full of honor and more experienced than many men of the [noble] order under which chance has placed him. I have seen many brave officers listen with pleasure and benefit from their advice; I could cite several traits of their intelligence and penetrating thought.[110]

Fauville pushed his noble peers to call forth their humanity and to extend it toward soldiers, recognizing in them the dignity inherent to the human race. In doing so, he underscored the inhumanity of their social prejudices, and by suggestion, classified such behavior as unpatriotic. More provocatively, by emphasizing the soldiers' utility and at times superior capacity and experience as defenders of the state, he associatively placed them in the same order as the *noblesse de l'épée* and characterized soldiers as more effective in their ability to pay the blood tax, *l'impôt du sang*. Coming full circle, and proposing an example of the successes that constructive emotions at war could create, Fauville insisted that Saxe and other great generals exhibited humanity in taking great care of their soldiers, down to the smallest details. "What particular care would he ever refuse his soldiers?" he asked. "Did he not give his attention to even the smallest detail?"[111] This humanity was mirrored back toward Saxe by his men, all of whom "clamored for the desire, the honor, and the glory to let their valor shine in the eyes of their general, whom they adored. Joy reigned, the soldiers were happy, service was duly observed, exercises were conducted frequently, the troops were superb, well-dressed in clean, proper military clothes; no closets full of powder or stinking grease on their heads, rather they were always well-combed, with hats on straight, marching with a virile assurance, persuaded that when they went to the enemy, they would defeat them, a situation . . . which occurred frequently."[112]

The Military Enlightenment's discourse on emotion and war is important for several reasons. It was the first profound and sustained discussion of military psychology in French history. It was also a vehicle through which reformers made a forceful denunciation of administrative corruption, social abuse, and the violation of human dignity in the French armed forces. The discourse ultimately led to a reform movement within the military that targeted corporal and capital punishment. This focus on active compassion and respect for the human body shows how the military sphere participated actively in the development of Enlightenment "rights talk."

From Humanity to Human Rights

The role of the French Enlightenment in the development of human rights has risen to the forefront of scholarly discussion of the history of rights. On the one hand, Lynn Hunt locates the "invention" of human rights in the eighteenth century, established by the pens of authors of sentimental novels. These writers exercised their readers in *sensibilité* and empathy, which set the stage for accepting what she qualifies as the required "three interlocking qualities" of human rights: "rights must be *natural* (inherent in human beings); *equal* (the same for everyone); and *universal* (applicable everywhere)."[113] On the other hand, Samuel Moyn argues against the possibility of writing a linear, *longue durée* history of human rights and posits that what we understand to be human rights did not coalesce until the 1970s. In his analysis, human rights are inextricably connected to the belief in or need for a (secular) supranational identity and authority following the violations of World War II and the failures of both political utopian plans like communism and institutions like the United Nations.[114]

Dan Edelstein takes a middle path. He casts doubt on *sensibilité* as a universalizing discourse (there are always villains and those who do not possess *sensibilité*). He also rejects Moyn's claims that human rights were "born" in the 1970s and that a longer history of human rights is untenable. Edelstein remarks instead that the eighteenth-century "philosophes' concept of rights was in fact more similar to the post-1970s understanding than [Moyn] allows: at both times, rights were believed to be supranational and could be appealed to above and beyond the nation-state."[115] He asserts that

> at an institutional level, Moyn's argument is correct: there were no international courts in the early modern era that could sanction states for rights violations. And the establishment of such courts was an essential development for human rights, in the late twentieth-century sense that Moyn attributes to them. But courts are not the only kind of supranational entities endowed with such powers. Enlightenment authors often went above the heads of their states by addressing the public directly and calling on an educated—and empathetic—cosmopolitan audience to denounce the transgressions of individual states. And in such instances, the authority they invoked to ground their attacks was often natural right.[116]

Treatises against slavery and against religious intolerance following the Calas affair in the 1760s, and, indeed, arguments against corporal and capital punishment in the military, appealed to a notion of natural or "human" rights that positive laws of states were violating. In looking at these examples, Edelstein concludes, "It is hard to see how they fundamentally differ, at a conceptual level, from the post-1970s view of rights that Moyn presents: 'entitlements that might contradict the sovereign nation-state from above and outside rather than serve as its foundation.'"[117] While not a universalizing discourse, *sensibilité* still played a key role in eighteenth-century rights talk. The laws of nature and the rights they imposed were not seen by eighteenth-century *philosophes* as accessible through the faculty of reason as *jusnaturalist* writers like Grotius had contended. As *philosophes*, both nonmilitary and military, vernacularized and popularized natural rights talk, they insisted that *sensibilité* was "the human faculty through which we gain access to the laws of nature," that higher than the authority of any king or nation was what Diderot called "the tribunal of conscience."[118]

It was precisely these presuppositions and dispositions that animated the military culture of *sensibilité* and humanity. In working to raze social abuses and diminish material inequalities within the armed forces while buttressing health and happiness through the rank and file, military thinkers were both participating in the rise of human rights and pushing to establish concrete manifestations of these rights in the military sphere.

These efforts came to a head in the 1760s and 1770s as the military and the broader intellectual community joined to fight capital and corporal punishment laws for desertion.[119] In debates about the military juridical and penal code, which saw numerous revisions during the second half of the eighteenth century, all parties agreed that desertion was a crime that needed appropriate punishment.[120] While the total number of deserters in any year cannot be calculated, extant records confirm the enormous proportions of the problem: nearly a quarter of all soldiers in the French army deserted during the War of Spanish Succession; sixty to seventy thousand men deserted during the War of Austrian Succession; and there were eight to nine thousand deserters per annum during the Seven Years' War.

In reaction to the exorbitant levels of desertion during the War of Spanish Succession, an ordinance was issued on July 2, 1716, ruling that deserters would be punished by death. Claude Le Blanc, who became minister of war and pushed the ordinance through Villars's Conseil de Guerre, was in some way aware of its excessive severity. He sought to mitigate it by a curious method of application, which was so arbitrary that it made the law ridiculous and ineffective. Rather than sentence all deserters to the death penalty, the guilty were to be punished in groups of three. These soldiers would draw straws (*tirer au sort*), and one would receive capital punishment, while the other two went to the galleys. If only one or two soldiers were caught at a time, then both were to be executed.[121] Regulations for desertion in the Gardes françaises were even more strict: one was considered a deserter if one had traveled more than two *lieues* from their company at any time, and, as of an ordinance issued on January 3, 1733, one was marked a deserter if absent from the two annual reviews that took place in Paris, even if the soldier was in the capital at the time.[122] Perhaps more disturbing was the mysterious system of amnesties and reintegrations into royal regiments that took place on a regular basis. Chagniot calculates that at least thirty-three sergeants in the Gardes françaises in 1750 who were eligible to be received at the grade of lieutenant in the Invalides were in fact deserters from other units who had obtained amnesties or certificates of pardon from the king or their previous commanding officers.[123] How could anyone be expected to respect, let alone fear, such a law?

The campaign against capital punishment began at the end of the War of Austrian Succession and was initiated within the military. In 1748 an officer named Barbançois wrote that the death penalty should be abolished and replaced with a system in which offenders in France became soldier-workers laboring on public work sites (*chantiers publics*) until they could reimburse the cost of their aborted military engagement.[124] A year later, d'Argenson brought together a committee to discuss this alternative mode of punishment. However, a critical mass of abolitionists did not arise until the aftermath of the Seven Years' War and the publication of Cesare Beccaria's (1738–1794) famed treatise *On Crimes and Punishments* (1764). Beccaria condemned torture and capital punishment, not only because of their brutality but also, in the case of the latter, because of its ineffectiveness as a deterrent. "The death of a criminal is a terrible but momentary spectacle," he avowed, "and therefore a less efficacious method of deterring others, than the continued example of a man deprived of his liberty, condemned, as a beast of burthen, to repair, by his labor, the injury he has done to society. If I commit such a crime, says the spectator to himself, I shall be reduced to that miserable condition for the rest of my life. A much more powerful preventative than the fear of death, which men always behold in distant obscurity."[125]

Many writers from the military community endorsed Beccaria's assessment. Their complaints targeted the ineffectiveness of capital punishment to dissuade desertion, the vain loss of life that such punishment caused, and the arbitrary system that lacked any proportionality between punishments and crimes.[126] Reformers discussed the pros and cons of inflicting different types of punishments, including forced work, the galleys, prison, isolation rooms, prolonged service, corporal punishment, and, indeed, death for traitors who deserted the French armed forces to serve the enemy. In their deliberations and reforms, military administrators and thinkers paid increasing attention to the military criminal's humanity and honor. They desired to develop a system that would encourage faithful service while punishing justly and efficaciously, though never to the point of destroying an individual's physical or mental well-being.[127]

Proposals for reform and public letters dating from the 1760s rode the wave of *sensibilité*-based moral philosophy, making the question into a veritable *cas de conscience*. In 1768 the vicomte de Flavigny wrote a public letter to Choiseul ("Réflexions sur la désertion et sur la peine des déserteurs en forme de lettre à Monsieur le duc de Choiseul") that he hoped would enflame "that compassionate pity by which *sensible* and generous souls respond to the voice of humanity" in the hearts of the minister and the public.[128] Partisans staged a publicity war against the administration, relaying heart-rending tales of unfortunate deserters who had been conscripted by force or whose deaths would orphan their helpless young children. Deserters were portrayed as victims rather than traitors of the nation. Investigations of soldierly emotions and psychology afforded a medical explanation and justification for why men in uniform deserted. According to one Merlet, who offered case studies from the War of Austrian Succession to support his claims, desertion was not the soldier's fault, since the cause of this action was "a sickness of the soul that suddenly took the soldier."[129] Soldiers and *philosophes* decried the death penalty and exculpated deserters by blaming the harsh treatment by officers as well as the unjust military. In their definition of *déserteur* in the *Encyclopédie*, Jaucourt and d'Alembert stated their case with a leading question: "We adopted the law of the death penalty against deserters from the Franks; and this law was good for a people whose soldiers went into war freely, took part in its honor and its spoils. Is this the same case with us?"[130]

Playwrights and *littérateurs* added to *le cri public*. Plays, pantomimes, and opéra comique had previously depicted the deserter as a comic figure, as in Louis Fuzilier's (ca. 1672–1752) *Arlequin déserteur* of 1715. However, by the 1760s the deserter had become a hero of *sensibilité*. Jean-Michel Sedaine's (1719–1797) opera *Le déserteur*, with music by Pierre-Alexandre Monsigny (1729–1817), was a smashing success from its début at the Théâtre de l'Hôtel de Bourgogne on March 6, 1769. It became a staple of the stage in Paris, Brussels, and provincial cities like Toulouse until the penultimate year of the Directorate and was a hit in theaters in the United States, England, and Germany. Mercier's play of the same name opened in Brest in 1771 but gained its popularity during the Revolution, playing constantly at major theaters in Paris for nine out of the ten years between 1789 and 1799. The only true villain of Mercier's play was the character who denounced the deserter, a moral formulation that *militaires philosophes* also utilized. "Who is the indelicate man who would report a deserter, who doesn't even help him to hide from the authorities?" asked Ferdinand Desrivières (b. 1734) in his "Réponse des soldats du régiment des Gardes françoises aux Loisirs d'une soldat du même régiment." "There is a sentence against this [deserting] man and a reward for the informer. It is true, there is money to be lost in saving him and to be gained by denouncing him. But in the first case, there is humanity and general approbation; in the second, opprobrium and nature revolts."[131]

Yet it was not only moral nature that revolted against capital punishment for the deserter; natural law was violated as well. Flavigny argued that natural law did not authorize the death penalty for "man born free [*l'homme né libre*]."[132] Relying on Beccaria's reading of Rousseau (who came to the opposite conclusion on this matter), Flavigny and later Servan de Gerbey in *Le soldat citoyen* (1780) argued that such penance represented a violation of the social contract. Flavigny wrote: "I believe that the assemblage of individual wills form the general will; that the general will is represented by the Sovereign and the Law; that the Sovereign and the Law consequently unite portions of will and of freedom that each individual puts in common for his security. That being posited, if I am right to believe that suicide is prohibited to man by divine and natural laws, if I can see as true the axiom that no one can give to others a right over him that he himself does not possess, I cannot define how the representative of the general will can exercise a right that he cannot have received."[133] To these abolitionists, capital punishment for deserters was morally and judicially unsound. It constituted a violation of human rights.

Louis XV and Choiseul did not budge. It was not until an ordinance of December 12, 1775, that the death penalty for desertion was repealed under the newly minted minister of war, the comte de Saint-Germain. Replacing it was a penal code that imposed a sentence of forced labor, with the number of years of punishment proportional to the circumstances of the soldier's desertion. Deserters were also given the right to return to their regiments within three days of their crime. In a strange Catholic-inspired twist, such deserters were permitted to "repent" upon their return, serve the minor punishment of fifteen days in prison, and then resume service.[134] Those who did not take advantage of this opportunity received longer punishments.

Public outcry turned into public celebration. Voltaire, writing a year before his death, heralded this victory of *sensibilité* and *humanité*: "[Louis XVI] took pity on [the deserters] and on France, who lost in them her defenders," he opined in the *Prix de la justice et de l'humanité*. "He absolved them of the death penalty and gave them means to repair their mistake by according them several days to return to the flag. And when they are punished, it is by punishment that chains them to serving the *patrie* that they abandoned. They are convicts for several years. We owe this military jurisprudence to a military minister who is as enlightened as he is good."[135]

But human rights enthusiasts did not have long to wait for a new battle. A mere three months later, another violation of the soldierly person was ratified by the crown in Saint-Germain's infamous ordinance of March 25, 1776. Following Prussian practice, for smaller offenses soldiers were to be struck repeatedly on the back—twenty-five to fifty forceful blows—with the flat side of a sword, *les coups de plat de sabre*. Once again, the swell of public outrage crested in Paris, giving rise to a new debate. The comte de Ségur described the ambiance of the moment in his memoir: "The court, the city [*la cour, la ville*] and the army disputed the pros and cons of this innovation with tenacity: some extolled it and others criticized it in fits of rage: the bourgeois, the military man, abbots, and even women, everyone dissertated and disputed on the subject."[136] According to a memoir by Jean-François de Pérusse, duc des Cars (1747–1822), women were instrumental in fomenting against Saint-Germain's ordinance. "His disciplinary ordinance excited numerous murmurs in the army, as it had done in different societies. Women agitated young people and many colonels against the punishment by *coups de plat de sabre* prescribed by this ordinance."[137]

Military officers also took issue with this means of punishment. While some executed the beatings without murmur or scruple, others not only condemned them but either refused to authorize them or did so as little as possible. Since military offenses were adjudicated on the ground as they occurred, officers (usually colonels) had great liberty in deciding how to apply the law in their units and whether to report them to the king and his *conseil de guerre*.[138] Guinier's study of penal records shows the range of responses to Saint-Germain's law. The regiment of Bourgogne was an outlier, having implemented sword flogging in 83 percent of punishments in 1777. The regiment of Béarn embodied the opposite extreme but was also more representative of the general disapproval of the *coups*: not a single man was submitted to a beating.[139] Between June and October of the same year, the first division of the Échêvés (which contained six infantry regiments, two regiments each of artillery and cavalry, and one regiment of dragoons) applied the beatings in 22 percent of 631 total punishments. The infantry regiments favored punishments involving isolation over the use of physical force, the cavalry used flogging in three out of twenty-eight punishments, and the artillery regiments did not implement beatings in any of the unit's 286 reprimands.[140] In the graphic narrative style popularized by Voltaire and *militaires philosophes*, memoirs decrying the *coups* depicted the brutal destruction of the human body and soul that the flogging inflicted. Colonel Étienne-François Girard (1766–1846) recounted the gruesome punishment of three grenadiers, one of whom was struck with such extreme force that blood came spurting out of his mouth and ears.[141] Descriptions like Girard's portrayed the *coups de plat de sabre* as morally dishonorable for the victim, but also as a violation of the rights and sanctity of the soldierly body.

Ironically enough, Saint-Germain promoted the *coups de plat de sabre* not only in the name of enforcing stricter discipline. Just as Antoine Louis (1723–1792) and later Joseph-Ignace Guillotin (1738–1814) sought to advance a more humane mechanism for capital punishment in the infamous guillotine, Saint-Germain instituted his means of corporal punishment believing it to be more honorable and thus in some way more humane than the whips, switches, and batons he attempted to replace.[142] Despite his progressive work to eliminate favoritism, luxury, venality, and social privilege from the French armed forces, Saint-Germain's Spartan and prussophilic notion of discipline was not suited for the age of *sensibilité*.[143] Under the crushing weight of criticism from within and without the military that took aim at different reforms, and most especially that of soldierly corporal punishment, Saint-Germain's ministry crumbled, and he resigned in 1777.

Humanity in Global War

If discourses of *sensibilité* and *humanité* were formidable forces in metropolitan discussions of military reform, they were even more so in global theaters.[144] These concepts were at the very heart of the human capacity for sociability, diplomacy, and cross-cultural bonds. They encouraged more nuanced ethnographic understanding and fueled indignation against injustices such as slavery. On the other hand, *sensibilité* and *humanité* were also moral and political weapons that justified institutionalized racism and the burgeoning notion of a French civilizing mission.

In Saint-Domingue, different groups engaged the discourses of *sensibilité* and *humanité* to support opposing claims about race and military service. In 1779, Charles d'Estaing, who had served a short and inglorious tenure as governor of Saint-Domingue from 1764 to 1766, returned to the island to recruit men to accompany him north to fight alongside the Americans in their war of independence. D'Estaing met with resistance from the local population, particularly white planters. Elite planters of all racial backgrounds had already raised a strong voice against conscription into the local militia, the constabulary, or French regular forces. In a treatise on the interior defense of Saint-Domingue, d'Estaing remarked upon the opposing priorities of colonists and the crown. The former were driven by personal interest and the desire to preserve their lands and fortune. As such, they would capitulate to any invading power as long as their lands would not be destroyed and they could continue to produce and sell crops. Metropolitan priorities focused on maintaining control over lucrative colonies like Saint-Domingue and instilling values that supported public interests.[145] Martial virtue and glory, it was hoped, could supplant the "liberal" economic virtue embraced by colonists.

As the eighteenth century progressed, the divide between liberal patriotism and martial patriotism became increasingly racialized. "White Saint-Dominguans had a different image of their civic role . . . Few white colonists dreamed of Spartan glory, and in 1779 white colonists chose a form of self-sacrifice consistent with their liberal notion of virtue."[146] Their contribution to any patriotic war effort was economic, either through voluntary monetary donations or by continuing to ensure that their plantations—and therefore the French Empire's economy—functioned to the highest capacity.[147] D'Estaing's recruiting efforts fell flat, mustering four companies for the all-white Volunteer Grenadiers. Instead of offering manpower, white elites collected money to offer the French navy a new state-of-the-art ship of the line. The local broadside publication, the *Affiches américaines*, lauded this effort, though not in terms of liberal virtue. Rather, it couched this type of service as the only viable means to serve the war while honoring humanity and the *sensibilité* of the elite white community: "To the honor of humanity, surely one will never again see a ferocious and barbarian mother send her son to his death with a dry eye, without emotion, see him again pale and bleeding and believe she owes this horrible sacrifice to the fatherland... These awful traits, so long admired by our fathers, are unnatural and make any respectable soul tremble."[148] While these statements convey a spirit of pacifism, this talk of *humanité* and *sensibilité* at once excused white elites from military service and declared their economic and racial superiority.

The insidious racism behind this statement of white *sensibilité* and *humanité* crystallized in several ways. First, failed efforts to recruit white manpower made d'Estaing and colonial administrations push even harder to recruit people of color. The Chasseurs volontaires, a unit of free colored men (commanded by white officers) first established in 1762 by Governor Armand, vicomte de Belzunce (d. 1763) and disbanded after the Seven Years' War, was reconstructed to ensure Saint-Dominguan manpower for the American War of Independence. While some free men of color, particularly wealthy planters, were reluctant to serve, others enlisted voluntarily or were coerced to do so by patrons and government bullying. They formed ten companies to the Grenadiers' four, such that when d'Estaing set sail for North America in August 1779, he was accompanied by three and a half times more free colored soldiers than white soldiers.

In addition to pushing more free men of color into military service, arguments of white *sensibilité* and *humanité* morally stigmatized free colored soldiers. These men and their families had answered the traditional call for patriotic action through military service, meaning that they were like the "ferocious and barbarian mothers" whose sons exhibited the "awful traits" described in the *Affiches*. Unlike the humane and *sensible* whites, free people of color were seen as emotionless, barbaric, and antiquated in their beliefs. "Even as royal volunteers, then," notes Garrigus, "free men of color were not 'respectable' or 'sensitive' citizens."[149]

Yet, certain *militaires philosophes* serving in Saint-Domingue reclaimed the discourse of *sensibilité* and *humanité* in support of free colored warriors. In his

Reflections, Colonel Lenoir de Rouvray, who positioned himself as a warrior-patriot and sentimental *père de famille*, described the physical and moral merit of the free people of color serving in the Chasseurs volontaires. Rouvray's arguments, albeit essentializing, claimed that not only were these men physically superior by a factor of four, but their moral qualities dwarfed those of white colonists. They are "robust, full of *sensibilité*, and pride," wrote Rouvray, describing free people of color as "infinitely more attached to their families than white people." He observed that "the bonds of blood and obedience were infinitely more respected" and that "free people of color would never desert except to go to their homes where they could easily be found."[150] It took one to know one in Rouvray's view of *sensibilité* and race. Rouvray described Belzunce, who had founded the original free colored unit, as an "âme sensible," part of a moral elite capable of recognizing the *sensibilité* and merit of free Saint-Dominguans of color.[151] Turning the tables again on white colonists, Rouvray reproached the racist "atrocious cabal" of white colonists who tried to stop Belzunce from mustering free men of color for the Chasseurs volontaires. The deplorable efforts undertaken by this cabal displayed the latter's lack of *sensibilité* and *humanité*, and also showed them to be "bad citizens."[152] As opposed to such colonists, free families of color were *sensibles*, courageous, and patriotic.

Militaire philosophes also evoked *sensibilité* and *humanité* in their attempts to loosen orientalist stereotypes about Indian leaders as cruel and despotic.[153] Russel conceded that, in his experience, Hyder Ali Khan was "insensible to friendship and to all of the sacrifices made for him" by his subjects and allies.[154] Russel explained that he had been "at infinite pains to make him understand that there were Laws of Nations [*droits des gens*], that when dealing with me he had engaged himself with my *patrie* and that he was obliged to uphold our conventions. It was only with much repetition, after four years that I accustomed him to not dismembering any of my soldiers and to paying them exactly each month."[155] However, Russel sought to give a more nuanced perspective on both Hyder and his son Tipu Sultan. Hyder lacked *sensibilité*, according to Russel, but still paid "weak homage to humanity" in his refusal to issue the death penalty. "I imposed this law upon myself one day," Hyder told Russel, "so that I would not have to repent punishing a good soldier or a faithful subject."[156] Tipu Sultan showed far greater *sensibilité* than his father and demonstrated "uprightness, delicacy, and gratitude."[157] Russel predicted that political and military ties between the French and the Mysorians, animated by shared moral sentiments and a polite comportment, would grow ever stronger (though history would soon tell otherwise).

In the colder waters of the Canadian Atlantic, *militaires philosophes* in Nouvelle France similarly defended the *sensibilité* and *humanité* of Amerindian peoples. Events and practices such as the ritual cannibalization following the attack of Pickawillany had long stoked metropolitan stereotypes. On June 21, 1752, Charles-Michel Langlade, a *métis* of French and Ottawa origins introduced in the previous chapter, led a force of French soldiers from Detroit and two hundred Ottawas and Ojibwas to Pickawillany, a town of strategic interest for distancing the English and enemy Amerindian tribes from French interests in the Ohio Country. Langlade's troops raided and then burned Pickawillany's impressive storehouses, took captives, and killed a number of people, including an Englishman and Memeskia, a Miami and Piankashaw chieftain. "Memeskia's demise proved the most arresting moment of the violence," writes Christian Crouch. "Surrounded and outnumbered, the old man finally succumbed, after which the Ottawas boiled and consumed him in front of the Miami chief's terrified followers. Feasting was not limited to indigenous flesh. 'One of the white men that was wounded in the belly, as soon as they got him, they stabbed and scalped, and took out his heart and ate it.'"[158]

Militaires philosophes complained that such incidents were exaggerated and sensationalized, and lacked any cultural understanding of Amerindian traditions and peoples. Contrary to widely accepted beliefs circulating in the metropole, wrote Zacharie de Bonneville, Amerindians "are not naturally *insensibles*" in physical or moral terms. To support this claim, Bonneville addressed a number of Amerindian practices and qualities in order to give a more culturally attuned interpretation to metropolitan readers and to the crown. "The anthropography of the Americans is not such a big deal," he wrote. Women and children were systematically spared, and the ritual had "no other motive than to consecrate the prisoners to the God of War. It is the *Te Deum* of the *sauvages*, and every person participating in the ceremony most often has less than half an ounce of flesh for his portion."[159] As Rouvray had done with free Saint-Dominguans of color, Bonneville communicated the physical and moral superiority of Amerindians, who "are not overly *sensibles* like Europeans and are not at all sexually debauched; they believe the men's vigor can be sapped by too much sex."[160] Antoine-Joseph Pernety (1716–1796), a naturalist and travel companion of Bougainville, also evoked the *sensibilité* of Amerindian peoples, which he found to be better attuned than that of Europeans. In the former, he saw "the sentiments of a humane heart, generous, those of veritable nobility. In ours, I see only a vulgar image, debased either by vanity or by cupidity."[161]

Certain metropolitan French officers exhibited the limits of their humanity during the American Revolutionary War, as they did not so much as bat an eye at slavery. In Newport, Rochambeau and his cadre all purchased slaves as domestic servants, replacing the white valets they would have hired on the

European continent. Crèvecoeur stated that at Yorktown "the Negroes who were not reclaimed by their masters found new ones among the French and we made a veritable harvest [*moisson*] of domestic servants. Those of us who didn't have a servant were very happy to find ones and for so cheap."[162]

Yet, fighting alongside American and French colonial slaves and free men of color was an experience that marked certain officers profoundly and likely played a role in turning them into abolitionists. American and British forces both employed African Americans in their armies. The latter engaged African Americans for labor until the end of the war, when low manpower forced them to train them for fighting units. American forces employed a greater number of African Americans, such that, according to the Baron Ludwig von Closen, they composed about one-quarter of the troops.[163] The Chasseurs volontaires of Saint-Domingue fought valiantly alongside metropolitan forces, though their service resulted in death or forced military service for nearly all of them.[164]

Though it is difficult to trace a causal relationship between racial intermixing at war and abolitionism, data such as the membership of the Société des amis des noirs (Society of the Friends of Blacks), founded in 1788 in France under the leadership of Jacques Brissot, sheds light on the question. The Société had ninety-five founding members, of whom between one-fifth and one-quarter were military officers of the army or navy. Of these military men, one-third had fought in the American Revolutionary War and were members of the Society of the Cincinnati. Laurent Jean-François, comte de Truguet (1752–1839), fought in d'Estaing's naval forces and witnessed the courage of the Chasseurs volontaires at engagements such as the siege of Savannah (1779). He later became the naval minister during the Directory and worked to enforce the abolition of slavery in Saint-Domingue as well as to establish a school near Paris for black and mixed-race children. He also became the most courageous and vehement voice in favor of maintaining the policy of abolition when Napoleon wanted to reinstate slavery in 1802. He combatted Napoleon's unabashed racism on the basis of humanity and human equality, but to no avail.

Humanity and New Heroism

Quantifying the occurrence of humanitarian acts in the military during the eighteenth century is not possible, making it difficult to substantiate to what extent such acts were a norm. There is also no linear trajectory toward humanity and sensibility in martial policy. Military administrations after that of Saint-Germain continued to grapple with creating a just taxonomy of crime and punishment with a fair, standardized implementation of the latter. Ultimately, however, an ordinance of 1786 formally legalized a gory list of penalties: fifty blows with the flat side of the sword for anyone who knew of a desertion plot but did not reveal it to commanders; whippings; carving a letter D into the skin of the ringleader in a band of deserters; cutting off the hand and hanging for anyone who defected to the enemy. At the battlefront and on campaign, gratuitous cruelty and the violation of human rights were rampant. Charles-Simon Favart wrote chillingly of a massacre in Flanders when on campaign with Saxe's army. The third duc de Richelieu earned himself the nickname "Father Marauder" for the extreme devastation he and his troops inflicted in Germany during the Seven Years' War, sacking towns like Celle, where all of the children in a local orphanage were killed.[165] Pillaging was practiced regularly, as was rape, which some officers claimed was in accordance with human nature rather than a violation of it. Even supposedly enlightened *militaires philosophes* like Turpin de Crissé used the all-too-familiar justification that victims were willing participants in rapes.[166] Laws against rape existed, but their enforcement was dubious at best. If the body of man in the space of war was seen as increasingly sacrosanct, the body of woman was not. The notions of humanity and *sensibilité* had devastating limits.

Yet, as the century progressed, questions of *humanité* and *sensibilité* became increasingly political. They ignited debate on patriotism, heroism, citizenship, and rights in the second half of the eighteenth century in France. Military humanitarianism, as expressed in Fauville's memoir, constituted a new type of patriotism: not one of virile, Spartan willingness to die for king and country, but one of compassion, *sensibilité*, and mutual respect for the talents, condition, and feelings of those with whom one shared the task of defending the nation. Increasingly, reformers acknowledged—in theory and in practice—that all warriors deserved recognition and reward, and that patriotism and heroism existed through the ranks and in different social classes, races, and sexes. Novels and popular plays, as well as political and military treatises, imagined an enlightened concept of heroism and a new vision of the nation.

CHAPTER 4

A Nation of Warriors
The Democratization of Heroism

The dust had hardly settled on the battlefield of Fontenoy when the Bourbon propaganda machine kicked into high gear. Four days after the battle, Louis XV, the Dauphin, and the cream of the French nobility sat among the ornately etched arches and pillars of the royal chapel at Versailles to celebrate the May 1745 victory in a Te Deum mass. Five days later, an enormous Te Deum was staged at Notre Dame in Paris with no less than forty bishops in attendance. By the end of the month, the celebratory mass was held in churches all across the kingdom, accompanied by festivities of unprecedented scale.

Also known as the Ambrosian Hymn, the Te Deum was a religious song of praise of the late fourth / early fifth century that became politicized in France during the seventeenth century. During the reign of Louis XIII, it was sung to give thanks to God on occasions such as royal weddings, births, and military victories. Louis XIV and his ministers, masterminds of royal propaganda, transformed what had been an intimate and pious celebration into a national event that Michèle Fogel terms a *cérémonie de l'information*, an informational ceremony.[1] The crown drafted an official royal account of the event to be commemorated, recorded it in a letter, and disseminated it to prelates in each diocese, where the letter was read and posted on the door of the church, and the event was feted with a Te Deum. But in order to amplify this sacred celebration into something that would attract a maximum of French subjects, profane spectacle and unbridled merriment were added to religious proceedings. Following the Catholic mass, lavish state-sponsored festivities took place in each town. There were rifle salutes, fireworks, light shows, banquets, and toasts. Food and drink were liberally distributed to townspeople, whose inebriated carousing went on until the wee hours of the morning.

As a *cérémonie de l'information*, the Te Deum had important political objectives. First, it brought royal words, imagery, and largesse to the people, who experienced the monarch's greatness and generosity as they took in the day's spectacles, victuals, and libations. It also represented one of the crown's attempts to control information and public opinion through royally sanctioned accounts of events. The lyrics of the hymn, which dated back to the epoch of the first race of the kings of France in the fourth century, reiterated the alliance between God and the French through the figure of the monarch, under whose auspices different joyous events took place: "Salvum fac populum tuum, Domine, et benedic hereditati tuae / Et rege eos, et extolle illos usque in aeternum" (O Lord, save thy people and bless thine heritage / Govern them and lift them up forever). Celebrating military victories had long reinforced the connection between divine power and royal agency. Since the king was the master of all armed forces, his martial triumphs were evidence that God favored the French monarch.[2]

Battle narratives and paintings of the period evince this traditional spotlighting of the king as the originary military hero.[3] The full account of the battle of Fontenoy published on May 29 in the *Gazette de France* articulates this with crystalline clarity. While the victory was a masterpiece of Maréchal Maurice de Saxe's military genius, the newspaper attributed all strategic and tactical agency to Louis XV.[4] The title itself announced the article to be "an account of the battle of Fontenoy and of the victory of the king's army, commanded by His Majesty, won over the allied army." The first lines of the narrative position the king as the decision maker and Saxe as mere executor: "The King, having resolved to begin the year's campaign in Flanders with a siege of the city of Tournai, his Majesty gave the command of his army to Maréchal Comte de Saxe, who left here at the beginning of last month to execute the orders that he received from the King" (figure 11).

A painting by Pierre L'Enfant (1704–1787) commemorating the battle featured customary iconography—the king mounted on a brilliant white steed and donning his royal red military regalia in the foreground of the image—to communicate this same message. Louis XV points at Saxe in a gesture reminiscent of Michelangelo's creation of Adam, indicating that he had designated Saxe to implement the orders that led to victory. The monarch looks straight out of the painting at the observer as if awaiting recognition for his excellent judgment. The king's own letter to Saxe written the day after the battle again articulated these principles regarding royal military agency and heroism. In it, Louis XV expressed his relationship to God, who gave the victory to him specifically. He acknowledged his troops in general terms and Saxe in highly oblique fashion: "My cousin, however great were the successes which it has pleased God to bestow on my arms during the last campaign, I have now received a more marked token of His mighty protection in the victory which I have just gained over my enemies. If I owe it to the valor of my troops, and especially my Household and Carabiniers, you have nonetheless contributed to it by your courage, counsel, and foresight."[5] With Saxe relegated to an advisory role, the one true hero, under God, is unmistakable (figure 12).

Yet, in addition to reaffirming the privileged relationship between God and the king as ultimate military agent and hero, the Te Deum and the royal battle account read aloud at church also legitimated the roles of the First and Second Estates and renewed justification for the society of orders.[6] Clergymen of the First Estate enacted their role as they thanked God through prayer for his grace in awarding victory. The noblemen of the Second Estate were marked as heroic military executors who fought for the king as well as the glory and preservation of France and its people. In the battle relation published in the *Gazette*, the first two pages were dedicated to the actions of the king and Saxe. Beginning on the third page, other noblemen were recognized (Louis Georges Érasme, marquis de Contades [1704–1795], Charles, duc de Fitz-James [1712–1787], and others), though usually in the expedient form of a list. Military heroism had a strict and rarified hierarchy. Those not royal or noble, white, male, and European were unseen.

Joining the fray of celebration, Voltaire "seized the occasion with the instinct of a born journalist," and contacted Minister of War d'Argenson to get details on the battle in order to compose a panegyric poem.[7] Voltaire wrote "Fontenoy," a cross between epic and "rhymed bulletin," in classical *alexandrin* (twelve-syllable verses) and published it on May 17, 1745, to wild popularity. It sold twenty-one thousand copies within days and came out in eight separate editions in the ten months after its original publication.[8] Voltaire followed the traditional formulas for attributing military agency and heroism. He began by heralding the courage of Louis XV in the first and second stanzas, then moved to Maurice de Saxe, and finally lauded "all of our heroes," which meant only high-ranked nobles. In the third stanza, he rather

RELATION
DE LA BATAILLE
DE FONTENOY,

Et de la Victoire que l'armée du Roy, commandée par Sa Majesté, a remportée sur l'armée des Alliez.

E ROY ayant resolu de commencer cette année la campagne en Flandres par le siege de la Ville de Tournay, Sa Majesté donna le commandement de son armée au Mareschal Comte de Saxe, lequel partit d'icy au commencement du mois dernier, pour executer les ordres qu'il avoit reçus du Roy.

Ce General fit sortir les troupes de leurs quartiers : il les divisa en plusieurs Corps, & par les diverses positions qu'il leur a fait prendre successivement, il a si parfaitement réussi à cacher aux ennemis le projet du Roy, que la Ville de Tournay fut investie le 25 du mois dernier, avant qu'ils eussent soupçonné que Sa Majesté se proposoit de faire attaquer cette Place.

Dés que les Alliez eurent appris cette nouvelle, ils rassemblerent à Cambron les troupes qui devoient composer leur armée, & ils publierent qu'ils alloient marcher au secours des Assiegez. Les dispositions des ennemis obligerent

A 4

FIGURE 11. Front page of the battle relation of Fontenoy, May 29, 1745. *La Gazette de France*, no. 24. Courtesy of the Bibliothèque nationale de France.

Figure 12. Pierre L'Enfant, "Battle of Fontenoy, May 11, 1745." Photo: Gérard Blot. Chateaux de Versailles et de Trianon. © RMN-Grand Palais / Art Resource, NY.

clumsily named these officers in a manner more akin to a grocery list than a panegyric that elucidates individual heroic actions:

> This blood of so many Kings, this blood of the Great Condé,
> D'Eu, by whom the French of Le Tonnerre cavalry unit is guided,
> Pentièvre whose zeal outdistanced his age
> Who had already signaled his courage by the river Main,
> Bavaria with de Pons, Boufflers et Luxembourg,
> Go each to their position to wait for this great day;

Each one brings joy to the warriors that he commands.
The fortunate Danoy, Chabannes, Gallerande,
The valiant Berenger, defender of the Rhine,
Colbert and du Chaila, all our heroes,
In the horror of the night, in that of silence,
They ask only that the peril begin.

Voltaire painstakingly named no less than fifty-one aristocratic officers in his 348-line poem. His name-dropping was so invasive and unpoetic that Cardinal Angelo Quirini (1680–1755), who was a correspondent of Voltaire's and had offered to translate the poem into Latin in order to further bolster its prestige, renounced the endeavor.[9]

Putting aside the author's social opportunism, Voltaire's "Fontenoy" regurgitated the heroic model conveyed by all other media sources, from the Te Deum and *La Gazette* to paintings like that of L'Enfant. These works celebrated the usual suspects in the usual ways and illustrated that the culture of military heroism was a prism that reflected the social, moral, and spiritual values of French society. They legitimated the divine power of the monarch and the privileges of the *noblesse d'épée* who served him in battle. These men were the face of the nation—but not for long.

There was something forced, something desperate, in the hyperbolic celebrations of Fontenoy. Louis XV ordered a whopping twelve Te Deums in the year of Fontenoy. This was the highest number of annual Te Deums sung in French history and was double the yearly average of six Te Deums ordered by his great-grandfather, the insatiable self-promoter Louis XIV.[10] After the feting of Fontenoy, the quantity of Te Deums celebrated dropped as precipitously as it had risen, from twelve in 1745 to seven during the Seven Years' War and only two during the American Revolution.[11] The frenzy of celebration belies an anxiety about the age-old cult of heroism, which had already begun to slip away. Louis XV and his ministers were clinging frantically to the status quo of military heroism and to the worldview it implied. However, the celebrations of Fontenoy had an opposite effect: they fueled opposition to the status quo and initiated a collective probing into what it meant to be a hero and who truly merited such a designation.

A grand public debate and cultural shift ensued, one that held great social, political, and military importance for the twilight of the *ancien régime* and the dawn of the French Revolution. *Philosophes, militaires philosophes,* and *littérateurs* reconsidered the primary attributes of a hero, setting forth "enlightened" moral criteria and discerning who—and by what circumstances, sentiments, and actions—could earn the moniker of hero. All voices chimed together to say that neither social status nor simply winning battles was sufficient. The heroism of the monarch came under scrutiny. High-ranking noble warriors were also challenged and deposed, as their heroism was deemed selfish, cruel, and arbitrary. At the same time, new faces came to populate the heroic imaginary—those of common soldiers and noncommissioned officers—and their acts were increasingly told through various secular and popular artistic media, especially novels and theater.[12] Popular plays such as Pierre-Laurent Buirette de Belloy's (1727–1775) *Le siège de Calais* (1665) and military writings championed the patriotic military fervor and potential for heroism of different social groups: common men of the Third Estate, French women, foreigners serving in the French armed forces, and religious and ethnic "Others" allied with the French. These new heroes and heroines were recognized in the cultural imaginary and, to some extent, in practice as members of the military moved to protect, acknowledge, and reward them for their service.

"Enlightened" heroism propelled two veins of significant cultural change in the final decades of the *ancien régime*. First, it was a democratizing force in the political imaginary, allowing commoners of the Third Estate, women, religious, and racial minorities to stake claims to citizenship and to representing the nation. In this, the king slowly faded as the ultimate source of political and military agency, while common citizens and their merit were increasingly recognized. "Enlightened" heroism is a lens that tracks a cultural process that one scholar calls "citizenizing," defining its contours and limits in terms of social class, gender, and race.[13] Second, the new heroism fostered a national culture of militarism by strongly rearticulating the link between patriotism and military service. A good citizen and patriot demonstrated the new heroic virtues, one of which was a willingness, if not enthusiasm, to fight and die for the *patrie*.[14] In the context of a socially democratizing view of heroism, militaristic patriotism engendered the notion of a nation at arms that was envisaged well before the French Revolution and its *levée en masse*, when conventional knowledge places its birth in France.[15] The spread of this morally superior and bellicose national identity prefigured the movement toward a culture of "total war" during the Revolutionary and Napoleonic periods.

Heroism Contested and Revitalized

The commemoration of Fontenoy was the initial battleground for destroying heroic traditions. Jean-Henri Marchand (d. 1785), lawyer, poet, and royal censor, was one of the first voices of dissent. Ventriloquizing as the vicar of Fontenoy, he penned a satirical poem, "Requête du curé de Fontenoy au

Roy," following the publication of Voltaire's poem. Marchand imagined the parish priest's complaints about shouldering the costs of treating the wounded, burying the dead, and hosting the throng of tourists who came to visit the site of the battle. He referenced Voltaire's poem directly, saying that the *philosophe* had done a great disservice by naming only the noblemen who fell on the battlefield, giving no mention of the six or seven thousand soldiers who gave their lives for France that day.[16]

Claude Godard d'Aucour (1716–1795), a tax farmer-general from Langres with literary aspirations, developed a more detailed and trenchant critique in his 1745 novel, *L'Académie militaire, ou les héros subalternes*. From the beginning of the novel, Godard d'Aucour communicated his goal to break with tradition and transform the landscape of military heroism from exclusivity to inclusivity. His anonymous narrator, "P***, an author following the army," told the story of a group of six common soldiers from different regions of France, aptly named Picard, Normand, Breton, Champenois, Bourguignon, and Parisien. These protagonists were not stereotypically crude, uneducated soldiers. Rather, Godard d'Aucour depicted them as *militaires philosophes*, possessing some level of education and interested in promulgating the Military Enlightenment through founding an academy of military history. The mission of this academy was to retrace the courageous acts of fellow common soldiers in order to democratize Glory, a goddess who was unequal and unjust in her blessings:

> Glory . . . is a proud Goddess who always marches at our head; she caresses all of our leaders, frolics around them, makes a list of their names that she entrusts to Fame to publish them all over the universe; but she deigns not turn her eyes onto us; it seems that we are not worthy of her.
>
> This prideful goddess is even more unjust knowing that she owes everything that she is to our arms; she is formed of our blood of our imperiled lives; it is in our victorious squadrons, on the bodies of our vanquished enemies that she is born, and hardly has this ingrate seen the light of day but she escapes from our breasts forever and flies toward our leaders with the sole care of immortalizing them and to credit their courage with that which in fact is most often a result of our own.[17]

This critique quickly escalated into a radical claim regarding the heroism and valor of the common soldier, positing their superiority over those of the noble officer:

> It is not that I propose to take away from officers the honor that is due; I know that we often see them offer up their lives, march first to the

perils in which they lead us; but if glory is the recompense for their valor, why is this same reward not the fruit of our own? Our days, are they not as valuable to us as those of officers?

I dare advance that we have more merit than they do because our courage alone makes us do things that officers do for valor, the shame of being dishonored, the hope of obtaining a brilliant new post and to acquire a famous name. They have ten motives to give their lives in battle to our single motive, yet we give our lives just the same.[18]

In these assertions, Godard d'Aucour turned the moral and heroic hierarchy on its head, revealing the military service of the common soldier to be born of pure courage and to be completely selfless compared to that of the officer, who fights for personal gain. Glory, like the French crown, which did not give soldiers, foreigners, or Protestants access to prestigious awards such as the Croix de Saint-Louis, was prideful, unjust, and arbitrary.

It is in response to this injustice that Parisien proposed to form a military academy whose charge was "to publish the *belles actions* of our subaltern heroes that the gazettes never talk about." The academy aimed to valorize the courage of individual soldiers and help the public to understand that soldiers were neither villains nor faceless, nameless pawns, but rather individuals with families, regional identities, merit, and pride. Academy publications would literally write such subaltern heroes into history, marking their humble families as dynasties of military honor akin to those of the *noblesse d'épée*. To do this, the academy would cite each hero by first and last name and record information about his family "so that if they have brothers or little nephews, they will be able to speak about how their relatives became sergeants on whatever specific occasion and because of whatever particular action, just as noblemen can cite with pleasure how, when, and why their ancestors received the baton of the maréchal of France."[19]

Provocatively, Godard d'Aucour bashed Voltaire's poem directly and offered a corrective to the prejudicial way the *philosophe* had celebrated the victory at Fontenoy. In the third part of the novel, Parisien reads a poem of his own composition to his follow academicians that integrates lines from Voltaire's poem but replaces all noble figures with *roturier* soldiers and subaltern officers. As per the academy's mission, each of these heroes has a biographical notice in the footnotes that commemorates their personalities, lineages, and posterity. These family genealogies, Godard d'Aucour insinuated, are as traceable and often as notable from the standpoint of military service as those of any noble officer. A soldier named l'Esperance (Hope) is listed as "the fourth of this same name, from the same city, and the same family to serve in the same regiment in this same war and [he] fought hard just like his relatives. May God ordain that he not die as they did."[20] The celebration of subaltern heroes was thus well under way by the time the abbé Gabriel-François Coyer (1707–1782) published his works on the *noblesse commerçante* in 1756 and 1757 and the abbé Pierre Jaubert (ca. 1715–ca. 1780) authored his *Éloge de la roture* in 1766.

Yet advocating for the democratization of heroism was a branch of a much larger critique in which generalized condemnations of warriors and military heroes increased exponentially from the War of Spanish Succession onward. These critiques of the moral fiber and true worth of the traditional hero—a man of war cut in the mold of the Homeric archetype—drew on a historic tradition. During the Renaissance, Montaigne had expressed his preference for Socrates (d. 399 BCE) over Alexander the Great (356–323 BCE) and championed an anti-hubristic conception of greatness bounded by human limits; of an *honnête homme* as opposed to a hero. Moralists of the seventeenth century, particularly La Bruyère and François de La Rochefoucauld, accentuated the difference between the *héros* and the *grand homme*, the latter having a much broader competence, while the former specialized only in the art of war. Fénelon followed with a Christian condemnation of the false glory of arms.

These writers laid the thematic groundwork that their eighteenth-century counterparts would build upon, though with a virulence and frequency unparalleled in French history.[21] Another Rousseau, the poet Jean-Baptiste (1671–1741), voiced the violence with which many denigrated and even demonized the figure of the military hero. In his "Ode to Fortune" of 1723, he wrote:

> What! Rome and Italy in ashes
> Will make me honor Sylla?
> I will admire in Alexander
> That which I abhor in Attila?
> I will call bellicose virtue
> What is in fact a murderous valiance
> That plunges its hands in my blood;
> And I could force my mouth
> To praise a savage hero,
> Born for the calamity of humans?
>
> What traits your splendor presents me,
> Merciless conquerors!
> Scorned vows, over-reaching projects,
> Kings vanquished by tyrants;
> Walls that flames ravish,
> Conquerors smoking in carnage,

Peoples abandoned to the sword;
Mothers, pale and bloodied,
Tearing their trembling daughters
From the arms of an unbridled soldier.

In addition to this ghastly vision of military action, Rousseau also called into question the veritable agency of the warrior hero. He submitted that the actions and traits of heroes were not of their doing, but should rather be attributed to fortune (thus the title of the poem). "Their most heroic virtues," he claimed, "are nothing but fortunate crimes" (*crimes heureux*). This concept of the "fortunate crime" was a fertile formulation that a number of *philosophes* reused. In his encyclopedia entry for *héros*, Jaucourt asserted that the term "hero" was "uniquely consecrated to warriors who bring military talents and virtues to the highest degree; virtues that through the eyes of wisdom often are nothing but fortunate crimes that usurped the name virtue."[22] Diderot made reference to a fragment by a moralist predecessor in his encyclopedia article on heroism, wryly averring that "most heroes, says La Rochefoucauld, are like certain paintings; in order to esteem them, one mustn't look at them too closely."[23] *Militaires philosophes* also adopted this disparaging vision of the warrior hero, and it reappeared in works by Turpin de Crissé, the chevalier de Berny, and others.

In this discourse, the figure of the *héros* or *homme illustre* was the foil of the vastly superior *grand homme*. "The *grand homme* is quite another thing," explained Jaucourt; "he conjoins most of the moral virtues to his talents and genius; he has only beautiful and noble motives in his conduct; he listens only to the good of the public [*le bien public*], the glory of his prince, the prosperity of the state, and the happiness of the people."[24] Turpin de Crissé added a number of details to this definition in his "Lettre sur la différence du grand homme au héros" published in the *Amusemens philosophiques*. Professing to prefer the *grand homme* to the *héros*, he affirmed:

> To be full of piety, severe and just in the distribution of punishments and recompense, exact in discipline, simple, humane, selfless, bringing all of the glory to his master and the wellbeing of the *patrie*, this is the *grand homme*. To love war alone, to aspire toward glory without sparing blood, to be prompt, impetuous, to brave dangers; joining audacity and pride to talent in warfare, to never give up, to stiffen in the face of difficulty, to be motivated by personal ambition rather than the glory and happiness of the *patrie*, this is the hero.[25]

Yet, in spite of professing to favor the *grand homme* over the *héros*, many of these same writers moved to offer a new, revitalized vision of the hero that broke down the diametric opposition and hierarchy between the two types. Diderot, Jaucourt, and others posited that a true hero combined characteristics of the *grand homme* and the *héros* or *homme illustre*. In his article on heroism, Diderot argued that the greatness of soul attributed to the *grand homme* is implicit in veritable heroism, that no true hero has a base or groveling heart. For Diderot, heroism was more than greatness of soul, since it included the latter and supplemented it with great feats that excite surprise and admiration.[26]

Jaucourt claimed that this combination of characteristics typified the term "hero" in its original meaning. "The term hero, in its origin, was consecrated to he who united warrior virtues with moral and political virtues, he who withstood challenges with constancy and faced perils with resolution. Heroism presupposes the *grand homme* worthy of sharing the cult of mortals with the gods. Such were Hercules, Theseus, Jason, and others."[27] In this way, even as he had insisted on a difference between *héros* and *grand homme* as they had evolved through human civilization, his vision of the superior individual was one possessed of both moral and military greatness. Most of the examples he cited in his article evince this integration, even those from his definition of the *grand homme*, since the majority were indeed military men: Trajan, Alfred the Great, Titus. Berny actively worked to destabilize both the distinction between the *héros* and the *grand homme* and the alleged superiority of the latter. If Coyer and the abbé de Saint-Pierre insisted on the superiority of the *grand homme*, a greater number of thinkers, including those mentioned here, embraced the new vision of the perfect hero as articulated by Jaucourt: "Overall, humanity, gentleness, patriotism united with talents are the virtues of the *grand homme*; bravura, courage, temerity, knowledge of the art of the war and military genius characterize the *héros*. However, the perfect hero is he who combines love and sincere desire for public happiness [*la félicité publique*] with his capacities and valor as *grand capitaine*."[28] Louis Basset de la Marelle's (ca. 1730–1794) treatment of the term *héros* in *La différence du patriotisme national chez les François et chez les Anglais* (1766) exemplifies the redefinition of heroism in the middle of the eighteenth century. Instead of relying on the contrast between the *grand homme* and the *héros* in order to discuss heroism, Basset de la Marelle modeled his discussion on two types of heroes: the warrior hero (*le héros guerrier*) and the patriot hero (*le héros patriote*).[29] This categorization was analogous to Jaucourt's differentiation between heroes and perfect heroes. The warrior hero was a self-interested and imperialistic conqueror animated by an "insatiable desire for glory." His ambitions led him to ruin the state rather than conserve it as he "dispensed the blood of his fellow citizens" and "depopulated the lands" without any thought of his *patrie*.[30] On the other hand, the patriot hero's "views, thoughts, deeds, fortune, and days are only for the *patrie* and the King."[31] "His actions adhere more to virtue" as well as honor, and he is "more interested in being a good man [*homme de bien*] than in appearing as one."[32]

The midcentury culture of patriotism, or "the cult of the nation," as David Bell puts it, played a key role in sharpening and propelling the new vision of heroism. Jay Smith shows that patriotism was a vector of grand rethinking during the French Enlightenment, a discussion that fostered a reconsideration of relationships between humanity and the divine, between modernity and antiquity, between social classes and categories, and between different political systems and their corresponding moral foundations (such as Montesquieu's monarchy/honor versus republic/virtue).[33] While scholars continue to contest the origins of what Edmond Dziembowski calls the "new patriotism," it is certain that its rumblings in the 1750s had exploded into a broad cultural discourse and a political program in the wake of the Seven Years' War.[34] Dziembowski traces the "slow maturation of ideas that radicalize at the end of the century" moving from "'aristocratic republican' patriotism (d'Aguesseau), to an 'English republican' patriotism (Montesquieu, and Mably to a certain extent), then to a 'Spartan republican' patriotism (Rousseau)."[35] The historiography of this evolution pinpoints the definitional aspects of patriotism: love of country, an ethics of self-sacrifice for the good of the public and *patrie*, a civic virtue that championed human rights and liberty.

The importance attached to patriotism and rather naïve faith in its effects cannot be underestimated. It was a primary element of successful warfare and government, as Jaucourt, Montesquieu, and others explained, citing English, Greek, and Roman history. Military thinkers, too, adopted patriotism as a generator of military effectiveness and worked to instill it in the French armed forces in the latter half of the century. In its noble selflessness and honorable public-mindedness, patriotism was seen to be such a pure sentiment that it could be a pillar of collective moral reform, the type the *médecins philosophes* sought to achieve. In his essay *Le patriote anglais* (1756), Jean-Bernard, abbé Le Blanc (1707–1781) presented patriotism as the very fabric of civil society: "True wisdom, along with true happiness, consists in the attachment to one's duties of all kinds, of which the first is love and consequently the defense of the *Patrie*. Certainly, patriotism, or that which is the same thing, love of our country, is the most eminent virtue that could adorn any man: it is, to speak correctly, the cardinal virtue on which civil society is founded. A good patriot is necessarily a good subject . . . He prefers the good of the public to his own."[36] In Le Blanc's formulation, being a patriot meant laying claim to a multilayered superiority: moral ("most eminent virtue"), intellectual ("wisdom"), emotional ("happiness"), political ("good subject"), and social ("good of the public"). Like *humanité* and *sensibilité*, true patriotism was active and even militant. There was a semiotic system of speech and action by which one signified one's patriotism, which found its most natural expression in military action: defense of the *patrie*. Love of country was seen to breed war, at least of the defensive ilk. The patriot was thus an incarnation of the "perfect hero" who united the virtues of the *grand homme* with those of the *héros*. The honor and superiority associated with patriotism made it integral to military reforms seeking to reap the practical benefits of patriotic armed forces. As Le Blanc remarked, "Vincit amor patriae" (love of country conquers).[37] These assumptions about patriotism therefore made it central to military change, to rehabilitating the image of the warrior, and to effecting broad moral revitalization in France following the losses of the Seven Years' War.

Yet, the means of igniting patriotism in the French armed forces and general population were not obvious. Montesquieu, the *Encyclopédistes*, and others had already remarked that patriotism was inherent to citizens of republican governments, not to silent subjects of absolute monarchies. With no large-scale political change in sight, many agreed that the best way to cultivate patriotism was through emulation inspired by images and tales of great individuals:

> In the last thirty years of the old regime, the French lived amidst a glittering company of ghosts. One could not belong to an academy, walk through the streets of central Paris, attend an artistic salon or visit a bookseller without coming across orations, odes, statues, paintings, engravings, and books glorifying the "great men" of France's past. Catinat and Bayard, Duguesclin and Suger, d'Aguesseau and Turenne, and many others passed ceaselessly in review. Their panegyrists placed infinite faith in the ability of images of national greatness to inspire further national greatness.[38]

As Bell, Dziembowski, and Smith demonstrate, a patriotic program—one that Bell thinks of as nationalist—was promulgated by the crown and taken up freely by *philosophes*, literati, and military officials. The patriotic and nationalist program took many forms: songs, orations, paintings, engravings, sculptures, essays, plays, anthologies of great French men and women, eloquence competitions, and more. These works celebrated French history, its protagonists, and the heroic qualities that they represented.

While scholars have shown that an ever-broadening range of activities was considered patriotic, military service to the *patrie* continued to occupy a central place. In 1758 the Académie française ordered that "great men of the nation" become the focus of the *concours d'éloquence* (eloquence competition), which had previously addressed religious topics. Bell keenly notes that this change occurred precisely and expressly as the events in the Seven Years' War were turning bad for France. The competition opened with a decidedly martial flavor, since the great man to be celebrated in the first *concours* was none other than Maurice de Saxe. This indeed set a trend. Of the sixteen men who were eulogized in the competitions between 1759 and 1787, a quarter of them were military figures, representing the largest single occupational group in the *concours* (double in quantity compared to French monarchs).[39] Military leaders such as Nicolas de Catinat (1637–1712), Anne Hilarion de Costentin, comte de Tourville (1642–1701), Turenne, and François-Henri de Montmorency, duc de Luxembourg (1628–1695) represented a third of the subjects selected for sculpture commissions made by de facto minister of arts Charles-Claude Flahaut de la Billarderie, comte d'Angiviller (1730–1810), in the prestigious art salons between 1777 and 1789.[40] Once again, these martial personalities dwarfed any other group represented.

In addition to the sheer number of warriors represented in this pantheon of patriots, equally significant was how these figures and their heroism were represented in the eulogies. Antoine Léonard Thomas (1732–1785), whose panegyrics for Maurice de Saxe and naval officer René Duguay-Trouin (1673–1736) won the *concours* in 1759 and 1761, respectively, cast these military men in the new mold of the enlightened "perfect hero." Saxe and Duguay-Trouin were at once *grands hommes* and *héros*, moral individuals dedicated to humanity and the *patrie* as well as martial idols whose derring-do was worthy of epic poetry.

In addition to speaking of their military prowess, Thomas mobilized a set of characteristics and conditions that had become widely accepted as characterizing the *grand homme*. The abbé de Saint-Pierre articulated these traits in a 1739 essay that compared the *grand homme* and the *homme illustre*. Saint-Pierre enumerated the three conditions necessary to earn the moniker *grand homme*: (1) great motivation or desire for the public good; (2) immense difficulties overcome, as much by the consummate constancy of a patient and courageous soul as by the remarkable talents of a just and broad mind (*esprit*) that is fertile in means; and (3) outstanding advantages procured to the public in general or to his *patrie* in particular.[41] Thomas appropriated these three characteristics in his descriptions. He repeatedly represented the motif of overcoming challenges, showing the *roturier* Duguay-Trouin as having faced numerous trials at sea—storms, battles, disease, his own brother dying in his arms—but also rising above social prejudice to attain his renown through merit and love for his monarch. Thomas reimagined the first time that Duguay-Trouin went to meet King Louis XIV after a victorious naval campaign. "It was neither the splendors of opulence, nor the names of his ancestors, nor noble titles that announce him; he is announced by his exploits . . . It was a strange spectacle for the lazy and disdainful courtiers that a seaman, without any title except his service, was transported directly from the helm of his vessel into the middle of the Court and was conversing with his King. Some of them perhaps remarked that he did not possess the grace and manners of the Court; Louis XIV remarked his valor and his genius."[42]

Thomas depicted Duguay-Trouin as a man animated by sociability, *sensibilité*, and humanity, primary elements of the new enlightened military ethos. "He inspired in his soldiers, by a foresight that penetrated everything, by a confidence that never doubted success, by dispositions that pushed his troops to be brave, by a severity in discipline that is for courage what a sober and frugal life is to the body, by an attention full of humanity to spare their blood, for in his eyes, soldiers were men."[43] Duguay-Trouin was an *âme sensible* and indeed a *patriote sensible*, who felt pain at the loss of human life in war and made manifest his care for his soldiers by fostering their heroism, disciplining them honorably, and doing all that he could to spare their lives.[44]

Similarly, in the *Éloge de Nicolas de Catinat*, written in 1775, Jean-François de la Harpe (1739–1803) continually underscored the marshal's humility and humanity in his efforts to attenuate the violence and bloodshed of war:

> Of all Louis XIV's generals, it was he who asked the least for himself, who best distributed rewards in his army, and who cost the least to the state. Being so frugal with the wealth of the *patrie*, how much more sparing must he have been with the blood of his children? It is true that this quality is not only born of a disposition of the soul, it also depends on the science of command; the art of sparing men from war is that of conducting them. Yet is it not too common in the history of military practice to see humanity sacrificed to glory? . . . Soul of Catinat! Pure and enlightened soul! Just ideas of duty and glory gave you more humane sentiments! O Catinat! For a sage like you, every victory that wasn't necessary was a crime! Alas, when war is necessary, it is still deplorable and Catinat made it a point of honor to make it less bloody.[45]

During and following the disastrous Seven Years' War, eulogists like Thomas and de la Harpe offered the Académie, the crown, and the French public an image of national redemption through the enlightened military hero.

While panegyrists wrote grandiose eulogies, other writers worked in more popular genres, especially theater, that could have a greater reach to the diverse peoples of France. These works often focused on subaltern officers and common soldiers who demonstrated the characteristics of the perfect hero as well as domestic virtues. Rehabilitating the soldiery and petty officer corps meant transforming these figures from odious to pitiable, nameless to familiar, wasteful to useful, respectable, and heroic. This metamorphosis was reflected both in patriotic literature and in the armed forces, which instituted policies to honor and render more citizenlike the soldier and subaltern.

Subalterns, Citizens, and Heroes

It was in early spring that widow Madame Luzere received lodging billets for two officers of the French army deployed near the tiny German village she called home. Soon thereafter, the officers arrived at her doorstep. The younger one was a stereotypical French swashbuckler, the type she had always heard about. He was haughty and loud, and immediately made eyes at Madame Luzere's teenage daughter. His superior was a middle-aged man and something of a foil to his self-important subordinate. He was kind, courteous, even humble. His eyes did not sparkle with pride in victories past and future, but were soft and seemed to hide a quiet grief beneath his furrowed brow. His name was Chevalier St. Franc, and once he and his hostess found themselves alone, he told her his story.

As a young man, he was destitute and had enlisted out of dire financial need. Through his bravery in battle he had risen through the ranks to attain a post as major, one that many young aristocratic officers coveted or deemed unjustly bestowed, focusing on his obscure social origins rather than the acts and scars that proved his merit. He said that he learned to overlook such pettiness, to fulfill his duty to his *patrie*, and to serve as a good example to his soldiers. But he hated war:

> Only senseless youth could make a game out of such a serious profession, one that must make us shed tears regardless of our successes. It is enough to be obliged to close our ears to the cries of nature and pity . . . The duty of combat! A cruel duty! But in the intervals between these bloody calamities, I become a man again and I feel the need for peace. My soul aspires toward some generous action. I try, assuaging the suffering of humanity, to repair the miseries of which I was a fatal and blind instrument. Ah! How could the sad spectacle of war and the painful scenes that it manifests not render the heart of a man more tender and more *sensible*?[46]

The chevalier's thoughts wandered, and after a few more words were exchanged, he went into a silent reverie. After what seemed an eternity, he looked back at Madame Luzere:

I do not enjoy the honors or the pleasures attached to my rank . . . I had a son whom I loved . . . When he came into the world, he had nothing to welcome him but the gifts of nature. All I had to offer to contribute to his destiny were my tears . . . Today fortune has smiled at me and I could create for him a better future, but I don't know what has become of him . . . His memory pursues me relentlessly. Inheritor of my misfortune! He was forced to enlist in the army. He wore the same soldier's uniform that my own men wear today. In each of them, I sometimes believe that I see and recognize my child . . . They are all dear to me . . . Maybe he is still alive, leading a painful and languishing life . . . But I lost him, Madame, and in such a tragic way as to make one almost desire never to see him again.[47]

The Chevalier St. Franc and his story, created and staged by Louis-Sébastien Mercier in his international hit drama *Le deserteur* (1770), can only take on their full meaning in the context of cultural debates on war and the military discussed in the previous chapters. St. Franc is a complex character, not quite an archetypal antihero or a classical hero, for his hatred of war seems nearly to overtake his patriotic fervor. He is *sensible*, humane, and modest, yet firm in justice and in his tenacity in fighting his way up through the ranks to become a major. He is a faithful and successful servant of the king, and, equally if not more importantly for his character, he is a father. It was his desire to provide for his son that led St. Franc to enlist in the first place. These paternal sentiments were indicative not only of a sensitive soul but also of the fibers of a true man and citizen. He was the epitome of the *patriote sensible* and perfect hero.

Domesticity was essential in the new heroism that St. Franc represents. Recent historiography on gender and family in eighteenth-century France suggests that the enlightened citizen was a loving father and a righteous master of the household who contributed to the state by expanding its population.[48] In addition to the link between fatherhood and citizenship, other historians have illuminated theories regarding marriage and citizenship, a subject that developed into a heated debate in reference to the military.[49] "Reformers and their opponents clashed repeatedly over how best to spur individuals to bravery," writes Jennifer Heuer. "Their debates reveal fundamental differences in contemporary understandings of masculinity, family, and the appropriate relationship between the army and the nation. For some, military men were to be considered citizens, invested in both war and domestic life; being a better warrior also meant being a husband and father. For others, soldiers were inherently set apart from other Frenchmen, either because of their particular social status or the violence of their profession; soldiers needed to be separated from both the obligations and temptations of domesticity."⁵⁰ According to the latter group, attachment to family would soften a soldier's will to fight and would likely provoke either desertion or the burden of managing his wife and children who followed the army. Proponents of military marriage, on the other hand, upheld that marriage would stoke courage and heroism, since men would feel responsible for financially supporting their families and would want to be seen as honorable, courageous, and patriotic.

Theatrical works like Mercier's *pièce à thèse*—a type of Diderotian *drame bourgeois* composed to convey a precise political message—lauded and spread the image of the military man as loving father and often used this sentimental character as a mechanism to gain empathy for the play's political message. Mercier's depiction of St. Franc as a relatable, meritorious, and enlightened hero served as a device to deliver his condemnation of capital punishment for desertion. St. Franc himself does not desert the French army in the play. Rather, it is his son Durimel. In the span of the drama, Durimel is denounced and caught, then brought to an officer in order to be executed for his crime. That officer is none other than St. Franc, his own father.

Durimel explains how he ended up in the army and why he deserted. His story—enlisting due to financial need, suffering the abuse of a commander, retaliating, and then running away—was familiar to the eighteenth-century public. Mercier constructed Durimel as a sentimental character, a victim of unfortunate life circumstances and of a dual cruelty in the military—an abusive colonel who caused Durimel to desert and then a penal code that sentenced him to death for it. However, Mercier was careful to show that both son and father were heroes: St. Franc for incarnating the perfect hero, and Durimel for insisting that his father follow orders and have his son killed by firing squad so as not to tarnish his hard-earned honor and rank as a major. St. Franc obeys, but in doing so he comes apart at the end of the play—clinging to his son, wailing in agony, and crying out to the firing squad not to ask him to give the final signal to shoot his own child (a scene recounted by the conceited young officer lodging with Madame Luzere, whose haughtiness gave way to genuine emotions of shame, outrage, and devastation).

Through the dénouement of the play, audiences across Europe, the Channel, and the Atlantic were brought to reflect on and to feel in their hearts the ways that war and military policies touched members of the armed forces and those around them. St. Franc could be a neighbor, an uncle, a friend, and Durimel could be one's own son. Such familiarity mended the image of the soldier and petty officer, replacing their unsavory reputation as nameless, faceless marauders with a virtuous identity and a status as a victim and martyr.

For Mercier, this familiarity also constituted a pillar of his strategy to engage audiences in his outcry against the death penalty for desertion.

The strategy of familiarization to elicit empathy was increasingly widespread in journalism and the arts of the mid-eighteenth century. During this time, as the Seven Years' War was fomenting, sentimental portrayals of military martyrs like that of French Canadian officer Joseph Coulon de Villiers, sieur de Jumonville (1718–1754), who was assassinated by forces led by George Washington, were deployed to galvanize patriotism and boost enlistments.[51] Popular theatrical works, especially opéra comique of the 1760s and 1770s, staged the details of military life, from recruitment to living in garrisons to preparing for battle. Louis-Guerin d'Azémar's one-act comedic opera *Les deux miliciens*, first staged at the Comédie des Italiens in August 1771, portrayed the process of recruitment for the regular army and for the militia with peasants drawing lots to see who would go to which service. Azémar, like other writers of the period, incorporated lessons about how to understand military service and servicemen through the eyes of patriotism. At the beginning of the play, characters lament the arrival of the military recruiter, comically named Frappedabord ("Hit-first"). However, Frappedabord reminds them that serving in the army makes them heroes in their villages:

> When a solder comes home from war,
> He is cherished! He is celebrated!
> People admire him, people respect him:
> Everyone is enchanted.
> ...
> "What an air! What traits!" each person exclaims:
> He is another man, my word . . ."
> A lad whose soul is broken in by war
> Is beautified by serving his King.[52]

While military audiences in Saxe's army in Flanders had grown used to such comedies and their messages, Azémar brought them to the Parisian public.

Louis Anseaume (1721–1784), who had a long-standing collaboration with Charles-Simon Favart and was the *sous-directeur* of the Opéra-Comique in Paris for a time, dedicated many plays to depicting military men as respectable well-doers during the early 1760s as the disasters of the Seven Years' War spiraled downward. His opéra comique entitled *Le soldat magicien* (*The Soldier Magician*) débuted at the Foire Saint-Laurent in 1760. It became a staple of European stages, including the Théâtre de l'Hôtel de Bourgogne and the Théâtre italien in Paris, as well as the Grand Théâtre de la Monnaie in Brussels from the 1760s through the end of the century. In this play, a soldier comes to lodge in the home of Monsieur and Madame Argant. This soldier is unnamed in order to show that he is a character type representing all soldiers rather than an individual. Upon arrival, he is immediately welcomed to the home by the valet Crispin, who announces that he loves and pities soldiers. The soldier quips that Crispin displays good taste in his appreciation of military men, but then queries why the valet pities them. When Crispin responds that servicemen have a difficult life, the soldier laughs and sings a merry, reassuring song about how the soldier is "tranquil in the middle of combat, despite the bombs that fall and explode into shrapnel . . . Nothing worries him, he dances to the sounds of the cannon like one dances to that of the accordion."[53]

Anseaume sought to depict the soldier as strong rather than pitiable, but also as smart, good-humored, and kind. Anseaume put forth this image in the main plot of the play, which is a romantic comedy about the unhappy marriage between Monsieur and Madame Argant. The clever soldier quickly ascertains the couple's problems: the husband's jealousy and abuse of his wife, who herself has come dangerously close to having an affair with a public prosecutor of their town. In a comedic feat of imposture, the soldier pretends to be a magician whose tricks reveal the follies of both husband and wife and help the couple rediscover a loving commitment to one another. Anseaume's soldier displays the new heroism, serving his *patrie* and countrymen on the battlefield as well as in thoughtful and kind domestic feats.

Anseaume showed soldiers and subaltern officers to exhibit this type of heroism. The extremely popular *Le milicien* (*The Militiaman*), which premiered for Louis XV at the Château de Versailles in 1762, starred a sergeant named La Branche. In a small country town, Lucas has mischievously maneuvered himself so as to receive a small family inheritance that should have been paid to Colette. He uses this money to pressure her into marrying him and to give up her love for militia captain Dorville. La Branche masterminds a plan to enlist Lucas and to retrieve Colette's inheritance so that she and Dorville can be happily married. La Branche displays his military sociability in aiding his superior to find happiness. He demonstrates his humanity and *sensibilité* in taking action to correct Lucas's injustice and in supporting Dorville and Colette's union. In these ways, as well as in his own military service, La Branche is portrayed by the playwright as a consummate patriot and hero.

Plays like *Le soldat magicien* and *Le milicien* were exceedingly popular and enjoyed expansive stage success from chronological and geographical perspectives. From its debut at Versailles in 1762, Anseaume's *Le milicien* was performed 135 times in twelve theaters located all over France and in two foreign countries in the second half of the eighteenth century.[54] This and similar plays spread images of the new heroism animating military men of all ranks. They participated in a process that Jay Smith calls the "nationalization of honor," spreading it from the king and the nobility, through the military ranks, and out to the French populace. Guibert wrote that

> from the court to the capital, the spirit of honor and courage will flow outward into the astonished provinces. The nobility, giving up the petty enjoyments of luxury and leisure, will abandon the cities to return to its chateaus; there it will find itself happier and less confused. It will regain the morals of its ancestors. While retaining its enlightened outlook, it will once again become warlike and gallant. The taste for arms and military exercises, rekindled in the nobility, will soon make its mark on the people. The bourgeoisie will no longer see the profession of the soldier as scornful. The young people in the countryside will no longer fear joining the militia.[55]

In Guibert's vision, the French population at large would become citizens and soldiers, leading to military and moral regeneration. "How easy it is to have invincible armies in a state where subjects are citizens who cherish their government, love glory, and do not fear hard work!"[56] The anonymous writer of the reform memoir "Reflections on Military Constitution" articulated it clearly: "To have good soldiers, it is necessary to begin by making good citizens, and to have good citizens [the government must] make them as contented as possible."[57] For *militaires philosophes* like Guibert and *philosophes* such as Rousseau, Servan, and Mably, the militarized citizenries of Rome, Sparta, and America furnished convincing examples of patriotic morality and military success.

The crown was willing to "nationalize" honor to a certain extent, especially within the soldiery. New policies were instituted to standardize recompense across the army, such as an award of 600 livres for taking an enemy cannon or flag. Particularly significant actions, such as capturing a high-ranking enemy officer, procured not only monetary award but also a promotion for those deemed to possess the appropriate military and leadership skills.[58] Yet the crown had no intention of legally making subjects into citizens and citizens into soldiers. Osman concludes that, as a result, state focus went toward making soldiers more culturally citizenlike, all the while eschewing any concept of the nation at arms.

Judging on military policy alone, this conclusion is legitimate. However, broadening sources to include the heroic arts, especially patriotic theater, a narrative of the nation at arms is clearly present. Buirette de Belloy's play *Le siège de Calais* of 1765 was by far the best known of these political plays. The remarkable enthusiasm and patriotic fervor generated by the play prompted the chronicler Louis Petit de Bachaumont (1690–1771) to write that it was "a sermon for the monarchy which the government must protect, spread, and make understood by the entire nation."⁵⁹ Louis XV undertook just that. He staged the play at Versailles a week after its Parisian début, and then ordered the Comédie française to offer a free performance of the work. *Le siège de Calais* swept through theaters across France in cities, towns, and military garrisons and was printed and distributed to regiments on the continent and in the colonies. The governor of Saint-Domingue himself paid to print copies of the play, with a self-congratulatory proclamation that it was "the first French play ever printed in the Americas."⁶⁰

The play recounted the well-known historical episode of the final days of the English siege of Calais in 1347. King Edward III of England (1312–1377) promised to spare the townspeople of Calais upon surrender, on the condition that they select six of their most prominent citizens to come before him in their nightgowns with the keys to the city. The burghers, or bourgeois, were to be executed, but according to Sir John Froissart's chronicles, Edward's queen consort, Philippa of Hainault (1314–1369), convinced her husband to show clemency and spare them.⁶¹ Rather than crediting the queen for this act of humanity, Belloy's Edward was swayed by the heroism of the six burghers, whom he endowed with enlightened public and private virtues of the "perfect hero." Belloy integrated patriotic and sentimental drama in order to educate audiences on the relationship between love of country and love of family. Like the protagonists in the play, audience members should love and cherish their family members, but when danger and war are imminent, they must learn to love their *patrie* first and foremost. Saint-Pierre demonstrates this evolution when his son is (falsely) reported dead in act 1, scene 2:

> He is dead and my tears . . . But what am I doing? O my country!
> When I will have saved you, I will be able to cry for my son!
> Love of the *patrie*, oh pure and vivid flame,
> Reignite in my breast your generous transports;
> Let my paternal tears be dried by your fire.
> It is my country, my king, it is France that calls me,
> And not the blood of a son that had to die for her.

Through such scenes, Belloy aimed to instruct and to elicit emulation. He wrote: "Let it not be said by those who come out of our theatre: 'The great men I have just seen played were Romans; I was not born in a country where I can emulate them.' Let it be said, sometimes at least: 'I have just seen a French hero; I can be such a one too.'"⁶² Belloy's ensemble of heroes included a variety of social groups—commoners of the Third Estate, aristocrats, the king, and to some extent women. Gender marked a tenuous space of exploration in the new constellation of patriotism, citizenship, and military service. While it may have been increasingly easy to accept these different male figures as perfect heroes, the figure of the heroine and attributes of female heroism, or "heroinism," remained problematic. Military policies and practices as well as the cultural imaginary expressed through theater illuminate the concurrent loosening and reaffirming of juridical and cultural norms of patriarchy.[63]

Women, War, and Heroinism

Deep-seated beliefs with regard to gender underscored perspectives on women's patriotism, citizenship, and military agency. Salic Law notwithstanding, age-old prejudices held that women were incapable of the sentiments of patriotism and of civic values. Even enlightened efforts to rethink such stereotypes revealed their persistence. In his *Essay on the Character, the Manners, and the Understanding of Women in Different Ages*, published in 1772, Antoine Léonard Thomas suggested examining "whether females, so alive to friendship, to love, and to compassion, can raise themselves up to the love of their country, which extends itself to all its citizens, and to the love of humankind, which includes all nations."[64] While Thomas agreed with the prevailing notion that women could not "raise themselves up to the love of their country," he blamed this on society as opposed to gender essentialism.[65] Women's exclusion from public life made them unable to experience patriotic sentiments. This was a problem of nurture, not nature. Yet Thomas's arguments quickly degenerated into essentializing logic. Women's minds were simply incapable of conceptualizing collectivities beyond the domestic sphere. Love of humanity and love of country, Thomas concluded, "these vast measures are for them beyond their nature."[66]

This sexist and essentialist mentality, one that Rousseau repopularized in *Émile* (1762), hampered the ability to imagine women as patriots. In the *Encyclopédie*, the word *citoyenne* or female citizen did not exist, and the article *citoyen* (male citizen) categorized servants, children, and women as dependents of a *paterfamilias*, or male head of household.[67] Historians have examined the concept of female citizenship and shown how it was considered oxymoronic, nonexistent, or, at best, only imagined as public absence or passivity, just as male citizenship was characterized by presence and action.[68]

Traditional notions of women as military agents were equally prejudicial. Complaints regarding the influence of women pitted "feminine" and "military" as mutually exclusive. Violence and martial activity were associated with the categories of male, nobility, life in the public sphere, and aggressive concepts of honor and self-sacrifice. Women, who were equated with the private sphere and a defensive conception of honor, could only "cross over" into the realm of male activity under exceptional circumstances and with certain enabling conditions in place. It could become a woman's duty to use violent means to defend her husband's property if he was absent (gone off to war, for example) and therefore unable to protect it himself. Such a woman acted on a kind of borrowed agency, taking the place of the man and gaining some of his privileges. This was the case of the Frondeuses-Amazones, the women who took part in the armed rebellions of the princes from 1650 to 1653.[69] Several enabling conditions of this "crossing over" were in place: these women were noble, and they were acting in the absence of their husband, most often in defense of his property or interests.[70] These circumstances sanctioned and legitimated a temporary gender transgression mainly because it did not truly challenge, let alone transform, the mentality or social system in place. Following the Frondes, gender codes returned to the status quo ante, and Louis XIV dramatically reduced the number of women permitted to participate in army life. Any woman attempting to serve in the French armed forces under an assumed male identity was punishable under the Ordinance of December 19, 1666, by which enlisted military men who hid their identities were sent to the galleys.

Popular plays like Belloy's *Le siège de Calais* halfheartedly challenged these norms and in many cases strongly reasserted them. The cast of characters made his work deceptively "feminist," for while recorded histories of the siege of Calais did not showcase French women, Belloy invented a female protagonist, Aliénor, for his play. Aliénor was the noble daughter of the comte de Vienne, governor of Calais, and was touted as "a model for her sex," primus inter pares in a France full of heroines:

> . . . you see bringing illustriousness to her ruins,
> France is now fertile with heroines:
> Edward's spouse and haughty Monfort
> Do not alone have the right to disdain death.
> (Act 2, scene 5)

Aliénor and the other women of Calais actively participate in military action through strategizing and executing their plans. Aliénor leads the town in devising two tactical plans to end the siege—either to set fire to the town and commit a noble suicide (act 1, scene 6) or to burn the town and wage a final attack so that the people of Calais die in glory (act 2, scene 5). She calls for the women of Calais to participate as direct military agents. For the collective suicide and attack, respectively, she promises the men of Calais:

> You will see, like me, your faithful spouses
> Encourage your happily cruel hands:
> And holding their fathers and spouses in their arms,
> From our flaming houses throw ourselves with you.
> (Act 1, scene 6)

> Come; you must arm your dear companions,
> Or keep the steel for your hardened hands,
> While torches that will burn Calais
> Will be thrown by us onto the English camp.
> (Act 2, scene 5)

Belloy's rhetoric of military heroism delineates a gender economy of equity—men and women can be heroes of France, and both can participate in military acts, though differently. Using stereotypical constructions of the gendered body, the arms of the faithful wives encourage and embrace, while the hands of their husbands and fathers are utensils of cruelty. In this way, any hint of radicalism that could have been perceived in Belloy's proposal for women's martial agency is undercut in the same breath that it was pronounced. Belloy repeated this formula in Aliénor's call to combat, which is addressed to the townsmen, not the townswomen. Women remained grammatically passive in every instance of their military "agency." It was men who granted female violence: "It is necessary to arm your dear companions."

This theme of men giving women the tools of violence and the permission to use them is evident in the very design of Aliénor's character. Like the Frondeuse-Amazone, she is a noblewoman who comes to stand in for an absent man (her father) in defending their territory and therefore legitimately gains access to military agency. Belloy made it abundantly clear that Aliénor's power was on loan from her father. In act 1, scene 5, the mayor of Calais, Eustache de Saint-Pierre, says it directly: "Give them your father by governing their zeal." Aliénor herself echoes the borrowed character of her mission in act 1, scene 6: "My father planned to make a noble sacrifice . . . what a joy that in his absence his daughter can accomplish it." Though Aliénor's temporary transgression allows her a certain degree of borrowed military agency, one that she envisages passing on to her fellow women of Calais, Belloy made a point of thwarting the most extreme proposal of militarism and heroism. In act 2, scene 5, Aliénor intimates her desire to follow the example of the three burghers of Calais who had already volunteered to be sacrificed to King Edward, a gesture of patriotic emulation that Belloy dramatically curtailed: Saint-Pierre addresses her as follows:

> Madame, stop. I understand your hope.
> Between our sexes, distinguish the duty.
> I can, without outraging the glory of yours,
> Reclaim an honor that only belongs to ours . . .
> Those who, with steel in hand, defended this rampart,
> All have the right to receive Edward's rigors before you.
> (Act 2, scene 5)

Belloy prohibited Aliénor's access to martyrdom and heroinism by reimposing structures of the patriarchal social system onto her body, which cannot be sacrificed in this way or accrue the related heroic honor. From this point through the end of the play, Belloy dismantled all aspects of Aliénor's heroic character, pushing her into a trajectory of roles that mark a dwindling agency—from Amazon, she goes to dutiful daughter-mediator, then hopeful wife, and finally takes on an impersonal, almost allegorical character celebrating humanity in the final scene. Belloy invented a citizenlike Amazon all the better to put her back in her place.

Jeanne d'Arc (Joan of Arc or the Maiden of Orleans) was also treated to character erasure and the dismantling of heroinism in epic poems of the seventeenth and eighteenth centuries. Jean Chapelain (1595–1674), writer, critic, and founding member of the Académie française, wrote a much-lampooned epic poem on Joan of Arc, *La Pucelle* (1656). In it, the story of Joan's heroinism is mitigated by a series of other plot lines involving a large cast of characters, and she is ultimately replaced as central protagonist by a male character. Yet this subtle devaluing of Joan's heroic qualities does not compare to the sardonic slander to which she was subject in Voltaire's mock epic *La Pucelle d'Orléans*, which began circulating in the 1730s. Overtly irreligious, fantastical, and lascivious, Voltaire declared in the first stanza of the poem that the most outstanding of Joan's feats had nothing to do with God, *patrie*, or military prowess. Her greatest heroinism was remaining a virgin for an *entire year*. After many lines displaying Joan's absolute stupidity, the poem ends in debauchery.[71] Voltaire's *La Pucelle* was condemned, censured, and burned all over Europe, which only seems to have fueled its popularity. After wide circulation in manuscript form for more than twenty-five years, the poem saw 135 editions, clandestine and authorized, between 1755 and 1860. Voltaire's unceremonious deflowering and desacralizing of Joan of Arc seemed a decisive blow to any progressive notions regarding women, war, citizenship, and heroinism.

Yet at the same time, artists, playwrights, and military officers of the eighteenth century advanced more inclusive perspectives that destabilized, and in some cases pushed beyond, gender stereotypes and tropes. At any given time during the *ancien régime*, some four thousand women were present in the French army.[72] Numerous women followed the army, and far lesser quantities followed *compagnies franches de la marine* or the navy, for obvious logistical reasons. Wives, children, and prostitutes accompanied the troops and in earlier times played an essential role in the pillage economy. Other noncombatant women served as *cantinières* and *vivandières* (sutlers who sold food, alcohol, and other goods) or *blanchisseuses* (laundresses).[73] A minority of women also served as combatants or *femmes soldats* (women soldiers), though they did so disguised as men.[74] Despite Louis XIV's Ordinance of December 19, 1666, studies have shown that a number of military officers sought not to punish women in uniform, but rather to explain, justify, and ultimately reward them for their service. Male officers who knew these female soldiers and had fought with them in their units often had a more lenient approach than the laws and centralized policing might have enforced. When the identities of women warriors such as Jeanne La Balle, Françoise Fidèle, Jeanne Bensac, Marguerite Goubler, and Madeleine Kellerin (all of whose birth and death dates are unclear) were revealed, their officers and other advocates came to their defense. They deployed three tropes that fostered some level of understanding and tolerance: the *guerrière héroïque* (the noble heroic woman warrior), the *sainte travestie* (the cross-dressed saint), and the *fille aguerrie* (the war-hardened girl).

The *guerrière héroïque* most resembled the Frondeuse of the seventeenth century as embodied by noblewomen like Anne Geneviève Bourbon-Condé, duchesse de Longueville (1619–1679), and "la Grande Mademoiselle," Anne Marie Louise d'Orléans, duchesse de Montpensier (1627–1693). Their aristocratic identity implied an ancestral heritage of war making and displays of martial generosity for the kings of France. Women could take part in this lineage and *mentalité*, albeit only in exceptional times of need. Jeanne La Balle, also known as the marquise de Lursan or Sister of the Cross, was arrested in 1729 and justified her military service via the *guerrière héroïque* trope. She said that it had been a lifelong dream to emulate her father and her ancestors, who had always served the king of France. She wrote about the generosity of her heart and the honor of her family, which made her assume a male identity in order to become a combatant.[75]

Yet, as her military name suggests, Jeanne La Balle was smart enough to deploy two tropes as a defense for her "displacement" into the realm of war: being a noble heroic warrior woman (marquise de Lursan) and a saintly warrior figure (Sister of the Cross) in the mold of Joan of Arc. Despite Voltaire's bawdy poem, the image of the pious virgin fighter still had clout in the military sphere and cultural imaginary. Françoise Fidèle, who had been serving in the Parisian militia, was discovered to be a woman by a medical surgeon in 1748 and was subsequently arrested by Police Inspector Poussot. In his report, Poussot defended her engagement in the militia, explaining that she was the alleged daughter of an Irish captain in the regiment of Dylon and that she came to serve out of need, since she was orphaned at age four. He lauded her education, her chastity, and her desire to enter a convent. Poussot painted her as a victim of circumstance and as a would-be nun in hopes that she would simply be imprisoned rather than condemned to the galleys. He succeeded.[76]

Advocates for Jeanne Bensac, who served for a year during the War of Spanish Succession, went even further than recommending leniency in punishment. They proposed that she be granted leave (as opposed to being arrested) and be given a small monetary reward to guarantee her safe passage to her hometown in Limousin. Bensac had champions in different corners. First, several captains of the second battalion of the regiment of Bourbon in which she had served supported her and signed a letter on her behalf. They insisted that no one knew she was a woman and that she had always been prudent (or indeed a prude) in her actions and words. A second supporter was the intendant Le Bret, who attached a personal letter to the secretary of war requesting that she be granted leave and a payment of 40 écus to rent a horse and return to her home. A final ally was Monsieur Humbert, chaplain at the royal hospital at Antibes, who used formulations of hagiography to represent her conduct as that of a veritable saint.[77]

The final trope used to justify women serving in the military was that of the *fille aguerrie*, or the war-hardened girl. The *fille aguerrie* was acclimated to military life, either by having been a soldier's daughter who grew up at the front or by working as a sutler or laundress. Françoise Fidèle and Jeanne Bensac were both presented as having spent their formative childhood years in the military. Fidèle had war in her blood, since she was an *enfant de troupe*, a child of the army troops, and both women had been acculturated as warriors due to their time in the service. Several woman warriors of the eighteenth century, such as Madeleine Kellerin and Marguerite Goubler, whose identities were discovered in 1745 and 1761, respectively, were *enfants de troupe*. Kellerin was given a gratification after she had her hand amputated following an injury incurred at the front. She was forced to declare her sex when she was committed to hospital, and the dénouement of her story was worthy of *comédie larmoyante*, or sentimental comedic theater: she was discharged from the service, received a military pension, married another injured veteran, and obtained the honor of moving into a state home for veterans in Strasbourg.

However, her discharge and gratifications from the state also entailed gender realignment: she took on a domestic role by becoming a wife, and was commanded to use her pension money to "acheter des habits convenables à son sexe" (buy clothing suitable to her sex).[78]

While a certain binarism persisted in perspectives on gender and warfare, *femmes soldats* simultaneously operated within and loosened prevalent gender stereotypes. No king or military administration encouraged women to serve in the French armed forces. However, their official acknowledgment, honorable discharge, and state-issued recompense mark some cultural shifting from hard-line exclusion and public condemnation. Examples of honorable discharge are particularly numerous. Françoise Courvoisy received 150 livres after five years of service in 1759, and Marguerite Goubler received 100 livres after one year of service in 1761.[79] The tropes of the *guerrière héroïque, sainte travestie,* and *fille aguerrie* can be seen not only as justifications for female militancy but also as tools of empowerment reclaimed in order to recognize honor, merit, and heroism.

At the same time, patriotic literature and art featured women with increasing prominence and explored female capacities for patriotism and heroic action. Historians have offered provocative reappraisals of "civic motherhood," the *citoyenne*, and the Spartan mother in eighteenth-century France. Rather than seeing female domesticity as an ideal that excluded women from the fabric of the nation, they argue that the figure of the Spartan mother gave women an important educational role. "Creating the bonds that attach all citizens to the state, the *citoyenne* acts as a linchpin for the ideal state grounded in the principles of social contract and equality."[80] A woman's domestic role in educating children was a type of citizenship and an expression of patriotism. What is more, since domesticity was also celebrated as a masculine trait and an important attribute of the enlightened hero, it no longer marked an absolute boundary of gender difference.

Anthologies of great women and collective biographies went a step further, connecting women and their service to France to national memory. Following in the footsteps of Pierre Le Moyne (1602–1671), whose *Galerie des femmes fortes* (*Gallery of Warrior Women*) was published in the early seventeenth century, historian abbé Claude-Marie Guyon (1699–1771) published his volume on women warriors entitled *L'histoire des Amazones anciennes et nouvelles* (1740). Works like this and others by Jean Zorobabel Aublet de Maubuy and Jean-François de La Croix were not novel in kind, but rather in function as pedagogical tools to foster patriotism. They reiterated a more visible role for women as participants in the nation's history and asserted women's capacity for patriotism. The theater represented such illustrious female figures, but was also more radical in portraying women as models of the new heroism in its patriotic, domestic, public, and military dimensions. These women became embodied and therefore "present" to audiences, encouraging women of the eighteenth century to emulate them. Barnabé Farmin de Rozoi (ca. 1745–1792), who later became principal editor for the *Journal militaire et politique*, charted the limits of this exploration of gender, war, and heroism in his own theatrical work on the siege of Calais. Unlike Belloy's play, Rozoi's *Décius français*, which was never performed, largely abandoned neoclassical ideologies and aesthetics to champion equality in the realms of military agency and heroism.

From the beginning of the play, Rozoi openly supported gender equality in politico-military agency and heroic capacity. In act 1, scene 2, Emilie, Eustache de Saint-Pierre's mother and one of the two female protagonists invented by Rozoi, is presented as a Spartan woman. Emilie makes remarks akin to the "Sayings of Spartan Women" of Plutarch's (40–120 CE) *Moralia* that learned audiences would have recognized. She tells the English officer-envoyé Talbot (who is in the historical role of Mauny or Manny) that she would kill her own son if he fled the English in cowardice. Remarking on Talbot's surprise at her statement, she affirms: "You are surprised, Talbot: but courage knows neither sex nor age." Unlike Aliénor, whose agency is borrowed from the father, Emilie is an autonomous agent who sees herself as a citizen, endowed with courage and an inalienable right to participate in the political and military affairs of Calais. Unsolicited and without replacing a man, she proposes herself as a hero and leader of the community of Calaisiennes, proclaiming that "each sex should have a hero as its leader."

In the mode of the perfect hero, Rozoi endowed Emilie with a combination of bellicose patriotism and *sensibilité*. He displayed this character in what he called "the combats of patriotism and nature," an internal battle in which Emilie's private feelings of maternal love for Eustache battle with her civic sentiments of courage, virtue, and patriotism. Emilie is a *patriote sensible* similar to Thomas's vision of Duguay-Trouin and Mercier's character St. Franc in *Le déserteur*, published years after Rozoi's play.[81] *Patriotisme sensible* underscores that the psychological challenge of sacrifice for the *patrie* is a mark of a great hero, as the comte de Vienne confirms: "These combats, Emilie, illustrate great hearts. The greatest heroes shed tears." Underscoring Emilie's greatness in a tacit reference to tearful epic warriors like Ulysses and Aeneas works to emphasize her heroic nature and the injustices done to her because of her gender. In act 4, scene 3, Emilie comes to the same stumbling block as Belloy's Aliénor when she is denied the right to sacrifice herself as one of the six burghers of Calais. However, Rozoi used this situation not to domesticate Emilie, as Belloy would do with Aliénor, but to issue a caustic critique of sexism in the military sphere. Emilie deplores women's status: they are virtuous, but never receive glory; they are great, but are never permitted to perform grand gestures on the battlefield. "Men, doubtless you feared us becoming your rivals, proud to be your equals if only for a day."

Emilie's feminist proclamations stand in stark contrast to the statements and figure of the other female protagonist, Julie, who is Eustache de Saint-Pierre's wife. Julie represents the Aristotelian archetype of the uncontrolled, irrational woman characterized by unbridled, selfish emotion and an incapacity to put public matters ahead of her own personal concerns—a classic misogynistic image of why Salic Law needed to be upheld in France. Rozoi constructed Julie as a selfish, emotional woman in order to stage a conflict between patriotic and unpatriotic women. Julie is weak and carnal, seeking first and foremost the transports of love and tenderness, while Emilie's response reiterates proper patriotic values and the realities of the political situation.

Yet Julie's character has a function greater than that of a simple foil, for it is through staging this female stereotype that Rozoi was able to debunk it. In a spectacular *coup de théâtre* in the final scene, the audience discovers that Julie has masterminded a way to become one of the six burghers of Calais by cross-dressing and passing as a man. Just before the executions are to start, the revelation occurs: Julie pulls off her helmet and reveals her identity. This image bridges the gap between the female body and patriotic martyrdom. Instead of being demoted or labeled an exception, her example becomes the general rule legitimating female military agency and heroism. Emilie also joins the group of soon-to-be-sacrificed burghers. This leads to a tableau that combines the goals of Diderot's *drame bourgeois* with those of patriotic theater as the extended Saint-Pierre family—Emilie, Eustache, Julie, and Julie's brother—stand together representing equal rights in patriotic agency and heroism. In Rozoi's version of the story of the siege of Calais, it is not Queen Philippa but rather this spectacle of egalitarian patriotism and heroism that convinces King Edward to pardon the burghers and recognize the greatness of France as the most patriotic nation on earth.

The reception history of Belloy's and Rozoi's plays is revealing about the politics of theater and the prevailing *mentalité* toward women, war, and heroism. Rozoi's *Décius français* was soundly rejected by the Comédie française, and its author was thrown in jail. Belloy's *Le siège de Calais* rose to unparalleled fame, and he was elected to the Académie française. The crown and the play's audiences, who saw performances of *Le siège de Calais* at Versailles, in Paris, in barracks across France, and in colonial outposts, seem to have felt very comfortable with the play's messages of male bourgeois heroism, the realignment of the *patrie* and the king, the reaffirmation of Salic Law, and a neoclassical image of female martial agency as exceptional and curtailed. Though the female protagonist in Belloy's play can borrow *logos* from a patriarchal authority, and even some of his military and political agency, any progressive movement is blocked at the female body and its public signification. On the other hand, and despite its many flaws, Rozoi's play advanced a nuanced vision of *patriotisme sensible* and a powerful image of gender equality in the political, military, and heroic space of the nation. The dénouement of his female-driven plot prefigures twentieth-century feminist critique in a dual rejection: first, of the male mode of individuation by a bringing together of its female characters; and second, in its rejection of the reductionist characterization of the "maternal-feminine" in favor of a vision of women as strong, complex beings engaged in a struggle of body and mind to reach equality and emancipation.

As male soldiers were made more citizenlike, female soldiers experienced a smaller but related shift. Also, just as male citizens like the six burghers of Calais were militarized in the patriotic imaginary, so were female citizens, at times in equal degree, though only in works like Rozoi's that were too radical for their day. Foreigners, free men of color, and indigenous allies of the French had a similar range of experiences in relation to heroism and citizenship.

Foreigners, Freemen, and the Nation

In mid-September 1746, a troupe of Indian singers arrived at the residence of Governor Joseph-François Dupleix in Pondicherry. Ananda Ranga Pillai had informed the governor that this group had composed a series of songs in the local language of Telugu to celebrate Dupleix's person and exploits. The songs glorified his patience and courage, his efficiency in making Pondicherry into a fortified French stronghold, and his military prowess in combat against the English, who had "fits of nervous diarrhea" at the mere mention of his name. Dupleix had become an epic hero of the Indian subcontinent.

For the performance, Dupleix had a special rug spread across the floor and invited a host of guests, including several European women who served as interpreters, translating the songs from Telugu into Tamil so that Madame Dupleix could translate from Tamil to French. The singers opened with a song about the British capture of two French ships, the *Jason* and the *Dauphin*, returning from China in February 1745. The British had sold the vessels to the Dutch, but when the French threatened a diplomatic crisis with the Dutch, the latter sent a friendly reimbursement for the value of both ships. Dupleix was not entirely pleased with this insufficiently heroic telling of events. He requested a number of modifications, including a line that detailed the exact amount of a penalty fee (15,000 pagodas) that the French forced the Dutch to pay and another line about how the French naval captain of the *Pondichéry* fired cannon at the British assailants when they arrived back in India with the stolen vessels, most likely killing the British commodore Curtis Barnett (who in fact died in 1746 of an illness). The singers agreed to modifications in this and other songs and returned to perform the new versions soon thereafter. Heroic reputation as expressed in local news and cultural media like these Telugu songs was an important part of Dupleix's strategy to cement his political, military, and economic clout on the subcontinent.[82]

Just as Dupleix gained access to heroic status in a foreign culture, so certain groups of foreigners who served in regular and auxiliary units slowly attained recognition and reward in France. Yet the culture of inclusivity in heroism and patriotism had a distinct boundary—usually that of race—that blocked aspirations to become heroes and citizens of France. In the colonies and France's overseas trade settlements, a double standard emerged by which the French were expected to become heroes in indigenous culture, but no Indian prince, Amerindian chief, or free man of color could become a hero in French culture.[83] Rewards such as the medals awarded to free men of color in Saint-Domingue and Amerindian *chefs à médaille* (medal chiefs) displayed openness and inclusivity. However, these rewards and special statuses also lodged hidden ambitions of the crown, which sought to influence and manipulate the actions of awardees. For these individuals, prizes and privileges always came with strings attached.

Foreign troops formed a significant part of the French armed forces during the *ancien régime*. They fought in designated foreign units of the regular metropolitan army and as auxiliaries recruited locally for colonial forces.[84] In the metropolitan army, thousands of soldiers hailed from eastern and northern Europe, Africa, Asia, and the Americas. Many were not Catholic and did not speak French. "By their very presence," writes Christopher Tozzi, "they defied many of the myths that legitimized the Bourbon state, highlighting the rich racial, religious, cultural and linguistic variety that characterized France under the Old Regime despite the fictions to which the Crown clung. These soldiers also demonstrated, through the special privileges that the monarchy extended to them, the ease with which one could 'become French' before 1789 by bearing arms for the king."[85]

The diversity of the French armed forces grew remarkably from the 1740s to the Revolution, such that in 1789, 32 of the army's 168 regiments, including 8 cavalry units and 24 infantry units, were designated as foreign. The majority of the foreigners in service of the French crown came from neighboring European countries such as Switzerland and different German principalities. There were also historic units of Irishmen, Scots, Hungarians, Italians, and Liègeois. These foreign troops possessed distinct privileges, including higher pay and exemption from some of the policies that applied to French soldiers, such as the inability to marry without permission from commanding officers. Tozzi contends that the crown increasingly worked to turn "foreigners into Frenchmen." Louis XIV made particular strides in this effort in a 1715 decree that granted all foreign servicemen of the army and marines who had served for more than ten years the rights of natural subjects, including the ability to pass on property to their heirs.[86]

Living for many years among the French, these foreigners were increasingly integrated socially and culturally. They often chose to spend their military leave in France instead of returning home, and in many cases they married French women. Despite his increasingly staunch Catholicism, Louis XIV also created policies of inclusion for Protestants that his successors followed and amplified. Protestants were prohibited from being accepted at the Invalides and were not eligible for military academies, awards, or decorations such as the Order of Saint-Louis. The Sun King began to slacken such policies by allowing Swiss Protestants to enter the Invalides toward the end of his reign. Louis XV went further to recognize the military service and heroism of Protestant military men. In 1759 he created the Order of Military Merit for Protestant heroes of the French armed forces and also set up a military academy for Protestant students.

Maurice de Saxe's regiment of volunteers, the Volontaires de Saxe, was formed in a spirit of curiosity and spectacle, but also with a conviction with regard to the martial prowess of "black" peoples. Levied during the War of Austrian Succession, the regiment was largely composed of eastern Europeans (Poles and Tartars) except for its first company, which was predominantly composed of "black" uhlans (light cavalry) from France's Caribbean colonies as well as Africa, Asia, and South America.

Saxe took great and deliberate pains to assemble this company once the king authorized the creation of the Volontaires on March 15, 1743.[87] He recruited them from other units in the French army, many of which had a single "black" *timbalier*, or timpanist, who played drums to control movements of troops. He had members of his entourage inquire about the whereabouts of these "black" soldiers, corresponded with their commanding officers, and offered handsome payoffs in order to acquire each soldier. He also took initiatives to get freemen or slaves who were from the colonies, but who were living or temporarily located in France. In the spring of 1747, Saxe was informed that twelve black prisoners who had been captured by French privateers were being held in a prison at Bayonne. Saxe beseeched the naval minister, le comte de Maurepas, to attain them for him, but the latter communicated that this was simply impossible due to the *loi générale du royaume* (the general law of the realm), which mandated no slave trade or slavery in France.[88] It was illegal for slaves to contract a military engagement with Saxe, since they were technically the property of their owners and could neither be sold nor traded in France. Thus, there was no legal way for Saxe to confiscate or purchase the twelve prisoners, whose ownership devolved onto the ship owner of the privateering vessel that captured them. In a similar effort, Saxe forwarded to Maurepas an anonymous memoir that he had received proposing a plan to recruit fugitive slaves. Maurepas answered desperately that this plan was not only ill advised, but "absolutely impracticable."

Saxe's recruitment for the Volontaires had attracted the attention of the colonial lobbyists in France, who were horrified that Saxe would willfully steal their "property" and were even more so at the thought that their former slaves would receive military training that they might one day decide to turn against their former masters. Yet despite this pressure and the laws in place, Saxe was not to be deterred and became savvy in manipulating the loopholes of the *loi générale*. In one instance, he was able to enlist two black slaves located in the Atlantic hub of Bordeaux, since they had not been registered properly, which nullified the ownership status of their masters.

Once Saxe had enlisted these men, he ensured that they were treated with absolute equality. From an administrative perspective, their contracts were the same as those of all other foreign soldiers; their identities were recorded in the *contrôles des troupes* like every soldier in the armed forces; they had the same types of beds and quality of uniform as their peers; and they were not segregated from the white men serving in the company. They had the same mortality rates and desertion rates as the white men of the company. They married and brought their wives with them on campaign, as did white French soldiers. These women also gained employment as laundresses like the wives of French soldiers. Corvisier tracked down documents attesting to the wedding of three "black" uhlans of Saxe's regiment at the church of Chambord. The officers of these men signed off on the marriages and most likely attended the ceremonies and the celebrations following them.[89]

Saxe's persistence in creating this company of "black" uhlans was driven to some extent by orientalism: Saxe's purposefully accentuating their skin color by outfitting the "black" light cavalrymen with gleaming white horses, his usage of the company as a kind of personal guard akin to those he had heard about in "the Orient," and his referring to this diversity of soldiers from different continents and ethnicities reductively as *nègres*. Yet Saxe also had a genuine curiosity and desire to learn about different religious, cultural, and racial groups and believed in their military prowess. In 1757 Saxe wrote to the count Heinrich von Brühl (1700–1763), prime minister of Saxony, asking him to send "six tovaritch Tartars, but true Mahometan Tartars. I will make them officers in my regiment of Uhlans . . . I dare to beg your Excellency once again that they all be of Mahometan religion."[90] Saxe seems to have planned to learn about the Islamic faith from these individuals and may well have done so in conversations that were never committed to written record. At the same time, he was animated by his belief in the merit of these men. As his letter to von Brühl made clear, he intended for these men to serve as commanding officers, not simply NCOs and soldiers to be led by white Europeans or Frenchmen, as had been done with militias, constabularies, and colonial auxiliaries in overseas theaters. Saxe was proud of his role in recruiting and promoting these men through the ranks. As he later wrote to von Brühl, "I am extremely happy and captain Babac was made lieutenant-colonel as soon as he arrived. I believe that he will be the first Muslim lieutenant-colonel that has ever been part of the service of his very Christian Majesty."[91]

Corvisier concludes that Saxe's "black" uhlans were born not only of an intention to be original, but also one that was "unconsciously revolutionary." Comments like those he made to von Brühl and his bold dismissal of the colonial lobby, however, make his intentions seem far from unconscious in their revolutionary character. The military administration squelched this from becoming a trend, and in the years following Saxe's death, the politically charged unit was disbanded. In the 1740s, white metropolitan soldiers struggled to be seen as heroes endowed with patriotism, civic and domestic virtues, and leadership qualities. Without the patronage of enlightened military figures like Saxe, people of color did not have a chance.

Questions of race, military service, heroism, and citizenship were far more politically tenuous in Saint-Domingue. Clashes on the character of colonial patriotism occurred in the middle decades of the eighteenth century. On one side, wealthy white planters shunned military service in favor of liberal virtue and economic patriotism as promulgated by Saint-Dominguan colonist Émilien Petit (1713–ca. 1780) in his work *Le patriotisme américain* (1750). Petit and his followers condemned French military government in the colony and claimed that "when rule of law liberated colonists from the arbitrary decisions of local military leaders, their rational self-interest would create prosperity, order, and strong attachment to the *patrie.*"⁹² Racial segregation was central to Petit's system, for "if whites and free people of color became too 'familiar,' that is, if they established viable families, creole patriotism might come to mean imperial autonomy or independence."⁹³ The naval ministry hired Petit and brought him to Versailles for twenty years to help mold colonial policy in the Antilles.

Contrary to these conservative voices of the colony, high-ranking military officers of the continent on assignment in Saint-Domingue—among them Charles d'Estaing and Lenoir de Rouvray—proved to be far more liberal. When d'Estaing arrived in the colony to serve as military governor, he brought with him a strong conviction regarding classical civic virtues and the merit of people of color, which John Garrigus describes:⁹⁴

> No previous colonial administrator had ever announced, to the degree he did, his belief in the moral worth of free men of color. He described them as loyal sons, proud, and frugal. He proposed a special "Prize of Valor" and "Prize of Virtue" for free colored soldiers with attached pensions, to be awarded during a special ceremony on the king's birthday. Moreover, he proposed that anyone of one-eighth or less African ancestry be considered officially white, immune from all legal discrimination. Insisting on the artificiality of color distinctions among successful creole families, he described this measure as merely "treating like Whites those who are, really." D'Estaing knew this proposal would cause political tumult. However, "to reject from the citizen class people so precious, especially in a country where men are so necessary, seemed to me to be a contradiction worth fighting." He believed that such a reform would strengthen the patriotism of the entire free population of color. Time and marriage with the descendants of Europeans would open full citizenship to qualified families.⁹⁵

D'Estaing's ideas caused such outrage that he was recalled to return to France only fifteen months after his arrival in Saint-Domingue. Nearly fifteen years later, however, d'Estaing returned to the colony to recruit military manpower in his mission to aid the Americans in their fight for independence. When he returned in the spring of 1779, he brought back his meritocratic ideology and support of egalitarian civic virtue, along with protégés like Lenoir de Rouvray and a propaganda system to help promulgate these ideas. In 1780, Captain Vincent, the supposedly 119-year-old veteran of the 1697 raid on Cartagena, was given full military honors at his burial, and the *Affiches américaines* newspaper lauded him as "new proof for those who need it that a truly great soul, no matter what shell it inhabits, is visible to all men and can silence even those prejudices that seem necessary."[96] The *Affiches* continued to tout egalitarian civic patriotism in these months of heavy recruitment, extolling the patriotic enthusiasm of free people of color who enlisted in the newly reformed Chasseurs volontaires and proclaiming that this martial love of the French *patrie* ignited the "zeal and good will of Citizens of every species [*espèce*]."[97]

The French crown used these words and rewards to stoke the hopes and patriotism of free people of color in Saint-Domingue, ultimately making them a tool of manipulation. A similar strategy for recruiting manpower and advancing metropolitan interests had also been used in North America through the system of *chefs à médaille*. Medals had been objects of diplomatic exchange between French and Amerindians; however, Versailles and colonial administrations attempted to change their cultural meaning to signify reward. Roughly twelve men of different Amerindian tribes per annum received a medal from the king rewarding them for their faithful allegiance to the Bourbon regime. While the medal recognized merit, it also aimed to make the winners into *chefs à alliance* (alliance chiefs).[98] The medals were clearly intended to coerce awardees into continued fidelity, and it was hoped that *chefs à médaille* would have a special status in their tribes, positioning them as leaders who could further French interests within indigenous communities. This plan backfired since rewards and status given by a European power were not necessarily respected within First Nations, where positions of leadership were determined independently and according to their own criteria.[99] Trapped in between two worlds, *chefs à médaille* were heroes neither of the French nation nor of their own tribes.

The Chasseurs volontaires of Saint-Domingue also found oblivion rather than glory or citizenship. Many died at the siege of Savannah in 1779, and others were dispersed throughout the French Empire, being forced to continue their service. Racist discourse spread across the colony and was materialized into its laws, wiping away notions of colored civic virtue, patriotism, and heroism. What was viewed as an "indelible stain" of African ancestry provided an excuse to make military service a burden of an inferior race rather than the privilege of a patriotic citizen. While Stewart King finds evidence for free colored men participating in a "military leadership class" in the Northern Province of Saint-Domingue, John Garrigus unearths no such evidence in the Southern Province, where liberal virtue reigned and colored military service was a mark of shame and lesser status.[100] Ultimately, free colored people shouldered the burdens of military service, but never reaped any reward or recognition in the pantheon of French heroes. The celebration of their heroism and recognition of their status as citizens would take a revolution.

Imagining the French Nation at Arms

The cult of military heroism participated in three major evolutions of the eighteenth century concerning national identity, the armed forces, and the citizenry. The first has to do with policies designed to uphold soldierly honor and improve the conditions of military service. In 1787 the newly formed Council of War with Guibert at its head worked to pass reforms that all hoped would resolve decades of dysfunction and debacle. Improving the lot of the soldier and rewarding him for his merit were top priorities. The council therefore passed a raise of six deniers (half a penny) per day to soldiers' salaries, improved the quality of military rations, offered higher pensions to senior soldiers, and required officers to address soldiers with the more formal and respectful "vous" as opposed to the informal "tu." Regiments were also required to establish schools to teach noncommissioned officers to read, write, and use basic arithmetic. The council reinstated corporal punishment for certain military crimes, but mandated that such punishments be administered in private so that the soldier's honor would not be violated by public humiliation.[101]

The 1780s were also the heyday of naval reform. In the final decade of the *ancien régime*, reforms moved from a largely scientific focus to include a human focus. Saxe's "details" that concerned caring for the human and material necessities of his men finally found a counterpart in the navy under the watchful eye of the naval minister, the marquis de Castries. Years of collaboration with Louis XVI resulted in the promulgation of a 458-page code in 1786 that redefined the naval constitution from top to bottom, including reforms by which the state provided better care for sailors and their families.[102] "No secretary of state, not even Colbert," writes Alain Berbouche, "had ever looked more attentively into [improving] the lot of seamen."[103]

While naval reforms were highly esteemed, those of the army were less successful. The reforms were well intentioned and reflected developments on the redeemed and deserving figure of the patriotic and heroic *soldat sensible*. The Council of War could never satisfy all demands for reform, many of which were competing and incompatible, nor was its championing of soldierly merit strong enough to abolish physical punishment. The Ségur Law of 1781 stipulated that all officer candidates had to furnish proof of four generations of nobility, showing that social caste prejudices continued to influence military reform until the eve of the French Revolution. Through the 1780s, growing disappointment fueled military insubordination and retirements.

The culture of heroism played a role in another important development relating to the relationship between military and nonmilitary individuals, between soldiers and "civilians." While theft, pillage, contraband, and violent crimes perpetrated by army men against civilians persisted, they represented only 5 percent of crimes reported in garrison and transit towns.[104] The program of "domesticating" the soldiery initiated by Louis XIV had met with some success. Garrisoning and an ever-improving military justice system, in combination with state propaganda and popular literature, rendered military figures—from great generals to subaltern officers and soldiers—increasingly familiar and less sinister. Between 68 and 88 percent of soldiers came from agricultural and artisan communities in France, which meant that they already held certain cultural and experiential ties to rural and village populations. The shared values and increasing respect between military men and rural people became manifest when the army was called in to quell grain riots, more than a dozen of which occurred between late 1787 and mid-1789. Though some officers agreed to lead their troops into rioting regions to subdue violence, other officers refused to carry out orders or even elected to resign from their posts. One such officer in Toulouse wrote a letter of resignation after being asked to quash rioting, stating that he preferred to leave the armed forces rather than to pursue such activity, since "it was not the business of the army to attack citizens."[105] As the notion of the perfect hero had dictated, military men were to be members and protectors of the citizenry.

New policies, ad hoc initiatives by officers, and the nationalist program of the post–Seven Years' War period fostered the third development of a democratization of heroism and an ever-stronger cultural ideal correlating citizenship with military service. French people from all walks of life could think of themselves not only as citizens, but as the makings of "enlightened" heroes animated by patriotism, social and domestic responsibility, and a strong martial spirit. They were ready to incarnate the dreams that had been voiced by Guibert in the *Essai général de tactique* and by the Chevalier d'Arc in *La noblesse militaire*: "I hear the murmuring of the Nation; thousands of voices cry out, to arms! O Frenchman . . . yes, you are worthy of the blood from which you have descended. You have the virtues of your ancestors, and some that they did not always demonstrate, such as moderation and humanity."[106] This image became real between 1787 and 1790 when an increasing number of ad hoc citizen armies came into being. These units were precursors to the National Guard, which became an official part of the army in Paris.[107] Well before cries of the *patrie en danger* and mass levies of the French Revolution, the Military Enlightenment generated an image of France as a nation of patriotic warriors.

CHAPTER 5

The Dialectic of Military Enlightenment
The Revolutionary and Napoleonic Eras

By the mid-nineteenth century, the blade of the Revolution's guillotine and the booming cannon of Napoleon's armies were distant memories. George Sand (1804–1876) and Victor Hugo (1802–1885) felt that the dream of perpetual peace was at hand. In *History of My Life* (1855), Sand wrote: "As for the philosophy of perpetual peace, it is in the *esprit* of the newest philosophical schools. Today, it would be ridiculous to find the abbé de Saint Pierre ridiculous or to speak without respect for him whom even his detractors called *l'homme de bien par excellence*."[1] Victor Hugo similarly remarked that "if no incident outside of our natural expectations comes to trouble the majestic march of the nineteenth century, civilization, already saved from so many storms and so many pitfalls, will distance itself further and further from this Charybdis that we call war and this Scylla that we call revolution."

Sand and Hugo expressed this optimism regarding the end of war despite evidence to the contrary. Recently enough, both writers had lived through the brief French invasion of Spain in 1823 and the July Revolution of 1830. Sand's championing of perpetual peace came after the lengthy and violent conquest of Algeria (1830–1847) and the 1848 Revolution in France, as well as the First Franco-Mexican War (1838–1839). In fact, the Crimean War (1853–1856) was in full swing when Sand's pacifist affirmation was published. Soon thereafter, Sand and Hugo would be confronted with further challenges to hopes of perpetual peace as the French government expanded global and colonial wars: the Second Italian War of Independence or Franco-Austrian War (1859), the Second Opium War in China (1856–1860), the Second Franco-Mexican War (1861–1867), the Franco-Prussian War and the Paris Commune (1870–1871). News of wars abroad, especially the American Civil War (1861–1865), was equally dismaying for French pacifists. Events occurring after their lifetimes, from the Dreyfus Affair (1894) to the world wars, would surely have dashed their hopes for the nineteenth century marking the arrival of humane and peaceful civilization. Perhaps Sand's and Hugo's optimism would have dissolved into the kind of sardonic pessimism that Voltaire expressed regarding Saint-Pierre's pacifistic "dreams of a good citizen": "He had the simplicity to harp on the most trivial moral truths in his books, and by another simplicity, he almost always proposed as practicable things that are impossible [such as] the project for perpetual peace."[2]

For some historians the notion of perpetual peace had far more nefarious implications than simplicity and impossibility. David Bell argues that at the beginning of the French Revolution, a hopeful belief that war was a relic of a backward monarchical past paradoxically fueled an apocalyptic culture of war. In this, some viewed conflicts of the 1790s as "wars to end all wars," which fostered strategies of annihilation. Other scholars do not believe that an essential shift in the understanding of warfare in human civilization had occurred, suggesting, as Jeremy Black does, that "the ready recourse to violence in France owed something to a politics of paranoia."[3] While historians do not agree on the causes of the escalation of warfare or whether the Revolutionary and Napoleonic Wars can be categorized as "total wars," most concur that the period between 1792 and 1815 saw warfare of unprecedented scale and sociopolitical impact.[4] Surveying all of the major European battles between 1490 and 1815, Gunther Rothenberg estimates that more than one-fifth were fought during the Revolution and the Napoleonic era.[5] Individual battles, such as the battle of Leipzig of October 16–19, 1813, engaged over half a million French, Polish, Italian, German, Russian, Austrian, Swedish, and Russian troops and left over one hundred thousand casualties. The *levée en masse* of 1793 called forth all French people to serve the nation's warring cause and seemingly made real the burgeoning myth of a martial Grande Nation, or Great Nation.[6] Research by Alan Forrest and Isser Woloch confirms that war was the most pervasive and even oppressive force in French society of the time.[7] Wars of nations, such as those of the Revolution, in which political survival was at stake, and conflicts of imperial conquest undertaken by Napoleon surpassed the parameters of early modern limited war. Any hope of perpetual peace seemed to give way to fleetingly euphoric triumphs and enduring devastations of perpetual war.

From a military standpoint, the wars of 1792 to 1815 demanded renewed efforts to optimize systems of logistics, manpower, tactics, technology, and medicine. The paradigms of reform of the Military Enlightenment continued to frame these efforts. The initial phase of the French Revolution invigorated military *esprit philosophique*, spreading it to an even wider group of actors. Men and women voiced grievances, proposed reforms, and drafted petitions. The French nation of warriors that *philosophes* and *militaires philosophes* had imagined crystallized into the Revolution's Grande Nation of citizen-soldiers, although the role of women, racial minorities, and foreigners as combatants and heroes of the nation continued to be debated. Napoleon's "militarizing process," to recast Norbert Elias's phrase, transformed the emblem of the citizen-soldier into that of the soldier-citizen, locating the source of French glory, power, and moral virtue in the army. Continued mutations in the relationship among citizens, the nation, and war led to a pervasive process of militarization and, indeed, militarism.[8]

Making French armed forces more effective and war more efficient, while at the same time less onerous, remained a goal, just as it had for participants in the Military Enlightenment. The importance of social relations within the armed forces was a focal point in this regard. Revolutionaries propounded the concept of fraternity as uniting all citizens and especially those of the army. The culture of military fraternity, combined with that of *sensibilité*, would become a springboard for what Brian Martin calls "Napoleonic friendship," a physical, psychological, and emotional intimacy that flowed horizontally and vertically through the ranks and that was most poignantly exhibited by the emperor-general himself toward his officers and soldiers. Napoleon manufactured military identity and effectiveness through a notion of care that was made manifest not only in social relations but also in improved living conditions and medical treatment as well as a meritocratic reward system that elevated, indeed ennobled, the deserving military man. The old notion of a military "band of brothers" that Enlightenment *militaires philosophes* had promulgated was anchored with "the institutionalized notion that to serve one's country was to live and die in the care of other men."[9]

Martial community was not only constructed on the foundations of *sensibilité* and *humanité*, however. The culture of sexual heroism and masculine "homosocial enactment" was a cornerstone of Napoleonic martial identity and "imperial virtue," according to Michael Hughes. Notorious for pillaging and rape, Napoleon's men built martial identity, community, and victory, at least in part, on the violation of women and civilians. If, as Howard Brown argues, the concept of atrocity in the space of war was sharpened during the Revolutionary period, it was because enlightening cultures of *sensibilité*, *humanité*, and *droits de l'homme* (rights of man) had become more deeply rooted in French collective consciousness and were being defiled in the space of war.

This chapter connects the themes and arguments of the preceding chapters to the history and historiography on military cultures and institutions of the Revolutionary and Napoleonic eras. Tracing threads of the Military Enlightenment through the period spanning 1789 and 1815 reveals that the "radical ruptures" of this epoch were in many cases neither ruptures nor radical.[10] Rather, Revolutionary and Napoleonic militaries and their cultural imaginaries represented a dénouement and a broader formalization of cultures and ad hoc practices that coalesced in the Military Enlightenment.

La Grande Nation

The constitution, moral standing, and effectiveness of French armed forces were of crucial import for the multiple regimes that governed France between the outbreak of the French Revolution in 1789 and Napoleon's overthrow of the Directory (1795–1799) and establishment of the Consulate in November 1799. Military reform was repeatedly invested with symbolic significance for domestic politics. It marked the passing of the Old Regime and the inauguration of a nation of citizens in the early years of the Revolution, and would later serve as an arena for conflicts between Montagnards and Girondins during the Convention. At other times, military reform efforts were attended with all of the urgency of a revolutionary movement and a nation whose very existence were at stake. Such was the case with reforms restaffing the army and navy after the mass emigration of nobles in 1791. Approximately 6,000 noble army officers fled France, and naval officers did the same, leaving 2 of 9 admirals, 3 of 18 rear admirals, 42 of 170 captains, and 356 of 530 lieutenants.[11] The Convention's famed *levée en masse* in August 1793 and subsequent surveillance of army generals by the Committee of Public Safety were also efforts toward sheer survival for the Republic. The Directory inherited an army in disarray, marred by years of disorganization, arbitrariness, and ineffectiveness, as well as hastily made and poorly enforced policies that had engendered indiscipline, insubordination, and even deadly mutinies among troops. While the Directory's comprehensive reform program was "highly unpopular," according to Rafe Blaufarb, it was nevertheless "necessary to instill order, stability, and regularity in the army."[12] The meteoric rise of Napoleon Bonaparte and his successful seizure and maintenance of power were evidence not only of his own propagandistic and bureaucratic masterminding but also of a cultural and political system that equated political legitimacy with military power. In this regard, the more things changed, the more they remained the same.

Historians have dedicated volumes to navigating the turbulent, rapid-fire changes to the constellation between nation, citizenry, and the armed forces during the Revolutionary era.[13] These complex transformations of the French Revolution's armed forces and the reforms and ideologies of the Military Enlightenment were closely imbricated. This is unsurprising given that figures like Napoleon were schooled during the last decades of the *ancien régime* and would come to take power during the decades after 1789. With enthusiasm and unshaken confidence that their positions would not be compromised by the new order, reform-minded officers believed that their voices and plans for reforming the armed forces would finally, and more thoroughly, materialize. "If we look beyond the radical decision to open careers to talent," writes Blaufarb, "it becomes clear that the Assembly's broader program of military reform, as well as the officers' response to it, was articulated within a conceptual framework inherited from the Old Regime."[14] Indeed, *militaires philosophes* of the early Revolution returned to the exact themes of the Military Enlightenment—sociability, *humanité* and *sensibilité*, merit, and a patriotic citizen army. Successive revolutionary administrations attempted to grappled with these ideas and how to institutionalize them.

The first carryover from the Military Enlightenment was a fresh outpouring of reform-minded fervor expressed in an explosion of written documents on the armed forces. Hopes for change that had been hung on Guibert and his Council of War had erupted in scandal and ended in dissatisfaction for officers and soldiers alike. When Louis XVI called for the drafting of *cahiers de doléances* (registers or lists of grievances) in the spring of 1789, French subjects from all parts of the country sent their complaints. Members of the Third Estate expressed their desire to serve at all ranks in France's army and navy, echoing discussions of citizen-armies and visions of military heroism among common French people that had circulated in patriotic theater, news reports from the American Revolution, and works by *philosophes* and *militaires philosophes*. Letters to the Estates General requested that provincial inhabitants should not only be given the chance to serve their *patrie* but to do so as officers rather than as simple soldiers or members of the universally reviled *milice*. Provinces like Limousin and bailiwicks such as that of Reims advocated for a meritocratic officer corps in which Frenchmen of all ranks could access the highest positions in the armed forces. The bailiwick of Nemours suggested that the privileges of the nobility were unjustified, since the burden of going to war was shared with the Third Estate, not just a few aristocratic officers who alone paid tax with their "blue blood."[15] Provinces suggested methods of recruitment for integrating members of the Third Estate up through the army's ranks and insisted that rather than being conscripted, patriotic Frenchmen would proudly volunteer their service and lives.

Members of the armed forces brandished their plumes as events of the summer of 1789 took a turbulent turn—voting conflicts, the Third Estate's takeover of the Estates General, the founding of the National Assembly, the storming of the Bastille, the Great Fear, and the abolition of privilege and the opening of military careers to talent on August 4, 1789. A new flood of memoirs, letters, and lists of grievances (regimental cahiers) were submitted to the National Assembly between August and October 1789, when Georges-Louis-Félix, baron de Wimpffen (1744–1814) convinced assemblymen to form a military subcommittee. These documents represent more than fifty regiments and seventy garrison towns from across the metropole.[16] With proposals coming from military and nonmilitary sectors, collective participation in the process of reforming the Revolutionary armed forces bears the marks of its enlightened forebear in both form and content.

The ideal of the citizen-soldier and a nation of warriors imagined by thinkers of the Military Enlightenment seemed first in line to pass from cultural imaginary to reality in the early phase of the Revolution. Members of the National Assembly, whom the regiment of Barrois referred to as "Warrior Citizens," had already abolished feudalism on the night of August 4–5, 1789, thereby transforming the relationship among members of the nation, the military, and the people. The regiment of Forez wrote to the National Assembly that "each soldier is [a] citizen and each citizen is [a] soldier: thus the nation in recovering liberty has a great interest in emancipating the soldier from the slavery in which he groans."[17] Soldiers and citizens had become one and the same, which meant that the soldier should be liberated from his previous military "slavery" just as the citizen was being liberated from former political "slavery."

Making each soldier a citizen and each citizen a soldier, all the while elevating the status of the latter, could take many forms. The prospect of doing so inaugurated a period of soul-searching, hypothesizing, and heated debate. The question of recruitment was vital and fiercely contested. One strain of thought, championed in the Assembly by Edmond Louis Alexis Dubois de Crancé (1747–1814), held that universal male conscription was the best path to realizing a French citizen army, since it would make military service an obligatory and thus definitional part of citizenship. It would also assure the availability of standing and reserve forces.[18] The majority, however, believed that the armed forces should recruit uniquely on the basis of voluntary enrollment. Based on free choice rather than coercion or outright force, voluntary enlistment seemed the best way to organize recruitment in a manner that evinced the new spirit of liberty and citizenship. Proponents of voluntary service felt confident that, as with the ancient Greeks and Romans and modern Americans, French love and willingness to die for the *patrie* would fill the ranks with enthusiastic and able warriors. While adherents of this perspective admitted that it would take time for old stigmas attached to soldiering to disappear, they trusted, as the officers of the regiment of Forez did, that better salaries and living conditions would boost the attractiveness and even pride of service in the minds of French people. Voluntary enrollment won the debate and was decreed by the National Assembly on July 22 on the grounds that obligatory service would have violated the personal liberty of citizens and that it would rob other industries of hard-working men who would relish other professions but make "mediocre soldiers."[19]

Yet, encouraging volunteers to enroll and inculcating civic values within them would require certain institutional changes, as military men and members of the military committee concurred. A number of these changes had long been part of suggested military reforms that were reiterated in the regimental cahiers. Given that the military committee itself was composed of twenty deputies, eighteen of whom were active or retired officers who had fought for the French in a number of global theaters, this sense of continuity is no surprise. In their work, they not only pored over recently submitted cahiers but also consulted memoirs, letters, and treatises that had been sent to the state throughout the eighteenth century.[20] Newly submitted documents once again invoked *humanité* and *sensibilité*, either openly or tacitly. Officers garrisoned at Lille and those writing from regiments like that of Rohan or Penthièvre agreed that soldiers required better food and clothing. Provisions for veterans, such as increased pensions and state care of army widows and orphans, would provide safety nets for soldiers that might well boost enrollment as well as demonstrate the government's appreciation of its citizen-soldiers. The state needed to invest in improving medical services to care for soldiers' physical and emotional health. The military penal code also received continued critique for arbitrariness and harshness.

The military committee and the National and Constituent Assemblies heeded many of these calls when the opportunity arose. After the violent mutinies of Nancy in August 1790, discussed later in this chapter, the National Assembly trumpeted its care for the wives and children of national guardsmen who fell while taking back the city. While the propagandistic purposes of this gesture were undeniable, it most likely brought some level of satisfaction to officers who had written on this issue only months before. The arena of military medicine also became a focal point of the state's efforts to preserve manpower, all the while exercising *sensibilité* and *humanité*. The total of 726 military doctors and surgeons active in 1788 swelled to over 8,000 by 1794.[21] Medical personnel continued to delve deeper in trying to understand battlefield psychopathology and sought treatments for soldiers and officers who suffered from mortal homesickness. These investigations seemed more and more pressing as international war broke out. One health officer estimated that *nostalgie*, or homesickness, was the cause of one in four fatalities at Verdun in 1793.[22]

Military penal law, by which the state risked injuring its own soldiers' honor or corporal integrity, was also addressed on several occasions. All agreed that a penal code was necessary to guarantee discipline. However, degrees of crime and appropriate punishment once again demanded rearticulation in light of new political ideology. The new code presented to the National Assembly on October 29, 1790, by lawyer and military committee member Jean-Baptiste-Charles Chabroud (1750–1816) tasked the state with protecting the soldier's honor, which he described as a "sensibilité, je ne sais quelle." Admixing discourses of *sensibilité*, honor, and citizenship, Chabroud declared that the state must be the guarantor of this *sensibilité* of honor—a "dignity of man and citizen that the soldier has not abdicated"—by clarifying and limiting the use of afflictive or defamatory punishments.[23] Further adjustments to successfully administer this objective and to control the abuse of the penal code by military superiors were articulated in 1792 before the ever-suspicious iron hand of the Terror's administration took hold with Louis-Antoine de Saint-Just's (1767–1794) and Philippe-François-Joseph Lebas's (1764–1794) Court of the Armée du Rhin, whose most frequent punishment was the death sentence.[24]

Charles H. Hammond asserts that an "enlightening" of the system of military justice did materialize as new codes succeeded in articulating: a categorization of offenses; proportionality in degree between crimes or misdemeanors and their corresponding punishments; improved efficiency in investigating and trying cases; and establishing France's first military appeals court. Demonstrating the structures and themes of the Military Enlightenment, experiments were conducted that brought civilians as jurors for court-martial, and when this failed, regular soldiers were given exceptional influence over verdicts. "The Revolution did not get to the bottom of jurisdictional problems, the composition of military court, or the overshadowing role of commanders," Hammond states, "but despite shortcomings, the 1857 Code of Military Justice owed much to the Revolution's enlightening work."[25]

In addition to reforms framed by questions of *sensibilité* and *humanité*, others harkened back to reform thinking of the Military Enlightenment as they targeted the issues of merit and equality as well as improving social relations in the armed forces. For many, particularly for soldiers and noncommissioned officers, access to more opportunities for reward and advancement, benefiting from greater respect and camaraderie between service members, and being included in and even viewed as heroes of Revolutionary political culture were lines of progress that went hand in hand.

Intra-nobiliary tensions and competition had been one of the most constant and destructive forces in the eighteenth-century army and navy, one that reforms by Ségur, Castries, and the Council of War did not quash. The military committee knew all too well that the recruitment and promotion of officers was a lasting gripe related to the old order. It necessitated rethinking if not urgent action in the case of reconstituting the postemigration officer corps. Reformers of the *ancien régime* had aimed to improve professionalism and curtail the influence of wealth, the culture of luxury, and political favoritism in appointments and promotions. The military committee adopted these same objectives. It proposed a more professional and largely meritocratic "composite system" of officer recruitment by which 75 percent of new commissions were awarded to citizens who achieved strong results on a rigorous exam. The remaining 25 percent of new commissions, especially at the level of second lieutenancies, were to be reserved for veteran noncommissioned officers who had already proven their mettle in service.[26] Opening officer careers to talent thus began to take form, though this process was mitigated by the persisting role of favoritism in nominations and by the retention of a significant number of pre-Revolutionary officers, including over 2,200 supernumeraries who had been forced out by Guibert's Council of War. Political and military upheaval, however, stopped this system from being implemented.

While many officers upheld that the nobility would retain an elevated status and influence through Revolutionary military reforms, others understood that their positions would shift and were willing to tolerate certain changes in the name of a greater public, as well as personal, good. Some poorer and middling noblemen expressed that the newfound equality between nobles and nonnobles was preferable to the mistreatment that they suffered from aristocratic grandees during the *ancien régime*. As Charles-Élie, marquis de Ferrières (1741–1804) wrote in October 1789, "I'd prefer that a common man think himself my equal than to have a grandee treat me as his inferior."[27] Persisting social prejudices, evidenced in escalating tensions and violence between officers and soldiers during the summer of 1790, soon became the target of the Jacobin movement. In January 1791 the two noble honorific military orders—the Ordre royal et militaire de Saint-Louis and the Institution du mérite militaire for Protestants—were eliminated and replaced with more broadly meritocratic Décoration militaire. In the winter and spring of

1791, the Jacobins (particularly members of the Marseille club) pressed for the *licenciement* measure, which would dissolve the standing officer corps in order to reconstitute it more democratically. The Constituent Assembly rejected the measure and resorted to recomposing the officer corps by means of nomination after thousands of noble officers emigrated.

These moves contributed to spurring the Convention's hard line on military reform, which aimed to snuff out the last traces of aristocracy and establish merit via a thoroughly republican military organization. In October 1792, a month after the monarchy had been abolished, the Décoration militaire was eliminated as a vestige of the *ancien régime*. The *amalgam*, discussed later in this chapter, and a system of democratic electoral advancement were decreed in February 1793. However, in the following eighteen months, political self-preservation increasingly took precedence over the ideals of merit and equal opportunity in the officer corps. After a period filled with government surveillance and purging of politically suspicious or threatening officers, on 1 Thermidor II (July 19, 1794) Bertrand Barère successfully pushed through a revised law on advancement that attributed one-third of advancements to election, one-third to seniority, and one-third to government appointment. This cycling of perspectives on recruitment and promotion, which oscillated between desiring to establish a merit-based system and a concomitant desire to wield state influence over the results, later repeated itself in the Directory both before and after the coup d'état of 18 Fructidor V (September 4, 1797) with more purges, another *amalgame*, and further decrees. Bonaparte would again reconstruct the system in what Blaufarb aptly calls "Napoleon's improbable synthesis: monarchy and meritocracy in the reconstruction of the officer corps."[28]

For soldiers and subaltern officers who remained in the army throughout this period, Drévillon observes that "the Revolution brought an immediate, tangible, and incontestable amelioration in [their] condition."[29] As Article 6 in the Declaration of the Rights of Man and Citizen made clear, "All the citizens, being equal in its eyes, are equally admissible to all public dignities, places and employments, according to their capacity and without distinction other than their virtues and their talents." While the emigration of noble officers and the necessary increase in military size with the coming of war both contributed to the accessibility of advancement within the ranks, the opening of careers to "all citizens" had an undeniable effect that is evidenced in statistics. Of the 119 *chefs de demi-brigade* in the line infantry during year II, 88 percent were Old Regime army men who had benefited from the new system of opening careers to talent and promotion by seniority. Among *chefs de corps*, who were on average forty-three years old and who had served for just shy of twenty years, 56 percent had been simple soldiers or NCOs in 1789.[30]

The crown jewel of the early Revolution's citizen-soldier ideal manifested in the National Guard. Pioneered in July 1789 immediately following the storming of the Bastille, the National Guard was born of the conviction that "the people should guard the people." The National Guard of Paris was to be an inclusive bourgeois-citizen militia like the one that spontaneously formed in Lille as the events of the Bastille reached the northern city. Lafayette was chosen to lead this force, which would be reminiscent of the citizen armies of the American Revolution he had fought alongside and championed for years. The National Guard of Paris, as well as those that sprung up around the country thereafter, drew enormous enthusiasm. Men from all walks of life enlisted, from individuals with no military background to soldiers, former members of the Gardes françaises, and even deserters from the Swiss regiment and other army units.[31] The Guard was an institution that commingled all French men. It offered citizens the chance to be first-time heroes protecting their *patrie* and offered a second chance to deserters, who were not marginalized, physically brutalized, or executed, but rather given an opportunity for redemption. Without the institutional burdens of the army or the detested history of the Old Regime militias, the National Guard was a shining manifestation of the new France, its people, and their values.

Despite the idealized image projected by the National Guard and merit-based systems of recruitment and promotion in the line army, these structures could go only so far in terms of creating a sentiment of common citizenry. Indeed, the National Assembly was aware that structures and laws alone could not dissipate tensions between old social identities that soldiers, officers, and nonmilitary men carried with them into the Revolutionary age. The question of fostering sociability and community—as well as establishing their limits—was again a concern, as it had been for reformers of the Military Enlightenment.

The cult of *fraternité* in the National Guard and the line army, whose rise Brian Martin traces, can be seen to combine elements of enlightened military identity—natural sociability, compassion, and devotion to *humanité*, a sense of masculine community, and civic and domestic patriotism—augmented by newfound bonds of national and political identity.[32] In what Simon Schama calls a "revolutionary obsession with oath swearing," thousands of national guardsmen, from the capital to the tiniest rural village in France, made public oaths of fraternity that Martin says "were intended to bind citizens, as brothers and equals, into a relationship of mutual respect and support."[33] To celebrate the first anniversary of Bastille Day, the mayor of Paris, Jean-Sylvain Bailly (1793–1736), proposed a great festival of federation that would unite all citizens as soldiers and brothers. The prospect of a crowd of thousands uniting as brotherly citizen-soldiers was politically threatening to the National Assembly, which rejected this version of the festival in favor of one that featured military fraternity within the army alone. Bishop and politician Charles-Maurice de Talleyrand (1754–1838), who celebrated a Catholic mass at the fête on July 14, 1790, made it clear that "it is France as an army that is going to gather together, not France as a deliberating body."[34]

Journalist and politician Camille Desmoulins's (1760–1794) report of the Fête de la Fédération, retold by Martin, relays that fraternal sentiment was expressed not only in words but also in actions. In his newspaper *Histoire des Révolutions de France et de Brabant*, Desmoulins detailed the preparations and unfolding of the event, which brought together 150,000 delegates at five in the morning in freezing winds and torrential rain. During the course of the oath and festival, Desmoulins reported witnessing soldiers "throwing themselves into one another's arms, making promises to each other of liberty, equality, fraternity."[35] Despite the Assembly's desire to contain the sentiment of fraternity to the *fédérés* themselves, those surrounding them could not help but join in the bonding, bringing different signs of affection and different types of embraces: "On their feet since five o'clock in the morning, the citizen-soldiers were dying of hunger. This became an occasion to show signs of fraternity that have never been seen before: loaves of bread thrown down from windows received on bayonets, cold meats, wine, brandy, etc. Women, young and old, came out of their houses to bring all kinds of refreshments to the *fédérés*. Without fearing incest, these 'sisters' received from their 'brothers' many patriotic embraces that had none of the innocence of fraternal kisses."[36] Through the concept of fraternity, those of *sensibilité*, sociability, and patriotism found a new vocabulary, new actors, and freer expression in the citizenship and soldiery of the early Revolution.

In addition to oaths and festivals like the Fête de la Fédération, bringing greater intimacy and integration into the army was orchestrated through military reforms enacted between 1791 and 1799. Once men were brought together in the army—the one hundred thousand volunteers of 1791 or the three hundred thousand bakers, merchants, clergymen, farmers, and petty bourgeois who enlisted (or were drafted) after the *levée en masse* of autumn 1793—required what Martin refers to as "fraternal integration." As they had in the *ancien régime*, differences in social class, profession, regional identity, and service history (the veteran *blancs* of the Royal Army versus the newly enlisted *bleus*) often ended in tension and intra-army violence. In the case of cavalry and artillery units, most new volunteers were integrated into established units, with some exceptions in which they formed independent squadrons for the former and companies for the latter. This was relatively straightforward, at least from an organizational standpoint. The line infantry posed the larger challenge. Lafayette, commander of the Armée du Nord for a short time, implemented ad hoc brigading, or *embrigadement*, which created a demi-brigade composed of one battalion of veteran line soldiers and two battalions of newly enlisted men. This practice fostered intermixing in the 1791 and 1792 levies, though it also brought forth tensions between the *blancs* and *bleus*.

By 1793 the Convention approved of brigading throughout the French army; however, it delayed broad implementation, such that the *amalgame* became the chosen method of integration. "The *amalgame* was an extension of ad hoc brigading, but it differed in two senses," explains John Lynn. "First, just as in Dubois-Crancé's earlier proposal, the *amalgame* would create permanent demi-brigades of three battalions each. Second, the *amalgame* would thoroughly mix the battalions together. They would be broken down into companies, which would be combined in such a manner so as to produce three entirely new battalions."[37] Dubois-Crancé insisted that the *amalgame* would "generalize the republican spirit" in the army, bringing veterans into close contact with volunteers.

Company- and section-level structures pioneered during the mid-eighteenth century also fostered social bonds and primary group cohesion. Details regarding daily chores and meals shared among men of the same *ordinaire* were directly imported into *règlements* of 1792 from the field service regulation of 1778.[38] Until around 1795, company-level groups of friends, family members, or men from the same town or region who enlisted together were permitted to remain together. This policy fostered bonds that were key to retention, morale, and combat effectiveness, as historical evidence relays. Citizen-soldier Joseph-Louis-Gabriel Noël (1764–1850) wrote of dreary days at camp during the rainy season and commented that "instead of complaining in the tent when it rains, all of us sing together as loud as we can; this makes a noise to drive the clouds away."[39]

Dubois-Crancé's new system of promotion also attempted to institutionalize merit and interpersonal respect through the ranks. One-third of promotions were based on seniority, and the other two-thirds were based on a process of election-selection, that is, men of a given rank would elect three peer candidates for a vacant position, and their superior officers would select one of them to receive the promotion. In theory, this meant that in hopes of advancement, soldiers and officers would be encouraged to display their merit to their peers and cultivate respectful, affectionate "fraternal" bonds with them.

Such bonds were also strengthened by improving living conditions and pay for all and by the Convention's political education and literacy campaign to indoctrinate the military. If previous royal subjects were to become republican citizens and warriors, this meant partaking in the patriotic mythmaking of the time. "The Republic implemented programs designed to transform the army into a 'school of Jacobinism' that taught its students the ideals of the Revolution," elucidates Michael Hughes. "To shape the values of French soldiers, civilian and military officials sent thousands of journals, pamphlets, and songbooks to the army, and organized festivals and other morale-building activities. The government in Paris also dispatched Representatives on Mission to the army who endeavored to develop the troops' devotion to the Revolution's cause."[40] A corollary to imparting this political education was literacy, so in 1794 (decree of 27 Pluviôse II) the Convention ruled that all those to hold the rank of officer or NCO, beginning with corporals, had to know how to read. All of this boosted the military's bonding to the Republic and intramilitary connectedness, since "foot soldiers could now look to their corporals and sergeants to share political news from the press, read their letters from family, and help them write their letters home. This afforded new opportunities for fraternal intimacy and great trust between soldiers."[41]

Martin summarizes: "More than a symbolic slogan for military festivals, *fraternité* thus became the ideological foundation for major policy reforms between 1791 and 1799 that were intended to create more loyal and cohesive fighting units." Thinkers of the Military Enlightenment had already laid extensive foundations for a socio-emotional approach to creating more loyal and cohesive fighting units. They had long before addressed the challenge of bringing men of disparate backgrounds together in the space of the army and advocated for these men to know and care for one another through applying their natural sociability, *sensibilité*, and *humanité*. Decades before the Revolution, these thinkers and practitioners wrote passionately about the importance of social and cultural unity in the forms of primary group cohesion and esprit de corps that fostered emotional resilience, emulation, pride, and, in the hopes of men like Fauville and Saxe, happiness—which in turn led to victory.

The Revolutionary culture of martial respect was not only promoted between military men. The government and the citizenry were to display these sentiments as well. A great outcry ensued when Dubois-Crancé—apparently not always a perfect champion of the soldier—referred to soldiers as "brigands" in a speech that was published in newspapers across France. Soldiers and officers in army regiments like those of Armagnac and Auvergne complained directly to the National Assembly. They decried Dubois-Crancé's slur and his disregard for soldierly honor. Dubois-Crancé responded speedily and apologetically. A clear communication had been made about the extent of soldierly honor. As early as February 1790, Alexandre Lameth had said as much, proclaiming that soldiers of the new order were not only to be given honor and respect by the state and the people, but should recognize their own merit so as to feel honor and respect for themselves. This economy of honor would be evident at all times in the soldiers' behavior, a Revolutionary version of the Enlightenment military hero as patriotic warrior and upstanding person in all arenas of his life: "The Nation will know through [soldiers'] conduct during peace and courage in war that the men honored by the *patrie* also know how to honor themselves."[42] The soldiers and officers who complained to the National Assembly regarding Dubois-Crancé's insult did exactly that.

The soldier's honor—a rising tide during the eighteenth century traced by Corvisier, Lynn, Guinier, Osman, and others—was finally becoming the rule. Members of the armed forces, and particularly the army, were shown as ideal representatives of the nation, an image that the government tried to bolster in reality through political propaganda. The Convention saw the army to be the ideal republic, one toward which the entire nation could aspire. Political and military ideals therefore coalesced in the notion of the citizen-soldier and in the myth of la Grande Nation, the Great Nation. Originally explored in Jacques Godechot's classic study, and later developed by Jean-Yves Guiomar and others, this national model upheld Revolutionary France as "a beacon of enlightenment that would bear liberty and civilization to the oppressed peoples of Europe."[43] This was a clearly imperialist concept of the Revolutionary French nation, inciting and justifying military, political, and cultural conquest in Europe and beyond. Being a member of la Grande Nation meant being a vehicle of a French civilizing mission, which, as Michael Hughes affirms, dovetailed perfectly with the image of a nation of warriors:

> This representation was reinforced by the legend of the nation-in-arms. The Revolutionaries created this legend by making their soldiers into symbols of patriotism that operated as a source of French national identity well into the twentieth century. The military and political culture of the French Revolution claimed that its armed forces were composed of brave young volunteers who left their families to answer the call of the *patrie*, which was threatened by the forces of tyranny. These men selflessly devoted themselves to the Republic and its political ideals, and shared the qualities of the centenary from which they came. As such, the armies formed of these citizen-soldiers truly represented the French nation, and their unique characteristics caused them to fight better than their opponents. According to Revolutionary propaganda, French soldiers, unlike the mercenaries recruited by their enemies, waged war to project their rights and the rights of others.[44]

Poised to fight for their *liberté, fraternité, égalité* and those of other peoples, citizen-soldiers of the French Revolution were imagined to be heroes of the nation and of humankind. La Grande Nation would accomplish the Military Enlightenment's dreams of progress (or so Revolutionary propaganda claimed), and Napoleon built on this narrative.

Reality was, of course, quite different. Militarily extending *liberté, fraternité, égalité* in France and its colonies proved easier in theory than in practice. Not everyone wanted to be a citizen-soldier. The almost limitless tidal wave of enthusiastic volunteers that the military committee, National and Legislative Assemblies, and Convention imagined simply did not exist. After the first levy of national guardsmen in 1791, levies had varying levels of success, especially with increasing awareness of possible unsavory deployments to quell domestic conflict in the Loire and the true risk to life and limb in battle with an ever-growing list of international enemies. Great victories like Valmy (September 20, 1792) and Jemappes (November 6, 1792) could be just as dissuading as they were convincing for individuals facing voluntary (or coerced) enrollment. The practice of purchasing a replacement to fill one's position that had been rampant in the *ancien régime* was still widespread in Revolutionary France.[45] Others sought exemption via marriage or physical ineligibility, ripping out their teeth, which would automatically exclude them from the ranks, since they could not quickly tear open paper cartridges of gunpowder between their teeth with bayoneted musket in hand.

If some did not want to be part of la Grande Nation, others plainly could not be. Successive Revolutionary regimes aimed to make real the citizen army of which Enlightenment intellectuals had dreamed. This meant nationalizing the army such that its ranks were full of French citizens and clinching the connection between military service and citizenship. Women, foreigners, and racial minorities posed a problem in this endeavor. What place could or should these groups play in a nationalized army, especially given the extreme need for manpower created by war? The stakes of allowing these "Others" to serve were high: If they served in the citizen army, were not they, too, citizens? As Revolutionary authorities grappled with these questions, they concocted a series of policies that optimized the manpower of these groups, all the while reducing their political weight and status.

Otherness, Exclusion, and the Coming of War

During the Revolution, the constellation of women, war, and citizenship found its contours in Enlightenment formulations. Women argued for equality in citizenship and access to armed service in a feminine framework of *patriotisme sensible*, like that of Farmain de Rozoi's character Emilie in his play *Décius français*. The National Assembly lauded these militant patriotic declamations and celebrated some of its early *héroïnes républicaines*. However, Revolutionary governments never considered women citizen-soldiers as plausible policy. Instead, they expunged women from the armed forces in an April 1793 decree. On the other hand, within military units, there was far more tolerance of the few women who served and even a championing of their heroism to Revolutionary administrations as officers tried to secure pensions and rewards for their deserving female soldiers. As it had during the Enlightenment, military meritocracy conflicted with the rigidity of policy and the symbolic threat of female service.

Women stepped forward as potential agents of political violence in the initial phase of the Revolution.[46] Women bore arms in the street and marched to Versailles. In 1791–1792, the National Assembly heard and applauded women like Olympe de Gouges (1748–1793), Pauline Léon (1768–1838), and Claire Lacombe (b. 1765), who suggested that women should be allowed to train in military arts on the Champs de Mars and form their own battalions or regiments of "Amazons." Songs about women warriors—some celebratory, some mocking—such as "Departure of the French Amazons for the Frontier" and "The Republican Heroines," circulated, as did pamphlets, broadsides, and petitions. A petition to the National Assembly filed in October 1789 made specific demands about women and feminine culture in the military. Asking to "repair the wrongs of a six-thousand-year injustice," the petition requested specific changes, including the right to "all positions, compensations, and military dignities. In this way the French will be truly invincible, when their courage is inspired by the joint themes of glory and love; we do not even make exception for the baton of a marshal of France; so that justice can be rendered equally, we order this instrument to be passed alternatively between men and women" (Article IX). Article VI requested the annulment of a more subtle and insidious military practice of gendered humiliation: "When a soldier has, out of cowardice, compromised French honor, he will no longer be degraded as is the present custom, by making him wear women's clothing; but as the two sexes are and must be equally honorable in the eyes of humanity, he will henceforth be punished by declaring his gender to be neuter."

While these female petitioners sought to break down gender stereotypes, they strategically embraced certain elements of feminine identity in order to temper what was seen to be the radical nature of their demands. In her address to the National Assembly on March 6, 1792, Pauline Léon reassured the male citizens of the Assembly that women warriors would not forsake their duties in the domestic sphere:

> Yes, Messieurs, it is arms that we need (applause); and we come to ask your permission to procure them. Let not our weakness be an obstacle: courage and intrepidness will rise above it; and love for the *patrie*, the hate of tyrants will make us brave all dangers easily (applause). Do not believe that our plan is to abandon the care of our family and our home, which is always dear to our hearts, in order to run to face the enemy.
>
> No, Messieurs, we want only to be the same as you in defense; you cannot refuse us and society cannot take away this right that nature gave us, unless you pretend that the Declaration of Rights has no application for women.[47]

Natural law, the rights of citizenship, and the traditional female role combined in the female citizen-soldier. Léon's ideal woman warrior was indeed a *patriote sensible* and an "enlightened" perfect hero. She embodied patriotic, militant, emotional, and domestic values at the same time.

Léon was correct in her acknowledgment of a potential blockage to her demands, which would come in the form of the Assembly "[pretending] that the Declaration of Rights had no application for women." While deputies responded by praising Léon and her fellow petitioners for their patriotism, this did not lead to officializing civic rights or military service. Rather they reinstated gender norms and boundaries. The Assembly's president commented that the women's petition should be registered in order to shame men who fled military service, meaning how shameful it was to be less patriotic and militant than a woman. Rather than breaking gender lines, the petition was used reinforced them. Antoine Dehaussy de Robecourt (1755–1828) countered Léon's nature narrative with the traditional patriarchal narrative: instead of nature granting women rights and capacities, nature dictated a strict order by which women were not meant to die in war, nor were their "delicate hands made for handling iron [swords] or for agitating homicidal pikes."[48] The discussion ended when a deputy cried out, "Send it to the Committee of Liquidations!" and the Assembly broke out into prolonged laughter. As Jennifer Heuer shows, Revolutionary oratory, songs, and iconography concerning women's relationship to war took the form of the stoic "Republican mother" or what we have called the maternal *patriote sensible*, like Rozoi's character Emilie. Both figures patriotically sacrificed their sons, husbands, and brothers for the *patrie en danger*.[49]

Disregard for petitions like Léon's did not stop women from joining the army, many still hiding their sex and others fighting openly as women.[50]

Women such as Renée "l'Angevin" Bordereau (1770–1824) fought as royalists in the Vendée. They enlisted alongside brothers and fathers, as was the case with the Fernig sisters Théophile (1775–1819) and Félicité (1770–1841). They went to battle alongside their husbands, as did Alexandrine "Rose" or "Liberté" Barreau (1773–1843). During the early years of Revolutionary warfare, military officers promoted the merit of these women, as their predecessors had done during the Enlightenment. The Fernig sisters were *filles aguerries*, daughters of a captain. They joined up as young teenagers, were trained, and served as officers at the rank of aide-de-camp under General Charles-François Dumouriez (1739–1823). They earned national acclaim as heroines for their courageous feats in combat at Valmy, Jemappes, and other battles. Rose Barreau, who fought disguised as a man and whose martial sobriquet was "Liberté," became a national celebrity after she fought bravely in an engagement against Spanish troops in July 1793, fighting until she had exhausted her ammunition supply and then dragging her wounded husband from the battlefield. Her superior officer hailed her as a republican heroine and worked with commanders to get her recognized by the National Convention. She and her husband were awarded an immediate bonus of 300 livres, she was celebrated in a local assembly, and her story was included in Léonard Bourdon's (1754–1807) propaganda publication, *Recueil des actions héroïques et civiques des républicains français* (History of Heroic and Civic Actions of French Republicans, 1793). Bourdon was sure to highlight Barreau's courageous acts as well as her desire to reinscribe herself in a typical female gender role following her service, quoting her as asking to retire "to go give to my children the care that I owe them as their mother now that I have rendered service to my husband and to my country to the best of my capacity."[51] Heroinism was made possible by women's initiative, followed by military leniency and advocacy, then a careful reinsertion of women into a traditional gendered ideal (figure 13).

Republican military heroines like the Fernig sisters and Barreau were rare, however. Figures of Marianne and Liberty as well as that of the Spartan woman extolled by Revolutionary leaders were only meant to be images that encouraged and justified the actions of men, not signs of political or military agency for women.[52] It was soon clear that women could not be citizens or soldiers, nor could they be workers, supporters, or bystanders at the front. Women on Revolutionary war campaigns were blamed for slowing down the troops— particularly after marriage laws were loosened—consuming precious food and supplies, and taking up space in wagons reserved for army baggage.[53] As a result, on April 30, 1793, Lazare Carnot (1753–1823) and the Convention finally ruled that all "useless" women be expelled and barred from camps and garrisons. Only four women were permitted per battalion as laundresses and

FIGURE 13. Engraving of Alexandrine "Rose" or "Liberté" Barreau (1771–1843) in *Fastes de la nation française et des puissances alliées, ou Tableaux pittoresques gravés . . . accompagnés d'un texte explicatif, et destinés à perpétuer la mémoire des hauts faits militaires, des traits de vertus civiques, ainsi que des exploits des membres de la Légion d'honneur* by Ternisien d'Haudricourt (1807). Courtesy of the Bibliothèque nationale de France.

sutlers. A woman could figuratively represent la Grande Nation, but a citizen-soldier she could not be.

Foreigners and racial minorities also posed a conundrum to the ideal of a national army of citizens, both on the continent and overseas. Chrisopher Tozzi examines the two opposing forces at play in the minds and policies of successive Revolutionary administrations. On the one hand was the desire to establish a strong connection between citizenship and military service so as to make an army of "true" French citizens, which translated to white, French-born men. On the other hand came both the ideology of *liberté, égalité, fraternité* and the pressing need for manpower in the armed forces, especially when levies fell short of numbers needed to sustain the French war effort. Foreign soldiers and racial minorities in France—including freemen and refugees from the colonies—were an important source to draw from in order to fill lacunae in recruitment. They were thought to be especially useful when deployed in dangerous operations in which mortality and casualty rates would likely be high, thus preserving the lives of "real" French citizens. As policies regarding foreign and minority troops took shape, so too did the strategy of forming them into specialized units. This separation allowed the French military to profit from their manpower, all the while downplaying the political significance of their engagement—military service did not mean citizenship—and preserving posts in the line army for French citizens.[54]

By the summer of 1792, the Revolutionary government had created a number of these special corps. They were referred to as "foreign legions" (*légions franches étrangères*), although their ranks contained Frenchmen of different races, including mixed-race aristocratic officers like Joseph Boulogne, chevalier de Saint-Georges (1745–1799), (figure 14) and the "black count," Thomas-Alexandre Dumas (1762–1806).[55] These two men were born of white noble French fathers and African slave mothers in Guadeloupe and Saint-Domingue, respectively, and received an education in France decades before the outbreak of the Revolution. The mixed-race Saint-Dominguan Julien Raimond (1744–1801) advocated for these men in his speeches to the National Assembly in early September 1792. These men were French, he argued, and should be considered citizens with full political rights, including that to muster and serve the Republic in war. The Assembly granted Raimond permission to assemble a unit of black and mixed-race soldiers, which became the Legion of the Americans and the Midi that Saint-Georges commanded with Dumas as one of his lieutenants. By November 7, 1792, the unit had enlisted 400 infantrymen and 150 cavalrymen.[56] The Legion of the Americans was a pathway to participating in the Revolution and allowed men of black and mixed-race origins to attain high-ranking officer positions for the first time in modern European history.[57] Dumas went on to be the highest-ranking officer of African-European mixed-race heritage of all time in any European army. "To be sure, their numbers were small and their existence as legionnaires was brief, but of much greater weight than their military contributions was their symbolic role in reinforcing the association between military service and citizenship for racial minorities," writes Tozzi. "They also set an important precedent for the corps of black soldiers that Napoleon later raised, as well as the tens of thousands of colonial troops who fought in France during the twentieth century."[58]

Despite the symbolic significance of such units, the precedent set by Revolutionary military policy also prefigured future regulations that would keep "foreign" units like the Legion of the Americans on an administrative footing separate from the rest of the army. Bernard Gainot notes that policies for the *légions franches étrangères* pushed "to the margins of the regular army the political question and the military employment" of both foreigners and racial minorities.[59] The exceptional and precarious status of these special units became clear on multiple occasions. The Legion of the Americans was on shaky ground from its inception. Saint-Georges was not allocated sufficient funds for equipment and horses for his troops, nor was he given enough time to train them

FIGURE 14. Portrait of the Chevalier de Saint-Georges (1745–1799) by William Ward (1766–1826) after Mather Brown (1761–1831), dated 1788. Courtesy of the Harris Brisbane Dick Fund, 1953, Metropolitan Museum of Art.

properly before he got notice from Minister of War Jean-Nicolas Pache (1746–1823) that the legion would be deployed to the battlefront. Saint-Georges responded to Pache, asserting that "short of horses, equipment and officers, I cannot lead my men to be slaughtered ... without a chance to teach them to distinguish their left from their right."[60] Shortly thereafter, and as happened to many foreign servicemen, Saint-Georges was denounced to the Committee of Public Safety as a potential royalist and a person to watch. He was cleared of these charges, but before he could make it back to his legion, it had been partially disbanded and was converted into the 13th Cavalry *chasseurs* unit of the regular army.

Members of the unit who remained in the service of the army had a more dubious fate ahead of them. The Ministry of War proposed to collect these soldiers and form a special detachment that would be removed from the European front and dispatched to the Caribbean. As conflict over this matter broke out in the Convention, advocates of black and mixed-race troops raised the specter of returning these men to slavery and claimed that the predicament of these men was "relevant for all true friends of liberty and humanity."[61] These arguments prevailed and thus prevented the Atlantic-bound unit from forming; however, the message was nevertheless clear: racial minorities were men and could fight in the French armed forces, but they were neither "true" citizens nor would they be heroes of the *patrie*.

This realization also had weight in Saint-Domingue, where citizenship, military service, and heroism were tied up in a debate on how and by whom the French Revolution would be rolled out in the colony. Questions of citizenship and race were, as many white colonists feared, intermixed with that of slavery. Propaganda by the Société des amis des noirs and the abbé Henri Jean-Baptiste Grégoire (1750–1831) made this enmeshment apparent and warned that if freedom and rights were not accorded to all inhabitants of the colony, they would be seized forcibly by the figure of a black "New Spartacus" of whom Mercier, Raynal, and Diderot foretold.[62] This was indeed prescient. Vincent Ogé (1755–1791), a wealthy Saint-Dominguan "quadroon" (one-quarter African, three-quarters white) and comrade of Julien Raimond's in the fight for free colored rights, attempted to become the first New Spartacus as he mustered three hundred free people of color to assure their participation in local elections. Ogé's actions led to an initial small-scale slave rebellion in 1790, but the revolt was quelled, and Ogé was brutally assassinated by white colonial authorities.[63] Ogé was a martyr for his class and for mixed-race people, but he was not cast as a hero who died to spread the values of the Revolution. Saint-Domingue's most recognized New Spartacus, François-Dominique Toussaint-Louverture (1743–1803), soon emerged.

In August 1791, the voodoo priest Dutty Boukman (d. 1791) instigated a massive slave uprising that would become the Haitian Revolution.[64] Within weeks, the rebellion had grown to one hundred thousand strong, scorching plantations and killing slave masters. Rebels controlled one-third of the island by 1792, and in 1793 Toussaint became a formidable military and political leader. Toussaint adopted the languages of vengeance, freedom, and equality in his declaration of Camp Turel on August 29, 1793, making himself into a Revolutionary hero on the island. Facing this powerful revolt, on April 4, 1791, the Legislative Assembly granted full citizenship and equality to free people of color, though it did not emancipate slaves. Desperate to control the uprising, secure his authority, and advance his egalitarian and abolitionist ideals, the civil commissioner of Saint-Domingue, Léger-Félicité Sonthonax (1763–1813), created the Legion of Equality and a number of volunteer units open to all citizens regardless of race. In June 1793, he promised freedom to all rebels willing to help him defeat the forces of François-Thomas Galbaud du Fort (1743–1801), who revolted against the commissioner. Then, in August 1793, Sonthonax freed the slaves of the Northern Province. Debates raged in Paris regarding military service by people of color and the racism of colonial armed forces, including the newly formed Legion of Equality. The Convention ratified the abolition act on February 4, 1794, and extended it to the entire French Empire, though it was not applied everywhere.

Establishing political enfranchisement and abolishing slavery were the result of a double motivation. On one side, political discussions in the Convention relay that these achievements were born of ideologies of humanity and racial equality in citizenship and military merit. On the other side, it is clear that enfranchisement and abolition were expedients to control slave and white colonist rebellions, permitting France to maintain control over Saint-Domingue. Toussaint's own destiny verifies this, since he was eventually arrested, shipped off to France, and then imprisoned until the end of his life in 1803. This ambiguity casts a shadow over the fact that freedom and citizenship were accorded to all male inhabitants of the island as one weighs the Revolutionaries' imperial ambition against their commitment to *sensibilité*, humanity, and the democratization of heroism.

Meanwhile, for the National Assembly and for those white French men who could and did join up, the nascent Revolutionary vision combining military fraternity, *sensibilité*, *humanité*, and citizen-soldiers was immediately put to the test. It shook and crumbled on multiple occasions. Samuel Scott has shown that what historians have referred to as *l'année heureuse* or the "year of peace" of 1790 (or the eighteenth months spanning fall 1789 and spring 1791) was far from peaceful outside of the well-policed capital.[65] Indeed, the National Guard and the regular line army quelled and instigated riots, violence, and murder throughout the country. Rivaling claims to political legitimacy flowed forth, as old hostilities from the *ancien régime* erupted anew and fresh antagonisms arose. Citizens did not simply turn into or automatically admire soldiers and national guardsmen, but rather fought against them, and vice versa. Townspeople rose up against local elites; government and law enforcement devolved into deadly mutinies.

Violent unrest broke out in the naval port cities of Toulon and Brest in the summer of 1789. Port workers joined with local petty bourgeois and members of political clubs to revolt against their miserable salaries and working conditions. This spirit soon moved from port to sea as mutinies took place on numerous vessels, from large ships like the *Duguay-Trouin* and the *Patriote* to frigates such as the *Capricieuse*, *Cybèle*, *Fortunée*, and *Neréide*, in addition to smaller ships. In 1790 more than one-third of regular army units experienced insubordination, which Scott characterizes as "unprecedented." Three-quarters of these cases, which ranged from desertion to large-scale mutiny, involved soldiers openly flouting their officers' command. Soldiers of the Royal Vaisseaux and La Couronne infantry units stationed at Lille ignored their commanding officers and engaged in battle against the Normandy Chasseurs and the Colonel-Général Cavalry, who themselves had rebuffed their officers' orders to disengage. Junior officers—one of whom was future Napoleonic marshal Louis Nicolas Davout (1770–1823)—led their soldiers into mutiny against superior officers.

Greater public accountability of regimental monies, as decreed by the National Assembly and the king in early August 1790, led to armed conflict between soldiers and officers suspected of misusing funds. Such was the famed Nancy Affair in which violence broke out between the Châteauvieux Swiss Infantry, the Du Roi Infantry, the Mestre de Camp Général Cavalry, local townspeople and politicos from the Jacobin Club, and national guardsmen who arrived on the scene to control the rioting. Officers were imprisoned and held for ransom; soldiers were beaten with musket straps; and heavy fire and street brawling ensued between Revolutionary soldiers, citizens, and the five-thousand-man force of General François Claude Amour, marquis de Bouillé (1739–1800), sent to suppress hostilities. As a result, scores of soldiers and citizens were sent to prison and sentenced to punishments ranging from death, to being broken on the wheel, to life in the galleys.[66] Fraternity and humane sentiment between members of the citizen army had clearly failed.

Ironically, General Bouillé blamed the Fête de la Fédération for the mutinous spirit and collusion of citizen and soldier witnessed at Nancy. While the National Assembly had hoped to draw distinct lines between soldiers and citizens during the event, the festival occasioned much military-civilian fraternizing. "The effect of this federation was to poison the troops," Bouillé claimed; "soldiers brought back from the capital all the seeds of corruption; they spread them throughout the army and fifteen days or a month later, the entire army was in a state of insurrection."[67] Officers now had to grow accustomed to the kinds of mistreatment that their ancestors—and some of the officers themselves—had long doled out to soldiers: threats, humiliating beatings and stonings, physical mutilation such as blinding, and murder. As their birthright and privileges drained away through successive Revolutionary decrees, officers felt increasingly disrespected, disempowered, and vulnerable. Many left France, as they judged that their status and their Military Enlightenment dreams of sociability, *humanité*, and *sensibilité* in the armed forces were not to be.

With time, it was not only soldiers and officers who doubted or abandoned the ideals of a volunteer citizen army of fraternal compatriots. The state itself soon gave up as well when leaders realized that relying solely on voluntary enlistment left the armed forces far short of the necessary manpower, especially with the outbreak of war in 1792. With the *patrie* in danger, voluntary enrollment gave way to the coercive *levée en masse* in 1793, and finally to conscription under the Directory. What is more, the concept of humanity led to violence, as the category of "enemy of the human race" (*hostis humani generis*) was evoked to justify exterminating internal and international enemies of the Revolution.[68] Ideals of the Military Enlightenment had been toppled, or so it seemed.

Yet, the military transformations of the Revolution, the myth of the Grande Nation, and persisting ideas of Military Enlightenment did not negate one another. Instead, they combined to create an expansive new culture of militarism and imperialism further molded by the hands of a soon-to-be emperor-warrior.

Progeny and Profaner of Military Enlightenment

Napoleon Bonaparte was literally schooled in the Military Enlightenment. After his father furnished proof of four generations of Bonaparte nobility, the nine-year-old Napoleon was enrolled at the École militaire de Brienne in the Champagne region. He studied there for five years and then was one of five in his class who successfully passed the entrance exam to be admitted into the École royale militaire in Paris. He matriculated in October 1784 for a one-year formation as a *cadet gentilhomme*. While his strength in mathematics qualified him for a post in the navy, in November 1785 he was assigned to the artillery regiment of La Fère garrisoned at Valence.

In his youth, Napoleon was a veritable *militaire philosophe*. After his formal education was finished, he continued to pursue military studies of his own accord, reading and writing about artillery and attempting to discern immutable, universal principles of war.[69] He took notes on existing practices and drafted his own list of "Principles of Artillery." He also read and wrote political and cultural histories of his native Corsica, as well as ancient Greece, England, France, Venice, Florence, and other states. In addition to military, social, and natural sciences, Napoleon had strong philosophical and literary sensibilities. He was an avid reader of literature, writing commentary on works by Bernardin de Saint-Pierre and others as well as authoring works such as the "Dialogue on Love." His early notes and writings display his deep engagement with many of the hot philosophical debates of the Enlightenment: on patriotism, glory, suicide, nobility, royal authority, the state of nature, and Rousseau's *Discours sur l'origine et les fondements de l'inégalité parmi les hommes*. Given his intellectual and literary activities, it is no surprise that Napoleon compared his own life to a novel.

Napoleon's formation as a man of the Military Enlightenment is also clear in his understanding of the martial enterprise in human terms, that is to say, his identifying the crucial role played by social, psychological, and physical conditions affecting military men. His ideas of the Grande Nation, heroism, and martial community evince this anthropocentric approach and its roots in Enlightenment and Revolutionary martial cultures. Napoleonic martial culture involved more innovation than invention; it intermingled familiar yet subtly redefined images of military men, the rationale behind martial endeavor, and ultimately, the French nation. Napoleon's successful deployment of this hybrid cultural system played a key part in the move from ideology to action in the form of militarization unprecedented in intensity and scale.

His first step was reframing the notion of the citizen-soldier, giving precedence to the latter and making it a requisite for the former. "During the Revolution, the ideal Frenchman was a devoted citizen of the *patrie* and soldier when needed. Under Napoleon, the citizen-soldier became a soldier citizen," explains Michael Hughes:

> The Napoleonic regime employed its vision of martial masculinity to forge a new kind of man defined by his military attributes, a man who was a soldier first, and who earned the benefits of being a citizen through military service. To accomplish this goal, Napoleon and his supporters mobilized every resource and institution at their disposal to disseminate military values among the population in France. In the arts, education, churches, the press, official awards, and public cele-

brations, the army became a model for society. Napoleonic propaganda portrayed its soldiers as the epitome of French manhood, as hypermasculine heroes whom all French men should strive to emulate.[70]

The enlightened military hero had been prepared to tearfully sacrifice himself and his loved ones for the *patrie*. By contrast, the ideal Revolutionary and Napoleonic citizen had a more monolithic exuberance and burning desire to sacrifice himself for the French nation. Yet, the rationale behind Revolutionary and Napoleonic patriotic martial desire was different. While Revolutionaries had mainly placed emphasis on defensive war to protect the progress of the Revolution and the *patrie en danger*, Napoleon largely forsook this remnant of traditional *jus ad bellum* in favor of open imperialism. Napoleon's soldier-citizens were cast as the martial curators of French honor and were charged with aggrandizing France's status in geopolitics via military conquest. The comparatively subtle crusade for Revolutionary values and liberty was replaced by unabashed imperialism in the name of self-entitled French dominance. The nation as a whole was portrayed as inherently bellicose. The French were defined by their virtue and their hunger for war, honor, and glory; thus the imperial impulse could be justified biologically. Napoleon's "patchwork" patriotism, by which he "combined Revolutionary virtue with the traditional martial values of honor and glory," fostered "a new synthesis that can best be described as Imperial virtue," according to Hughes.[71] Imperial virtue was naturalized as an intrinsic quality of the French and formed the basis of a nationalist program of militarism. The initial phases the program had already been embarked upon during the Revolution; Napoleon expanded this basis exponentially through a multipronged effort.

First, military service was a means of social engineering through which citizens could be made into soldiers who embraced imperial virtue. Napoleon's great wars gave ample opportunity for the armed forces to serve as a mechanism of cultural and political indoctrination of French youth. Second, Napoleon's creation of the knightly order of the Légion d'honneur (Legion of Honor) in 1802 and the incremental reestablishment of ennobling titles between 1804 and 1808 anchored institutions that placed power and recognition in the hands of faithful military servants. Of the newly ennobled, 67.9 percent were soldiers, making them the dominant social category in the Empire's elite. Henri de Carrion-Nizas (1767–1841), one of Napoleon's schoolmates at Brienne who was a member of the Tribunat, made stirring speeches to support founding the Légion d'honneur so as to militarize the nation. "Let us watch over and conserve with care this warrior attitude, this spirit of military honor, in which our true grandeur resides . . . All the arts have their excellence and their beauty, without a doubt; but the arts of honor and victory are the true [arts] of the French people. So nature would have it, Providence even."[72] According to Pierre-Louis Roederer, Napoleon's "director of public spirit," the new nobility and *légionnaires* were also meant to serve as intermediaries "through whom acts of power can be carefully and faithfully conveyed to public opinion and through whom opinion can reach [central] power."[73] Members of these institutions were vehicles of militarism and channels of information back to the emperor.

Third, through festivals, monuments, proclamations, and publications, Napoleon trumpeted a military-based cult of heroism that celebrated *le bon soldat*, the good soldier. *Le bon soldat*, like the enlightened perfect hero, not only performed glorious feats of derring-do but also exhibited patriotism through his willingness to die for France and his acts of kindness toward his compatriots. Théophile-Malo Corret de La Tour d'Auvergne (1743–1800) was one such hero. A veteran of the Royal Army and a recipient of the Croix de Saint-Louis, he became the leader of the "Infernal Column" of grenadiers during the Revolution. He was so dedicated to the Revolutionary cause and to selfless patriotic service that he refused all promotions and led an entire division with the rank of captain. After being imprisoned by the British for two years, he retired in 1795 because he had lost his teeth in captivity. However, La Tour d'Auvergne reenlisted in 1799 for an extraordinary reason: he replaced the recently drafted son of a close friend who would have fallen into destitution had his son gone off to war. The martial, patriotic, and moral characteristics of *le bon soldat* associated with the emperor and his *grognards* were boasted of far and wide. Festivals like that celebrated after the Treaty of Tilsit (1807) promulgated the ideal of heroism and imperial virtue as well as that of the public's gratitude for this service. In this way, the culture of militarism not only spread military values into the populace but at the same time further galvanized the armed forces around Napoleon's heroic self-image.

The imperial virtue of Napoleon's men harkened back to *ancien régime* notions of heroism in other ways. Napoleonic heroism had a highly gendered and sexualized component. It could best be seen not only in the Frenchman's generosity toward fellow citizens and his insatiable belligerence, but also in his sexual appetite. Napoleon's propaganda machine created a vision of French heroism based on the age-old connection between the lust for war and lust for sex. While Revolutionary soldierly masculinity was Spartan and stoic, the Napoleonic counterpart was seductive and lustful, recalling the military identity cultivated by Maurice de Saxe. Napoleonic martial masculinity was also inculcated through methods similar to those deployed by Saxe. Songs and other media that circulated through military units not only propagated this martial ideal but also brought men together as a community that sang of their shared identity, glory, honor, and masculinity. Hughes's analyses of Napoleonic songs reveal the same tropes in military songs and plays of the eighteenth century, like those of Favart. The French military man was a conqueror whose prowess was evidenced on the battlefield and in the bedroom. Both French and foreign women could not but find the French soldier's masculine and moral charms irresistible. This sexual heroism was utilized as a means of motivation, just as it had been in Saxe's army. These songs functioned like Favart's vaudeville provocatively sung by an actress on the eve of Rocoux; they encouraged soldiers and officers to fight for French glory and to win so that they could return and "jouir des fruits de la victoire," *jouir* meaning both "to enjoy" and "to have an orgasm."

If martial masculinity was built by a power differential and an ultimate disrespect for women's bodies and personas, enlightened *sensibilité* and *humanité* combined with Revolutionary *fraternité* and *égalité* to fortify relations between military men. Napoleon viewed these forces of interrelationship as purveyors of moral virtue and martial identity, but also as *sensibilité*- and *sociabilité*-based survival strategies for men facing the adversities of campaign, battle, and military life. Following the discoveries and reform proposals of the eighteenth century, Napoleon's regime institutionalized the notion that, to repeat Martin's phrase, "to serve one's country was to live and die in the care of other men."[74] Napoleonic friendship, in which "shared suffering and success in combat depended on greater trust and intimacy between soldiers in the Grande Armée," was an inheritor of the Military Enlightenment.[75] Deep emotional affection and caring actions to bolster the welfare of one's comrades were encouraged and flamboyantly exhibited by Napoleon himself in his relationships with Marshal Jean Lannes (1769–1809), General Géraud Christophe Duroc (1772–1813), and General Jean-Andoche Junot (1771–1813). According to Martin, the "military marriage of mutual admiration and affection" and the demonstrations of care that this marriage entailed became models of military friendship for the entire army.[76] Their example sanctioned three new modes of intimacy: horizontally between equals at any rank, vertically downward from a superior officer toward those serving under him, and vertically upward from soldiers and lower-ranking officers to their superiors.[77]

Historians have documented Napoleon's extraordinary efforts to cultivate intimate relationships and a feeling of camaraderie—real or imagined—between himself and those who served him, particularly soldiers. In order to be an effective motivational force, this affection and intimacy required proofs in action, which Napoleon furnished on a regular basis. He showed his belief in equality and his respect for his soldiers by not putting himself above them.

He joked with his *grognards*, referred to them by name, and allowed them to address him informally. He wore a simple military uniform and lived through the same hardships that they did, fighting among them on the battlefield, enduring long marches, sleeping in the same camps. He responded to requests from officers and soldiers alike and undertook numerous efforts to fulfill the Military Enlightenment goal of improving the social, psychological, and physical conditions of military service in order to make his men victorious and happy. He guaranteed and improved their pay and supplied better foodstuffs and uniforms. He awarded field promotions by dramatically pinning his own military decorations to men's coats and he cared for veterans' families at his own expense.

The reestablishment of ennoblement and the creation of the Légion d'honneur offered significant merit-based titles and pensions to military men. Prioritizing work ethic and deservedness over social prejudice, he approached his men and framed his authority through merit—he had risen through the ranks by way of talent and hard work, as any soldier (theoretically) could. Napoleon displayed his *sensibilité* by using paternal terms and making countless gestures of affection and goodwill. On occasion, such as in a proclamation to his troops as they marched to meet the Russians in 1805, he went so far as to lay claim to prioritizing the Military Enlightenment's goal of sparing men: "My entire concern will be to obtain victory with the least amount of bloodshed: my soldiers are my children."[78] Brotherly and paternal love waxed sentimental to the point of sounding romantic at times, as in his desperate kisses on the face of the dying Lannes and in declarations to his men. "SOLDIERS," he boomed in an 1806 address to the Grande Armée, "I cannot express the sentiments that I have for you better except to say that I bear the love for you in my heart that you show me every day."[79] As Hughes aptly concludes, "The emperor forged a bond with his *grognards* by touching their imaginations as well as their hearts."[80]

Imperial Expediency and Enlightenment Curtailed

Napoleon's efforts to strengthen his armed forces and to some extent justify his imperialism through sociability, *sensibilité*, and merit had serious repercussions and shortcomings, not the least of which were the brutal conquest and deaths of between five and seven million combatants and civilians. Internal contradictions plagued Napoleon's military cultural system. The Légion d'honneur in its very creation asked for conflicting fidelities from its members, who were obliged to swear upon their honor to dedicate themselves to the

Empire, to the Emperor himself, to the laws of the Republic, to squelching any return to feudalism, and to liberty and equality in general. The Empire was increasingly dictatorial at the expense of republican values. Absolute devotion to the forces of imperial conquest and the related "civilizing" subjugation of peoples could be seen to fly in the face of values such as liberty and equality. What is more, the Légion itself as well as the newly reinstated orders of nobility were clear throwbacks to the feudal past. These types of ideological contradictions were also inherent to the Military Enlightenment, as were practical concerns on subjects such as establishing the limits of esprit de corps. Just as manifestations of esprit de corps and its accompanying sentiment of collective honor had been the fodder for intra-army rivalry during the eighteenth century (before and during the Revolution), a sense of mortal competition attended esprit de corps in Napoleon's military. As the captain Elzéar Blaze has shown, soldiers' and officers' personal memoirs reveal an epidemic of "duellomania" in Napoleonic military men whereby individuals defended the honor of their unit or service branch.[81] Blaze attributes this penchant for dueling to the plethora of corporate identities that had become firmly rooted in the armed forces of the period. Success in the project of sociability and collective identity at the unit level translated directly to interunitary competition and violence. It was an insurmountable challenge to locate the appropriate limits of esprit de corps so that units could reap the benefits of collective identity but not be pulled into deadly rivalry.

The navy did not experience the same satisfaction of victory and glory as the army. After semisuccessful efforts to reconstitute the fleet in year II of the Revolution and before the expedition to Egypt in 1798, the navy experienced a slow decline.[82] It was marred by mediocrely trained men and subpar materials that led to aborted missions and spectacular defeats, like that of Trafalgar (1805). If lower-ranking naval officers of humble social origins were seduced by Napoleon's aggrandizing propaganda, higher-ranking officers remained skeptical of Napoleon and his regime, especially since their experience "was the inverse of the formidable Napoleonic epic" lived by men of the army.[83] Napoleon made some effort to improve naval training, creating two "floating schools" at Brest and Toulon in 1810; however, according to the historian Philippe Masson, the Napoleonic navy was composed of "parade squadrons."[84] What is more, Napoleon made none of the efforts to foster social relations in the navy that he did in the army. Instead, he tried to force maritime effectiveness at the expense of social unity by haphazardly intermixing all seamen: French, those from vassal territories, the merchant marine, the Grand Corps, new recruits, and so on. One officer spoke of the social discord that reigned: "The officers, all of different origins, liked each other very little.

There was no *esprit de corps*. From the most ignorant to the most educated, a kind of complacency, presumption, and most ridiculous pridefulness reigned; subordination was more than compromised . . . I think that it was correct to blame this spirit of insubordination for the lack of unity that marred the battles of our squadrons and that was the principal cause of our maritime disasters."[85]

Sociability, *sensibilité*, and merit were also compromised, and in some cases openly refused, in relation to indigenous peoples, foreign troops, and racial minorities. In this, Napoleon's actions were somewhat paradoxical. On the one hand, they seemed to manifest a cosmopolitanism and *esprit philosophique* passed on from an enlightened age. Napoleon relied on foreign peoples to supply guidance in local terrain and customs, linguistic translation services, and especially military manpower. He restored foreign regiments and reinstated some of the rights that foreign members of the French armed forces had benefited from during the *ancien régime*, including a potentially greater access to French nationality, then defined as "a personal relationship between the ruler and the ruled."[86] In the Egypt campaign, Maltese, Greek, and Coptic legions of volunteers were formed and were later reconfigured in 1802 as the battalion of *chasseurs de l'Orient* comprising Greek, Coptic, Egyptian, and Syrian soldiers who remained in the service of the French army. A squadron of "Mamelukes" composed of Middle Eastern refugees was also formed and served as a part of Napoleon's personal Imperial Guard until 1814. A group of sub-Saharan African troops were enlisted for the Egypt expedition, having been purchased from slave traders. A small number of these African soldiers joined their Mediterranean counterparts as members of the French army.

Napoleon's campaign in Egypt also included a scientific expedition of 167 engineers, mathematicians, naturalists, physicists, chemists, botanists, geologists, and more. The Institut d'Égypte (the Egypt Institute) was founded in 1798 with Napoleon as its vice president. It had forty-eight members organized in four sections: mathematics, physics and natural history, political economy, and the arts. In and outside of the institute, members of the scientific expedition and *militaires philosophes* set up the first printing press in Egypt along with scientific journals like the *Décade égyptien* and the *Courrier égyptien*. They also established libraries, laboratories, bilingual dictionaries, museums, gardens, hospitals, observatories, and archeological digs. It was in fact a French military engineer, Pierre-François Bouchard (1771–1822), who discovered the Rosetta Stone.

Yet these same policies and projects also belied Napoleon's prioritizing of his own power over any enlightened principle. Napoleon made very little effort to establish a "middle ground" with indigenous peoples, marking a break with many *militaires philosophes* of the *ancien régime*. Imperial to the core, he was most interested in asserting, publishing, and growing his own power. His launching of a printing press was not done in the name of cosmopolitan sharing of technology, but rather so that he could advance a publicity campaign to garner the support of—and especially subordination of—the Egyptian people. Skeptics also viewed the scientific work he sponsored as a propagandistic effort aimed to make an appearance of enlightened pursuits overshadow his project of conquest.

Napoleon's imperial intentions and disinterest in a "middle ground" were made abundantly clear in multiple ways. He imposed French municipal structures in Cairo and other cities, published proclamations in shockingly poor Arabic, posed as a liberator of Egyptian peoples, and hypocritically declared the supremacy of Islam and his own adherence to the principles of the Quran. Memoirs written by Louis Antoine Fauvelet de Bourrienne (1769–1834), childhood friend and private secretary to Napoleon during the Egypt expedition, remarked that the emperor's feeble efforts toward gaining any cultural understanding of Egyptians was born of pure political self-interest:

> I confess that Bonaparte frequently conversed with the chiefs of the Mussulman religion on the subject of his conversion; but only for the sake of amusement. The priests of the Koran, who would probably have been delighted to convert us, offered us the most ample concessions. But these conversations were merely started by way of entertainment, and never could have warranted a supposition of their leading to any serious result. If Bonaparte spoke as a Mussulman, it was merely in his character of a military and political chief in a Mussulman country. To do so was essential to his success, to the safety of his army, and, consequently, to his glory. In every country he would have drawn up proclamations and delivered addresses on the same principle. In India he would have been for Ali, at Thibet for the Dalai-lama, and in China for Confucius.[87]

Napoleon's foreign troops were "potent symbols of the emperor's exotic, cosmopolitan ambitions," but they were also viewed through an orientalist perspective and deployed ornamentally.[88] They were objects of xenophobia, handed down from the Revolution. While the *ancien régime* held foreign troops in esteem, neither the Revolutionaries nor Napoleon followed suit. "Imperial commanders almost never celebrated the foreign units as symbols of the state's prestige or diplomatic clout," writes Tozzi, and "most foreign units were dismissed by Napoleonic officials as marginal components of the army that could be useful only when subject to strict supervision by French natives."[89] Frenchmen therefore occupied most officer and NCO positions in foreign units. Their loyalty and true worth in question, foreign troops were put under constant surveillance. By the end of the Empire, they were disarmed and expunged from the army in great numbers.

Napoleon's views on race also became transparent over time. Purchasing slaves to serve as soldiers in the Egypt expedition was both politically and morally ambiguous. It could be seen as a manifestation of egalitarian values and as a policy that fostered manumission. At the same time, it legitimated state participation in slave trading, since the military blatantly rejected French antislavery law. Less ambiguous were Napoleon's declarations and actions regarding Saint-Domingue. In a declaration to the citizens of the island issued on Christmas Day in 1799 (4 Nivôse VIII), Napoleon proclaimed that "the Consuls of the Republic, announcing to you the new social pact, declare to you that the sacred principles of liberty and equality of black people [*noirs*] will never be subject to infringement or modification." However, his motivations became clear in the following paragraph, in which he flattered black Saint-Dominguans and asked for their loyalty before issuing a veiled threat about their freedom and the looming presence of slavery in the Caribbean: "If there are malevolent men in the colony of Saint-Domingue or those who maintain ties with enemy powers, brave Blacks [*braves noirs*], remember that the French people alone recognize your liberty and the equality of your rights."[90]

Shortly thereafter, Napoleon revealed the hypocrisy of his "new social pact" as he considered reinstating slavery on the island. In a well-known debate, admiral and former minister of the navy Laurent Truguet was the most outspoken voice for maintaining abolition on moral and ideological grounds. Napoleon's response was trenchant and directly addressed the question of *humanité*:

> Well, Monsieur Truguet, if you had come to Egypt preaching the liberty of Blacks or Arabs, we would have hung you from a ship's mast. We abandoned all the Whites to the ferocity of the Blacks and we don't even want them to be unhappy about it! Eh! Well, if I had been in Martinique, I would have been for [our sworn enemies] the English, because above all one must save one's life. I am for Whites because I am white; I have no other reason and that is the right one anyway. How could we have accorded liberty to Africans, to men who had no civilization, who had no idea what a colony was or what France was? It is simple that those who wanted liberty of Blacks wanted the enslavement of Whites. What is more, do you think that if the majority of the Convention had known what it was doing and had known the colonies, it would have given liberty to Blacks? Without a doubt, no. But few people were capable of

foreseeing the results and a sentiment of humanity is always powerful on the imagination. But nowadays, [it is ridiculous] to still adhere to such principles!⁹¹

Humanity was a relic of an idealistic and naïve past. Equality itself was also inconceivable, since whichever way one chose to go on the question of abolishing slavery, one of the two races would end up enslaved. The subsequent expeditions of Charles Victor Emmanuel Leclerc (1772–1802) and Donatien-Marie-Joseph de Vimeur, vicomte de Rochambeau (1755–1813) to reestablish slavery and French authority in the colony ultimately failed, but Napoleon had made it obvious that in his eyes, Enlightenment values of *sensibilité* and *humanité* were dead.

Like the limits of equality and merit with regard to race, those concerning gender were utterly clear-cut. A simple male citizen could transform into a hero, but women were not accorded this opportunity. In fact, women were unequivocally excluded and furthermore denigrated by the cult of military masculinity and imperial virtue. Women were shown instead to be weak, emotional, and often unpatriotic, as was the character Julie in the first acts of Rozoi's *Décius français*.⁹² French and foreign women described in Napoleonic songs were like the actresses who entertained Saxe's army: they were to be objects of the military man's affections whether they liked it or not. Hughes shows that rape was intimated in many of these songs, and that in practice the laws relating to rape recorded in the military code of 1803 were not necessarily applied. Military men who committed rape were to be arrested, tried by military tribunals, and punished depending on the nature of the rape (inclusion of an accomplice, the use of "excessive force," or killing the victim) and the victim's identity (whether she was considered a "child," meaning fourteen years old or younger). The names of those charged with rape and the verdict of their trials were to be announced in the orders of the day, yet there is little record of such pronouncements on rape, indicating an unofficial toleration of it as long as it excluded homicide or manslaughter, excessive violence, rape of a minor, or general public disorder.⁹³ The virtuousness of "imperial virtue" was, in this and many other ways, highly dubious.

Following in the footsteps of the Revolutionary armies, Napoleon simply ignored the rules of conduct that had become standard practice during the eighteenth century, especially regarding pillage and devastation; he embraced a "slash and burn philosophy."⁹⁴ Despite official policy that forbade pillaging, Napoleon supported it and encouraged it. He expressed to his brother Joseph Bonaparte (1768–1844), whom he had appointed king of Naples, that "the security of your dominion depends on how you behave in the conquered province. Burn down a dozen places which are not willing to submit themselves. Of course, not until you have first looted them; my soldiers must not be allowed to go away with their hands empty." Napoleon also expressed this directly to his troops in an infamous and oft-quoted speech to the Armée d'Italie that Paddy Griffith has called "one of the most brazen and barefaced incitements to pillage that has ever been issued in the whole history of warfare":

> Soldiers! You are naked and underfed. The government owes you much, but it can give you nothing. Your patience, and the courage you display among these bare rocks, are admirable; but they bring you no glory and shed no brilliance upon you. I want to lead you into the most fertile plains in the world. Rich provinces and great cities will fall under your power: there you will find honor, glory and riches. Soldiers of the 'Italie,' will you fail to show courage or constancy?[95]

This speech was recounted in the *Mémorial de Sainte-Hélène* some twenty-five years after the fact, leaving some doubt as to whether or not Napoleon actually spoke to his men in these terms in 1796. However, the impetus behind these statements and Napoleon's proud retelling of this memory (however faulty) to his biographer Las Casas make them important and representative of his former ideas and practices. "By succumbing to the temptation of pillaging," Tuba Inal states, "the French Army sacrificed its military security, its moral rectitude and revolutionary virtue."[96] What is more, this barbaric violation "set the international standard for pillaging . . . [driving] forward a notable degradation in the professionalism of warfare and the valuation of life."[97] All other European armies, notably the Russians and Prussians on French soil, indeed followed suit. A dynamic of total war was at work, as J. T. Johnson conveys, as "Napoleon utilized the powers of the nation at his disposal to their utmost to carry on war 'without slackening for a moment until the enemy was prostrated.'"[98] Inal appositely concludes that "it was like a 'regress' in a world of 'progress,' from the eighteenth century, when not only ideas about the progress of European civilization became very popular but also practical rules about the conduct of warfare started to take root, to the Revolutionary Wars where human barbarity along with this kind of insecurity returned."[99]

The need to curb such abuses and violations through international law would become the objective of international conferences from the Congress of Vienna (September 1814–June 1815) to the Hague Conferences of 1899 and 1907. The legal scholar John Westlake (1828–1913) wrote that after the Napoleonic Wars, a return to the values of Military Enlightenment occurred.

A "remarkable development of the sentiment of pity," an "enthusiasm for humanity," and a "recognition of human brotherhood" reemerged and informed policies and institutions of armed forces and international law during the nineteenth, twentieth, and twenty-first centuries.[100] Yet devastating violations of humanity also awaited, and perpetual peace remained a far-off dream.

Epilogue
The Modern Heritage

> *An institution or reform movement that is not selfish must originate in the recognition of some evil that is adding to the sum of human suffering, or diminishing the sum of happiness.*
>
> —Clara Barton (1821–1912), founder of the American Red Cross

The French Military Enlightenment died with Antoine-Henri de Jomini (1779–1869); at least, that is the traditional narrative in the history of military thought. Jomini and Napoleon embodied the last believers in reason-based universal principles of war, a perspective that was eclipsed by German—and in particular Clausewitzian—doctrines influenced by turn-of-the-century intellectual movements like romanticism and historicism. The alleged predictability of warfare associated with French neoclassical and Enlightenment *esprit de système* was supplanted by an essential belief in the contingencies and influence of human factors in warfare: troop motivation and morale, battlefield emotions, patriotic sentiments. Technological advancements in armaments such as Perkins's steam gun, the Congreve rocket, and improvements to the musket occurred alongside a shift toward operational as opposed to tactical thinking of the eighteenth century. These developments in military thought, doctrine, and practice brought an end to the French Military Enlightenment.

Yet, like many narratives of rupture, this one was concocted by the successors of the Military Enlightenment who hoped to distinguish themselves from the generations that preceded them. Writers associated with the Counter-Enlightenment and the "German movement" appear as oppositional to those of the French Military Enlightenment only if one accepts a narrow view of the latter as bounded by a focus on "pure reason" and universal principles. The themes examined in this book show a much more comprehensive perspective that disrupts the traditional account. Martial sociability and collective identity; human rights and international humanitarian law; military medicine (physical, psychological) and human emotion in war; patriotism, citizenship, democratizing heroism—these themes of the Military Enlightenment gave shape to modern institutions, practices, and thought on war. They constitute central paradigms of inherited knowledge about military experience with which future *militaires philosophes*, political leaders, and activists have engaged from the late eighteenth century until today in a transhistorical military enlightenment.

Even the work of the most celebrated thinkers of the Counter-Enlightenment and German movement reveal a narrative of continuity despite shifting national contexts.[1] In his *Reflections on the Art of War, Its Progress, Contradictions, and Certainty*, the first volume of which appeared in 1796, the Counter-Enlightenment writer Georg Heinrich von Berenhorst (1733–1814) insisted that immutable laws could not be depended on to understand war. A multiplicity of unpredictable and uncontrollable contingencies related to human emotion, will, and "spirit" was the dominating force. He rejected the notion of soldiers as automatons and viewed them as vibrant human beings capable of patriotic inspiration and fierce courage. These ideas align him more with the French Military Enlightenment than previously acknowledged.[2] Likewise, the work of Gerhard Johann David Scharnhorst (1755–1813), whom Clausewitz called the "father and friend of my spirit," reveals the influence of Maurice de Saxe in his empirical stance, his insistence on accepting the "nature of things," and his claim that an "infinity of circumstances," in this case cultural, political, geographical, and strategic, are at play in warfare.[3]

Clausewitz also carried on the legacy of Enlightenment military thought in certain ways. Clearly a man of his time and place, Clausewitz was influenced as much by his experiences in the Napoleonic Wars as he was by the German intellectual landscape animated by historicism, romanticism, idealism, and other movements. His canonized work *On War* (1832) advanced many developments that were new and different when compared to those of the century before: his theory on the relationship between politics and war, his focus on military engagements, his downplaying of professional knowledge and privileging of personality, his avoiding of ethical questions that he preferred to "leave . . . to the philosophers."[4] However, important continuities with Military Enlightenment thought also pervade his work, including his strong recognition of the contingencies in engagements and the decisive role played by moral forces within the army. The diametric opposition between the Military Enlightenment and the Counter-Enlightenment, the German movement, and "military romanticism" is the result of exaggeration and simplification. The influence of the Military Enlightenment has indeed been pervasive throughout the nineteenth and twentieth centuries and to this day in the French armed forces and beyond. Tracing a few themes evinces this continuous impact. First, contemplations of psychology, emotion, camaraderie, and collective identity in war have remained active and interrelated lines of inquiry. Soon after the demise of the *ancien régime*, Jomini, Clausewitz, and other theorists sought a greater understanding of social factors in combat effectiveness, believing that, as Napoleon asserted, "battles cannot be won by troops possessing no *esprit de corps.*" Later in the nineteenth century, Colonel Charles Ardant du Picq (1821–1870), who fought in the Crimean War and later in Syria, Algeria, and the Franco-Prussian War, drew pointed attention to the psychological effects of combat and the importance of cohesion between soldiers. In his *Études sur le combat: Combat antique et moderne (Battle Studies*, published partially in 1880; complete text published in 1902), Ardant du Picq articulated his belief that human fear and powerful passions, as opposed to discipline or will, were of the greatest consequence to combat effectiveness and that social bonds between servicemen were the key buttresses to soldiers in combat. Echoing the words of the chevalier de Montaut, he wrote that "The habit of living together, obeying the same leaders, commanding the same men, sharing fatigue and privations" fosters "fraternity, union, professionalism, palpable emotions, in a word, an intelligent solidarity."[5]

Ardant du Picq was seemingly inspired in this conviction by the work of Louis-Jules Trochu (1815–1896), who was an aide-de-camp to Ardant du Picq's mentor, Maréchal Thomas Robert Bugeaud (1784–1849). Trochu also emphasized the centrality of psychological aspects of warfare in his enormously successful *L'armée française en 1867*, which saw ten editions printed in a few months and amounted to twenty in 1870. Echoing Saxe, Trochu asserted that knowledge of human beings and emotions formed the foundations of military command: "I understand this generalized experience in the practice of commanding during peacetime and war to have its origins in the study of the human soul [*l'âme humain*] and the passions which are particular to armed masses in the many diverse situations, often violent and forced, where one must conduct and command them."[6]

Continued reflections on the human soul and moral support in war led later *militaires philosophes* to again consider the primacy of affection and caregiving among men of the military. In his work *Le rôle social de l'officier* (*The Social Role of the Officer*, 1891), Marshal Louis Hubert Lyautey (1854–1934) championed "affectionate leadership." He believed, as eighteenth-century thinkers did before him, that commanders had to gain the confidence, love, and respect of their men by showing them these same sentiments. Such sentiments could be expressed by observing and acknowledging the abilities of individual men, working with them closely, and addressing their needs. Lyautey thus advocated not only for a lateral affection between servicemen of the same rank, but also for a highly personalized form of vertical affection that spanned the military hierarchy. Lyautey, too, echoed words that Maurice de Saxe had written more than 150 years before him in his insistence that officers must build not only "military intelligence" but also "military heart."

With figures like Trochu, Ardant du Picq, and Lyautey as intermediaries, the modern conception of the "band of brothers" in a military unit is a direct descendant of Military Enlightenment explorations of martial sociability and emotion. Yet today, as in the eighteenth century, the diversity of the French military raises challenges to such solidarity. While official policy regarding homosexuality in the ranks is that of tolerance, commanders and psychiatrists reserve the right to discharge homosexual individuals whom they deem disruptive or socially alienated.[7] France also has the highest percentage of women in the military of any country in Europe. Women represent 15 percent of the combined armed forces; however, the Ministry of Defense has acknowledged that strong efforts are necessary to eliminate discrimination, harassment, and sexual assault.[8] While the "Don't ask, don't tell" and the combat exclusion policies in the United States were repealed in 2011 and 2013, respectively, discrimination, harassment, and assault remain pervasive.[9] The French and American militaries, as well as others around the world, must continue to contemplate on what premises and on what omissions military participation and solidarity are based, recognizing normative cultural forces and instituting preventive and punitive measures.

Turning to a second set of interconnected themes of the Military Enlightenment, service in the armed forces, citizenship, and heroism have remained tightly interwoven and highly conflictual in what Gary Wilder terms the "French imperial nation-state."[10] In 1996 President Jacques Chirac announced his intention to end peacetime military conscription, replacing it with the Journée d'appel de préparation à la défense (JAPD, Call to Prepare for Defense Day). In 2001 he terminated compulsory military service altogether, officially ending the policy of creating citizen-soldiers. Nevertheless, military service has been an enduring vehicle of expanding the French citizenry—at least in theory. This is evident in military institutions such as the Légion étrangère, or Foreign Legion. Commanded by French officers, the Légion was originally established by King of the French Louis-Philippe (1773–1850) in 1831 and was composed of members of the Royal Army's disbanded foreign regiments. The law creating the Légion stipulated that these foreign soldiers of Swiss, Polish, German, Italian, Spanish, and other origins could not serve on French soil, so the unit was first deployed to enforce French rule in newly conquered Algeria. The Légion fought in France's wars of colonization and decolonization around the globe, from Mexico to Vietnam to Africa, and saw combat in the world wars, the Persian Gulf, and the war on terror. In recognition of and recompense for their service, the French government established a path for members of the unit to acquire French citizenship. Légionnaires qualified to apply for naturalization after three years of service and, as of a 1999 provision, can apply immediately following injury, becoming *français par le sang versé*, French by bloodshed.

The Légion étrangère cannot be branded a mechanism of inclusiveness, however. It was also a means of exclusion and stigma compared to regular army units. Foreign nationals who had not acquired citizenship, even those who had spent most of their lives in France, could enlist only in the Légion. They could not serve in regular units, which were reserved for "real" Frenchmen, predominantly white male French-born citizens. While these foreign nationals considered France their home, they were forced to serve as foreigners until their service won them naturalization. Many never succeeded in becoming citizens or did so only after extraordinary effort. The distinction between "real French" and "non-French" played no small part in the Dreyfus Affair (1894–1906), in which anti-Semitism and xenophobia against a French citizen formed a perfect storm surrounding the young artillery captain, Alfred Dreyfus (1859–1935). At a broader level, this distinction continues to plague France and its first-, second-, and third-generation immigrants; it has played a role in radicalizing disaffected youth and made France a target of numerous terrorist attacks in 2015, 2016, and 2017.

Historians have increasingly probed these complexities surrounding race, nationality, and military service in units other than the Légion étrangère, such as the Army of Africa and colonial troops deployed throughout the empire and in the metropole.[11] In his study of the latter in World War I, Richard Fogarty examines how colonial power dynamics and racial stereotyping followed colonial troops who came to serve in France. Dark-skinned Africans from below the Sahara were viewed as brutal savages (making them excellent fighters), while Indochinese were viewed as meek and physically weak, thus less suited for war. Fogarty describes how these stereotypes were sometimes applied with good intentions by French military officers and government officials who attempted to be culturally aware and sensitive as they made distinctions about the groups that composed the colonial forces. Upon observing North African troops stationed in Aix-en-Provence and Arles, one officer noticed the tensions between troops from the three countries of the Maghreb and interpreted these tensions through the lens of an old adage in Arabic that

"Moroccans are warriors, Algerians [are] men, and Tunisians [are] women." "To some extent, the French absorbed these attitudes from the images they believed North Africans had of themselves," comments Fogarty. However, attributing racist and sexist statements to indigenous cultural judgments was a convenient justification, and Fogarty warns that these "classifications corresponded neatly with French perceptions during the war."[12]

During this same war, however, France was the only European power to bring colonial soldiers to fight in Europe and also trained and deployed African American units for combat, which the U.S. Army had not done, preferring to assign them to labor battalions. The regiments of the 92nd Division (the "Buffalo Soldiers Division") and the 93rd Division (the "Blue Helmets," of which the 369th Infantry, the celebrated "Harlem Hellfighters," was a part) fought valiantly against the Germans and were duly recognized by the French military and government. The 369th was awarded a Croix de Guerre for taking Sechault (1918), and two of its members, Privates Henry Johnson (1892–1929) and Needham Roberts (1901–1949), were the first Americans to win individual Croix de Guerre. They became international heroes whose story of bravery in staving off a German unit that attacked them at an isolated outpost on the western front was recounted in newspapers. One hundred and seventy-one members of the 369th received individual medals. At the Bastille Day parade in Paris on July 14, 1919, detachments from units of *troupes indigènes* as well as of all of France's allies in World War I were invited to march behind Foch, Joffre, and Pétain in the victory parade on the Champs-Élysées. In 1971 female personnel were included in the parade, and they can now serve in all posts (including combat infantry), save serving on submarines and in riot-control gendarmeries. Fulfilling the unfulfilled dreams of the Military Enlightenment, twentieth-century French ideals of heroism could be meritocratic and egalitarian.

Yet this egalitarianism in heroism and in rewarding foreign and racial "Others" for their service to France was fraught, to say the least. In 2009 the BBC's *Document* program unearthed papers from World War II attesting to the fact that "black colonial soldiers—who made up around two-thirds of Free French forces—were deliberately removed from the unit that led the Allied advance into the French capital," which was freed on August 25, 1944. De Gaulle clearly stated that he wanted French units to lead the charge in liberating Paris. Allied High Command agreed, but on the condition that the units be all-white, initiating a debate on what units could most easily be purged of all nonwhite members.[13] Since the nineteenth century, fiery debates have surrounded the liberal republican promise—and, according to some, obligation—to bestow citizenship on *troupes indigènes* who had served the French nation.

Opponents to the recompense of naturalization worried that individuals from indigenous units would never be "French" enough and ultimately could not be assimilated into French mores and civilization in satisfactory measure (itself a problematic proposition). "In the final analysis," writes Fogarty, "French assimilationist principles often gave way before what many regarded as insoluble racial, cultural, and religious differences," which resulted in "limited access to naturalization in the colonies after the war" and the stunting of any "transforming colonial subjects into French citizens."[14]

Rachid Bouchareb's film *Indigènes* (*Days of Glory*, 2006) and Gregory Mann's work *Native Sons* both brought broader awareness to the fact that North and West African veterans of the French armed forces had their pensions frozen at their 1959 rate, receiving €61 a month compared to €690 a month for metropolitan veterans as of 2006. The French government declared this institutionalized discrimination illegal in 2001, but failed to remediate the situation until 2010. As the twenty-first century progresses and the country's diversity continues to develop while old symbols and prejudices persist, France must confront questions asked since the eighteenth century: Who can join and represent the imagined community of the nation, and what is the place of military service in ideal French citizenship?

Sensibilité and humanity, also themes of the Military Enlightenment, have been motivators for change in the domains of the armed forces and international law. In his 1864 work *International Charity on the Battlefield*, Henri Dunant (1828–1910) directly linked the creation of the Red Cross and the Geneva Conventions to cultures of sentiment and humanity as well as to the cartels struck between eighteenth-century generals at battles like Dettingen. The preambles to the Second (1899) and Fourth (1907) Hague Conventions, which aimed to codify new regulations regarding international humanitarian law, both referenced universal "laws of humanity" now referred to as the Martens Clause. The Military Enlightenment origins of the clause are unmistakable, as it established human values and conscience as the basic standard to which individuals and nations were to adhere:

> Until a more complete code of the laws of war is issued, the High Contracting Parties think it right to declare that in cases not included in the Regulations adopted by them, populations and belligerents remain under the protection and empire of the principles of international law, as they result from the usages established between civilized nations, from the laws of humanity and the requirements of the public conscience.
> —Convention with Respect to the Laws of War on Land (Hague II), July 29, 1899

Until a more complete code of the laws of war has been issued, the High Contracting Parties deem it expedient to declare that, in cases not included in the Regulations adopted by them, the inhabitants and the belligerents remain under the protection and the rule of the principles of the law of nations, as they result from the usages established among civilized peoples, from the laws of humanity, and the dictates of the public conscience. —Laws and Customs of War on Land (Hague IV), October 18, 1907

Citizens were to be spared, prisoners of war were not to be mistreated, and the Red Cross was to be permitted to operate as a neutral humanitarian organization. The focus on humanity in war would form the foundation for defining the categories of war crimes, especially crimes against humanity, whose first accusation was articulated in a joint statement of the Allied Powers against Turkey in 1915 regarding the Armenian genocide. It was not until the Nuremburg Trials after World War II, however, that crimes against humanity were defined as "murder, extermination, enslavement, deportation, and other inhumane acts committed against any civilian population, before or during the war, or persecutions on political, racial or religious grounds in execution of or in connection with any crime within the jurisdiction of the Tribunal, whether or not in violation of the domestic law of the country where perpetrated." The gentlemanly cartels and moral tenets of the Military Enlightenment constituted the first generation in this genealogy.

Humanité and sensibilité also framed the birth and development of military psychology. Physicians diagnosed nostalgia in colonial warriors of the nineteenth century, shell shock in those of World War I, and post-traumatic stress disorder (PTSD) in warriors of our own time.[15] Also following the Military Enlightenment's model, soldiers were not viewed as replaceable pawns in a war game of masses. Rather, they were seen as individual people and citizens whose lives and battle experiences were significant. Hervé Drévillon shows several manifestations of this turn toward the individual, including developments in military medicine and surgery and the greater attention brought to calculations of deaths and casualties.[16] He also points to mid- and late nineteenth-century debates surrounding necessary and unnecessary wars and the role played by technology and tactics in defining soldiers as numbers in a nameless mass or individuals whose lot should be of official concern.[17] The decree of May 28, 1895—the infamous doctrine of *offensive à outrance* or "all-out attack"—sharpened these questions. The rationale for this offensive tactic was that a violent and liberating charge was the only way to confront the new reality of battle in which soldiers could no longer see where gunfire was coming from.[18] The consequences of this belief, which drew a direct historical line from Napoleon to Clausewitz to the *offensive à outrance* and was naïvely cast as the victory of humanity over technology—would soon be reckoned with when France tallied its horrific number of casualties and deaths in World War I.

Humanity in war has come under criticism since the turn of the twenty-first century. Noam Chomsky condemned what he called the "new military humanism," by which humanitarianism was evoked as a justification for U.S. and NATO involvement in Kosovo in 1999. According to Chomsky, the banner of "humanism" hid the true economic and political objective, which was to confirm the economic and military hegemony of Western democratic superpowers. Chomsky argues that the paralegal status of eighteenth-century humanitarian cartels and conventions set the precedent for the new military humanism of the late twentieth century, privileging moral imperative over international law. Chomsky's reproach of humanitarian interventionism was wrong in that, as a United Nations–administered Supreme Court acknowledged, crimes against humanity and violations of the laws of war were indeed committed in Kosovo, therefore legitimizing U.S. and NATO intervention. However, Chomsky's view on the dangers of the rhetoric of humanity in relation to the rule of law raises categorical problems that continue to plague international laws of war. Analyzing the juridical concept of *hostis humani generis* (enemy of the human race), Dan Edelstein illustrates that it set up the framework for "totalitarian justice" as exemplified by the Terror of the French Revolution and later the Soviet and Nazi regimes. This form of justice involved "the coexistence of two parallel justice systems," one for ordinary crimes and one for "inhuman" individuals, groups, and crimes that were considered *hors-loi* (outside of the law).[19] Being an enemy of humanity meant being outside of the law, which allowed totalitarian regimes to strip individuals and groups of the protections furnished by legal or natural rights.

Wars on terrorism in the post-9/11 era have amplified the difficulty and dangers of categorizing individuals in order to apply the international laws of war. Regarding the Geneva Conventions, terrorists represent a gray area, since they can be construed as "unlawful combatants." This denies them formal prisoner of war status when detained. As such, terrorist detainees are deprived of the third convention, pertaining to the proper treatment of prisoners of war, which has opened the door to objectionable interrogations and treatment, even torture. Egregious government-sponsored violations of human rights ensued, such as the U.S. Army and Central Intelligence Agency's use of waterboarding (which the United Nations categorized as torture, but the United States did not) and multiple violations of detainees in the Abu Ghraib prison in Iraq, including murder, torture, physical and sexual abuses, and rape. What is more, war tactics in conflicts around the world—Syria, Yemen, Iraq, Afghanistan, Mali, the Ivory Coast—have included numerous violations of the Geneva Conventions as well as crimes against humanity. Bombarding hospitals, sexually assaulting civilians, summarily executing detainees, and using chemical warfare are tactics in circulation that defy the laws of war. This defiance itself is a cornerstone of modern terrorism. "It adds up," says International Committee of the Red Cross (ICRC) president Peter Maurer, "to a long list of disrespect which is of course shattering the system as a whole of the Geneva Conventions."[20]

Efforts to protect civilians and spare the lives of combatants are well intentioned, but have opened up new ambiguities and, in some instances, backfired completely. Distinguishing between citizens and militants in circumstances of total war, guerrilla war, and resistance to occupying forces was a critical subject of debate in international legal discussions of war during the twentieth century. More recently, the doctrine of surgical warfare and the use of unmanned combat aerial vehicles (UCAVs), commonly referred to as drones, are primary examples. Against the backdrop of atomic warfare as experienced in World War II, surgical tactics allegedly aim to better deliver on the demands of the Geneva Conventions to limit civilian casualties, not to mention environmental ones. Better identification of targets and speedy, decisive "surgical" strikes should translate to fewer civilian lives at risk and less physical and mental trauma from "boots on the ground" battle. Opponents of drone warfare dismiss it as "neither cheap, nor surgical, nor decisive."[21] Hospitals, schools, and civilian locales have been accidental targets, and significant issues of accountability have arisen. Who is at fault when there is no "man in the loop" to deploy the weapon, or when this individual is a civilian rather than a member of the military, or when the thousands of miles between the "man in the loop" and the target prevent him or her from properly distinguishing conditions surrounding the target? What is more, instead of sparing members of the military from mental anguish, the stress of this role has been tracked in the rising rate of psychological trauma and PTSD in UCAV operators.[22] More "advanced" autonomous weapon systems that remove the "man in the loop" and function on artificial intelligence alone were condemned in an open letter that as of March 18, 2017 has 3,105 AI/Robotics Researcher signatories and 17,701 other endorsers, including Nobel laureates Stephen Hawking and Frank Wilczek.[23]

Thinkers of the Military Enlightenment believed that war was, as Voltaire put it, "an inevitable scourge" of human civilization. With this in mind, participants embraced a two-part objective: first, to find ways to wage war effectively and efficiently in order achieve martial goals while sparing costs and precious resources, especially manpower; and second, to wage war humanely and in a fashion that reflected the rationality, compassion, morality, and dignity of the human race. Did the French armed forces achieve this objective? During the eighteenth century, as today, the answer is yes and no. War was and continues to be extremely costly in financial, political, and human terms, and military effectiveness is determined by "an infinity of circumstances that human prudence could never predict," as Saxe put it hundreds of years ago. Waging war more humanely was and continues to be a struggle, from defining what humane treatment entails and who deserves it, to facing warring parties whose tactics purposefully violate human rights.

Yet the debates and practices of the Military Enlightenment led to a more profound understanding of war and of social, psychological, and political elements that affect military experience. And, however embattled, the laws of war create near miracles every day by setting up parameters for conduct and providing numerous forms of humanitarian aid: reuniting family members scattered by armed conflict; administering medical treatment; and furnishing food, water, shelter, and clothing. Helen Durham, director of international law and policy at the ICRC, has said that she "wonder[s] at the hubris of a legal framework that attempts to reduce suffering during times of armed conflict," a hubris, optimism, or naivety that participants in the Military Enlightenment also exhibited. However, as Dunham insists, despite the law being a "clumsy tool for change" that "does not revolutionize human behavior," the laws of war "are more than an aspirational framework for our better hearts, they actually do work."[24] The Military Enlightenment tells us that these laws are necessary, but that only the empathy and behavior of individuals, combatants and civilians alike, can complete the important mission of setting limits on the devastations of war. Until the time that Kant's and the abbé de Saint-Pierre's dream of perpetual peace can be realized, this must remain among the most important and noble goals for human civilization.

Notes

Introduction

1. René-Louis de Voyer de Paulmy d'Argenson, *Mémoires du marquis d'Argenson, ministre sous Louis XV* (Paris: Baudin Frères libraires, 1825), 21–22. All translations are the author's own unless otherwise noted.

2. The notion of military enlightenment itself was long ago pioneered and developed by John Lynn and Azar Gat; however, their work has still not been sufficiently integrated into broader histories of the Enlightenment. See John Lynn, *Battle: A History of Combat and Culture from Ancient Greece to Modern America* (Cambridge, MA: Westview Press, 2003), and Azar Gat, *A History of Military Thought from the Enlightenment to the Cold War* (Oxford: Oxford University Press, 2001). See also Armstrong Starkey, *War in the Age of Enlightenment, 1700–1789* (Westport, CT: Praeger, 2003), and Christopher Duffy, *The Military Experience in the Age of Reason* (London: Routledge, 1987).

3. Julie C. Hayes offers a useful distinction between historical and philosophical accounts of the Enlightenment in "Fictions of Enlightenment: Sontag, Süskind, Norfolk, Kurtzweil" in *Questioning History: The Postmodern Turn to the Eighteenth Century*, ed. Greg Clingham (Lewisburg: Bucknell University Press, 1998). Philosophically, the Enlightenment as intellectual movement has been associated with a normative set of ideals including secular liberalism, civic humanism, and rational scientific or philosophical inquiry (*esprit philosophique*) in the name of human progress and happiness. Yet a general application of these tenets, or an account of the Enlightenment as a unified philosophy, phenomenon, or project, has largely been deemed untenable. Instead, many scholars contend that a multiplicity of "Enlightenments" unfolded during the long eighteenth century: French, Scottish, Catholic, Protestant, Newtonian, Cartesian, Atlantic, Mediterranean, and so on. Classical studies such as those of Ernst Cassirer (*The Philosophy of the Enlightenment*, 1932) and Peter Gay (*The Enlightenment: An Interpretation: The Rise of Modern Paganism* and *The Science of Freedom* of the 1960s) have been supplanted by postmodern approaches born of the cultural and linguistic "turns" in scholarly methodology. A recent exception is Dan Edelstein, *The Enlightenment: A Genealogy* (Chicago: University of Chicago Press, 2010) that rehabilitates Peter Gay's analysis and argues for a unitary perspective of the Enlightenment's definition and French origins. The strong push against such unitary accounts of the Enlightenment is evident in the criticisms of Jonathan Israel's multivolume history. See his *Radical Enlightenment: Philosophy and the Making of Modernity, 1650–1750* (Oxford: Oxford University Press, 2002), *Enlightenment Contested: Philosophy, Modernity, and the Emancipation of Man, 1670–1752* (Oxford: Oxford University Press, 2009), and *Democratic Enlightenment:*

Philosophy, Revolution, and Human Rights, 1750–1790 (Oxford: Oxford University Press, 2013). For critiques of Israel's approach and an ideological definition of the Enlightenment, see "Democratic Enlightenment," special issue, *H-France Forum* 9, no. 1 (Winter 2013). The classic statement of the notion of multiple "Enlightenments" is expounded in *The Enlightenment in National Context*, ed. Roy Porter and Mikuláš Teich (Cambridge: Cambridge University Press, 1981). This diversity grounds J. G. A. Pocock's argument that scholars should drop the definite article that precedes "Enlightenment," since no single, unitary entity or process can be identified. J. G. A. Pocock, "Historiography and Enlightenment: A View of Their History," *Modern Intellectual History* 5 (2008): 83–96. Also on Enlightenment and history, see Daniel Brewer, *The Enlightenment Past: Reconstructing Eighteenth-Century French Thought* (Cambridge: Cambridge University Press, 2008). For synopses on the historiography of the Enlightenment, see James Schmidt, "Enlightenment as Concept and Context," *Journal of the History of Ideas* 75, no. 4 (2014): 677–85; and Schmidt, "What Is Enlightenment?," chap. 1 in Dorinda Outram, *The Enlightenment* (Cambridge: Cambridge University Press, 2013).

4. For more on this argument, see Edelstein, *The Enlightenment*, 21, 28.

5. Edelstein, *The Enlightenment*, 2.

6. *This Is Enlightenment*, ed. Clifford Siskin and William Warner (Chicago: University of Chicago Press, 2010), 12–18.

7. Outram, *The Enlightenment*, 3.

8. Madeleine Dobie, "The Enlightenment at War," *PMLA* 124, no. 5 (October 2009): 1851–54.

9. The role of defending the kingdom defined the noble Second Estate as "ceux qui combattent" (those who battle) in the feudal society of orders of the *ancien régime*. First Estate was composed of men of the church ("ceux qui prient," those who pray) and the Third Estate contained all of the working classes ("ceux qui travaillent," those who work) in the French population.

10. See Daniel Brewer, ed., *The Cambridge Companion to the French Enlightenment* (Cambridge: Cambridge University Press, 2014), and its advertising blurb.

11. See Christian Ayne Crouch, *Nobility Lost: French and Canadian Martial Cultures, Indians, and the End of New France* (Ithaca, NY: Cornell University Press, 2014); Julia Osman, *Citizen Soldiers and the Key to the Bastille* (New York: Palgrave, 2015); Hervé Drévillon, *L'individu et la guerre: Du chevalier Bayard au Soldat inconnu* (Paris: Éditions Belin, 2013); Arnaud Guinier, *L'honneur du soldat: Éthique martiale et discipline guerrière dans la France des Lumières, 1748–1789* (Ceyzérieu: Champ Vallon, 2014); Louis Tuetey, *Les officiers sous l'ancien régime; nobles et roturiers* (Paris: Plon, Nourrit et Cie, 1908); André Corvisier, *L'armée française à la fin du XVIIème siècle au ministère de Choiseul: Le soldat*, 2 vols. (Paris: Presses Universitaires de France, 1964); Emile G. Léonard, *L'armée et ses problèmes au XVIIIème siècle* (Paris: Pion, 1958); Jean Chagniot, *Paris et l'armée au XVIIIe siècle* (Paris: Economica, 1985); Michel Foucault, *Discipline and Punish: The Birth of the Prison* (New York: Vintage Books, 1977); and Naoko Seriu, "The Paradoxical Masculinity of French Soldiers: Representing the Soldier's Body in the Age of the Enlightenment," EUI Working Paper, Max Weber Programme (Florence: European University Institute, 2009).

12. Nonmilitary *philosophes* and military reformers—martial intellectuals or *militaires philosophes*—undertook what would later be understood as the Kantian enterprise of releasing the military domain from its "self-incurred tutelage." They imagined "enlightening" the martial enterprise, bringing metaphorical light and critical reflec-

tion where darkness and ignorance had reigned. The metaphor of light recurs incessantly in the writings of military thinkers of the period. See, for example, Maurice de Saxe's *Mes rêveries suivies d'un choix de correspondance politique, militaire et privée* (Paris: Commission française d'histoire militaire / Institut de stratégie comparée / Economica, 2002), 89–90.

13. On the culture of war, see David A. Bell, *The First Total War: Napoleon's Europe and the Birth of War as We Know It* (Boston: Houghton Mifflin, 2007), 11–17.

14. Article "War" in Voltaire's *A Philosophical Dictionary*, derived from *The Works of Voltaire: A Contemporary Version*, trans. William F. Fleming, 21 vols. (New York: E. R. DuMont, 1901) and hosted in an ebook by the University of Adelaide, Australia. https://ebooks.adelaide.edu.au/v/voltaire/dictionary/chapter475.html, accessed March 23, 2017.

15. Edna Hindi Lemay, "La guerre dans la vision ethnographique du monde au XVIIIe siècle," in *La bataille, l'armée, la gloire 1745–1871: Actes du colloque international de Clermont-Ferrand*, vol. 1, ed. Paul Viallaneix and Jean Ehrard (Clermont-Ferrand: Association des publications de la Faculté des lettres et sciences humaines de Clermont-Ferrand, 1985), 109–18.

16. Cited in Hamish Scott, "The Fiscal-Military State and International Rivalry during the Long Eighteenth Century," in *The Fiscal-Military State in Eighteenth-Century Europe: Essays in Honour of P. G. M. Dickson*, ed. Christopher Storrs (Farnham, UK: Ashgate, 2009), 47. Scott cautions against overstating the importance of colonial possessions in the political calculations of eighteenth-century monarchs. See also Daniel Baugh, "Withdrawing from Europe: Anglo-French Maritime Geopolitics," *International History Review* 20 (1998): 1–32.

17. See James Q. Whitman, *The Verdict of Battle: The Law of Victory and the Making of Modern War* (Cambridge, MA: Harvard University Press, 2012), 17.

18. See ibid., 10.

19. Scott, "The Fiscal-Military State," 29–30.

20. While there were no pan-European wars between 1714 and 1741 or between 1763 and 1792, there were major bilateral conflicts during these "peaceful" periods.

21. Joël Félix and Frank Tallett, "The French Experience, 1661–1815," in Storrs, *The Fiscal-Military State*, 151. For a discussion of this subject in a later eighteenth-century context, see Jeremy J. Whiteman, *Reform Revolution and French Global Policy: 1787–1791* (Aldershot, UK: Ashgate, 2002).

22. On *gloire*, see John Lynn, *The Wars of Louis XIV, 1667–1714* (London: Routledge, 1999), and in a broader history, Robert Morrissey, *Napoléon et l'héritage de la gloire* (Paris: Presses Universitaires de la France, 2010).

23. Scott, "The Fiscal-Military State," 29.

24. These figures represent wartime troop numbers adjusted down from theoretical strength following the "douze pour vingt" rule, meaning that one had to recruit twenty men in order to put twelve into the field. For a discussion of historiographical debates on the French army in war and peacetime between the Wars of Religion and the War of Spanish Succession, see John A. Lynn, "Revisiting the Great Fact of War and Bourbon Absolutism: The Growth of the French Army during the Grand Siècle," in *Guerra y sociedad en la monarquía hispanica: Política, estrategia y cultura en la Europa moderna (1500–1700)*, ed. Enrique Garcia Hernán and Davide Maffi, vol. 1 (Madrid: CSIC, Laberinto, Fundación Mapfre, 2006), 49–74.

25. Félix and Tallett, "The French Experience," 154–55. For perspectives on French naval expansion and contraction during the reign of Louis XIV, see Benjamin Darnell, "Naval Policy in an Age of Fiscal Overextension" in *The Third Reign of Louis XIV, C. 1682–1715*, ed. Julia Prest and Guy Rowlands (Abingdon: Routledge, 2016), 68–81.

26. Guillaume Le Blond, "Guerre," in *Encyclopédie, ou Dictionnaire raisonné des sciences, des arts et des métiers*, ed. Jean le Rond d'Alembert and Denis Diderot, 7:985.

27. The history of just war theory dates from the eighth or ninth century BCE to today. See ongoing online publications in the *Oxford Handbook of Ethics of War*, ed. Helen Frowe and Seth Lazar (New York: Oxford University Press, 2015). DOI: 10.1093/oxfordhb/9780199943418.001.0001, accessed March 23, 2017.

28. Hervé Drévillon, *L'individu et la guerre*, 16.

29. On the Wars of Religion, see Jean Paul Barbier-Mueller, *La parole et les armes: Chronique des guerres de religion en France 1562–1598* (Geneva: Hazan-Musée international de la Réforme, 2006); Olivia Carpi, *Les guerres de religion 1559–1598: Un conflit franco-français* (Paris: Ellipses, 2012); Jean-Marie Constant, *Les Français pendant les guerres de religion* (Paris: Hachette Littératures, 2002); Denis Crouzet, *Dieu en ses royaumes: Une histoire des guerres de religion* (Seyssel: Champ Vallon, 2008); Crouzet, *Les guerriers de Dieu: La violence au temps des troubles de religion (v. 1525–v. 1610)* (Seyssel: Champ Vallon, 2005); Crouzet, *La genèse de la Réforme française 1520–1562* (Paris: SEDES, 1999); Barbara B. Diefendorf, *Beneath the Cross: Catholics and Huguenots in Sixteenth-Century Paris* (Oxford: Oxford University Press, 1991); Mark Greengrass, *France in the Age of Henry IV* (London: Longman, 1986); Greengrass, *The French Reformation* (London: Blackwell, 1987); Greengrass, *Governing Passions: Peace and Reform in the French Kingdom, 1576–1585* (Oxford: Oxford University Press, 2007); Mack P. Holt, *The French Wars of Religion, 1562–1629* (Cambridge: Cambridge University Press, 2005); Arlette Jouanna, Jacqueline Boucher, Dominique Biloghi, and Guy Thiec, *Histoire et dictionnaire des guerres de religion* (Paris: Laffont, 1998); Robert J. Knecht, *The French Wars of Religion, 1559–1598* (New York: Longman, 1996); Knecht, *The Valois: Kings of France, 1328–1589* (New York: Hambledon Continuum, 2007); Knecht, *The Rise and Fall of Renaissance France, 1483–1610* (Oxford: Blackwell, 2001); and Knecht, *The French Civil Wars* (New York: Longman, 2000). For a French military perspective on the Thirty Years' War, see David Parrott, *Richelieu's Army: War, Government and Society in France, 1624–1642* (Cambridge: Cambridge University Press, 2001), and Stéphane Thion, *French Armies of the Thirty Years' War* (Auzielle: Little Round Top Editions, 2008). See also Richard Bonney, *The Thirty Years' War, 1618–1648* (Oxford: Osprey Publishing, 2002); Georges Livet, *La Guerre de Trente Ans* (Paris: Presses Universitaires de France, 1994); Geoffrey Parker, *The Thirty Years' War* (London: Routledge and Kegan Paul, 1984); Henri Sacchi, *La Guerre de Trente Ans* (Paris: Harmattan, 2003); Yves Krumenacker, *La Guerre de Trente Ans* (Paris: Ellipses, 2008).

30. On *sensibilité* in the French Enlightenment and the American Revolution, respectively, see Anne C. Vila, *Enlightenment and Pathology: Sensibility in the Literature and Medicine of Eighteenth-Century France* (Baltimore: Johns Hopkins University Press, 1998), and Sarah Knott, *Sensibility and the American Revolution* (Chapel Hill: University of North Carolina Press, 2009). For a perspective on *sensibilité* in the allegedly modern view of war as revelation, see Yuval Noah Harari, *The Ultimate Experience: Battlefield*

Revelations and the Making of Modern War Culture (Houndmills: Palgrave Macmillan, 2008).

31. John Locke, *An Essay concerning Human Understanding* (1690); David Hume, *A Treatise of Human Nature* (1739–1740), *An Enquiry concerning Human Understanding* (1748), and *An Enquiry concerning the Principles of Morals* (1751); Étienne Bonnot de Condillac, *Essai sur l'origine des connoissances humaines* (1746); Adam Smith, *Theory of Moral Sentiments* (Oxford: Oxford University Press, 1976).

32. Dan Edelstein, *The Terror of Natural Right: Republicanism, the Cult of Nature, and the French Revolution* (Chicago: University of Chicago Press, 2009), 15.

33. Joan DeJean, *Ancients Against Moderns: Culture Wars and the Making of a Fin de Siècle* (Chicago: University of Chicago Press, 1997), 82.

34. John Gillingham, "War and Chivalry in the History of William the Marshal," in *Thirteenth Century England II: Proceedings of Newcastle upon Tyne*, ed. Peter R. Coss and Simon D. Lloyd (Woodbridge, UK: Boydell and Brewer, 1988), 1–14; Richard W. Kaeuper, *The Book of Chivalry of Geoffroi de Charny: Text, Context, and Translation* (Philadelphia: University of Pennsylvania Press, 1996); Kaeuper, *Chivalry and Violence in Medieval Europe* (Oxford: Oxford University Press, 1999); Kaeuper, *Holy Warriors: The Religious Ideology of Chivalry* (Philadelphia: University of Pennsylvania Press, 2014); Kaeuper, *Medieval Chivalry* (Cambridge: Cambridge University Press, 2016).

35. The historian Geoffrey Parker contends that most modern conventions for restraint in war appeared in Europe between 1550 and 1700, first in theory and more slowly in practice. These restraints were formed by multiple influences—legal, personal interest, and the aristocratic code of honor. State, military, and international legislation and legal theory conjoined to define *jus or ius ad bellum* (the lawful initiation of war) and *jus in bello* (lawful conduct within war). For more on the evolution of laws of war, see Richard Tuck, *The Rights of War and Peace: Political Thought and the International Order from Grotius to Kant* (Oxford: Oxford University Press, 1999), and Michael Howard, George J. Andreopoulos, and Mark R. Shulman, eds., *The Laws of War: Constraints on Warfare in the Western World* (New Haven, CT: Yale University Press, 1994), especially chaps. 2–4. See also Geoffrey Best, *Humanity in Warfare* (New York: Columbia University Press, 1983). For more on cultures of noble honor and violence in early modern France, see Brian Sandberg, *Warrior Pursuits: Noble Culture and Civil Conflict in Early Modern France* (Baltimore: Johns Hopkins University Press, 2010); Pascal Brioist, Hervé Drévillon, and Pierre Serna, *Croiser le fer: Violence et culture de l'épée dans la France modern, XVIe–XVIIIe siècle* (Seyssel: Champ Vallon, 2002); Arlette Jouanna, *Le devoir de révolte: La noblesse française et la gestation de l'état modern, 1559–1661* (Paris: Fayard, 1989); Stuart Carroll, *Blood and Violence in Early Modern France* (Oxford: Oxford University Press, 2006); Kristen B. Neuchel, *Word of Honor: Interpreting Noble Culture in Sixteenth-Century France* (Ithaca, NY: Cornell University Press, 1989).

36. See Hedley Bull, ed., *Hugo Grotius and International Relations* (Oxford: Oxford University Press, 1990) and Christopher A. Ford, "Preaching Propriety to Princes: Grotius, Lipsius, and Neo-Stoic International Law," *Case Western Reserve Journal of Law*, vol. 28, no. 2 (1996): 313–66.

37. Dobie, "The Enlightenment at War," 1853.

38. On merit in the armed forces, see Jay M. Smith, *The Culture of Merit: Nobility, Royal Service, and the Making of Absolute Monarchy in France, 1600–1789* (Ann Arbor: University of Michigan Press, 1996); Jay M. Smith, *Nobility Reimagined: The Patriotic*

Nation in Eighteenth-Century France (Ithaca, NY: Cornell University Press, 2005); Rafe Blaufarb, *The French Army, 1750–1820: Careers, Talent, Merit* (Manchester, UK: University of Manchester Press, 2002).

39. Charles Perrault, *Parallèle des Anciens et des Modernes, en ce qui regarde les arts et les sciences*, vol. 2 (Paris, 1692), 30.

40. Michel Foucault, "What Is Enlightenment?," in *The Foucault Reader*, ed. Paul Rabinow (New York: Pantheon Books, 1984), 32–50; quotes from pp. 35 and 42, respectively.

41. The pioneering historian of global warfare Jeremy Black asserts that "viewed in a global context . . . developments in Europe were not exceptional." Jeremy Black, *War and the Cultural Turn* (Cambridge: Polity Press, 2012), 167.

42. On Germany, see Gat, *A History of Military Thought*, chap. 4, and Elisabeth Krimmer and Patricia Anne Simpson, eds., *Enlightened War: German Theories and Cultures of Warfare from Frederick the Great to Clausewitz* (Rochester, NY: Camden House, 2011).

43. Gat, *A History of Military Thought*, chap. 5, and the discussion of Manfried Rauchensteiner in B. K. Kiraly, G. Rothenberg, and P. Sugar, *East Central European Society and War in the Pre-Revolutionary Eighteenth Century*, vol. 2 of the series War and Society in East-Central Europe (New York: Social Science Monographs, 1982), 75–82.

44. On France's finances and military enterprise, see Guy Rowlands, *The Dynastic State and the Army under Louis XIV: Royal Service and Private Interest, 1661–1701* (Cambridge: Cambridge University Press, 2010); Rowlands, *The Financial Decline of a Great Power: War, Influence, and Money in Louis XIV's France* (Oxford: Oxford University Press, 2012); and Rowlands, *Dangerous and Dishonest Men: The International Bankers of Louis XIV's France* (London: Palgrave, 2014), as well as a number of his articles.

45. David A. Bell, *The Cult of the Nation in France: Inventing Nationalism, 1680–1800* (Cambridge, MA: Harvard University Press, 2003); Edmond Dziembowski, *Le nouveau patriotisme français 1750–1770: La France face à la puissance anglaise à l'époque de la Guerre de Sept Ans*, Studies on Voltaire and the Eighteenth Century (Oxford: Voltaire Foundation, 1998); J. M. Smith, *Nobility Reimagined*.

46. Félix and Tallett, "The French Experience," 152–53.

47. Ibid., 155. On financing war under Louis XIII, see Parrott, *Richelieu's Army*, and for war and finance under Louis XIV, see Rowlands, *The Dynastic State*.

48. Félix and Tallett, "The French Experience," 155.

49. France also has a flourishing black market. See Michael Kwass, *Contraband: Louis Mandrin and the Making of a Global Underground* (Cambridge, MA: Harvard University Press, 2014). Kwass also wrote on daring initiatives in the crown's eighteenth-century taxation policy in *Privilege and the Politics of Taxation in Eighteenth-Century France: Liberté, Égalité, Fiscalité* (Cambridge, UK: Cambridge University Press, 2009).

50. Ibid., 151–52.

51. Scott, "The Fiscal-Military State," 41.

52. See Rowlands, *Dangerous and Dishonest Men*.

53. Scott, "The Fiscal-Military State," 39, 45. See also James C. Riley, *The Seven Years War and the Old Regime in France: The Economic and Financial Toll* (Princeton, NJ: Princeton University Press, 1986), and Joël Félix, *Finances et politique au siècles des Lumières: Le ministère d'Averdy, 1763–1768* (Paris: Comité pour l'histoire économique et financière de la France, 1999).

54. Many of David Bien's most important English-language essays have been assembled into a collection, *Interpreting the Ancien Régime*, ed. Rafe Blaufarb, Michael S.

Christofferson, and Darrin M. McMahon, with a preface by Keith Baker, Oxford University Studies in the Enlightenment (Oxford: Voltaire Foundation, 2014). On the topic of French finances of the period, see also Gail Bossenga, "Financial Origins of the French Revolution" in *From Deficit to Deluge: The Origins of the French Revolution*, ed. Thomas E. Kaiser and Dale K. Van Kley (Stanford: Stanford University Press, 2010), 66.

55. Félix and Tallett, "The French Experience," 158.

56. See Lynn, *The Wars of Louis XIV*, 362–67 on limited war. On the aristocratic culture associated with limited war, see chap. 1 in Bell, *The First Total War*.

57. Corvisier, *L'armée française*, 2:737.

58. Ibid., 736.

59. Despite these devastating and state-threatening defeats, the French were fortunate to come out of this war with their territory relatively intact because the allied forces of England and Austria could not capitalize on these French losses. Such "indecisiveness" of battle was typical in the early modern system of so-called limited war. See Lynn, *The Wars of Louis XIV*, 266–360, on the French involvement in and perspective on the War of Spanish Succession. For a discussion of the decisiveness of battle in the early eighteenth century, see Jamel Ostwald, "The 'Decisive' Battle of Ramillies, 1706: Prerequisites for Decisiveness in Early-Modern Warfare," *Journal of Military History* 64 (2000): 649–77.

60. David D. Bien, "The Army in the French Enlightenment: Reform, Reaction, and Revolution" *Past and Present*, vol. 85 (November 1979): 68–98.

61. Voltaire, "Précis du siècle de Louis XV," in *Oeuvres complètes de Voltaire*, vol. 4 (Paris: Furne, 1843), 407.

62. On war and public opinion during the reign of Louis XV, see Tabetha Leigh Ewing, *Rumor, Diplomacy and War in Enlightenment Paris*, Oxford University Studies in the Enlightenment (Oxford: Voltaire Foundation, 2014), and Lisa Jane Graham, *If the King Only Knew: Seditious Speech in the Reign of Louis XV* (Charlottesville: University of Virginia Press, 2000).

63. On the nationalization of honor, see J. M. Smith, *Nobility Reimagined*.

64. See David D. Bien, "Military Education in 18th Century France: Technical and Nontechnical Determinants," in *Science, Technology, and Warfare*, Proceedings of the Third Military History Symposium, United States Air Force Academy, 1969, ed. Monte D. Wright and Lawrence J. Paszek (Washington, DC: U.S. Government Printing Office, 1971), 51–84.

65. See Robert Quimby, *The Background of Napoleonic Warfare: The Theory of Military Tactics in Eighteenth-Century France* (New York: Columbia University Press, 1957).

66. See John A. Lynn, "The Treatment of Military Subjects in Diderot's *Encyclopédie*," *Journal of Military History* 65, no. 1 (January 2001): 131–65.

67. See Gat, *A History of Military Thought*.

68. J. B. Schank, *The Newton Wars and the Beginning of the French Enlightenment* (Chicago: University of Chicago Press, 2008); Ken Alder, *Engineering the Revolution: Arms and Enlightenment in France, 1763–1815* (Chicago: University of Chicago Press, 2010); Alain Berbouche, *L'histoire de la Royale: La marine française et la politique au siècle des Lumières (1715–1789)* (Saint-Malo: Pascal Galodé, 2012); and Berbouche, *Marine et justice: La justice criminelle de la marine francaise sous l'Ancien Régime* (Rennes: Presses Universitaires de Rennes, 2010).

69. James E. McClellan III and François Regourd, *The Colonial Machine: French Science and Colonization in the Ancien Regime* (Turnhout, Belgium: Brepols, 2012). On

colonial medicine, see James E. McClellan III, *Colonialism and Science: Saint-Domingue in the Old Regime* (Baltimore: Johns Hopkins University Press, 1992); Pierre Pluchon, ed., *Histoire des médecins et pharmaciens de marine et des colonies* (Toulouse: Privat, 1985); Caroline Hannaway, "Distinctive or Derivative? The French Colonial Medical Experience, 1740–1790," in *Mundializacion de la ciencia y cultura nacional*, ed. Antonio Lafuente, Alberto Elena, and Maria Luisa Ortega (Madrid: Doce Calles, 1993), 505–10; Michael Osborne, *The Emergence of Tropical Medicine in France* (Chicago: University of Chicago Press, 2014); Erica Charters, *Disease, War, and the Imperial State: The Welfare of the British Armed Forces during the Seven Years' War* (Chicago: University of Chicago Press, 2014). For an overview of French colonialism during this period, see Pierre Pluchon, *Histoire de la colonialisaion française*, vol. 1, *Le premier empire colonial* (Paris: Fayard, 1991).

70. Outram, *The Enlightenment*, 54.

71. See Michèle Duchet's classic work, *Anthropologie et histoire au siècle des Lumières: Buffon, Voltaire, Rousseau, Helvétius, Diderot* (Paris: François Maspero, 1971).

72. For more on this flash point, see Outram, *The Enlightenment*, chap. 5, and Duchet, *Anthropologie et histoire au siècle des Lumières*. On Raynal's *Histoire des deux Indes and eighteenth-century expressions of ambivalence toward commerce*, see Anoush F. Terjianian, Commerce and Its Discontents in Eighteenth-Century French Political Thought (Cambridge: Cambridge University Press, 2013).

73. See the two-volume study published by the Académie des sciences d'outre-mer under the direction of Philippe Bonnichon, Pierre Gény, and Jean Nemo, *Présences françaises outre-mer (XVIe–XXIe siècles)* (Paris: Éditions Karthala/ASOM, 2012).

74. On different responses to French empire during the eighteenth century, see Sankar Muthu, *Enlightenment against Empire* (Princeton, NJ: Princeton University Press, 2003); Jennifer Pitts, *A Turn to Empire: The Rise of Imperial Liberalism in Britain and France* (Princeton, NJ: Princeton University Press, 2005); Madeleine Dobie, *Trading Places: Colonization and Slavery in Eighteenth-Century Culture* (Ithaca, NY: Cornell University Press, 2010); and Sunil Agnani, *Hating Empire Properly: The Two Indies and the Limits of Enlightenment Anticolonialism* (New York: Fordham University Press, 2013), among others.

75. See Jared Diamond, *Guns, Germs, and Steel: The Fates of Human Societies* (New York: Norton, 1997). Works that debunk this vision of the Spanish model include Mathew Restall, *Seven Myths of the Spanish Conquest* (Oxford: Oxford University Press, 2004); Ross Hassig, *Mexico and the Spanish Conquest*, 2nd rev. ed. (Norman: University of Oklahoma Press, 2006); Laura Matthews, *Indian Conquistadors: Indigenous Allies in the Conquest of Mesoamerica* (Norman: University of Oklahoma Press, 2007).

76. Wayne E. Lee, "Projecting Power in the Early Modern World," in *Empires and Indigenes: Intercultural Alliance, Imperial Expansion, and Warfare in the Early Modern World*, ed. Wayne E. Lee (New York: New York University Press, 2011), 2.

77. Lee, "Projecting Power," 1.

78. See Richard White, *The Middle Ground: Indians, Empire, and Republics in the Great Lakes Region, 1650–1815* (Cambridge: Cambridge University Press, 1991). Scholars have contested and continue to contest White's concept of the "middle ground" and its applicability in the geography he examined. White addresses some of these critical debates in the preface to the twentieth anniversary edition of the book published by Cambridge in 2011. On French experiences with Amerindians and warfare during this

period, see Crouch, *Nobility Lost*; Arnaud Balvay, *L'épée et la plume: Amérindiens et soldats des troupes de la marine en Louisiane et au Pays d'en Haut (1683–1763)* (Quebec: Presses Universitaires de Laval, 2006); Gilles Havard, *Empire et métissages: Indiens et Français dans le Pays d'en Haut, 1660–1715* (Quebec: Septentrion, 2003); and Armstrong Starkey, *European and Native American Warfare, 1615–1815* (London: University of Oklahoma Press / UCL Press, 1998), among others.

79. See John Garrigus, *Before Haiti: Race and Citizenship in French Saint-Domingue* (New York: Palgrave Macmillan, 2006), and Garrigus, "Catalyst or Catastrophe? Saint-Domingue's Free Men of Color and the Savannah Expedition, 1779–1782," *Review/Revista Interamericana* 22 (Spring/Summer 1992): 109–25, among others.

80. On war and society, see M. S. Anderson, *War and Society in Europe of the Old Regime, 1618–1789* (Montreal: McGill-Queens University Press, 1998); Geoffrey Best, *War and Society in Revolutionary Europe, 1770–1870* (Montreal: McGill-Queens University Press, 1998); Jeremy Black, *A Military Revolution? Military Change and European Society, 1550–1800* (Atlantic Highlands, NJ: Humanities Press, 1991); Black, *European Warfare, 1660–1815* (London: UCL Press, 1994); Black, *European Warfare in a Global Context, 1660–1815* (London: Routledge, 2006); André Corvisier, *Armies and Societies in Europe, 1494–1789*, trans. A. T. Siddall (Bloomington: Indiana University Press, 1979); Frank Tallett, *War and Society in Early Modern Europe: 1495–1715* (London: Routledge, 1997). In addition to those already mentioned in this introduction, a number of historians have played a pivotal role in ushering in the cultural study of war, notably John Keegan, Victor Davis Hanson, John W. Dower, Richard W. Kaeuper, Kenneth M. Pollack, Ralph D. Sawyer, and Ronald Takaki.

81. For a study on the 1M series at the SHD, see *Les lumières de la guerre*, ed. Hervé Drévillon and Arnaud Guinier (Paris: Éditions de la Sorbonne, 2015), vols. 1 and 2.

1. The French Military Enlightenment

1. John Lynn, *Battle: A History of Combat and Culture from Ancient Greece to Modern America* (Cambridge, MA: Westview Press, 2003), xv.

2. Martin Fitzpatrick, Peter Jones, Christa Knellwolf, and Iain McCalman, eds., *The Enlightenment World*. (New York: Routledge, 2004), 442. Jonathan Israel reproduces this refusal in *Democratic Enlightenment: Philosophy, Revolution, and Human Rights, 1750–1790* (Oxford: Oxford University Press, 2013), which leaves France out of its chapter on enlightened despotism. Israel, *Democratic Enlightenment*, chap. 10, 270–301.

3. John A. Lynn, *Giant of the Grand Siècle: The French Army, 1610–1715* (Cambridge: Cambridge University Press, 1997). Norman Davies, *Europe: A History* (Oxford: Oxford University Press, 1996), 627.

4. See David Parrott, *Richelieu's Army: War, Government and Society in France, 1624–1642* (Cambridge: Cambridge University Press, 2001), and Lynn, *Giant of the Grand Siècle*.

5. For more on d'Argenson, see Yves Combeau, *Le comte d'Argenson (1696–1764)* (Paris: Librairie Droz, 1999).

6. For more on this history of the *noblesse d'épée*, see Ellery Schalk, *From Valor to Pedigree: Ideas of Nobility in France in the Sixteenth and Seventeenth Centuries* (Princeton, NJ: Princeton University Press, 1986), and chap. 2 of this volume.

7. César Chesneau Dumarsais, "Education," trans. Carolina Armenteros, in *The Encyclopedia of Diderot & d'Alembert Collaborative Translation Project* (Ann Arbor: Michigan

Publishing, University of Michigan Library, 2007), http://hdl.handle.net/2027/spo.did2222.0000.390, accessed December 20, 2016; translation of "Education," in *Encyclopédie, ou Dictionnaire raisonné des sciences, des arts et des métiers*, vol. 5 (Paris, 1755). On the curriculum of the École militaire, see David D. Bien, "Military Education in Eighteenth Century France: Technical and Nontechnical Determinants," in *Science, Technology, and Warfare, Proceedings of the Third Military History Symposium, United States Air Force Academy, 1969*, ed. Monte D. Wright and Lawrence J. Paszek (Washington, DC: U.S. Government Printing Office, 1971), 51–84. For another officer's perspective on what the curriculum should entail, see "Projet d'une nouvelle école militaire addressé à Monsieur le Maréchal duc de Belle-Isle," with commentary by Aude Mayelle, in *Les Lumières de la guerre*, ed. Hervé Drévillon and Arnaud Guinier, vol. 1 (Paris: Éditions de la Sorbonne, 2015), 117–52.

8. See Marie Jacob, "L'École royale militaire: Un modèle selon l'*Encyclopédie?*," *Recherches sur Diderot et sur l'Encyclopédie* 43 (2008): 105–26.

9. http://www.dems.defense.gouv.fr/dems/connaitre-la-dems/histoire-de-l-ecole-militaire/article/la-construction-de-l-ecole-et-ses. Accessed on March 23, 2017.

10. Quoted on page 287 in Robert Laulan, "La fondation de l'École militaire et Madame de Pompadour," *Revue d'histoire moderne et contemporaine* 21, no. 2 (April–June 1974): 284–99.

11. For more on these reforms, which are but barely summarized here, see Alain Berbouche, *L'histoire de la Royale: La marine française et la politique au siècle des Lumières (1715–1789)* (Saint-Malo: Pascal Galodé, 2012), and Berbouche, *Marine et justice: La justice criminelle de la marine française sous l'ancien régime* (Rennes: Presses Universitaires de Rennes, 2010). See also Jean Meyer, "La marine française au XVIIIe siècle," in *Histoire militaire de la France*, under the direction of André Corvisier, vol. 2 (Paris: Presses Universitaires de France, 1992).

12. Quoted in Jean Meyer, "La marine française au XVIIIe siècle," 2:162.

13. Ibid., 152.

14. *Le militaire philosophe ou difficultés sur la religion proposées au Reverend Père Malebranche* (London, 1768), 8. See also Jean Chagniot, *Paris et l'armée au XVIIIe siècle* (Paris: Economica, 1985), 629–31.

15. Armstrong Starkey, *War in the Age of Enlightenment, 1700–1789* (Westport, CT: Praeger, 2003), 87.

16. Ibid.

17. Ira Gruber, *Books and the British Army in the Age of the American Revolution* (Chapel Hill: University of North Carolina Press, 2010).

18. Christopher Duffy, *The Army of Frederick the Great* (New York: Hippocrene Books, 1974), 47–50; Charles Royster, *A Revolutionary People at War: The Continental Army and the American Character, 1775–1783* (Chapel Hill: University of North Carolina Press, 1979), 88–89; Sarah Knott, *Sensibility and the American Revolution* (Chapel Hill: University of North Carolina Press, 2009); Robert Darnton, *The Great Cat Massacre and Other Episodes in French Cultural History* (New York: Viking, 1984), 242.

19. See Napoleon Bonaparte, *Manuscrits inédits*, ed. Frédéric Masson and Guido Biagi (Paris: Société d'éditions littéraires et artistiques, 1907).

20. For more on theories of how to wage war, especially the siege, in seventeenth- and early eighteenth-century France, see Jamel Ostwald, *Vauban under Siege: Engineering Efficiency and Martial Vigor in the War of the Spanish Succession* (Leiden: Brill, 2007).

21. See Arnaud Guinier, "Le mémoire comme projet de réforme au siècle des Lumières," in Drévillon and Guinier, *Les Lumières de la guerre*, 23–112.

22. Service Historique de la Défense (SHD) 1M 1709, no author, "Projet d'un militaire," n.d. (after 1763), 2–3.

23. Jürgen Habermas, *The Structural Transformation of the Public Sphere: An Inquiry into a Category of Bourgeois Society* (1962; reprint, Cambridge, MA: MIT University Press, 1991).

24. Azar Gat, *A History of Military Thought from the Enlightenment to the Cold War* (Oxford: Oxford University Press, 2001), 27. See also Johann Pohler, *Bibliotheca historico-militaris: Systematische Uebersicht der Erscheinungen aller Sprachen auf dem Gebeite der Geschichte der Kriege und Kriegswissenschaft seit Erfindung der Buchdruckerkunst bis zum Schluss des Jahres 1880*, 4 vols. (Leipzig, 1887–1897), 3:583–610.

25. Chevalier de Folard, *Nouvelles découvertes sur la guerre dans une dissertation sur Polybe, où l'on donne une idée plus étendue du commentaire entrepris sur cet auteur, et deux dissertation importantes détachées du corps de l'ouvrage* (1724); *Histoire de Scipion l'Africain, pour servir de suite aux hommes illustres de Plutarque. Avec les observations de M. le chevalier de Folard sur la bataille de Zama* (1738); *Histoire d'Épaminondas pour servir de suite aux hommes illustres de Plutarque, avec des remarques de M. le Chevalier de Folard sur les principales batailles d'Épaminondas, par M. l'abbé Séran de la Tour* (1739); *Histoire de Polybe, nouvellement traduite du grec par Dom Vincent Thuillier, avec un commentaire ou un corps de science militaire enrichi de notes critiques et historiques par F. de Folard* (1729); *Abrégé des Commentaires de M. de Folard sur l'histoire de Polybe* (1754).

26. For more on discussions of shock tactics in France, see Arnaud Guinier, in *Combattre à l'époque moderne*, ed. B. Deruelle and B. Gainot (Paris: Éditions du CTHS, 2013), 84–93. http://cths.fr/ed/edition.php?id=6559, accessed March 8, 2017.

27. See Frederick's *Histoire du chevalier de Folard tiré de ses commentaires tirés de l'Histoire de Polybe pour l'usage d'un officier, de main de maître* (Leipzig, 1761).

28. Lancelot Turpin, comte de Crissé et de Sanzay, *Essay on the Art of War*, vol. 1 (London, 1761), 1–2.

29. Paul-Gédéon Joly de Maïzeroy, *Theorie de guerre* (Lausanne, 1777), lxxxv–lxxxvi.

30. Paul-Gédéon Joly de Maïzeroy, *Essais militaires, où l'on traite des armes défensives* (Amsterdam: Gosses,1762); *Traité des stratagèmes permis à la guerre, ou remarques sur Polyen et Frontin* (Metz: Joseph Antoine, 1765); *Institutions militaires de l'empereur Léon le philosophe* (Paris: Merlin, 1771); *Cours de tactique théorique, pratique et historique*, 2 vols. (Paris, 1766); *La tactique discutée et réduite à ses véritables principes*, 4 vols. (Paris: Claude-Antoine Jombert, 1773); *Mémoire sur les opinions qui partagent les militaires, suivi du traité des armes défensives* (Paris: Claude-Antoine Jombert, 1773); *Théorie de la guerre* (Lausanne, 1777); *Traité sur l'art des sièges et des machines des anciens* (Paris: Claude-Antoine Jombert, 1778); *Tableau général de la cavalerie grecque, composé de deux mémoires et d'une traduction du traité de Xénophon intitulé Le Commandant de la cavalerie* (Paris: L'imprimerie royale, 1780).

31. Pierre Joseph de Bourcet, *Mémoires historiques sur la guerre que les Français ont soutenue en Allemagne depuis 1757 juqu'en 1762*, 3 vols. (Paris: Maradan, 1792); *Mémoires militaires sur les frontières de la France, du Piémont et de la Savoie, depuis l'embouchure du Var jusqu'au Lac de Genève* (Paris: Levrau et frères, an X); *Principes de la guerre de montagnes* (1760) (Paris: Imprimerie Nationale, 1888); *Carte géométrique du Haut Dauphiné et de la frontière ultérieure, levée par ordre du Roi, sous la direction de M. de Bourcet, maréchal*

de camp, par MM. les ingénieurs ordinaires et par les ingénieurs géographes de sa Majesté pendant les années 1749 jusqu'en 1754. Dressé par S. Villaret, capitaine ingénieur du roi Limites du Piémont (Paris, 1758); *Projet de ville-forteresse, à Versoix, inspiré des réalisations de Vauban* (1767).

32. For more on celebrity during this period, see Antoine Lilti, *Figures publiques: L'invention de la célébrité, 1750–1850* (Paris: Fayard, 2014).

33. Gat, *A History of Military Thought*, 45–46.

34. Ibid., 54.

35. For more on the growth of the novel as a genre during this period, see Ian Watt, *The Rise of the Novel* (Berkeley: University of California Press, 2000).

36. Choderlos de Laclos, *Les liaisons dangereuses*, 4 vols. (Paris: Durand Neveu, 1782), letter CLIII. For analyses of military influences on the novel, see Joan DeJean, *Literary Fortifications: Rousseau, Laclos, Sade* (Princeton, NJ: Princeton University Press, 1984); Christy Pichichero, "Battles of the Self: War and Subjectivity in Early Modern France" (PhD diss., Stanford University, 2008); Julia Osman, "A Tale of Two Tactics: Laclos's Novel Approach to Military Reform," *Eighteenth Century Fiction* 22, no. 3 (Spring 2010): 503–24.

37. Georges Festa, "La bataille, l'armée, la gloire dans l'oeuvre de Sade," in *La bataille, l'armée, la gloire 1745–1871: Actes du colloque international de Clermont-Ferrand*, vol. 1, ed. Paul Viallaneix and Jean Ehrard (Clermont-Ferrand: Association des publications de la Faculté des lettres et sciences humaines de Clermont-Ferrand, 1985), 83.

38. Ibid., 84.

39. Lancelot Turpin de Crissé and Jean Castilhon, *Amusemens philosophiques et littéraires* (Paris: Prault, 1754), 6.

40. See Turpin de Crissé's biography in *Biographie universelle, ancienne et moderne, ouvrage rédigé par une société de gens de lettres*, vol. 47 (Paris: L. G. Michard, 1827), 98–100. Quote from page 99.

41. Christian Ayne Crouch, *Nobility Lost: French and Canadian Martial Cultures, Indians, and the End of New France* (Ithaca, NY: Cornell University Press, 2014), 69–70.

42. Ibid., 15.

43. Quoted in Leah Hochman, *The Ugliness of Moses Mendelssohn: Aesthetics, Religion and Morality in the Eighteenth Century* (New York: Routledge, 2014), 91.

44. Zacharie de Pazzi de Bonneville, *De l'Amérique et des Américains: ou Observations curieuses du philosophe La Douceur, qui a parcouru cet hémisphere pendant la dernière guerre, en faisant le noble métier de tuer des hommes sans les manger* (Berlin: S. Pitra, 1771), 4–6.

45. Ibid., 43.

46. Crouch, *Nobility Lost*, 70.

47. Ibid., 71. See Charles Coste, ed., *Aventures militaires au XVIIIe siècle d'après les mémoires de Jean-Baptiste d'Aleyrac* (Paris, 1935).

48. Jean Jacques, chevalier de Cotignon, *Mémoires du chevalier de Cotignon: Gentilhomme nivernais, officier de marine de Sa Majesté Louis le Seizième* (Grenoble: Éditions des 4 Seigneurs, 1974), 341.

49. There is a long and detailed historiography on Lafayette in France and America. Important works include Louis Gottschalk, *Lafayette Comes to America* (Chicago: University of Chicago Press, 1935), *Lafayette Joins the American Army* (Chicago: University of Chicago Press, 1937), *Lafayette and the Close of the American Revolution* (Chicago: University of Chicago Press, 1942), *Lafayette between the American and*

the French Revolution (1783–1789) (Chicago: University of Chicago Press, 1950), and, with Sarah Maddox, *Lafayette in the French Revolution through the October Days* (Chicago: University of Chicago Press, 1969) and *Lafayette in the French Revolution from the October Days through the Federation* (Chicago: University of Chicago Press, 1973); Lloyd Kramer, *Lafayette in Two Worlds: Public Cultures and Personal Identities in an Age of Revolutions* (Chapel Hill: University of North Carolina Press, 1996). For a recent biography of Lafayette, see Laura Auricchio, *The Marquis: Lafayette Reconsidered* (New York: Knopf, 2015).

50. For more on these documents, see Jean-Jacques Fiechter, "L'aventure américaine des officiers de Rochambeau vue à travers leurs journaux," in *Images of America in Revolutionary France*, ed. Michèle R. Morris (Washington, DC: Georgetown University Press, 1990), 65–82.

51. Louis-Jean Christophe, baron de Closen, "Baron von Closen Journal," Library of Congress, Manuscript Division, vol. 2, 56–57.

52. Jean-Baptiste-Antoine de Verger, "Journal des faits les plus importants arrives aux troupes françaises aux orders de Monsieur le comte de Rochambeau," manuscript, Brown University, Anne S. K. Brown Military Collection, 61–62.

53. Jean-François-Louis Crèvecoeur, comte de Clermont, *Journal de la guerre d'Amérique pendant les années 1780–1783*, trans. Howard Rice and Anne Brown (Providence, RI: Rhode Island Historical Society, 1972), 38–39. Fiechter, "L'aventure américaine," 78.

54. Author's translation.

55. Blaise Pascal, *Pensées* (Paris: Gallimard, 1997), 83.

56. Ibid., fragment 56, p. 87.

57. See Jean de La Bruyère, *Les caractères, ou les moeurs de ce siècle* (Paris: Gallimard, 2002), chap. 10, fragment 9, p. 207, and chap. 11, fragment 119, pp. 307–8.

58. Though his pacifism is generally presented with a certain amount of gentleness in his literary oeuvre, Fénelon penned an extraordinary letter to Louis XIV dated 1694 expressing aggressive, provocative, and almost subversive words condemning the king's policies of war. Wisely, Fénelon never sent the letter. For more on Fénelon, his life, and pacifism, see David A. Bell, *The First Total War: Napoleon's Europe and the Birth of War as We Know It* (Boston: Houghton Mifflin, 2007), 54–62.

59. Fénelon, *Les aventures de Télémaque* (Paris: Gallimard, 2000), 200–201.

60. See Pichichero, "Battles of the Self." In his seminal book on the Enlightenment novel of worldliness, Peter Brooks took note of the presence of war in the system of "mondanité," though he did not analyze it or delve into its potential importance. Peter Brooks, *The Novel of Worldliness: Crébillon, Marivaux, Laclos, Stendhal* (Princeton, NJ: Princeton University Press, 1979).

61. I recently developed this perspective for a lecture entitled "Watteau's Soldiers: Bodies, War, and Enlightenment," delivered at the Frick Collection on September 21, 2016, in association with an exhibition entitled "Watteau's Soldiers" (July 12–October 2, 2016). On Watteau's military works, see, for example, Hal Opperman, "The Theme of Peace in Watteau," in *Antoine Watteau: The Painter, His Age and His Legend*, ed. François Moreau and Margaret Morgan Grasselli (Paris: Champion-Slatkine, 1987); Julie Anne Plax, *Watteau and the Cultural Politics of Eighteenth-Century France* (Cambridge: Cambridge University Press, 2000); Arlette Farge, *Les fatigues de la guerre* (Paris: Gallimard, 1996); Thomas E. Kaiser, "The Monarchy, Public Opinion,

and the Subversions of Antoine Watteau," in *Antoine Watteau: Perspectives on the Artist and the Culture of His Time*, ed. Mary D. Sheriff (Newark: University of Delaware Press, 2006), 63–75.

62. For more on Rousseau's perspectives regarding warfare, see Catherine Larrère, "L'état de guerre et la guerre entre les états: Jean-Jacques Rousseau et la critique du droit naturel," in Viallaneix and Ehrard, *La bataille, l'armée, la gloire 1745–1871*, vol. 1, 135–47.

63. Montesquieu, *Considérations sur les causes de la grandeur des romains et de leur décadence* (Oxford: Voltaire Foundation, 2000), 102, 141.

64. Arnaud Guinier, *L'honneur du soldat: Éthique martiale et discipline guerrière dans la France des Lumières, 1748–1789* (Ceyzérieu: Champ Vallon, 2014), 224–31.

65. Charles Rollin, *The Ancient History of the Egyptians, Carthaginians, Assyrians, Babylonians, Medes and Persians, Macedonians, and Grecians*, trans. unknown, 7 vols. (London, 1780), 2:243. For more on these writers, see Julia Osman, *Citizen Soldiers and the Key to the Bastille* (New York: Palgrave, 2015), 59–60.

66. For more on the publication history of the *Encyclopédie*, see Robert Darnton, *The Business of Enlightenment: A Publishing History of the Encyclopédie, 1775–1800* (Cambridge, MA: Belknap Press of Harvard University Press, 1979).

67. Louis de Jaucourt, "Guerre," in *Encyclopédie*, 7:995.

68. John A. Lynn, "The Treatment of Military Subjects in Diderot's *Encyclopédie*," *Journal of Military History* 65, no. 1 (January 2001): 133; and Jean Ehrard, "L'*Encyclopédie* et la guerre," in Viallaneix and Ehrard, *La bataille, l'armée, la gloire*, 1:93–101.

69. Lynn, "The Treatment of Military Subjects in Diderot's *Encyclopédie*," 136–37.

70. Ibid., 142.

71. Jean-François Marmontel, "Gloire," in *Encyclopédie*, 7:716.

72. David M. Vess, *Medical Revolution in France, 1789–1796* (Gainesville: University Presses of Florida, 1974); Laurence Brockliss and Colin Jones, *The Medical World of Early Modern France* (Oxford: Clarendon Press, 1997); and Erica Charters, "Colonial Disease, Translation, and Enlightenment: Franco-British Medicine and the Seven Years' War," in *The Culture of the Seven Years' War: Empire, Identity, and the Arts in the Eighteenth-Century Atlantic World*, ed. Frans de Bruyn and Shaun Regan (Toronto: University of Toronto Press, 2014), and Charters, *Disease, War, and the Imperial State: The Welfare of the British Armed Forces during the Seven Years' War* (Chicago: University of Chicago Press, 2014).

73. Charters, "Colonial Disease, Translation, and Enlightenment," 75.

74. Michael Osborne, *The Emergence of Tropical Medicine in France* (Chicago: University of Chicago Press, 2014); and Charters, "Colonial Disease, Translation, and Enlightenment."

75. Charters, "Colonial Disease, Translation, and Enlightenment," 75.

76. See Marc Martin, *Les origines de la presse militaire en France à la fin de l'ancien régime et sous la Révolution: 1770–1799* (Vincennes: Éditions du Service historique de l'Armée de Terre, 1975); and Brockliss and Jones, *The Medical World*, 699–700.

77. On the French press of the eighteenth century, see, for example, Jack Censer, *The French Press in the Age of Enlightenment* (New York: Routledge, 1994); Jack Censer and Jeremy Popkin, eds., *Press and Politics in Pre-revolutionary France* (Berkeley: University of California Press, 1987); Norman Fiering, "The Transatlantic Republic of Letters: A Note on the Circulation of Learned Periodicals to Early Eighteenth-Century America," *William and Mary Quarterly* 33, no. 4 (1976): 642–60.

78. Jeremy Popkin, *News and Politics in the Age of Revolution* (Ithaca, NY: Cornell University Press, 1989), 48, 121. See also Osman, *Citizen Soldiers*, 82.

79. Popkin, *News and Politics*, 129–31. Osman, *Citizen Soldiers*, chap. 4.

80. See Edmond Dziembowski, *Le nouveau patriotisme français 1750–1770: La France face à la puissance anglaise à l'époque de la Guerre de Sept Ans* (Oxford: Voltaire Foundation, 1998).

81. The rise of military journals in France can be explained by four factors: (1) the popularity of military subjects in the period between the War of Austrian Succession and the French Revolution; (2) the growth of Parisian and provincial presses; (3) the impetus to foster the diffusion of knowledge contained in the *Encyclopédie*; and (4) the profusion of specialized journals focusing on technical and scientific subjects. Martin, *Les origines de la presse militaire*, 67–75.

82. Ibid., 31–32.

83. Ibid., 33–36.

84. Ibid., 75.

85. Ibid., 37. Martin also counted forty-seven out of one hundred infantry regiments and seven out of seventeen dragoon regiments as subscribing to the journal.

86. Ibid., 38–48.

87. Ibid., 53–55.

88. Ibid., 55–59.

89. Antoine Lilti, *Le monde des salons: Sociabilité et mondanité à Paris au XVIIIe siècle* (Paris: Fayard, 2005), especially 287–95. On the *république des lettres* during this period, see Dena Goodman, *The Republic of Letters: A Cultural History of the French Enlightenment* (Ithaca, NY: Cornell University Press, 1994), and Laurence Brockliss, *Calvet's Web: Enlightenment and the Republic of Letters in Eighteenth-Century France* (Oxford: Oxford University Press, 2002), among others.

90. Lilti, *Le monde des salons*, 288.

91. See letter from Julie de Lespinasse to Guibert dated 16 August 1773.

92. Benedetta Craveri, *The Age of Conversation*, trans. Teresa Waugh (New York: New York Book Review, 2005).

93. Lilti, *Le monde des salons*, 227.

94. See Julia Landweber, "'This Marvelous Bean': Adopting Coffee into Old Regime French Culture and Diet," *French Historical Studies*, vol. 38, no. 2 (2015): 193–223.

95. For more on the general subject of cafés and public architecture, see Christoph Grafe and Franziska Bollerey, eds., *Cafes and Bars: The Architecture of Public Display* (New York: Routledge, 2007).

96. On Masonic friendship, see Kenneth Loiselle, *Brotherly Love: Freemasonry and Male Friendship in Enlightenment France* (Ithaca, NY: Cornell University Press, 2014). See also Lilti, *Le monde des salons*, 70–72, on sociability and Masonic lodges.

97. Harlow Giles Unger, *Lafayette* (New York: Wiley, 2002), Kindle ed., loc. 565–81.

98. Marc-Marie, Marquis de Bombelles, *Journal du marquis de Bombelles*, 8 vols. (Geneva: Éditions Droz, 1978–2013), 1:315–16.

2. Before Fraternity

1. *Oeuvres du comte P. L. Roederer publiées par son fils*, vol. 8 (Paris: Imprimeurs de l'institut, 1859), 494.

2. Elzéar Blaze, *Military Life under Napoleon*, ed. and trans. John R. Elting (Chicago: Emperor's Press, 1995), 176.

3. Brian Joseph Martin, *Napoleonic Friendship: Military Fraternity, Intimacy, and Sexuality in Nineteenth-Century France* (Lebanon: University of New Hampshire Press, 2011), 5–6.

4. See Michael J. Hughes, *Forging Napoleon's Grande Armée: Motivation, Military Culture, and Masculinity in the French Army, 1800–1808* (New York: New York University Press, 2012).

5. On the French defeat at Rossbach, see " 'La malheureuse affaire du 5': Rossbach ou la France à l'épreuve de la tactique prussienne," in *La Bataille, Du fait d'armes au combat idéologique, XIe - XIXe siècle*, ed. A. Boltanski, Y. Lagadec, F. Mercier, (Rennes: Presses Universitaires de Rennes, 2015), 231–44.

6. On *nostalgie*, see Thomas Dodman, *What Nostalgia Was: War, Empire, and the Time of a Deadly Emotion* (Chicago: University of Chicago Press, 2017).

7. Shakespeare coined the expression "band of brothers" in *Henry V* (1600) to mean comrades in arms. Nelson famously used it to describe his fellow naval officers to relay their collective excellence in seamanship and elite status. An awareness of the importance of bonds between military comrades dates back to the *Epic of Gilgamesh* (ca. 2100 BC), and Plato famously suggested that an army should be composed of lovers in the *Symposium* (ca. 385–370 BC). Developments in this chapter show how the modern understanding of "band of brothers" took form through a continual investigation and institutionalization of the mechanisms of social and emotional bonding: eating and sleeping in close quarters for extended periods, doing chores together, and experiencing the hardships of life on campaign and the horrors of battle alongside one another.

8. This is an imaginative rewriting of a passage from John A. Lynn's book *The Wars of Louis XIV, 1667–1714* (Harlow, UK: Longman, 1999), 216–18. For more on Louis XIV's self-fashioning as the "king of war," see Joël Cornette, *Le roi de guerre: Essai sur la souveraineté dans la France du Grand Siècle* (Paris: Payot, 1993), and Peter Burke, *The Fabrication of Louis XIV* (New Haven, CT: Yale University Press, 1992).

9. David A. Bell, *The First Total War: Napoleon's Europe and the Birth of War as We Know It* (Boston: Houghton Mifflin, 2007), chap. 1.

10. See Carl von Clausewitz, "Bekenntnisdenkschrift," in *Schriften, Aufsätze, Studien, Briefe*, ed. Werner Hahlweg, vol. 1 (Göttingen: Vandenhoek and Ruprecht, 1966), 750.

11. See Ellery Schalk, *From Valor to Pedigree* (Princeton, NJ: Princeton University Press, 1986), 21; Jay M. Smith, *The Culture of Merit: Nobility, Royal Service, and the Making of Absolute Monarchy in France, 1600–1789* (Ann Arbor: University of Michigan Press, 1996), 46; and Jonathan Dewald, *The European Nobility, 1400–1800* (Cambridge: Cambridge University Press, 1996).

12. Joseph Quincy, *Mémoires du Chevalier de Quincy*, 3 vols., ed. Léon Lecestre (Paris: Librairie Renouard, 1898–1900), 2:198.

13. In addition to values such as honor, glory, and virtue, the aristocratic ethos in the military sphere was also grounded in a physicality of self-control and expertise. See Kate Van Orden, *Music, Discipline, and Arms in Early Modern France* (Chicago: University of Chicago Press, 2005), 8, 54, 57–62. See also my concept of "technicity" in Christy Pichichero, "Battles of the Self: War and Subjectivity in Early Modern France" (PhD diss., Stanford University, 2008), chap. 1.

14. Benedetta Craveri, *The Age of Conversation*, trans. Teresa Waugh (New York: New York Book Review, 2005), 6. Ironically, the precise rules of the domain of style adopted by nobles could of course be mastered by the newly ennobled and wealthy bourgeois as well, a process related to the treatises of politeness and the salon milieu that we shall study in chapter 3.

15. Schalk, *From Valor to Pedigree*, 6.

16. Bell, *The First Total War*, 36.

17. Up to 25 percent of officers were of *roturier* origins by the end of Louis XIV's wars, a nonnegligible percentage that was alarming to members of the *noblesse d'épée*, whose family roots were grounded more deeply in the past. Hervé Drévillon, *L'individu et la guerre: Du Chevalier Bayard au Soldat inconnu* (Paris: Éditions Belin, 2013), 96.

18. L. Dussieux, *Les grands généraux de Louis XIV* (Paris: Lecoffre, 1888), 187.

19. Quoted in Émile-Guillaume Léonard, *L'armée et ses problèmes au XVIIIème siècle* (Paris: Plon, 1958), 41.

20. Pichichero, "Battles of the Self."

21. SHD 1M 1701, M. de Saint-Hilaire, "Traitté de la guerre où il est parlé des moyens de rédiger les troupes et y restablir l'ancienne et bonne discipline" [1712].

22. For more on Tissot's medical theory, see Anne C. Vila, *Enlightenment and Pathology: Sensibility in the Literature and Medicine of Eighteenth-Century France* (Baltimore: Johns Hopkins University Press, 1998), 188–96.

23. Ibid., 192.

24. For a discussion of gender and French mores, see David A. Bell, *The Cult of the Nation in France* (Cambridge, MA: Harvard University Press, 2001), chap. 5.

25. Translated in ibid., 149.

26. Louis-Sébastien Mercier, *Tableau de Paris*, vol. 3 (Amsterdam: n.p., 1782), 89.

27. See Christy Pichichero, "Moralizing War: Military Enlightenment in Eighteenth-Century France," in *France and Its Spaces of War: Experience, Memory, Image*, ed. Daniel Brewer and Patricia Lorcin (New York: Palgrave Macmillan, 2009).

28. Lauzun, quoted in Alain Berbouche, *L'histoire de la Royale: La marine française et la politique au siècle des Lumières (1715–1789)* (Saint-Malo: Pascal Galodé, 2012), 343.

29. SHD 1M 1703, le comte d'Argenson, "Raisonnemens sur ce que le lieutenant Colonel d'un Regimen, commandant de corps, ou capitaine doit observer pour le bien du service, avec un détail de l'état de l'officier, de sa vie et de sa conduite" [ca. 1743–1750].

30. See "Lettre de Jolly du 1er avril 1776" and "Lettre de Jolly du 4 avril 1776," in SHD A^4 44; quoted in Arnaud Guinier, *L'honneur du soldat: Éthique martiale et discipline guerrière dans la France des Lumières, 1748–1789* (Ceyzérieu: Champ Vallon, 2014), 303–4.

31. Paul-Henri Thiry, Baron d'Holbach, *La Morale universelle, ou les devoirs de l'homme fondés sur sa nature* (Amsterdam: Marc-Michel Rey, 1776), part 2, p. 127.

32. SHD 1M 1702, anonymous, untitled [1736].

33. SHD 1M 1703, anonymous, "Mémoire concernant les premières opérations à faire à la paix, tant dans le corps de la vieille infanterie que dans celuy des milices afin de pouvoir tirer de l'un et de l'autre des avantages considérables pour le service du Roy," also entitled "Mémoire contenant les moyens de porter le corps de l'infanterie françoise au plus haut point de perfection" [May 24, 1748].

34. SHD 1M 1708, Dossier Bombelles, "Mémoire contenant les moyens de remedier aux défauts qui se trouvent dans le corps de l'infanterie françoise et de le porter au plus haut point de perfection" (1756).

35. François Furet, *Interpreting the French Revolution* (Cambridge: Cambridge University Press, 1981), 192.

36. Bernardin de Saint-Pierre, *Études de la nature*, vol. 1 (Paris, 1804; first published 1784), 29. Cited in Daniel Gordon, *Citizens without Sovereignty: Equality and Sociability in French Thought, 1670–1789* (Princeton, NJ: Princeton University Press, 1994), 28.

37. Denis Diderot, "Réfutation de l'ouvrage d'Helvetius intitulé L'Homme," in *Oeuvres complètes*, vol. 2 (Paris, 1975; first published 1774), 382; cited in Daniel, *Citizens without Sovereignty*, 29.

38. Jean-Luc Quoy-Bodin, *L'armée et la Franc-maçonnerie: Au déclin de la monarchie sous la Révolution et l'empire* (Paris: Economica, 1987), 59.

39. Ibid., 40.

40. Ibid., 60–67.

41. Ibid., 62.

42. Ibid., 66.

43. Ibid., 67.

44. Ibid., 70.

45. Ibid., 59.

46. Pierre-Yves Beaurepaire, "Officiers 'moyens,' sociabilité et Franc-maçonnerie: Un chantier prometteur," *Histoire, Économie et Société* 23, no. 4 (October–December 2004): 541–50; quote and previous details on military lodges from 549.

47. Quoted in Quoy-Bodin, *L'armée et la Franc-maçonnerie*, 97.

48. Ibid., 54–55.

49. "Société," in *Encyclopédie ou dictionnaire raisonné des sciences, des arts et des métiers, par une Société de gens de lettres* (Paris, 1751–1772) 15:252.

50. Ibid., 253.

51. After rule number four, the author returns to the subject of social differences: "It is necessary to give not only the good that belongs to him, but also the degree of esteem and honor that he is owed according to his station and rank because subordination is the link of society and that without it there would be no order in families nor in civil government . . . But if the public good demands that inferiors obey, the same public good requires that superiors conserve the rights of those who submit to them and [that they] govern only to render them happier . . . This is the formal or tacit contract between men; some are above and the others are below in their difference of condition in order to render their society as happy as it can be." Ibid., 253–54.

52. Quoy-Bodin, *L'armée et la Franc-maçonnerie*, 77.

53. Quoted in ibid.

54. See chapter 4 in Kenneth Loiselle, *Brotherly Love: Freemasonry and Male Friendship in Enlightenment France* (Ithaca, NY: Cornell University Press, 2014).

55. Quoy-Bodin, *L'armée et la Franc-maçonnerie*, 79–83.

56. La Rochefoucauld, *Maximes et réflexions diverses* (Paris: Gallimard, 1976), 163.

57. Ibid.,163–66.

58. Carolyn Lougee, *Le Paradis des Femmes: Women, Salons, and Social Stratification in Seventeenth-Century France* (Princeton, NJ: Princeton University Press, 1976), 52.

59. Translated and quoted in ibid., 54.

NOTES TO PAGES 82–85   259

60. In *The Republic of Letters: A Cultural History of the French Enlightenment* (Ithaca, NY: Cornell University Press, 1995), Dena Goodman argues that utility did become a parameter in sociability of salons of the eighteenth century in which female heads (or *salonnières*) promoted the agendas in human progress of the Enlightenment and the Republic of Letters (53–54).

61. Gordon, *Citizens without Sovereignty*, 38.

62. SHD 1M 1703, M. de Lamée, "Essay sur l'art militaire dessein de l'ouvrage" [1742].

63. SHD 1M 1702, Lagarrigue, "Mémoire" [1733–1736].

64. César Chéneaux Du Marsais, "Philosophe," in *Encyclopédie*; my translation. For more on the term *honnête homme* and its connection to the mid-eighteenth-century definition of the *philosophe* in the *Encyclopédie*, see Daniel Brewer, "Constructing Philosophers," in *Using the Encyclopédie: Ways of Knowing, Ways of Reading*, ed. Daniel Brewer and Julie Candler Hayes, (Oxford: Voltaire Foundation, 2002): 21–35.

65. SHD 1M 1703, le comte d'Argenson, "Raisonnemens. . . ."

66. For more on *société*, see "Enlightenment and the Institution of Society: Notes for a Conceptual History," in *Main Trends in Cultural History*, ed. W. F. B. Melching and W. R. E. Velema (Amsterdam: Rodopi, 1994), 95–120.

67. See Samuel, Baron von Pufendorf, *De Jure Naturae et Gentium* (Lund, Sweden, 1672), book 2, chap. 3; and Gordon, *Citizens without Sovereignty*, 62–63, for a discussion of the work and its relation to other theories of natural law and sociability.

68. Antoine Lilti, *Le monde des salons: Sociabilité et mondanité à Paris au XVIIIe siècle* (Paris: Fayard, 2005), 86.

69. SHD 1M 1703, M. de Lamée, "Essay sur l'art militaire dessein de l'ouvrage" [~1742].

70. Ibid.

71. SHD 1M 1703, le comte d'Argenson, "Raisonnemens. . . ."

72. In both Lamée's definition and this one, essential human equality was the precondition for subordination, which itself was a practical organizing principle rather than a reflection of a profound inequality between men. Keith Baker has connected this theory of natural equality and functional inequality to Claude Buffier's *Traité de la société civile* (1726); see "Enlightenment and the Institution of Society."

73. Previously, absentee officers plagued the armed forces until the end of the *ancien régime*. Officers invented reasons for taking leave (health, weddings, lawsuits, etc.) and also abused the provision of the *semestre*, which granted leave from October to May for a percentage of officers. David D. Bien, "The Army in the French Enlightenment," *Past and Present* 85 (1979): 72.

74. For more on this history of garrisoning in France, see François Dallemagne, *Les casernes françaises* (Paris: Picard, 1990); John A. Lynn, *Giant of the Grand Siècle: The French Army, 1610–1715* (Cambridge: Cambridge University Press, 1997), 158–60; and André Corvisier, *L'armée française: De la fin du XVIIème siècle au ministère de Choiseul; le soldat* (Paris: PUF, 1964), 849–50.

75. In 1788 an ordinance permitted a *sage liberté* (judicious freedom) for garrisoned men, clarifying which men had free passage and allowing one-half of the soldiers in any unit to leave the garrison at any one time. Arnaud Guinier specifies that this freedom was framed as a right and not a question of royal grace, replacing harsh surveillance and arbitrary ad hoc decisions with a system based on just rules and increased trust in individual self-policing. Guinier, *L'honneur du soldat*, 309.

76. See André Corvisier, *Les contrôles de troupes de l'ancien régime* (Paris: État-major de l'armée de terre, Service historique, 1968) *with later volumes published* from 1968 through the early 1970s, and Guinier, *L'honneur du soldat*, 299–303.

77. For more on esprit de corps, see Guinier, *L'honneur du soldat*, 303–13.

78. SHD 1M 1703, anonymous, "Réflexions politiques" (ca. 1749).

79. Saxe, *Mes rêveries*, 150–51.

80. SHD 1M 1711, chevalier de Folard, "Sisteme nouveau de tactique" (ca. 1762–1776).

81. For more on theories of emulation in relationship to discipline, honor, and esprit de corps, see chaps. 9, 11, and 12 in Guinier, *L'honneur du soldat*.

82. See "Esprit de corps," in *Encyclopédie méthodique*, vol. 2 (Paris: Panckoucke, 1785), 312–14, and Guinier, *L'honneur du soldat*, 304, for these classifications.

83. Historian Clifford Rogers has informed me (pers. comm., June 2007) that during the fifteenth century in Europe people began to attribute the increasing ability of certain infantries to defeat opposing cavalries in battle to something akin to primary group cohesion. They advocated putting kin and neighbors together in infantry formations for the encouragement in valor and the shame in cowardice that close relations can exact on others. They ascertained that infantries that defeat cavalries often came from places with strong community cultures, such as Switzerland, Flanders, and England.

84. SHD 1M 1703, Chevalier de Montaut, "Réflexions sur la manière de former de bons soldats d'infanterie" (ca. 1747/1748).

85. The structures put in place by these ordinances were maintained into the Revolution. See SHD 1M 1897, "Service des armées en campagne: Comparaison des règlements antérieurs à 1809, jusqu'à et y compris 1809."

86. John A. Lynn, *The Bayonets of the Republic: Motivation and Tactics in the Army of Revolutionary France, 1791–1794* (Boulder, CO: Westview, 1996), 163, 169.

87. SHD 1M 1709, M. de Melfort, "Observations sur les différents détails relatifs à la nouvelle formation," (ca. 1762–1770).

88. Ibid.

89. A. P. C. Favart, *Mémoires et correspondence littéraires, dramatiques, et anecdotiques de C. S. Favart*, vol. 1 (Paris: Léopold Collin, 1808), 22.

90. On French national character and the gendering of their mores, see Bell, *The Cult of the Nation in France*, chap. 5.

91. See chapter 3 in this book; on medical philosophies of sensibility more broadly, see Vila, *Enlightenment and Pathology*.

92. Quoted in Albert de Broglie, *Maurice de Saxe et le marquis d'Argenson* (Paris: C. Lévy, 1893), 331.

93. Maurice de Saxe à Folard, May 5, 1746; quoted in ibid.

94. Louis Tuetey, Émile Léonard, David Bien, Rafe Blaufarb, John Lynn, David Bell, and others including myself have analyzed this in our scholarship. See Louis Tuetey, *Les officiers sous l'ancien régime: Nobles et roturiers* (Paris: Plon-Norrit, 1908); Corvisier, *L'armée française*; Léonard, *L'armée et ses problèmes*. In addition to these older works, see more recent research by Bien, "The Army in the French Enlightenment," 68–98; J. M. Smith, *The Culture of Merit*; and Rafe Blaufarb, *The French Army, 1750–1820: Careers, Talent, Merit* (Manchester, UK: Manchester University Press, 2002).

95. "Opéra comique," in *Encyclopédie*, 11: 495–96.

96. Antoine Le Camus, *La médecine de l'esprit* (Paris, 1753), 324.
97. Ibid., 246.
98. Ibid., 321.
99. Ibid., 322.
100. Ibid., 321.
101. Favart, *Mémoires et correspondence*, 26.
102. Ibid., 24.

103. It has been thought that, outside of his impromptu pieces on events at the front, Favart simply recycled material from the Parisian theater and replayed it in the Low Countries. However, closer examination of the plays themselves and comparative analyses that consider differences between the earlier Parisian versions of Favart's plays and the versions played and printed in Brussels uncover that this was not entirely the case.

104. My studies reveal that he also mitigated the tone of his *comédies militaires*, replacing some of the more violent words and expressions with less aggressive ones.

105. Hughes, *Forging Napoleon's Grande Armée*, 131.

106. For a history about actresses of the French theater, see Lenard Berlanstein, *Daughters of Eve: A Cultural History of French Theater Women from the Old Regime to the Fin de Siècle* (Cambridge: Harvard University Press, 2001).

107. Darrin McMahon, *Happiness: A History* (New York: Grove Press, 2006), 200.

108. Arnaud Balvay, *L'épée et la plume: Amérindiens et soldats des troupes de la marine en Louisiane et au Pays d'en Haut (1683–1763)* (Quebec: Presses Universitaires de Laval, 2006), 142.

109. For a cultural study of the rise of diplomacy in early modern Europe, see Timothy Hampton, *Fictions of Embassy: Literature and Diplomacy in Early Modern Europe* (Ithaca: Cornell University Press, 2009). On diplomacy and the performing arts, see Ellen R. Welch, *A Theater of Diplomacy: International Relations and the Performing Arts in Early Modern France* (Philadelphia: University of Pennsylvania Press, 2017).

110. See, among many others, works by Richard White, Gilles Havard, and Arnaud Balvay (previously cited) and Christian Ayne Crouch, *Nobility Lost: French and Canadian Martial Cultures, Indians, and the End of New France* (Ithaca, NY: Cornell University Press, 2014).

111. Amerindians often functioned as auxiliary troops in French military engagements and remained structurally separate entities from French forces. This configuration, in combination with the irregular style of warfare in North America, meant that social cohesiveness in battle was not pertinent as it was in the metropolitan army.

112. Christian Ayne Crouch, *Nobility Lost*, 44.

113. Jean Bernard Bossu, *Nouveaux voyages aux Indes occidentales*, vol. 1 (Paris: Le Jay, 1786), 123.

114. Zacharie de Pazzi de Bonneville, *De l'Amérique et des Américains: ou Observations curieuses du philosophe La Douceur, qui a parcouru cet hémisphere pendant la dernière guerre, en faisant le noble métier de tuer des hommes sans les manger* (Berlin: S. Pitra, 1771), 36.

115. See Cornelius J. Jaenen, "Amerindian Views of French Culture in the Seventeenth Century," *Canadian Historical Review* 55, no. 3 (September 1974), 261–91.

116. Crouch, *Nobility Lost*, 72–73.

117. These culture clashes and the efforts necessary to create a "middle ground" with Amerindian tribes would leave a lasting mark as Choiseul embarked on new projects for colonial expansion in islands of the Pacific Rim and the Indian and South

Atlantic Oceans. Bougainville and other officers who had served in the North American campaigns of the Seven Years' War propagated narratives of Amerindians as "brutal savages" whose strength, pride, and domineering spirit made holding onto Nouvelle France far too difficult. With this image in mind, Bougainville sent home visions of the docile, sociable, and sensuous people of Tahiti in his *Voyage around the World*. Given their temperament, the Tahitians would be much easier to interact with, and ultimately to dominate, than the proud Amerindian tribes of North America. For more on Bougainville's vision of the Tahitians in relation to his writings on indigenous tribes of North America, see chap. 6, "Paradise," in Crouch, *Nobility Lost*. While Diderot would mock Bougainville's Eurocentric imperialist vision of Tahitians, and while, as Sankar Muthu has shown, other intellectuals chimed together in a bid against empire, delusions and the desire for colonial domination would continue to be at the heart of French foreign policy. See Muthu, *Enlightenment against Empire* (Princeton, NJ: Princeton University Press, 2003).

118. See Jean-Jacques de Cotignon, *Mémoires du Chevalier de Cotignon: Gentilhomme nivernais officier de la marine de sa majesté Louis le seizième*, ed. Adrien Carré (Grenoble: Éditions des 4 Seigneurs, 1974), 360, for descriptions of the social life of a French officer serving on the Indian subcontinent.

119. Archives nationales (hereafter, AN) COL C/2/80, f° 72.

120. SHD A1 3541; SHD A1 3765; SHD 1 M 249^1; SHD 1 M 249^2; SHD 1 M 1106.

121. SHD 1 M 249^2, "Mémoire de Russel sur l'Inde" (1781), 56–57.

122. See *Memoirs of Hyder and Tippoo: Rulers of Seringapatam, Written in the Mahratta Language by Ram Chandra Rao "Punganuri," Who Was Long in Their Employ*, trans. Charles Philip Brown (Madras: Advertiser Press, 1849).

123. In an entry dated July 19, 1748, Pillai recorded a strained conversation between himself and the governor that displays the difficulties of managing information, business, and potentially conflicting friendships. *The Diary of Ananda Ranga Pillai, Translated from the Tamil by Order of the Government of Madras*, ed. H. Dodwell, vol. 5 (Madras: Government Press, 1917), 147–49.

124. SHD 1 M 232, "Mémoire sur l'Inde" (1757).

125. Cotignon, *Mémoires du Chevalier de Cotignon*, 341. The French hired, trained, and conducted thousands of sepoys in military operations in India during the eighteenth century. Because the French lacked sufficient European manpower, sepoys were essential for all martial endeavors. Cotignon expressed opinions about sepoys that Lally and some officers shared: they were learning discipline, but they were physically weak and cowardly. Cotignon said that fifty thousand French men could rout six hundred thousand sepoys, who should only be used for labor. Other officers, however, had much higher appraisals of sepoys' martial skills, bravery, and effectiveness. See SHD 1M 232.

126. SHD A1 3541; SHD A1 3629.

127. See John Garrigus, *Before Haiti: Race and Citizenship in French Saint-Domingue* (New York: Palgrave Macmillan, 2006), and Garrigus, "Catalyst or Catastrophe? Saint-Domingue's Free Men of Color and the Savannah Expedition, 1779–1782," *Review/Revista Interamericana* 22 (Spring/Summer 1992): 109–25; Stewart R. King, *Blue Coat or Powdered Wig: Free People of Color in Pre-Revolutionary Saint Domingue* (Athens: University of Georgia Press, 2001), among others.

128. AN Col. F3 188, Rouvray's "Reflexions."

129. Ibid.

130. Louis-Jean Christophe, baron de Closen, "Baron von Closen Journal," Library of Congress, Manuscript Division, vol. 2, 386.

131. Jean-François-Louis Crèvecoeur, comte de Clermont, *Journal de la guerre d'Amérique pendant les années 1780–1783* (Providence: Rhode Island Historical Society), 64.

132. Jean-Jacques Fiechter, "L'aventure américaine des officiers de Rochambeau vue à travers leurs journaux," in *Images of America in Revolutionary France*, ed. Michèle R. Morris (Washington, DC: Georgetown University Press, 1990), 76.

133. Ibid., 76–77.

134. For more on the political and social significance of the society in France, see Julia Osman, *Citizen Soldiers and the Key to the Bastille* (New York: Palgrave, 2015), 103–5.

135. Bell, *The Cult of the Nation in France*, 150 and chap. 5.

3. Humanity in War

1. For a broader though somewhat antiquated history on this subject, see Geoffrey Best, *Humanity in Warfare* (New York: Columbia University Press, 1983).

2. Jean Chagniot, "Une panique: Les Gardes françaises à Dettingen (27 juin 1743)," *Revue d'histoire moderne et contemporaine* 24 (1977): 78–95.

3. The duc de Choiseul commanded a regiment at Dettingen and wrote of its influence on the military reforms he proposed to the king in 1763. See *Mémoires du duc de Choiseul*, ed. Fernand Calmettes (Paris, 1904), 10.

4. See, for example, Reed Browning, *The War of the Austrian Succession* (New York: St. Martin's, 1993), 140.

5. Articles 1 and 6 of the 1864 convention read, respectively: "Ambulances and military hospitals shall be recognized as neutral, and as such, protected and respected by the belligerents as long as they accommodate wounded and sick," and "Wounded or sick combatants, to whatever nation they may belong, shall be collected and cared for."

6. Quoted in Michael Orr, *Dettingen, 1743* (London: Charles Knight, 1972), 4.

7. On the genealogy of humanity, see Richard Reitzenstein, *Werden und Wesen der Humanität im Altertum: Rede zur Feier des Geburtstages Sr. Majestät des Kaisers am 26. Januar 1907* (Strasbourg, 1907). On the sentimental turn, see William Reddy, *The Navigation of Feeling: A Framework for the History of Emotions* (Cambridge: Cambridge University Press, 2001), and Joan DeJean, *Ancients against Moderns: Culture Wars and the Making of a Fin de Siècle* (Chicago: University of Chicago Press, 1997).

8. *Encyclopédie ou Dictionnaire raisonné des sciences, des arts et des métiers*, ed. Denis Diderot and Jean-le-Rond d'Alembert (Paris: Briasson, David, Le Breton, 1751–1766), 15:52. I use the words *sensibilité* and sensibility interchangeably in this chapter.

9. *Encyclopédie*, 8:348.

10. Dan Edelstein has pointed to the antique origins of this paradox of humanity and has indicated multiple ways in which it provided a juridical justification for violence from the Renaissance through to the Terror during the French Revolution. See Dan Edelstein, *The Terror of Natural Right: Republicanism, the Cult of Nature, and the French Revolution* (Chicago: University of Chicago Press, 2009), 26–42.

11. Ibid., 15. This expression was coined by Marivaux in *La vie de Marianne* (1731–1735).

12. Ira Gruber, *Books and the British Army in the Age of the American Revolution* (Chapel Hill: University of North Carolina Press, 2010); Christopher Duffy, *The Army of*

Frederick the Great (New York: Hippocrene Books, 1974), 47–50; Armstrong Starkey, *War in the Age of Enlightenment, 1700–1789* (Westport, CT: Praeger, 2003), 86–89; Charles Royster, *A Revolutionary People at War: The Continental Army and the American Character, 1775–1783*, 2nd ed. (Chapel Hill: University of North Carolina Press, 1996); and Sarah Knott, *Sensibility and the American Revolution* (Chapel Hill: University of North Carolina Press, 2009).

13. On the genesis of this moral system and the book that Rousseau had planned to write on the subject, see the ninth book of Jean-Jacques Rousseau, *Confessions*, and Anne C. Vila, *Enlightenment and Pathology: Sensibility in the Literature and Medicine of Eighteenth-Century France* (Baltimore: Johns Hopkins University Press, 1998), 182–86.

14. See Vila, *Enlightenment and Pathology*, and Lynn Hunt, *Inventing Human Rights: A History* (New York: Norton, 2007), especially chap. 1.

15. This expression was first developed in Christy Pichichero "Le Soldat Sensible: Military Psychology and Social Egalitarianism in the Enlightenment French Army." *French Historical Studies* 31, no. 4 (Fall 2008), 553–80.

16. See Dan Edelstein, "Enlightenment Rights Talk," *Journal of Modern History* 86, no. 3 (September 2014): 530–65.

17. Michel Foucault, *Discipline and Punish: The Birth of the Prison* (New York: Vintage Books, 1977), 169.

18. Ibid., 140.

19. Ibid., 239.

20. Ibid., 151.

21. See Naoko Seriu, "The Paradoxical Masculinity of French Soldiers: Representing the Soldier's Body in the Age of the Enlightenment," EUI Working Paper, Max Weber Programme (Florence: European University Institute, 2009). On the subject, see also Arnaud Guinier, *L'honneur du soldat: Éthique martiale et discipline guerrière dans la France des Lumières, 1748–1789* (Ceyzérieu: Champ Vallon, 2014); Guinier, "Discipliner les corps dans l'armée française de la seconde moitié du xviiie siècle: L'héritage de surveiller et punir," in *Le corps dans l'histoire et les histoires du corps*, ed. M. Bouffard, J.-A. Perras, and E. Wicky (Paris: Hermann, 2013), 161–73; Guinier, "Les enjeux de la formation du soldat: Le problème de la métaphore mécanique dans les mémoires d'officiers de la seconde moitié du xviiie siècle," in *La construction du militaire: Savoir et savoir-faires militaires en Occident. 1494–1870: La formation du militaire*, ed. B. Deruelle and B. Gainot (Paris: Presses de la Sorbonne, 2013), 119–42; Guinier, "De guerre et de grâce: Le pas cadencé dans l'armée française de la seconde moitié du xviiie siècle (1750–1791)," *e-Phaïstos: Revue d'histoire des techniques* 4, no. 1 (2015): 15–26. For a broader perspective on the body, drill, and music, see William McNeill, *Keeping Together in Time: Dance and Drill in Human History* (Cambridge, MA: Harvard University Press, 1997).

22. Sabina Loriga, *Soldats—Un laboratoire disciplinaire: L'armée piémontaise au XVIIIe siècle* (Paris: Mentha, 1991), and Guinier, *L'honneur du soldat*, especially chap. 9.

23. Maurice de Saxe, *Mes rêveries suivies d'un choix de correspondance politique, militaire et privée* (Paris: Commission française d'histoire militaire / Institut de stratégie comparée / Economica, 2002), 91.

24. Ibid., 90.

25. Ibid., 12.

26. Ibid., 143.

27. On this subject, see DeJean, *Ancients against Moderns*, chap. 3, "A Short History of the Human Heart," 78–123.

28. Saxe, *Mes rêveries*, 3.

29. Ibid., 90–91.

30. Ibid., 90.

31. For a similar analysis and perspective on details, see Thomas W. Laqueur, "Bodies, Details, and the Humanitarian Narrative," in *The New Cultural History*, ed. Lynn Hunt (Berkeley: University of California Press, 1989), 176–204.

32. See DeJean, *Ancients against Moderns*, 82–89.

33. Guillaume Lamy, *Explication mécanique et physique des forces de l'âme sensitive, des sens, des passions, et du mouvement volontaire* (Paris: Lambert Roulland, 1678), and Étienne-Simon de Gamaches, *Système du coeur* (Paris: M. Brunet, 1708). For more on these works, see DeJean, *Ancients against Moderns*, 88–89.

34. John Locke, *An Essay concerning Human Understanding* (1690); David Hume, *A Treatise of Human Nature* (1739–1740), *An Enquiry concerning Human Understanding* (1748), and *An Enquiry concerning the Principles of Morals* (1751); and Étienne Bonnot de Condillac, *Essai sur l'origine des connoissances humaines* (1746).

35. The best genealogy of sensibility and philosophical medicine is in Vila, *Enlightenment and Pathology*.

36. Théophile de Bourdeu, *Recherches sur le tissu muqueux* (1767), in *Oeuvres complètes* (Paris: Chaille et Ravier Libraires, 1818), 187; quoted in Elizabeth A. Williams, *The Physical and the Moral: Anthropology, Physiology, and Philosophical Medicine in France, 1750–1850* (Cambridge: Cambridge University Press, 1994), 37.

37. Williams, *The Physical and the Moral*, 80–81. See also Peter Gay, "The Enlightenment as Medicine and Cure," in *The Age of the Enlightenment: Studies Presented to Theodore Besterman*, ed. W. H. Barber et al. (Edinburgh: St. Andrews University Publications, 1967), 375–86.

38. Laurence Brockliss and Colin Jones, *The Medical World of Early Modern France* (Oxford: Clarendon Press, 1997), 415.

39. Ibid., 408.

40. Ibid., 409. For more on medical commercialization and consumerism, see ibid., chap. 10, "Medical Entrepreneurialism in the Enlightenment," 622–70.

41. See R. S. Bray, *Armies of Pestilence: The Impact of Disease on History* (Cambridge: James Clarke, 1996), 144. Quote from Voltaire, *Histoire de la guerre de 1741* (Paris: Garnier, 1971), 33, cited in Browning, *The War of the Austrian Succession*, 120.

42. For more on the "Black Legend," see Colin Jones and Michael Sonenscher, "Social Functions of the Hospital in Eighteenth-Century France: The Case of the Hôtel-Dieu of Nîmes," *French Historical Studies* 13, no. 2 (Autumn 1983): 172–214. See also Brockliss and Jones, *The Medical World of Early Modern France*, 717–25.

43. Diderot, "Hôtel-Dieu," in *Encyclopédie*, 8:319–20.

44. See Jones and Sonenscher, "Social Functions of the Hospital," 175.

45. Quoted in L. G. Eichner, "The Military Practice of Medicine during the Revolutionary War," *Tredyffrin Easttown Historical Society History Quarterly* 41, no. 1 (Winter 2004): 25–32; quote on 28.

46. Ibid.

47. Erica Charters, "Colonial Disease, Translation, and Enlightenment: Franco-British Medicine and the Seven Years' War," in *The Culture of the Seven Years' War:*

Empire, Identity, and the Arts in the Eighteenth-Century Atlantic World, ed. Frans de Bruyn and Shaun Regan (Toronto: University of Toronto Press, 2014), 71.

48. On biological warfare during the eighteenth century, especially in North America, see Sheldon J. Watts, *Epidemics and History: Disease, Power, and Imperialism* (New Haven, CT: Yale University Press, 1997); Elizabeth A. Fenn, "Biological Warfare in Eighteenth-Century North America: Beyond Jeffrey Amherst," *Journal of American History* 86, no. 4 (March 2000), 1552–80; Paul Kelton, *Cherokee Medicine, Colonial Germs: An Indigenous Nation's Fight against Smallpox, 1518–1824* (Norman: University of Oklahoma Press, 2015). Amherst quote from the Bouquet papers, cited in Kelton, *Cherokee Medicine*, 103.

49. On efforts to manage naval disease specifically, see *Histoire des médecins et pharmaciens de marine et des colonies*, ed. P. Pluchon (Toulouse: Éditions Privat, 1985); Étienne Taillemite, *L'histoire ignorée de la marine française* (Paris: Librairie académique de Paris, 1988), 268–69; O. H. K. Spate, *Paradise Found and Lost: The Pacific since Magellan*, vol. 3 (Minneapolis: University of Minnesota Press, 1988), 191–96.

50. For background on France's corporative medical community, see chapters 3 and 8 in Brockliss and Jones, *The Medical World of Early Modern France*, and for commentary on the conflicts and debates between war commissioners, military physicians, and surgeons, see David M. Vess, *Medical Revolution in France, 1789–1796* (Gainesville: Florida State University Press, 1975), 27–28. For an overviews of French military and naval medicine, see Monique Lucenet, *Médecine, chirurgie et armée en France: Au siècle des Lumières* (Sceaux, France: I&D, 2006), and Brockliss and Jones, *The Medical World of Early Modern France*, 689–700.

51. Erica Charters contends that "although the history of medicine in the armed forces brings out underlying similarities between Britain and France during this period, these have not been studied as points of convergence. Medical developments in the British Army and the Royal Navy resembling those in French medicine are displayed as competing runners in a race, rather than teammates. Likewise, histories of eighteenth-century Europe as a cosmopolitan republic of letters consider war as an interruption and an obstacle, events that forced scholars to retreat into their national rivalries. As a result, there remains a gulf between military histories of eighteenth-century Europe and intellectual histories of the same period. This interdisciplinary consensus on Europe clashes with a more integrated view of war and scientific exchange beyond Europe's shores: while much work has been done on knowledge exchange between Europeans and non-Europeans, even in times of war, there are few studies that examine wars as opportunities for intra-European knowledge sharing and learning." She seeks to remedy this lacuna in her article "Colonial Disease, Translation, and Enlightenment"; quote from p. 74.

52. See Vess, *Medical Revolution in France*. Brockliss and Jones are skeptical of Vess's claim, just as many scholars have been of Geoffrey Parker's argument in *The Military Revolution: Military Innovation and the Rise of the West, 1500–1800* (New York: Cambridge University Press, 1988).

53. For more on the rise of surgery in Paris, see Brockliss and Jones, *The Medical World of Early Modern France*, chap. 9, "The Rise of Surgery," 553–621.

54. Théophile de Bordeu, *Recherches sur l'histoire de la médecine* (1764), in *Oeuvres complètes* (Paris: Chaille et Ravier Libraires, 1818), 504.

55. See Vess, *Medical Revolution in France*, 26–27.

56. Quoted in ibid., 27.

57. For more on the creation and implementation of the flying ambulance, see Dominique Larrey, *Memoirs of Military Surgery, and Campaigns of the French Armies*, vol. 1, trans. R. W. Hall (Baltimore: Joseph Cushing, 1814).

58. Dominique Larrey, *Memoirs of Military Surgery, and Campaigns of the French Armies*, vol. 2, trans. R. W. Hall (Baltimore: Joseph Cushing, 1814), 123.

59. Numerous works in French and English have been written on the history of the Invalides. See, for example, *Les Invalides: Trois siècles d'histoire* (Paris: Musée de l'armée, 1974); Isser Woloch, *The French Veteran from the Revolution to the Restoration* (Chapel Hill: University of North Carolina Press, 1979); and André Corvisier, *L'armée française de la fin du XVIIIe siècle au ministère de Choiseul: Le soldat* (Paris: Presses Universitaires de France, 1964). Hervé Drévillon and others have warned with legitimacy that the "caring" stance communicated by the state in forming the Invalides should be taken with a grain of salt, since other documents reveal the intent to control veterans who were seen as a threat and a social liability. See Hervé Drévillon, *L'individu et la guerre: Du Chevalier Bayard au Soldat inconnu* (Paris: Éditions Belin, 2013), 104, 118. Rather than viewing these tendencies as mutually exclusive, it may be preferable to see that the crown at once wanted to control and care for veterans, or at the very least wanted to be perceived as caring for its veterans.

60. See Jean Colombier, *Code de médecine militaire pour le service de terre* (Paris, 1772), v–ix.

61. Ibid., x. This notion of the "caring fiscal-military state" has been examined in the English context by Erica Charters in *Disease, War, and the Imperial State: The Welfare of the British Armed Forces during the Seven Years' War* (Chicago: University of Chicago Press, 2014), and Charters, "The Caring Fiscal-Military State during the Seven Years War, 1756–1763," *Historical Journal* 52: 4 (2009): 921–41

62. See Brockliss and Jones, *The Medical World of Early Modern France*, 692–700.

63. *Journal des Sçavans*, June 1767, 376; review of Richard de Hautesierck's *Recueil d'observations de médecine des hôpitaux militaires*. Quoted in Charters, "Colonial Disease, Translation, and Enlightenment," 73.

64. Antoine Poissonnier-Desperrières, *Traité sur les maladies des gens de mer* (Paris: Lacombe, 1767), 8.

65. Ibid., 14–15.

66. "Hygiène," in *Encyclopédie*, 8:385.

67. Louis, chevalier de Jaucourt, "Health," trans. Victoria Meyer, in *The Encyclopedia of Diderot and d'Alembert Collaborative Translation Project* (Ann Arbor: Michigan Publishing, University of Michigan Library, 2013), July 15, 2014, http://hdl.handle.net/2027/spo.did2222.0002.721 (translation of "Santé," in *Encyclopédie, ou Dictionnaire raisonné des sciences, des arts et des métiers*, vol. 14 [Paris, 1765]).

68. Paraphrased from "Hygiène," in *Encyclopédie*, 8:385.

69. Antoine Le Camus, *La médecine de l'esprit* (Paris, 1769), 303.

70. Ibid., 303–4.

71. Ibid., 142.

72. Ibid., 315.

73. Ibid., 325–26. These and other hygienic prescriptions can seem to belie a Foucauldian drive to construct and control the soldierly body. While such a disciplinary drive may have been present, and the imperative to preserve manpower was clear, doctors

and surgeons often related these objectives directly to an individualized ethics of care and humanity. For more on the subject of food and science during the Enlightenment, see Emma Spary, *Eating the Enlightenment: Food and the Sciences in Paris, 1670–1760* (Chicago: University of Chicago Press, 2012).

74. Jean Colombier, *Préceptes sur la santé des gens de guerre, ou Hygiène militaire* (Paris: Lacombe, 1775), 2–3.

75. As we saw in the previous chapter, discussions of the moral and physical degeneracy of the urban noble class abounded in eighteenth-century France, with critics railing about the sumptuousness of their surroundings, frequent pleasures, and leisurely lifestyles. Colombier added trending *sensibilité*-based ideas on neonatal care and childhood education to this discussion of noble health. Following Rousseau and others, he asserted that mothers should nurse their children rather than outsourcing to wet nurses; that caregivers should avoid subjecting infants to restrictive clothing, soft bedding (firm surfaces made of straw or horsehair were preferable), and warm, hermetically sealed rooms (which should rather be colder and ensure air circulation). See Rousseau's *Emile*, books 1 and 2. For more on female citizenship and motherhood, including breast-feeding, during the eighteenth century, see Annie K. Smart, *Citoyennes: Women and the Ideal of Citizenship in Eighteenth-Century France* (Newark: University of Delaware Press, 2011). As for military education for grandees and court nobles, Colombier's submissions echoed long-standing practices of noble martial education, some of which dated back to Vegetius, to whom the author referred directly. In this, predictably, the would-be warrior should engage in arms training, equestrian pursuits, hunting, and dancing.

76. On Monro and his work, specifically with patients deemed insane, see Jonathan Andrews and Andrew Scull, *Undertaker of the Mind: John Monro and Mad-Doctoring in Eighteenth-Century England* (Berkeley: University of California Press, 2001).

77. Colombier, *Préceptes*, 31–32.

78. Ibid., 37–48.

79. Ibid., 50–51.

80. Saxe, *Mes rêveries*, 62.

81. Ibid., 148.

82. Ibid., 141, 148.

83. Ibid., 141–42.

84. Scholars across the disciplines have been increasingly interested in the historical study of emotions in relation to early modern war. Previous work, such as that of Kennedy and McNeil, maintained that during the Revolutionary Age and prior to it the emotional and psychological toll of battle and of military life was either not a consideration or "deemed a defect of character or cowardice." *Military Psychology: Clinical and Operational Applications*, ed. Carrie H. Kennedy and Eric A. Zillmer (New York: Guilford, 2006), 2. For an intellectual history of cowardice and bravery, see William Ian Miller, *The Mystery of Courage* (Cambridge, MA: Harvard University Press, 2002). On war and emotion, see *Kulturgeschichte der Schlacht* (Krieg in der Geschichte) 78, ed. Marian Füssel and Michael Sikora (Paderborn: Schöningh, 2014). For a general presentation of the subject and for more on the context of eighteenth-century France, see Philip Shaw, *Suffering and Sentiment in Romantic Military Art* (Aldershot: Ashgate, 2013); and Thomas Dodman, *What Nostalgia Was: War, Empire, and the Time of a Deadly Emotion* (Chicago: University of Chicago Press, 2017). See also Nicole Eustache, *Pas-*

sion Is the Gale: Emotion, Power, and the Coming of the American Revolution (Chapel Hill: University of North Carolina Press, 2008), and R. D. Johnson, Seeds of Victory: Psychological Warfare and Propaganda (Aglen, PA: Schiffer, 1997).

85. See Peter N. Stearns and Carol Z. Stearns, "Emotionology: Clarifying the History of Emotions and Emotional Standards," *American Historical Review* 90, no. 4 (1985): 813–30.

86. DeJean, *Ancients against Moderns*, 9–81. In *The Passions of the Soul* (1649), Descartes advocated for replacing the existing vocabulary of *passion* and *affection* with a more vigorous term. See René Descartes, *Les passions de l'âme* (1649), in *Oeuvres philosophiques*, ed. Ferdinand Aliquié, vol. 3 (Paris: Garnier, 1973), 962. For more, see DeJean, *Ancients against Moderns*, 79–81.

87. David Denby, *Sentimental Narrative and the Social Order in France, 1760–1820* (Cambridge: Cambridge University Press, 1994), and Daniel Gross, *The Secret History of Emotion: From Aristotle's Rhetoric to Brain Science* (Chicago: University of Chicago Press, 2008).

88. I, 2, 11 §106 in Condillac, *Essay on the Origin of Human Knowledge* (Cambridge: Cambridge University Press, 2001), 69.

89. For example, SHD 1M 1703, anonymously written memoir dated May 24, 1748, "Mémoire concernant les premières opérations à faire à la paix, tant dans le corps de la vieille infanterie que dans celuy des milices afin de pouvoir tirer de l'un et de l'autre des avantages considérables pour le service du Roy," also entitled "Mémoire contenant les moyens de porter le corps de l'infanterie françoise au plus haut point de perfection."

90. In addition to medical, Christological, and affective definitions, the fourth edition of the dictionary of the Académie française offers a definition of passion as movement: "Mouvement de l'ame excité par quelque objet, dans ce que l'ancienne philosophie appelle la partie concupiscible, & la partie irascible de l'ame."

91. Descartes, *Les passions de l'âme*, 3:962.

92. Quoted in Seriu, "Fabriquer les sentiments: L'incitation au 'regret' par l'autorité. Armée française et désertion au XVIIIe siècle." *Nouveaux mondes, mondes nouveaux— Novo Mundo Mundos Novos—New World, New Worlds*. Online publication of IIe Journée d'Histoire des Sensibilités EHESS, March 10, 2005, https://nuevomundo.revues.org/850, accessed March 8, 2017. My translation.

93. For more on French national character and the debate on whether column or line formation (*l'ordre profond* or *l'ordre mince*) was more suitable, see Robert Quimby, *The Background of Napoleonic Warfare: The Theory of Military Tactics in Eighteenth-Century France* (New York: Columbia University Press, 1957).

94. Gross, *The Secret History of Emotion*.

95. My translation. SHD 1M 1709, M. de Montegnard, "Observation sur l'état actual de l'infanterie" (1764).

96. SHD 1M 1709, M. de Melfort, "Observations sur les différents détails relatifs à la nouvelle formation" (ca. 1762–1770).

97. Manuscript source quoted in Farge, *Les fatigues de la guerre* (Paris: Gallimard, 1996), 37.

98. SHD 1M 1709, le chevalier de Rochelambert, "Meditation militaire" (1760).

99. SHD 1M 1709, No author, "Reflexions sur la constitution militaire" (n.d.). For more on the emotion of ennui, see Pascale Goetschel, Christophe Granger, Nathalie

Richard, and Sylvain Venayre, eds., *L'ennui, histoire d'un état d'âme. XIXe–XXe siècles* (Paris: Presses Universitaires de la Sorbonne, 2012).

100. Montegnard, *Observation sur l'état actual de l'infanterie*.

101. Jacques-Antoine-Hippolyte de Guibert, "Essai général de tactique," in *Écrits militaires: 1772–1790* (Paris, Copernic, 1977), 64.

102. Saxe, *Mes rêveries*, 101.

103. SHD 1M, no. 17, anonymous, "Mémoire concernant les premières opérations à faire à la paix, tant dans le corps de la vieille infanterie que dans celuy des milices afin de pouvoir tirer de l'un et de l'autre des avantages considérables pour le service du Roy," also titled "Mémoire contenant les moyens de porter le corps de l'infanterie françoise au plus haut point de perfection" (May 24, 1748).

104. The Croix de Saint-Louis, a symbolic honor created by Louis XIV, was only for officers, as were titles and other monetary rewards bestowed on military men of this period.

105. GR 1M 1703, Chevalier de Montaut, "Réflexions sur la manière de former de bons soldats d'infanterie" (ca. 1747/1748).

106. SHD 1M 1709, M. de Montegnard, "Observation sur l'état actual de l'infanterie."

107. Charles de Mattei, marquis de Valfons, *Souvenirs du marquis de Valfons* (Paris: E. Dentu, 1860), 328.

108. SHD 1M 1709, M. de Melfort, "Observations sur les différents détails."

109. SHD series 1M, no. 1703, anonymous, "Mémoire concernant les premières opérations à faire à la paix, tant dans le corps de la vieille infanterie que dans celuy des milices afin de pouvoir tirer de l'un et de l'autre des avantages considérables pour le service du Roy," also entitled "Mémoire contenant les moyens de porter le corps de l'infanterie françoise au plus haut point de perfection" [May 24, 1748].

110. SHD 1M 1711, M. de Fauville, "Réfléxion militaire," (June 30, 1771), 14–15.

111. Ibid., 15.

112. Ibid.

113. Hunt, *Inventing Human Rights*, 20.

114. See Samuel Moyn, *The Last Utopia: Human Rights in History* (Cambridge, MA: Harvard University Press, 2010).

115. Edelstein, "Enlightenment Rights Talk," 533.

116. Ibid., 557.

117. Edelstein, "Enlightenment Rights Talk," 558, quoting Moyn, *Last Utopia*, 13.

118. Ibid., 541. See Diderot's article "Droit naturel" in *Encyclopédie* (1755), 5:115–16.

119. For a summary of this movement, see Jean Chagniot, *Paris et l'armée au XVIIIe siècle* (Paris: Economica, 1985), 618–28.

120. For more on these revisions, see Guinier, *L'honneur du soldat*, chap. 10.

121. For a period summary of the punishments associated with desertion, see Le Blond's article on the subject in the *Encyclopédie* (4:880).

122. Chagniot, *Paris et l'armée*, 621.

123. Ibid.

124. Ibid., 626.

125. Cesare Beccaria, *An Essay on Crimes and Punishments*, 4th ed. (Boston: Branden Books, 1992), 65–66. Beccaria's theory of punishment figures prominently in Foucault's genealogy of the prison in *Discipline and Punish*, since for him it represented a "new

strategy for the exercise of the power to punish" by which "to make of the punishment and repression of illegalities a regular function, coextensive with society; not to punish less, but to punish better; to punish with an attenuated severity perhaps, but in order to punish with more universality and necessity; to insert the power to punish more deeply into the social body." Foucault, *Discipline and Punish*, 81–82. Foucault here highlights the paradox of humanity conveyed by Diderot, which can be recognized without diminishing the importance of the move away from capital and corporal punishment for which Beccaria and others advocated.

126. Guinier, *L'honneur du soldat*, 271–72.

127. The impetus to improve the justice and effectiveness of the penal system did not mean that proposals for proper punishment were humane. Some ideas were not only cruel but downright grotesque. See, for example, Gratien-Jean-Baptiste-Louis, vicomte de Flavigny, *Réflexions sur la désertion et sur la peine des déserteurs en forme de lettre à Monsieur le duc de Choiseul* (1768), 33–34. Also in Chagniot, *Paris et l'armée*, 621 and 626.

128. Flavigny, *Réflexions sur la désertion*, 2–3. Also in Chagniot, *Paris et l'armée*, 623.

129. Chagniot, *Paris et l'armée*, 625.

130. Jaucourt and d'Alembert, "Déserteur," in *Encyclopédie*, 4:881.

131. Ferdinand Desrivières, *Réponse des soldats du régiment des Gardes Françoises aux loisirs d'une soldat du même regiment* (Paris: Chez Saillant, 1767), 46. Chagniot, *Paris et l'armée*, 624.

132. Chagniot, *Paris et l'armée*, 624.

133. Flavigny, *Réflexions sur la désertion*, 29–30. Also in Chagniot, *Paris et l'armée*, 624.

134. For an analysis of this practice of inciting regret, see Seriu, "Fabriquer les sentiments."

135. Voltaire, *Prix de la justice et de l'humanité* (London, 1777), 112.

136. Louis-Philippe, comte de Ségur, *Mémoires ou souvenirs et anecdotes*, vol. 1 (Paris: Eymery, 1825), 131–2, cited in Naoko Seriu, "Du feminine dans les discours militaires au XVIIIe siècle," *Genre et histoire*, no. 1 (Autumn 2007): 8 (sec. 16).

137. Duc des Cars, *Mémoires du duc des Cars*, vol. 1 (Paris: Plon, 1890), 144, cited in Seriu, "Du feminine," 8 (sec. 17).

138. For more on the evolving juridical system, see Guinier, *L'honneur du soldat*, 250–70.

139. Ibid., 284.

140. Ibid., 283–84.

141. See Étienne-François Girard, *Les cahiers du colonel Gérard*, ed. Pierre Desachy (Paris: Club des Éditeurs, 1961), 16–18. While Guinier insists that most military writings decrying the *coups* did so in citing violations of military honor (a claim that he does not support with evidence), it is equally important to note the role played by the defense of human rights.

142. In particular, St. Germain aimed to keep soldiers out of prisons, which were unsanitary in the extreme. On the guillotine, see Alister Kershaw, *A History of the Guillotine* (New York: Barnes and Noble, 1993).

143. For more on St. Germain's reforms, see Rafe Blaufarb, *The French Army, 1750–1820: Careers, Talent, Merit* (Manchester, UK: Manchester University Press, 2002), 28–33.

144. For more on notions of universal human nature versus a recognition of diversity, see Henry Vyverberg, *Human Nature, Cultural Diversity, and the French Enlightenment* (Oxford: Oxford University Press, 1989).

145. D'Estaing papers, Archives Nationales (AN) 562AP/19.

146. John D. Garrigus, *Before Haiti: Race and Citizenship in French Saint-Domingue* (New York: Palgrave Macmillan, 2006), 208.

147. For a microhistory on one eighteenth-century planter family in Cul de Sac, Saint-Domingue, see Paul Cheney, *Cul de Sac: Patrimony, Capitalism, and Slavery in French Saint-Domingue* (Chicago: University of Chicago Press, 2017).

148. *Affiches américaines*, Tuesday, March 30, 1779, no. 13; Bibliothèque nationale 4, lc 12 20/22. Quoted in Garrigus, *Before Haiti*, 209.

149. Garrigus, *Before Haiti*, 209.

150. AN Col. F3 188, Rouvray's "Reflexions," 29.

151. Ibid., 5.

152. Ibid., 6. Acquiescing to white colonists' fears about arming free people of color, Rouvray limited his racial egalitarianism to the space of the military. If some white people "fear that *gens de couleur* in the status of soldier would forget the respect that they must have for the color white or think they are equal to whites, here is my response: in civil status the *chasseur volontaire homme de couleur* is not less subject to laws and prejudices of colony. Once he is no longer a soldier, he returns to his civil status" (29–30).

153. On orientalism during the Enlightenment with particular attention to literature, see Srinivas Aravamudan, *Enlightenment Orientalism: Resisting the Rise of the Novel* (Chicago: University of Chicago Press, 2011); Madeleine Dobie, *Foreign Bodies: Gender, Language, and Culture in French Orientalism* (Stanford: Stanford University Press, 2002); and Julia Douthwaite, *Exotic Women: Literary Heroines and Cultural Strategies in Ancien Régime France* (Philadelphia: University of Pennsylvania Press, 1992).

154. SHD 1 M 249^2, "Mémoire de Russel sur l'Inde" (1781), 49.

155. Ibid., 50–51.

156. Ibid., 48.

157. Ibid., 55–56.

158. Ibid., 42.

159. Bonneville, *De l'Amérique et des Américains: ou Observations curieuses du philosophe La Douceur, qui a parcouru cet hémisphere pendant la dernière guerre, en faisant le noble métier de tuer des hommes sans les manger* (Berlin: S. Pitra, 1771), 48.

160. Ibid., 42–43.

161. Antoine-Joseph Pernety, *Dissertation sur l'Amérique et les Américains* (Berlin: G.J. Decker, ca. 1770), 105.

162. Jean-François-Louis Crèvecoeur, comte de Clermont, *Journal de la guerre d'Amérique pendant les années 1780–1783*, trans. Howard Rice and Anne Brown (Providence, RI: Rhode Island Historical Society, 1972), 64.

163. Both American and British armies used the promise of freedom from slavery to black, mixed-race, and Amerindian slaves in order to entice them into enlisting.

164. See John Garrigus, "Catalyst or Catastrophe? Saint-Domingue's Free Men of Color and the Savannah Expedition, 1779–1782," *Review/Revista Interamericana* 22 (Spring/Summer 1992): 109–25.

165. Starkey, *War in the Age of Enlightenment*, 94.

166. Ibid., 97.

4. A Nation of Warriors

1. See Edmond Dziembowski, *Le nouveau patriotisme français 1750–1770: La France face à la puissance anglaise à l'époque de la Guerre de Sept Ans*, Studies on Voltaire and the Eighteenth Century (Oxford: Voltaire Foundation, 1998), 373, and Michèle Fogel, *Les cérémonies de l'information dans la France du XVIe au milieu du XVIIIe siècle* (Paris: Fayard, 1989).

2. Referring to the king as head and possessor of the armed forces was not new to the eighteenth century. This was rather a long-standing tradition, as battle accounts always marked the king as the essential and originary agent even when he was not present at the battlefield. For seventeenth-century examples of this, see David Parrott, *Richelieu's Army: War, Government and Society in France, 1624–1642* (Cambridge: Cambridge University Press, 2001).

3. For a history of traditions in battle painting from Louis XIV to the early eighteenth century, see Julie Anne Plax, *Watteau and the Cultural Politics of Eighteenth-Century France* (Cambridge: Cambridge University Press, 2000), chap. 2. For Louis XIV's image as *roi de guerre*, or king of war, see Joël Cornette, *Le roi de guerre: Essai sur la souveraineté dans la France du Grand Siècle* (Paris: Payot, 1993), and Peter Burke, *The Fabrication of Louis XIV* (New Haven, CT: Yale University Press, 1992).

4. For a modern narrative and analysis of the battle of Fontenoy, see Armstrong Starkey, *War in the Age of Enlightenment, 1700–1789* (Westport, CT: Praeger, 2003), 105–31.

5. Letter from Louis XV to Maurice de Saxe, May 12, 1745, quoted in Francis Henry Skrine, *Fontenoy and Great Britain's Share in the War of the Austrian Succession, 1741–1748* (Edinburgh: Blackwood, 1906), 215.

6. Dziembowski, *Un nouveau patriotisme*, 373.

7. Skrine, *Fontenoy and Great Britain's Share*, 214.

8. Ibid.

9. See *Oeuvres complètes de Voltaire*, ed. Jean Michel Moreau, Louis Moland, Georges Bengesco, and Adrien Jean Quentin Beuchot (Paris: Garnier Frères, 1877), 372.

10. Michèle Fogel, "Célébrations de la monarchie et de la guerre: Les Te Deum de victoire en France de 1744 à 1743," in *La bataille, l'armée, la gloire, 1745–1871*, vol. 1 (Clermont-Ferrand: Association des publications de la Faculté des lettres et science humaines de Clermont-Ferrand II, 1985), 35–44; statistics on p. 35.

11. Ibid., 36.

12. The crown, too, turned toward the theater for propagandistic purposes. See Jeffrey Ravel, *The Contested Parterre: Public Theater and French Political Culture, 1680–1791* (Ithaca, NY: Cornell University Press, 1999).

13. See Julia Osman, *Citizen Soldiers and the Key to the Bastille* (New York: Palgrave, 2015). On citizen soldiers, see also Arnaud Guinier, "De l'autorité paternelle au despotisme légal: pour une réévaluation des origines de l'idéal du soldat-citoyen dans la France des Lumières," *Revue d'Histoire Moderne et Contemporaine*, vol. 2, n. 61–2 (2014): 151–76.

14. On dying for the patrie, see Elisabeth Guibert-Sledziewski, "Pour la patrie: mort héroïque et redemption," in *La bataille, l'armée, la gloire*, vol. 1, 199–208.

15. While David Bell has argued that militarism arose due to an increasing stigmatization of war as exceptional and a concomitant separation between military and civilian spheres, this chapter's narrative shows a similar end reached by a strikingly

different path. See Bell, *The First Total War: Napoleon's Europe and the Birth of War as We Know It* (Boston: Houghton Mifflin, 2007).

16. Jean-Henri Marchand, "Requête du curé de Fontenoy au roy" (Fontenoy, 1745), 7.

17. Claude Godard d'Aucour, *L'académie militaire, ou Les héros subalterns* (N.p., 1745), 19–21. On the literature of "subaltern heroes" and "citizen nobility," see André Corvisier, "Les 'héros subalternes' dans la littérature du milieu du XVIIIe siècle et la réhabilitation du militaire," *Revue du Nord*, vol. 66 (1984): 827–38 and Jay M. Smith, *Nobility Reimagined: The Patriotic Nation in Eighteenth-Century France* (Ithaca: Cornell University Press, 2005), esp. chapter 4.

18. Godard d'Aucour *L'académie militaire*, 19–21.

19. Ibid., 23.

20. Ibid., 393. The biographical notices explain the nicknames given to soldiers, recognize the accomplishments of future generations of their families (such as La Brie's younger brother, who is producing outstanding work at school and who already has an impressive punch), and make suggestions on how to care for surviving family members, like the newly widowed *vivandière* Fanchon, who could perhaps be married to another upstanding soldier in the regiment (395–96).

21. For more evolving perspectives regarding the *héros*, *homme illustre*, and *grand homme*, see Pierre-Jean Dufief, ed., *L'écrivain et le grand homme* (Paris: Droz, 2005).

22. Jaucourt, "Héros," in *Encyclopédie, ou Dictionnaire raisonné des sciences, des arts et des métiers*, 8:182.

23. Diderot, "Héroïsme," in *Encyclopédie*, 8:181.

24. Jaucourt, "Héros," 8:182.

25. Turpin de Crissé, *Amusemens philosophiques et littéraires de deux amis* (Paris: Prault, 1754).

26. Diderot, "Hérosime."

27. Jaucourt, "Héros."

28. Ibid.

29. See Louis Basset de la Marelle, *La différence du patriotisme national chez les François et chez les Anglais* (Lyon: Chez Aimé Delaroche, 1762). For a discussion of these categories of hero, see 9–12, and Jay M. Smith, *Nobility Reimagined*, 166–68.

30. La Marelle, *La différence du patriotisme national*, 10.

31. Ibid., 9.

32. Ibid., 10.

33. Smith, *Nobility Reimagined*, 7–9.

34. For a discussion of the origins of eighteenth-century French patriotism, see Dziembowski, *Un nouveau patriotisme*, 344–47.

35. Ibid., 342.

36. John Tell Truth, *Le patriote anglois, ou Réflexions sur les hostilités que la France reproche à l'Angleterre et sur la réponse de nos ministres au dernier Mémoire de S. M. T. C.*, translated into English by Abbé Jean-Bernard Le Blanc (Geneva: 1756), iv–v.

37. Ibid., 2.

38. David A. Bell, *The Cult of the Nation in France: Inventing Nationalism, 1680–1800* (Cambridge, MA: Harvard University Press, 2003), 107. Quote by Antoine-Léonard Thomas from *Essai sur les éloges* (Paris, 1829), 40–41.

39. Bell, *The Cult of the Nation*, 111–12.

40. Ibid., 109–11.

41. Abbé de Saint-Pierre, "Discours sur les différences du grand homme et de l'homme illustre," in *Histoire d'Epaminondas pour server de suite aux hommes illustres de Plutarque* (Paris, 1739), xxi–xliv.

42. Antoine-Léonard Thomas, *Éloge de René Duguay-Trouin* (Paris: Imprimeur de l'Académie française, 1761), 19–20.

43. Ibid., 38.

44. Ibid., 59.

45. Jean-François de la Harpe, *Éloge de Nicolas de Catinat* (Paris: Chez Demonville, 1775), 27–28.

46. Louis-Sébastien Mercier, *Le déserteur* (Paris, 1770), 32–33.

47. Ibid., 35–36.

48. See, for example, Leslie Tuttle, "Celebrating the Père de Famille: Fatherhood in Eighteenth-Century France," *Journal of Family History* 29, no. 4 (2004): 66–381; and Tuttle, *Conceiving the Old Regime: Pronatalism and the Politics of Reproduction in Early Modern France* (Oxford: Oxford University Press, 2010); Meghan K. Roberts, "Philosophes Mariés et Epouses Philosophiques: Men of Letters in Eighteenth-Century France," *French Historical Studies* 35, no. 3 (2012): 509–39; Roberts, "Cradle of Enlightenment: Family Life and Knowledge Making in Eighteenth-Century France" (PhD diss., Northwestern University, 2011); and Roberts, *Sentimental Savants: Philosophical Families in Enlightenment France* (Chicago: University of Chicago Press, 2016).

49. On military marriage, see Jennifer Ngaire Heuer, "Celibacy, Courage, and Hungry Wives: Debating Military Marriage and Citizenship in Pre-Revolutionary France," *European History Quarterly* 46, no. 4 (October 2016): 648–67. On marriage more broadly, see, for example, Sian Reynolds, *Marriage and Revolution: Monsieur and Madame Roland* (Oxford: Oxford University Press, 2012); Dena Goodman, "Making Choice and Marital Success: Reasoning about Marriage, Love and Happiness," in *Family, Gender, and Law in Early Modern France*, ed. Jeffrey Merrick and Suzanne Desan (University Park: Pennyvania State University Press, 2009), 26–61; Denise Davidson, "'Happy' Marriages in Early Nineteenth-Century France," *Journal of Family History* 37, no. 1 (2012): 23–35; and Suzanne Desan, *The Family on Trial in Revolutionary France* (Berkeley: University of California Press, 2004).

50. Heuer, "Celibacy, Courage, and Hungry Wives," 3.

51. See Bell, *The Cult of the Nation*, chap. 3.

52. Louis-Guerin d'Azémar, *Les deux miliciens ou l'orpheline villageoise* (Paris, 1771), 6.

53. Louis Anseaume, *Le soldat magicien* (Paris, 1775), 11–12.

54. These numbers are drawn from the CÉSAR (Calendrier électronique des spectacles sous l'ancien régime et sous la revolution), http://www.cesar.org.uk/cesar2/home.php.

55. Antoine-Hippolyte de Guibert, "*Essai général de tactique*," in *Écrits militaires: 1772–1790* (Paris, Copernic, 1977), 14.

56. Ibid., xvii.

57. SHD 1M 1704, "Réflexion sur la constitution militaire."

58. Arnaud Guinier, *L'honneur du soldat: Éthique martiale et discipline guerrière dans la France des Lumières, 1748–1789* (Ceyzérieu: Champ Vallon, 2014), 338.

59. Quoted in Ravel, *The Contested Parterre*, 197.

60. Ibid., 198.

61. *The Chronicles of Froissart*, trans. John Bourchier, Lord Berners, edited and reduced into one volume by G. C. Macaulay (London, 1924), chap. 146, "How the Town of Calais Was Given Up to the King of England," 155. For more on Belloy's play, see Clarence Brenner, *L'histoire national dans la tragédie française du XVIIIe siècle* (Berkeley: University of California Press, 1929); Margaret M. Moffat, "*Le siège de Calais* et l'opinion publique en 1765," *Revue d'Histoire littéraire de la France* 39, no. 3 (1932): 339–54; Anne Boës, *La lanterne magique de l'histoire* (Oxford: Voltaire Foundation, 1982); Jean-Marie Moeglin, *Les bourgeois de Calais* (Paris: Albin Michel, 2002).

62. Quoted in Bell, *The Cult of the Nation*, 122.

63. See Du Verdier's *Roman des dames* (1629, republished in 1632 as *Les Amazones de la cour*), Le Maire's *La Prazimène* (1638), and Gomberville's *Polexandre* (1632), as well as Le Moyne's *La gallerie des femmes fortes* (1647), to which Joan DeJean makes reference in *Tender Geographies: Women and the Origins of the Novel in France* (New York: Columbia University Press, 1991), 24–29. For lists and analyses of such novels, their characters, and collective biographies, see Maurice Magendie, *Le roman français au XVIIe siècle: De l'astrée au grand Cyrus* (Paris: Droz, 1932); Ian Maclean, *Woman Triumphant: Feminism in French Literature, 1610–1652* (Clarendon Press, 1977); and Natalie Zemon Davis, "'Women's History' in Transition: The European Case," *Feminist Studies* 3, no. 3/4 (Spring 1976): 83–103.

64. Antoine-Léonard Thomas, *Essai sur le caractère, les moeurs et l'esprit des femmes dans les différents siècles* (Amsterdam: Aux dépens de la Compagnie, 1772). This and further quotes come from the English translation, *An Essay on the Character, the Manners, and the Understanding of Women in Different Ages*, trans. Mrs. Kindersley, with two original essays (London: J. Dodsley, 1781), 144.

65. Thomas, *Essai sur le caractère*, 144–46.

66. Ibid., 146.

67. Annie Smart, *Citoyennes: Women and the Ideal of Citizenship in Eighteenth-Century France* (Newark: University of Delaware Press, 2011), 1.

68. Ibid., 1–2. See William H. Sewell Jr., "Le Citoyen/Citoyenne: Activity, Passivity, and the Revolutionary Concept of Citizenship," in *The French Revolution and the Creation of Modern Political Culture*, vol. 2, *The Political Culture of the French Revolution*, ed. Colin Lucas (New York: Pergamon Press, 1987–1989), 105–23; Joan Wallach Scott, *Only Paradoxes to Offer: French Feminists and the Rights of Man* (Cambridge, MA: Harvard University Press, 1996); Carole Pateman, *The Sexual Contract* (Stanford: Stanford University Press, 1988), and Pateman, *The Disorder of Women: Democracy, Feminism and Political Theory* (Stanford: Stanford University Press, 1989).

69. On women and the Fronde, see Faith Beasley, *Revising Memory: Women's Fiction and Memoirs in Seventeenth-Century France* (New Brunswick, NJ: Rutgers University Press, 1990); DeJean, *Tender Geographies*; Dominique Godineau, "De la guerrière à la citoyenne: Porter les armes pendant l'Ancien Régime et la Révolution française," *CLIO* 20 (2004): 43–69; and Sylvie Steinberg, *La confusion des sexes: Le travestissement en France à l'époque moderne, XVIe–XVIIIe siècles* (Lille: ANRT, 1999); as well as the following works by Sophie Vergnes: *Les Frondeuses: Une révolte au féminin, 1643–1661* (Seyssel, Champ Vallon, 2013); "Anne d'Autriche pendant la Fronde: Une régente dans la tourmente devant le tribunal de ses contemporains," in *Le bon historien sait faire parler les silences* (Toulouse: Méridiennes, 2012), 77–90; "Braver Mazarin: La duchesse de Bouillon dans la Fronde," *Clio* 33 (Spring 2011): 259–78; "La duchesse de Longueville et ses frères pendant la Fronde: De la

solidarité fraternelle à l'émancipation féminine," *Dix-septième Siècle*, no. 251 (April 2011): 309–32; "Les dernières Amazones: Réflexions sur la contestation de l'ordre politique masculin pendant la Fronde," *Les Cahiers de Framespa*, no. 7 (2011), http://framespa.revues.org/674, accessed March 10, 2017; "Des discours de la discorde: Les femmes, la Fronde et l'écriture de histoire," *Études Epistémè*, no. 19 (2011): 69–84; "De la guerre civile comme vecteur d'émancipation féminine: L'exemple des aristocrates frondeuses (France 1648–1653)," *Genre et Histoire*, no. 6 (Spring 2010), http://genrehistoire.revues.org/932, accessed March 10, 2017; "The Princesse de Condé at the Head of the Fronde des Princes: Modern Amazon or Femme Prétexte?," *French History* 22, no. 4 (December 2008): 406–24. See also Guyonne Leduc, ed., *Réalité et représentations des Amazones* (Paris: Harmattan, DL, 2008). Vergnes distinguishes two categories of Frondeuses: "intriguantes et médiatrices," schemers and mediators, who acted as diplomats and power brokers; and Frondeuses-Amazones, who participated directly in martial violence.

70. See Dominique Godineau, "De la guerrière à la citoyenne," bullet points 5–7 in the online version of the article.

71. On Chapelain's and Voltaire's epic poems, see chap. 1 in Nora M. Heimann, *Joan of Arc in French Art and Culture, 1700–1855* (Aldershot: Ashgate, 2005). See also Jennifer Tsien, *Voltaire and the Temple of Bad Taste: A Study of "La Pucelle d'Orléans"* (Oxford: Voltaire Foundation, 2003).

72. See Thomas Cardoza, "'Habits Appropriate to Her Sex': The Female Military Experience in France during the Age of Revolution," in *Gender, War, and Politics: Transatlantic Perspectives, 1775–1830*, ed. Karen Hagemann, Gisela Mettele, and Jane Randall (New York: Palgrave Macmillan, 2010), 192.

73. While *femmes soldats* have received more scholarly attention than sutlers and laundresses, the latter far outrepresented the former at warfronts (eight *vivandières* and seven to ten *blanchisseuses* per regiment). These women provided vital services to the army and, as *filles aguerries* who were often *enfants de troupe*, they became female soldiers when necessary. See Thomas Cardoza, *Intrepid Women: Cantinières and Vivandières of the French Army* (Bloomington: Indiana University Press, 2010), 12, 15.

74. Steinberg has found forty-four such cases, though there are surely many more who went undocumented or were never discovered within their units. See John Lynn, *Women, Armies, and Warfare in Early Modern Europe* (Cambridge: Cambridge University Press, 2008); Cardoza, *Intrepid Women*; Steinberg, *La confusion des sexes*.

75. Steinberg, *La confusion des sexes*, 83–84. Steinberg named the tropes discussed in this section.

76. Arsenal, Arch. Bastille, MS 10136, pp. 143–144. Steinberg, *La confusion des sexes*, 51–52.

77. SHD A1 1768. Steinberg, *La confusion des sexes*, 55–56.

78. SHD Y^a 507, dossier Kellerin. See also Steinberg, *La confusion des sexes*, 53, and Cardoza, "'Habits Appropriate to Her Sex.'"

79. Steinberg, *La confusion des sexes*, 53.

80. Smart, *Citoyennes*, 3.

81. Rozoi argued in his preface that "if the different affections of an *âme sensible* did not signal a conflict between patriotism and nature, Eustache wouldn't be interesting at all," which is true of Emilie as well (xi).

82. *The Diary of Ananda Ranga Pillai*, ed. H. Dodwel, vol. 2 (Madras: Government Press, 1917), 314–18.

83. The same cannot be said for George Washington, who did become a hero and something of a myth in French culture. See Julia Osman, "Cincinnatus Reborn: The George Washington Myth and French Renewal during the Old Regime," *French Historical Studies* 38, no. 3 (2015): 421–46.

84. Colonial and naval forces had numerous iterations and regroupings during the eighteenth century, particularly following the Seven Years' War. See René Chartrand, *Louis XV's Army*, vol. 5, *Colonial and Naval Troops* (Oxford: Osprey, 1997).

85. Christopher Tozzi, *Nationalizing France's Army: Foreign, Black, and Jewish Troops in the French Military, 1715–1831* (Charlottesville: University of Virginia Press, 2016), 17. See also "The Nation and the Army: Foreigners and Minorities in French Military Service, 1715–1831" (PhD. diss., Johns Hopkins University, 2011).

86. See Tozzi, *Nationalizing France's Army*, chap. 1.

87. See André Corvisier, "Les soldats noirs du maréchal de Saxe: Le problème des Antillais et Africains sous les armes en France au XVIIIe siècle," *Revue Française d'Outre-Mer* 55, no. 201 (1968): 367–413.

88. This same law did permit colonists to bring or send their slaves to France for a maximum of three years for the purposes of serving their masters or pursuing vocational training as long as slave owners went through a strict process of declaring and registering each slave. See Pierre H. Boulle and Sue Peabody, *Le droit des noirs en France au temps de l'esclavage* (Paris: L'Harmattan, 2014).

89. Corvisier, "Les soldats noirs du maréchal de Saxe," 395–97.

90. SHD A^1 3200, quoted in ibid., 377.

91. Ibid.

92. Garrigus, *Before Haiti: Race and Citizenship in French Saint-Domingue* (New York: Palgrave Macmillan, 2006), 112.

93. Ibid., 113.

94. He proposed a much derided plan to reinstate generalized militia service, which at once violated liberal virtue and also denied the chance for free men of color to demonstrate their civic virtue by serving voluntarily rather than by government mandate. See ibid., 119–24.

95. Ibid., 123.

96. *Affiches américaines*, March 21, 1780, no. 12, quoted in Garrigus, *Before Haiti*, 206.

97. *Affiches américaines*, April 6, 1779, no. 14.

98. Balvay, *L'épée et la plume*, 252.

99. Ibid., 247–52.

100. Stewart R. King, *Blue Coat or Powdered Wig: Free People of Color in Pre-Revolutionary Saint Domingue* (Athens: University of Georgia Press, 2001).

101. Osman, *Citizen Soldiers*, 117.

102. For more on these reforms, see Alain Berbouche, *L'histoire de la Royale: La marine française et la politique au siècle des Lumières, 1715–1789* (Saint-Malo: Pascal Galodé, 2012), 280–82.

103. Ibid., 284.

104. Drévillon, *L'individu et la guerre: Du Chevalier Bayard au Soldat inconnu* (Paris: Éditions Belin, 2013), 117.

105. Jean-Paul Bertaud, *La révolution armée: Les soldats-citoyens et la Révolution française* (Paris: Robert Laffont, 1979), 41–42. Osman has found numerous examples in which soldiers sided with grain rioters and on several occasions refused to enforce

higher grain prices. "Throughout this time of upheaval, French soldiers became markedly closer to civilian inhabitants, whose rioting had usually garnered a more violent state-sponsored reaction from soldiers." See Osman, *Citizen Soldiers*, 121.

106. Translated on page 366 in Jay M. Smith, "Social Categories the Language of Patriotism, and the Origins of the French Revolution: The Debate over noblesse commerçante," *Journal of Modern History* 72, no. 2 (June 2000): 339–74.

107. Osman, *Citizen Soldiers*, 124.

5. The Dialectic of Military Enlightenment

1. George Sand, *Oeuvres complètes de George Sand: Histoire de ma vie* (Paris: Lévy, 1892), 49.

2. Voltaire, *Catalogue des écrivains* vol. 9 (1733), in *Le siècle de Louis XIV* (Geneva: Cramer et Bardin, 1775), 11–13.

3. Jeremy Black, *War and the Cultural Turn* (Cambridge: Polity Press, 2012), 167.

4. Scholars also disagree on how to define "total war" and on whether it constitutes a useful analytical category. I agree with David A. Bell that the term "total war" is most useful when viewed as a production of a broader cultural and political context. On total war and the historiographical debate regarding it, see, for example, David A. Bell, *The First Total War: Napoleon's Europe and the Birth of War as We Know It* (Boston: Houghton Mifflin, 2007); Michael Broers, "The Concept of 'Total War' in the Revolutionary-Napoleonic Period," *War in History* 15, no. 3 (2008): 247–68; Roger Chickering, "Total War: The Use and Abuse of a Concept," in *Anticipating Total War: The German and American Experiences, 1871–1914*, ed. Manfred F. Boemeke, Roger Chickering, and Stig Förester (Washington, DC: German Historical Institute, 1999), 13–28; Eugenia C. Kiesling, "'Total War, Total Nonsense' or 'The Military Historian's Fetish,'" in *Arms and the Man: Essays in Honor of Dennis Showalter*, ed. Michael S. Neiberg (Leiden: Brill, 2011), 215–42; Hervé Drévillon, *L'individu et la guerre : Du Chevalier Bayard au Soldat inconnu* (Paris: Éditions Belin, 2013); Jean-Yves Guiomar, *L'invention de la guerre totale: XVIIIe–XXe siècle* (Paris: Le Félin Kiron, 2004). See also the forum: David Bell, Annie Crépin, Hervé Drévillon, Olivier Forcade, and Bernard Gainot, "Autour de la guerre totale," *Annales historiques de la révolution française*, no. 366 (2011): 153–70; and Erica Charters, Eve Rosenhaft, and Hannah Smith, *Civilians and War in Europe, 1618–1815* (Liverpool: Liverpool University Press, 2012).

5. See Gunther E. Rothenberg, *The Art of Warfare in the Age of Napoleon* (Bloomington: Indiana University Press, 1978), 61; the methodology of this calculation has seen some criticism. On Napoleon's wars specifically, see Charles Esdaile, *Napoleon's Wars: An International History* (New York: Penguin, 2009).

6. While Jean-Yves Guiomar has shown that the moniker "la Grande Nation" dated to the beginning of the French Revolution, he stipulates that "for France to be designated as 'la Grande Nation' with the character of exclusivity and absolutes signified by the definite article, one must wait until August 1797." See Guiomar, "Histoire et signification de 'la Grande Nation' (August 1797–Autumn 1799): Problèmes d'interprétation," in *Du Directoire au Consulat*, vol. 1, *Le lien politique local dans la Grande Nation*, ed. Jacques Bernet et al. (Lille: Centre de Recherche sur L'Histoire de l'Europe du Nord-Ouest, 1999), 317–27; quote from p. 317.

7. See Alan Forrest, *Conscripts and Deserters: The Army and French Society during the Revolution and Empire* (New York: Oxford University Press, 1989), and Isser Woloch, *The New Regime: Transformations of the French Civic Order, 1789–1820s* (New York: Norton, 1994).

8. For more on the rise of militarist discourse, see Wolfgang Kruse, "La formation du discours militariste sous le directoire," *Annales historiques de la Révolution française* 360, no. 2 (2010): 77–102.

9. Brian Joseph Martin, *Napoleonic Friendship: Military Fraternity, Intimacy, and Sexuality in Nineteenth-Century France* (Lebanon: University of New Hampshire Press, 2011), 2.

10. Compared to previous chapters, this chapter focuses primarily on secondary sources to make its arguments.

11. Philippe Masson, "La marine sous la Révolution et l'Empire," in *Histoire militaire de la France*, vol. 2, 375.

12. Rafe Blaufarb, *The French Army, 1750–1820: Careers, Talent, Merit* (Manchester, UK: University of Manchester Press, 2002), 133.

13. See ibid., chaps. 2–5; Samuel Scott, *The Response of the Royal Army to the French Revolution: The Role and Development of the Line Army, 1787–93* (Oxford: Oxford University Press, 1973); Jean-Paul Bertaud, *La Révolution armée: Les soldats citoyens de la Révolution française* (Paris: Robert Laffont, 1979); Bertaud, *La vie quotidienne des soldats de la Révolution, 1789–1799* (Paris: Hachette, 1985); Forrest, *Conscripts and Deserters*; John A. Lynn, *The Bayonets of the Republic: Motivation and Tactics in the Army of Revolutionary France, 1791–94* (Boulder, CO: Westview Press, 1984); Howard G. Brown, *War, Revolution, and the Bureaucratic State: Politics and Army Administration, 1791–1799* (Oxford: Clarendon Press, 1995); and Brown, *Ending the French Revolution: Violence, Justice, and Repression from the Terror to Napoleon* (Charlottesville: University of Virginia Press, 2006), among others.

14. Blaufarb, *The French Army*, 46.

15. *Archives parlementaires de 1787–1860*, Series 1, ed. J. Mavidal and E. Laurent (Paris: 1867–1913, 1985), 5:v, 533 and 4:120–338. See also Julia Osman, *Citizen Soldiers and the Key to the Bastille* (New York: Palgrave, 2015), 122–23.

16. SHD 1M 1718. On the regimental cahiers and military committee, see Blaufarb, *The French Army*, 52–60; Osman, *Citizen Soldiers*, chap. 6.

17. SHD 1M 1718, "Adresse du regiment de Forez à l'Assemblée National, 5 7bre 1789," quoted in Osman, *Citizen Soldiers*, 134.

18. On conscription in the French army, see in particular Annie Crépin, *Défendre la France: Les Français, la guerre et le service militaire, de la guerre de Sept Ans à Verdun* (Rennes: Presses Universitaires de Rennes, 2005); Crépin, *Histoire de la conscription* (Paris: Gallimard, 2009); and on the transformations of the army during this period, see her chapter "The Army of the Republic: New Warfare and a New Army," in *Republics at War, 1776–1840: Revolution, Conflicts, and Geopolitics in Europe and the Atlantic World*, ed. Pierre Serna, Antonio de Francesco, and Judith A. Miller (Basingstoke: Palgrave Macmillan, 2013).

19. *Archives parlementaires de 1787–1860*, 17:298; Osman, *Citizen Soldiers*, 138.

20. Blaufarb, *The French Army*, chap. 2.

21. Drévillon, *L'individu et la guerre*, 220.

22. Archives Historiques du Service de Santé de l'Armée au Val-de-Grâce, carton 28, dossier 6. Thirion, "Mémoire justificatif aux citoyens composants le conseil de santé," December 1793, cited in Thomas Dodman "Homesick Epoch: Dying of Nostalgia in Post-Revolutionary France" (PhD diss., University of Chicago, 2011), 120.

23. Jean-Baptiste-Charles Chabroud, *Rapport et projet de loi sur les délits et les peines militaires* (Paris: Imprimerie Nationale, 1791), 22.

24. See Drévillon, *L'individu et la guerre*, 155–56.

25. Charles H. Hammond, "The French Revolution and the Enlightening of Military Justice," *Proceedings of the Western Society for French History* 34 (2006): 134–46.

26. Blaufarb notes that only 12.5 percent of such commissions were actually awarded based on seniority and that the other commissions were to be filled via nomination by regimental cadres. Blaufarb, *The French Army*, 72.

27. "Lettre à Madame de Medel" (October 8, 1789), *Marquis de Ferrières, correspondance inédite (1789, 1790, 1791)*, ed. Henri Carré (Paris: Armand, Colin, 1932), 120. Cited in Blaufarb, *The French Army*, 57.

28. Title for chap. 6 in Blaufarb, *The French Army*, 164.

29. Drévillon, *L'individu et la guerre*, 157.

30. Ibid.

31. Osman, *Citizen-Soldiers*, 127.

32. For a brief survey of the meaning of fraternity during the Enlightenment, see Martin, *Napoleonic Friendship*, 20–22.

33. Simon Schama, *Citizens: A Chronicle of the French Revolution* (New York: Vintage, 1990), 502; and Martin, *Napoleonic Friendship*, 23.

34. Mona Ozouf, *La fête révolutionnaire* (Paris: Gallimard, 1976), 55–56, cited in Martin, *Napoleonic Friendship*, 23.

35. Camille Desmoulins, *Révolutions de France et de Brabant*, 8 vols. (Paris: Garnery, 1789–1791), 35:510, cited in Martin, *Napoleonic Friendship*, 26.

36. Camille Desmoulins, *Révolutions de France et de Brabant*, 35:509, cited in Martin, *Napoleonic Friendship*, 25.

37. Lynn, *The Bayonets of the Republic*, 59.

38. On *l'ordinaire* and motivation, see ibid., chap. 7.

39. Quoted in ibid., 168.

40. Michael J. Hughes, *Forging Napoleon's Grande Armée: Motivation, Military Culture, and Masculinity in the French Army, 1800–1808* (New York: New York University Press, 2012), 81. See also Bertaud, *La Révolution armée*, 109–229; Lynn, *The Bayonets of the Republic*, 119–82; Alan Forrest, *Napoleon's Men: The Soldiers of the Revolution and Empire* (London: Hambledon, 2002), 89–124. For a broader study on politics and popular culture, see Laura Mason, *Singing the French Revolution: Popular Culture and Revolutionary Politics, 1787–1799* (Ithaca, NY: Cornell University Press, 1996).

41. Martin, *Napoleonic Friendship*, 36. On Napoleon's soldiers and their correspondence, see Forrest, *Napoleon's Men*.

42. *Archives parlementaires de 1787–1860*, 17:76. Cited in Drévillon, *L'individu et la guerre*, 157.

43. Hughes, *Forging Napoleon's Grande Armée*, 98. See Jacques Godechot, *La Grande Nation: L'expansion révolutionnaire de la France dans le monde 1789–1799*, 2nd ed. (Paris: Éditions Aubier Montaigne, 1983); Guiomar, "Histoire et significations de 'la Grande Nation,'" 317–28. See also Otto Dann and John Dinwiddy, eds., *Nationalism in the Age of the French Revolution* (London: Hambledon Press, 1988).

44. Hughes, *Forging Napoleon's Grande Armée*, 99.

45. Replacement was a complicated issue. The practice was widespread, but it could also be illegal, and people trying to get replacements or serve as replacements could be turned away. Replacement was initially permitted until the *levée en masse* outlawed it. It remained officially forbidden when the Directorial government instituted conscription

in late 1798 and then was made legal once again in 1799. See Bernard Schnapper, *Le remplacement militaire en France: Quelques aspects politiques, économiques, et sociaux du recrutement au XIXe siècle* (Paris: S.E.V.P.E.N., 1968).

46. On the historiographical debate regarding women during the Revolution, see, among others, Suzanne Desan, *The Family on Trial in Revolutionary France* (Berkeley: University of California Press, 2004); Dominique Godineau, *The Women of Paris and Their French Revolution* (Berkeley: University of California Press, 1998); Jennifer Ngaire Heuer, *The Family and the Nation: Gender and Citizenship in Revolutionary France, 1789–1830* (Ithaca, NY: Cornell University Press, 2005), and Heuer, "Citizenship, the French Revolution, and the Limits of Martial Masculinity" in *Gender and Citizenship in Historical and Transnational Perspective: Agency, Space, Borders*, ed. Anne Epstein and Rachel G. Fuchs (London: Palgrave, 2017); Olwen Hufton, *Women and the Limits of Citizenship in the French Revolution* (Toronto: University of Toronto Press, 1992); Lynn Hunt, *The Family Romance of the French Revolution* (Berkeley: University of California Press, 1992); Joan Landes, *Women and the Public Sphere in the Age of the French Revolution* (Ithaca, NY: Cornell University Press, 1988); Sara E. Melzer and Leslie W. Rabine, eds., *Rebel Daughters: Women and the French Revolution* (Oxford: Oxford University Press, 1992); Dorinda Outram, *The Body and the French Revolution: Sex, Class and Political Culture* (New Haven, CT: Yale University Press, 1989); Candice E. Proctor, *Women, Equality, and the French Revolution* (Westport, CT: Greenwood Press, 1990); Shirley Elson Roessler, *Out of the Shadows: Women and Politics in the French Revolution, 1789–95* (New York: Peter Lang, 1996); Joan Wallach Scott, *Only Paradoxes to Offer: French Feminists and the Rights of Man* (Cambridge, MA: Harvard University Press, 1997).

47. *Archives parlementaires de 1787–1860*, 39:423.

48. Ibid.

49. Jennifer Heuer, "'No More Fears, No More Tears'? Gender, Emotion and the Aftermath of the Napoleonic Wars in France," *Gender and History* 28, no. 2 (August 2016): 438–60.

50. On women warriors during the French Revolution, see Dominique Godineau, "De la guerrière à la citoyenne: Porter les armes pendant l'Ancien Régime et la Révolution française," *CLIO* 20 (2004): 43–69; Sylvie Steinberg, *Le travestissement en France à l'époque moderne: XVIe–XVIIIe siècles* (Lille: ANRT, 1999); Rudolf Dekker and Lotte C. Van de Pol, "Republican Heroines: Cross-Dressing Women in the French Revolutionary Armies," trans. Judy Marcure, *History of European Ideas* 10, no. 3 (1989): 353–63. See also Thomas Cardoza, "'Habits Appropriate to Her Sex': The Female Military Experience in France during the Age of Revolution," in *Gender, War, and Politics: Transatlantic Perspectives, 1775–1830*, ed. Karen Hagemann, Gisela Mettele, and Jane Randall (New York: Palgrave Macmillan, 2010); Cardoza, *Intrepid Women: Cantinières and Vivandières of the French Army* (Bloomington: Indiana University Press, 2010); David Hopkin, "The World Turned Upside Down: Female Soldiers in the French Armies of the Revolutionary and Napoleonic Wars," in *Soldiers, Citizens and Civilians: Experiences and Perceptions of the French Wars, 1790–1820*, ed. Alan Forrest, Karen Hagemann, and Jane Rendall (Basingstoke: Palgrave Macmillan, 2009), 77–98; Jean-Clément Martin, "Travestissements, impostures, et la communauté historienne: A propos des femmes soldats de la Révolution et de l'Empire," *Politix: Revue des sciences sociales du politique* 19, no. 74 (2006): 31–48.

51. Léonard Bourdon, *Recueil des actions héroïques et civiques des républicains français; présenté à la Convention nationale* (La Grenette: Destéfanis, 1793), 8.

52. On gendered images of the nation, see Joan Landes, *Visualizing the Nation: Gender, Representation, and Revolution in Eighteenth-Century France* (Ithaca, NY: Cornell University Press, 2001); on Spartan women, see Hughes, *Forging Napoleon's Grande Armée*, 118–21.

53. See Cardoza, *Intrepid Women* and "'Habits Appropriate to Her Sex'"; Jennifer Heuer, "Celibacy, Courage, and Hungry Wives: Debating Military Marriage and Citizenship in Pre-Revolutionary France," *European History Quarterly* 46, no. 4 (October 2016): 648–67.

54. For an overview of this debate regarding foreign and minority troops, citizenship, and military service, see the introduction to Christopher Tozzi, *Nationalizing France's Army: Foreign, Black, and Jewish Troops in the French Military, 1715–1831* (Charlottesville: University of Virginia Press, 2016).

55. See Bernard Gainot, *Les officiers de couleur dans les armées de la République et de l'Empire, 1792–1815* (Paris: Éditions Karthala, 2007), and chap. 3 in Tozzi, *Nationalizing France's Army*. On Dumas's life, see the Pulitzer Prize–winning biography by Tom Reiss, *The Black Count: Glory, Revolution, Betrayal, and the Real Count of Monte Cristo* (New York: Crown, 2012).

56. Tozzi, *Nationalizing France's Army*, chap. 3.

57. Ibid. See also Pierre Boulle, "Les gens de couleur à Paris à la veille de la Révolution," in *L'image de la Révolution française: Congrès mondial pour le Bicentenaire de la Révolution*, Sorbonne, Paris, July 6–12, 1989, vol. 1 (Paris: Pergamon Press, 1989), 159–68; and J. C. Raguet, "Du pionniers noirs au Royal-Africain 1802–1813: Histoire d'une unité noire sous le Consulat et le 1er Empire" (master's thesis, Enseignement militaire supérieur de l'armée de terre, Paris, 1991); rosters of 30 Vendémiaire year III, 26 Brumaire year III, and 13 Frimaire year III, SHD Xi 71.

58. Tozzi, *Nationalizing France's Army*, 110.

59. Gainot, *Les officiers de couleur*, 32.

60. SHD Dossier 13e Chasseurs, Xc 209/211, letter dated February 13, 1793.

61. Quote by Joseph Serre on May 19, 1793, in Tozzi, *Nationalizing France's Army*, 110.

62. For more on this subject, see Laure Marcellesi, "Louis-Sébastien Mercier: Prophet, Abolitionist, Colonialist," *Studies in Eighteenth Century Culture* 40 (Spring 2011), 1–27.

63. See chap. 8 in John Garrigus, *Before Haiti: Race and Citizenship in French Saint-Domingue* (New York: Palgrave Macmillan, 2006). See also John Garrigus, "Vincent Ogé Jeune (1757–1791): Social Class and Free Colored Mobilization on the Eve of the Haitian Revolution," *Americas* 68, no. 1 (2011): 33–62.

64. For more on the Haitian Revolution and its impact, see David Geggus, *The Haitian Revolution: A Documentary History* (Indianapolis: Hackett, 2014); Geggus, *Haitian Revolutionary Studies* (Bloomington: Indiana University Press, 2002); Geggus, ed., *The Impact of the Haitian Revolution in the Atlantic World* (Columbia: University of South Carolina Press, 2002); Geggus and Norman Fiering, *The World of the Haitian Revolution* (Bloomington: Indiana University Press, 2009); Carolyn Fick, *The Making of Haiti: The Saint Domingue Revolution from Below* (Knoxville: University of Tennessee

Press, 1990); Laurent Dubois, *Avengers of the New World: The Story of the Haitian Revolution* (Cambridge, MA: Belknap Press of Harvard University Press, 2005); and Dubois, *A Colony of Citizens: Revolution and Slave Emancipation in the French Caribbean, 1787–1804* (Chapel Hill: University of North Carolina Press, 2004), among others.

65. Samuel F. Scott, "Problems of Law and Order during 1790, the 'Peaceful' Year of the French Revolution," *American Historical Review* 80, no. 4 (October 1975): 859–88.

66. Ibid., 865–68.

67. François Claude Amour, marquis de Bouillé, *Mémoires sur la Revolution française*, vol. 1 (London: Cadell and Davies, 1797), 134.

68. Dan Edelstein, *The Terror of Natural Right: Republicanism, the Cult of Nature, and the French Revolution* (Chicago: University of Chicago Press, 2009), 260–63.

69. For a recent work on the Napoleonic theory of war, see Bruno Colson, *Napoleon: On War* (Oxford: Oxford University Press, 2015).

70. Hughes, *Forging Napoleon's Grande Armée*, 111.

71. Ibid., 106.

72. Speech published in the *Moniteur* of 30 Floréal year X; quoted in Hughes, *Forging Napoleon's Grande Armée*, 110.

73. *Motifs due projet de loi exposés devant le Corps legislative par le Conseiller d'État Roederer* (25 Floréal year X).

74. Martin, *Napoleonic Friendship*, 2.

75. Ibid., 6.

76. Ibid., 44.

77. Ibid., 49.

78. Order of the day, Grande Armée, Elchingen, 29 Vendémaire year 14; quoted in Hughes, *Forging Napoleon's Grande Armée*, 156.

79. Proclamation of the Emperor and King, Potsdam, October 26, 1806, quoted in Hughes, *Forging Napoleon's Grande Armée*, 159.

80. Hughes, *Forging Napoleon's Grande Armée*, 157.

81. Elzéar Blaze, *La vie militaire sous l'Empire ou moeurs de la garnison, du bivouac et de la caserne*, vol. 1 (Paris: Bureau de l'album des théâtres, 1837), 303.

82. See Joseph Martray, *La destruction de la marine française par la Révolution* (Paris: Éditions France Empire, 1988); Martine Acerra and Jean Meyer, *Marines et révolution* (Rennes: Éditions Ouest-France, 1988); Etienne Taillemite, *L'histoire ignore de la marine française* (Paris: Librairie Académique Perrin, 1988); William S. Cormack, *Revolution and Political Conflict in the French Navy, 1789–1794* (Cambridge: Cambridge University Press, 1995).

83. Masson, "La marine sous la Révolution et l'Empire," 2:388.

84. Ibid.

85. Quoted in ibid.

86. Tozzi, *Nationalizing France's Army*, 170. On the subject of language in Napoleon's and the previous eighteenth-century army, see Tozzi, "One Army, Many Languages: Foreign Troops and Linguistic Diversity in the Eighteenth-Century French Military," in *Languages and the Military: Alliances, Occupation and Peace Building*, ed. Hilary Footitt and Michael Kelly (Basingstoke: Palgrave Macmillan, 2012): 12–24.

87. Louis Antoine Fauvelet de Bourrienne, *Memoirs of Napoleon Bonaparte*, ed. R. W. Phipps, vol. 1 (New York: Charles Scribner's Sons, 1889), 168–69.

88. Tozzi, *Nationalizing France's Army*, 153.

89. Christopher Tozzi, "Citizenship, soldiering and revolution: Foreigners and minorities in the French military, 1750–1831" (PhD diss., Johns Hopkins University, 2013), 400.

90. *Correspondance de Napoléon Ier: Publiée par ordre de l'empereur Napoléon III*, vol. 6 (Paris: H. Plon, J. Dumaine, 1861), 42.

91. Translated from quote in Yves Benot, *La démence coloniale sous Napoléon* (Paris: Éditions la découverte, 1992), 89.

92. See Heuer, "'No More Fears, No More Tears,'" on the depiction of weak, emotional women and the reality of their active resistance to the Napoleonic war machine.

93. Hughes, *Forging Napoleon's Grande Armée*, 128.

94. Fritz Redlich has theorized on the reasons for this disregard; see *De Praeda Militari: Pillage and Booty, 1500–1815* (Wiesbaden: Franz Steiner, 1956). Tuba Inal also discusses these reasons in *Looting and Rape in Wartime: Law and Change in International Relations* (Philadelphia: University of Pennsylvania Press, 2013), 48–49.

95. Paddy Griffith, *The Art of War of Revolutionary France, 1789–1802* (London: Greenhill Books, 1998), 55.

96. Inal, *Looting and Rape in Wartime*, 49.

97. Griffith, *The Art of War of Revolutionary France*, 42.

98. J. T. Johnson, "Lieber and the Theory of War," in *Francis Lieber and the Culture of the Mind*, ed. Charles R. Mack and Henry H. Lesesne (Columbia: University of South Carolina Press, 2005), 62–63.

99. Inal, *Looting and Rape in Wartime*, 50.

100. *The Collected Papers of John Westlake on Public International Law*, ed. L. Oppenheim (Cambridge: Cambridge University Press, 1914), 279.

Epilogue

1. Yuval Noah Harari concurs with this sense of continuity, but goes so far as to view all generations of military thinkers from 1740 to 1865 as indistinguishable in their sensibility-based epistemological positioning. See Yuval Noah Harari, *The Ultimate Experience: Battlefield Revelations and the Making of Modern War Culture* (Houndmills: Palgrave Macmillan, 2008), 127–96.

2. On Berenhorst, see Azar Gat, *A History of Military Thought from the Enlightenment to the Cold War* (Oxford: Oxford University Press, 2001), 152–57.

3. See *Development of the General Reasons for the French Success in the Wars of the Revolution* (1797) by Gerhard von Scharnhorst and Friedrich von der Decker. On Scharnhorst, see Gat, *A History of Military Thought*, 158–69.

4. See Carl von Clausewitz, *On War*, ed. and trans. M. Howard and P. Paret (Princeton, NJ: Princeton University Press, 1976), 479.

5. Charles Ardant du Picq, *Études sur le combat: Combat antique et combat moderne* (Paris: Champ Libre, 1978), 53. Quoted in Brian Joseph Martin, *Napoleonic Friendship: Military Fraternity, Intimacy, and Sexuality in Nineteenth-Century France* (Lebanon: University of New Hampshire Press, 2011), 8.

6. Louis-Jules Trochu, *L'armée française en 1867* (Paris: Amyot, 1870), 101–2.

7. Geoffrey W. Bateman, "Military Culture: European," *Glbtq Encyclopedia*, 2015, http://www.glbtqarchive.com/ssh/military_culture_eur_S.pdf.

8. See "Lutte contre le harcèlement, les discriminations et les violences sexuels" on the French Ministry of Defense's website. http://www.defense.gouv.fr/portail-defense/vous-et-la-defense/egalite-femmes-hommes/lutte-contre-le-harcelement-les-discriminations-et-les-violences-sexuels/bilan-perspectives-et-plan-d-action, accessed May 19, 2016.

9. See, for example, the discovery in March 2017 that male members of the U.S. Marines were secretly sharing photographs of female service members in varying states of undress. Male marines continued to share these photos even after the story had broken and investigations began. See the article CNN article by Eliott C. McLaughlin and AnneClaire Stapleton and dated March 9, 2017: "Secret Marines group is still sharing nude photos amid scandal." http://www.cnn.com/2017/03/08/politics/marines-united-photos-investigation/, accessed March 17, 2017.

10. See Gary Wilder, *The French Imperial Nation-State: Negritude and Colonial Humanism between the Two World Wars* (Chicago: University of Chicago Press, 2005).

11. On the history of French colonial soldiers, see for example Charles John Balesi, *From Adversaries to Comrades-in-Arms: West Africans and the French Military, 1885–1918* (Waltham, MA: Crossroads Press, 1979); Marc Michel, *L'appel à l'Afrique: Contributions et reactions à l'effort de guerre en AOF, 1914–1919* (Paris: Publications de la Sorbonne, 1982); Myron Echenberg, *Colonial Conscripts: The Tirailleurs Sénégalais in French West Africa, 1857–1960* (Portsmouth, NH: Heinemann, 1991); Joe Lunn, *Memoirs of the Maelstrom: A Senegalese Oral History of the First World War* (Portsmouth, NH: Heinemann, 1999); Gregory Mann, *Native Sons: West African Veterans and France in the Twentieth Century* (Durham, NC: Duke University Press, 2006); Richard S. Fogarty, *Race and War in France: Colonial Subjects in the French Army, 1914–1918* (Baltimore: Johns Hopkins University Press, 2008).

12. Fogarty, *Race and War in France*, 77–78.

13. See Mike Thomson, "Paris Liberation Made 'Whites Only,'" April 6, 2009, http://news.bbc.co.uk/2/hi/europe/7984436.stm.

14. Fogarty, *Race and War in France*, 233.

15. See Thomas Dodman, "Un pays pour la colonie: Mourir de nostalgie en Algérie française, 1830–1880," *Annales: Histoire, Sciences Sociales* 66, no. 3 (2011): 743–84.

16. Hervé Drévillon, *L'individu et la guerre : Du Chevalier Bayard au Soldat inconnu* (Paris: Éditions Belin, 2013), 219–28, esp. 226.

17. Ibid., 228–33.

18. For more on this subject, see chapter 8 in ibid.

19. Dan Edelstein, *The Terror of Natural Right: Republicanism, the Cult of Nature, and the French Revolution* (Chicago: University of Chicago Press, 2009), 269. For more on the rise of totalitarianism and questions of human rights in the context of World War II, see the work of Hannah Arendt, especially *The Origins of Totalitarianism* (New York: Schocken Books, 1951).

20. See "Will New Forum Boost Compliance with the Rules of War?," *IRIN*, December 4, 2015, https://www.irinnews.org/fr/node/255777.

21. William J. Astore, "Drone Warfare: Neither Cheap, Nor Surgical, Nor Decisive," March 25, 2013, https://www.thenation.com/article/drone-warfare-neither-cheap-nor-surgical-nor-decisive/.

22. See, for example, David Zucchino, "Stress of Combat Reaches Drone Crews," *Los Angeles Times*, March 18, 2012; and Rachel Martin, "Report: High Levels of 'Burnout' in U.S. Drone Pilots," NPR, December 19, 2011.

23. The open letter dated July 28, 2015 can be found on the Future of Life Institute's website: http://futureoflife.org/AI/open_letter_autonomous_weapons#signatories, accessed March 18, 2017.

24. Helen Durham, "The Limits of War," TEDxSydney, May 21, 2015. The talk can be accessed from the website of the International Committee of the Red Cross: https://www.icrc.org/en/document/tedxsydney-even-wars-must-have-limits, accessed March 16, 2017.

Index

Note: Italic page numbers refer to illustrations.

Académie de chirurgie, 124
Académie de marine, 17, 35
Académie des inscriptions et belles-lettres, 29, 40
Académie française, 164–66, 177, 182
Académie royale de musique, 91
Académie royale des sciences, 29, 56, 126
Affiches américaines, 146, 188–89
Africa, 19, 22, 23, 48, 122
Algeria, 192, 234
Almanach royal, 58, 69
American Civil War (1861–1865), 193
American Revolutionary War (1775–1783): citizen armies of, 202; and d'Estaing, 20, 106, 145, 188; and French Freemason lodges, 78; French troops in, 122, 145–46; journals of French military men serving in, 24, 49–50; and Lafayette, 49, 63, 252–53n49; and military journals, 59; and newspapers, 58, 196; and slavery, 148–49, 272n163; and sociability, 107–9; and Te Deum mass, 156
Amerindian tribes: as auxiliary troops, 261n111; and *chefs à alliance*, 189; and *chefs à médaille*, 184, 189; and heroism, 184, 189; and *militaires philosophes*, 45–48, 50, 99–101, 147–48; and *sensibilité*, 147–48; and slavery, 272n163; and smallpox, 123; and sociability, 99–101, 261n111, 261–62n117
ancien régime: and absentee officers in armed forces, 207, 259n73; civilian hospitals of, 126; cultural readings of, 24; and foreign troops of French armed forces, 184, 224, 278n84; and heroism, 156, 157, 220; hierarchical society of, 23, 66, 68; and military education, 196; and military medicine, 56, 126; and military reforms, 190, 200, 201, 225; passing of, 195, 232;

social divisions during, 66, 216; value systems of, 68, 256n11, 257n27; women's military service during, 178
anoblis (recently ennobled), 14, 71
Anseaume, Louis, 170–72
Antilles, 48, 52, 97, 99, 106, 188
Archives nationales, 20, 23
Archives nationales d'outremer, 20
Ardant du Picq, Charles, 232, 233
aristocratic code of honor, 66, 67–68, 70, 71, 245n35
Aristotle, 133, 182
armed forces, 10–11, 15. *See also* French armed forces

"band of brothers" concept, 67, 80, 194, 233, 256n7
Barreau, Alexandrine "Rose" "Liberté," 210, *211*
Bayard, chevalier de, 25–26
Beccaria, Cesare, 141, 142, 270–71n125
Belle-Isle, Charles Louis August Fouquet, duc de, 33
Belloy, Pierre-Laurent Buirette de, 157, 172–77, 181, 182, 183
Belzunce, Armand, vicomte de, 146, 147
Bensac, Jeanne, 178, 179
Berenhorst, Georg Heinrich von, 231
Berny de Nogent, Pierre-Jean-Paul, chevalier de, 44–45, 161, 162
Biron, duc de. *See* Lauzun, Armand Louis de Gontaut, duc de
Blaze, Elzéar, 65–66, 67, 223
Bonaparte, Joseph, 227–28
Bonneville, Zacharie de Pazzi de, 47–48, 100–101, 148
Bordeu, Théophile de, 115, 120, 121, 124
Bossu, Jean Bernard, 99–100, 109

289

INDEX

Bougainville, Louis Antoine de, 18, 48, 73, 100, 148, 262n117
Bouillé, François Claude Amour, marquis de, 216–17
Bourbon monarchs, 13, 14, 91, 151–52, 184, 189
Brissot de Warville, Jacques, 26, 149
Britain: armed forces of, 36–37, 50, 266n51; community culture in, 260n83; constitutional system of, 28; economy of, 14; French competition with, 19–20; military academies of, 17; military expenditures on navy, 12; military medicine in, 266n51; navy of, 34, 35; population of, 13; taxation in, 14; and War of Austrian Succession, 247n59
Broglie, Victor François, duc de, 14–15, 41
Buddenbrock, Johann Heinrich, baron of, 113, *114*
Buffon, George-Louis Leclerc, comte de, 47, 98
Bussy, Charles Joseph Patissier, marquis de Castelnau, 102–3, 105, 122

Calais, English siege of (1347), 173, 175, 181
Canada, 22, 97, 99, 101
Caribbean, 19, 20, 122, 185, 214
Carnot, Lazare, 210–11
Castries, Charles Eugène Gabriel de La Croix, marquis de, 35, 190, 200
Catinat, Nicolas de, 165, 166
cérémonie de l'information, 151–52
chivalric code, 8–9, 68, 100
Choiseul, Étienne-François, duc de: and colonial expansion, 261–62n117; on colonial power, 5; and French navy, 35; and military education, 41; on military penal code, 141, 143; and military professionalism, 59; and military reform, 33, 88, 111, 134, 263n3; and salons, 61–62; on *société militaire*, 85, 86
citizenship: and citizen-soldiers, 194, 197–98, 202–3, 206–7, 208, 211, 218–19; and *fraternité*, 203; and heroism, 157, 190; marriage linked to, 168–69; and military penal code, 199; and military service, 191, 207, 212, 234, 235–36; public debates on, 16, 22, 150, 157; and racial minorities, 214; in Revolutionary era, 197–98; and women, 174, 177, 180, 207–8, 209, 211
civility, 8, 12
classical republicanism, 109
Clausewitz, Carl von, 230–32, 238

Clermont, Louis de Bourbon-Condé, comte de, 77, 91
Clermont-Crèvecoeur, Jean-François-Louis, comte de, 49, 50, 108, 149
le coeur humain (human heart), 115, 131
Colbert, Jean-Baptiste, 6, 13, 35, 190
Colombier, Jean, 125–26, 128–30, 268n75
colonialism: and Military Enlightenment, 18–22, 23; and "Others," 10–11; revisionist narrative of, 21–22; and war, 5, 243n16
Comédie française, 91, 173, 182
Committee of Public Safety, 195, 214
commoners (*roturiers*): and heroism, 157, 158–60, 165, 166–67, 169–71, 172, 173–74, 190, 196; and military medicine, 129; and military service, 30, 41, 196–97, 201–2; noble military officers' attitudes toward, 70, 76; rich commoners in officer corps, 71, 257n17
Compagnie des Indes, 19, 102
Condillac, Étienne Bonnot de, 8, 119, 132
Conseil de Guerre (Council of War), 71–72, 85, 140, 144, 190, 196, 200
Constituent Assembly, 198, 201
cosmopolitanism: and critiques of war, 53; and Freemason lodges, 62; and human rights, 139; of *médecins philosophes*, 56; and military medicine, 123, 266n51; and Napoleon, 224, 225; of noble military officers, 12, 108; rise of, 12; and sociability, 75
Cotignon, Jean Jacques de, 48–49, 262n125
Counter-Enlightenment, 230, 231
Coyer, Gabriel-François, 160, 162
Crimean War (1853–1856), 192, 232
Croix de Guerre, 235
Croix de Saint-Louis, 159, 220, 270n104
cross-culturation, 18, 21, 99, 145

d'Alembert, Jean-Baptiste le Rond, 7, 29, 42, 54, 55, 58, 142
d'Argenson, Marc-Pierre de Voyer de Paulmy, comte: on conversation, 84; on humanity, 89; and military reforms, 29–30, 31, 33, 41, 74, 83–85, 141; on relations within French army, 74, 75, 83; on sociability, 83–84, 85, 109; and Voltaire, 29, 153
d'Argenson, René-Louis de Voyer de Paulmy, marquis, 1–2, 90
Declaration of the Rights of Man and Citizen, 201, 209
Décoration militaire, 200–201
De Gaulle, Charles, 235

de Pauw, Cornelius, 47–48
Descartes, René, 37, 39, 132, 269n86
d'Estaing, Charles-Hector, comte, 20, 73, 106, 145–46, 149, 188, 278n94
Dettingen, battle of (1743), 110–11, *111*, 112, 133, 236, 263n3
Dettingen cartel (1743), 112, 113, 236
d'Harcourt, comte, 26, *27*
d'Holbach, Paul-Henri Thiry, Baron, 36, 55, 74, 109
Dictionnaire de l'Académie française (1694), 7, 8, 98, 112, 117, 127, 269n90
Dictionnaire philosophique (Voltaire), 58
Diderot, Denis: on Bougainvilles, 262n117; and Marc-Pierre d'Argenson, 29; and *drame bourgeois*, 169, 182; on heroism, 161, 162; on Hôtel-Dieu hospital, 121–22; on humanity, 112–13, 271n125; on military subjects, 54, 55; on Richardson, 113; on Saint-Domingue, 214; on *sensibilité*, 8; on sociability, 75–76, 109; *Supplement to Bougainville's Voyage*, 18; on tribunal of conscience, 139; on war, 7, 55, 58
Document (BBC program), 235
domestic sphere. *See* public sphere / domestic sphere
Dost Ali Khan, 104–5
Dreyfus, Alfred, 234
Dreyfus Affair (1894), 193, 234
Dubois de Crancé, Edmond Louis Alexis, 197, 204, 205, 206
du Deffand, marquise, 61–62
Duguay-Trouin, René, 165, 181
Dumarsais, César Chesneau, 30–31, 38, 39
Dumas, Pierre-Benoît, 102, 104–5
Dumas, Thomas-Alexandre, 212
Dumont de Montigny, Jean-François-Benjamin, 99, 101
Dupleix, Joseph-François, 102–4, 183–84
Durham, Helen, 240
Dutch War (1672–1678), 6, 13

École des ingenieurs-constructeurs de la marine, 34–35
École militaire de Brienne, 37, 217
École royale d'artillerie de La Fère, 43
École royale du génie de Mézières, 16, 30
École royale militaire, 17, 30–31, 33, 35, 37, 125, 217
emotions, and military psychology, 131–33, 134, 135, 137, 138, 142, 232, 233, 239, 269n86

Encyclopédie, ou dictionnaire raisonné des sciences, des arts et des métiers (Diderot and d'Alembert): on citizenship, 174; dedication to Marc-Pierre d'Argenson, 29; and diffusion of knowledge, 255n81; on health, 127–28; on humanity, 112–13; on hygiene, 127; on Marathas, 103; on military penal code, 142; military subjects in, 17, 30, 53, 54–55, 59; on *philosphes*, 83; publication of, 58; and sociability, 109; "Société," 79–81, 258n51; on war, 7
Encyclopédie méthodique (1782–1832), 58, 87
Encyclopédie militaire, 58–59, 255n85
enfants de troupe, 179, 277n73
Enlightenment: centrality of war and the military in, 3, 6, 24; and exploration and cross-cultural contact, 18; and forms of communication, 2–3; French Enlightenment, 3, 4–5, 138, 163; Guibert influenced by, 42; historical definition of, 2, 241–42n3; multiple Enlightenments, 241–42n3; and Napoleon, 218; operationalization of thought, 11. *See also* French Military Enlightenment; Military Enlightenment
environmentalist theories, 97–98
equality: in ambulatory medical treatment, 125; and Freemason lodges, 78–79, 81; and French Revolution, 207, 211, 221; and functional inequality, 84, 259n72; and functional social hierarchy, 80, 81; gender equality, 181, 182; and human rights, 138, 139; La Rochefoucauld on, 82; and Napoleon, 221–22, 223, 226, 227; racial egalitarianism, 147, 272n152; relationship to empire, 98–99, 106–7; and *société militaire*, 84–85, 259n72; and women, 207–8
esprit de corps, 10, 67, 86–87, 205, 223–24, 232
esprit de finesse, 4
esprit de métier, 10, 83
esprit de système, 4, 230
esprit philosophique: and French Revolution, 194; Military Enlightenment embracing, 2, 4, 11, 18, 28, 39, 242–43n12; and Napoleon, 224; and war, 4, 45–51, 98, 242–43n12
Estates General, 196, 197
ethnography: and geographical discovery, 18; and *militaires philosophes*, 98; proto-ethnographic works, 20, 28, 39, 46, 49, 50–51
Eugene of Savoy, Prince, 15

European states: and desertion of armed forces, 15; early modern colonialism of, 21; and global theaters of war, 19; military conflicts in eighteenth century, 6, 243n20; pan-European value systems, 12, 246n41

faiseurs de systèmes, 39–40, 41, 42
Fauville, M. de, 137–38, 150, 205
Favart, Charles-Simon, 90, 91, 93–94, 97, 109, 150, 170, 221, 261nn103, 104
Fénelon, François de Salignac de la Mothe-, 53, 80, 160, 253n58
Fête de la Fédération, 202–3, 216–17
Fidèle, Françoise, 178, 179
filles aguerries (war-hardened girls), 178, 179–80, 210, 277n73
First Estate, 153, 242n9
First Franco-Mexican War (1838–1839), 192
Flanders, 90–91, 260n83
Flavigny, vicomte de, 141, 142–43
Folard, chevalier de, 25, 39, 54, 87, 91, 117
Fontenoy, battle of (1745), 1, 90, 151–53, 154, 155–56, 155, 157, 158, 159
Foucault, Michel, 11, 113, 116–17, 126, 132, 267n73, 270–71n125
France: black market of, 246n49; colonial interests of, 18–20; credit used by, 13, 16; economy of, 14, 15–16; fiscal-military state of, 12, 13, 14–15, 71; military expenditures of, 6, 13–16; and national character, 12, 90, 133; and national identity, 157, 202, 206; nationalism in, 12, 16, 164, 190, 191, 219; population of, 13–16; and terrorist attacks, 234. *See also specific wars*
Franco-Austrian War (1859), 193
François I (king of France), 128
Franco-Prussian War, 193
fraternité, as concept of French Revolution, 66, 67, 194, 202–5, 207, 211, 215, 216, 217, 221
Frederick the Great of Prussia, 28, 39, 42, 57, 77, 91
Freemason lodges: charitable activities of, 81; as conversation venue, 57, 61, 62–64; and equality, 78–79, 81; and French armed forces, 12, 38, 77–78, 80–81; as ideal cultural models, 67; and military friendship, 76–81; Napoleon on, 65
free people of color: in American Revolutionary War, 149; and citizenship, 188, 189, 215; and desertions, 147; d'Estaing on, 188–89; and French Revolution, 211–12, 214–15; and heroism, 184, 189; and patriotism, 189; and race theories, 98, 106; racial acceptance of, 115; in Saint-Domingue, 22, 106–7, 146–47, 148, 212, 214–15; and Saxe's regiment, 185–87. *See also* race and racism
French armed forces: and absentee officers, 85, 86, 259n73; and *amalgame*, 201, 204; casualties and deaths related to combat, 1, 15–16, 121, 125–26; and citizen armies, 191, 196, 197–98, 202, 207, 216, 217; conditions of camp life, 53–54, 89, 117–18, 129–30, 133–38, 190, 194, 198, 204, 218, 222, 268n64, 84; crimes against civilians, 190–91; crisis in leadership of, 15–16, 38, 67, 70–75; cultural and political indoctrination of, 219; desertion in, 15, 18, 57, 66, 74, 85–86, 115, 135, 136, 140, 141–44, 169, 216; during Revolution, 196–97, 216; dysfunction in, 66, 76, 91; foreigners serving in, 157, 159, 184–85, 194, 207, 211–12, 214, 224, 225–26, 233–36, 278n84; and foreign legions, 212, 233–34; and Freemason lodges, 12, 38, 77–78, 80–81; free people of color serving in, 185–89; and grain riots, 191, 278n105; growth of, 6; king as head and possessor of, 152, 273n2; and Légion d'honneur, 219, 222–23; and merit-based system, 30, 70, 136, 196, 197, 200, 201, 202, 204, 208, 222, 224, 227; noncombatant women serving in, 178, 277n73; and patriotism, 163, 164; pay and retirement benefits of, 133–35, 136, 140, 190, 204, 208, 222, 236; and pillaging, 150, 178, 190, 194, 227–28; professionalization of, 16–17, 30, 37–38, 59, 83, 200, 228; and purchasing replacement to fill position, 207, 281–82n45; recognition, reward, and advancement in ranks for, 30, 63, 71, 73, 133, 135, 136, 153, 159, 172, 184, 185, 188, 189, 190, 194, 196–97, 200, 201, 202, 204, 208, 281n26; and recruitment, 197–98, 200, 201, 202, 207, 211; reform culture of, 23, 28–29, 60, 64, 66, 82–83, 85–88, 115, 133, 138, 194; social relations within, 70, 194, 199–201, 203, 204–5, 221–22, 223; and women's military service, 22, 175, 178, 180, 186, 207, 208–11, 233, 235, 277n73. *See also* French military men; noble military officers
French army: class divisions in, 30, 41, 54, 66, 67–68, 70, 71, 74–75, 76, 90, 108, 109, 190, 200, 203–4, 257n17; and *contrôles des troupes*, 85–86; and "docile body," 116–19;

INDEX 293

and duties of officers, 38; and Freemason lodges, 77, 78; historiography of, 24; and priority of continental dominance, 34; refinement and civility of, 68, 69, 70; reforms of, 35, 38, 74, 190; and regional differences, 75; and *sage liberté* for garrisoned men, 85, 259n75

French diaspora, 22–23

French Enlightenment, 3, 4–5, 138, 163

French mercantile empire and overseas colonies, map circa 1750, xiv–xv

French military archive, and role of indigenous peoples in colonialism, 21

French Military Enlightenment: and Berenhorst, 231; and conversation venues, 57, 61–64; cultural contributions to, 18; ending of, 230–31; and epistolary communication, 57, 61; and fiscal-military state, 12, 13, 14–15, 71; and historiography of French army, 24; ideologies of, 196, 217, 223; and Jomini, 230; means and spaces of, 57–64; and *militaires philosophes*, 36–45; and military journals, 58–60, 255nn81, 85; and Napoleon, 217, 218, 221, 222; and print media, 57–61; reforms of, 16, 23, 28–31, 33–35, 194, 196–200, 202, 205, 217; and Revolutionary and Napoleonic era, 16, 195, 196–97, 199, 206

French military men: and citizenship, 168–69; conditions of, 218; effect of empire and diaspora on careers of, 20; first-hand accounts of, 21, 22; memoirs of, 38, 48, 49, 57, 60, 103, 131, 134, 137–38, 144, 150, 172, 223; as *militaires philosophes*, 20–21, 27–28, 36–45, 46, 48–50; and military journals, 59; on military penal code, 144; professionalization of, 30, 33, 37–38, 200; and *sensibilité*, 22, 169; Sergent's portraits of, 25–26, 27, 104; travel narratives of, 18, 20, 46, 48; war journals of, 49. See also noble military officers

French navy: in American Revolutionary War, 59–60; casualties from disease in, 121; and class divisions, 73; and Freemason lodges, 77, 78; hospitals of, 126; and mass emigration of nobles in 1791, 195; mutinies on vessels, 216; and Napoleon, 223–24; refinement and civility of, 68, 70; reform of, 29, 34–35, 38, 78, 190; in Seven Years' War, 15, 19–20, 52, 121; and sociability, 99

French Revolution (1789–1799): and Bastille, 202; and citizen-soldiers, 194, 197–98, 202–3, 206–7, 208, 215, 218; Convention, 195, 201, 203–6, 207, 214, 215; and *fraternité*, 66, 67, 194, 202–5, 207; French Military Enlightenment's influence on, 16, 195, 196–97, 199, 206; ideals of, 205, 218; and *levée en masse*, 157, 193, 203–4, 217, 281n45; and military reforms, 195, 196–201, 204–5; and myth of martial Grande Nation, 193, 195–207, 206, 207, 211, 217, 218, 279n6; and Nancy Affair, 198, 216–17; National Assembly, 197, 198, 199, 202–3, 207, 208–9, 212, 215–17; Terror of, 238; violent unrest in port cities, 216; wars of, 15, 193; and women, 207–8

French Revolution (1848), 192

Friedlingen, battle of (1702), 118, 133

Frondeuses-Amazones, 175, 176, 178

Gardes françaises of the Maison du Roi, 111, 112, 129, 140, 202

Gazette de France, 58, 60, 152, 153, 154, 156

Gazette de Leyde, 58

gender: and essentializing logic, 174–75; gendered humiliation as military punishment, 208; and heroism, 157, 174, 183, 221; and military culture, 220–21; and patriarchal narrative, 177, 183, 209; relationship with empire, 101, 106; and sociability, 109; stereotypes of, 178, 180, 182, 183, 208–9, 210; and worldliness, 72. See also masculine identity; women

Geneva Conventions, 101, 112, 236, 238–39, 263n5

George II (king of England), 110, 112

German movement, 230, 231

German principalities, 185

Girard, Étienne-François, 144

gloire: and colonial power, 5; culture of, 6; democratization of, 158, 159; and Napoleon, 219, 221; as noble value, 68, 70, 73, 256n13; *philosophes* on, 55–56

Godard d'Acour, Claude, 158–60, 274n20

Goubler, Marguerite, 178, 179, 180

grain riots, 191, 278n105

Gramont, Louis, duc de, 110, 111

grands hommes, 161, 162, 164, 165

Grotius, Hugo, 9, 139

Guadeloupe, 19, 122, 212

guerrière héroïque (noble heroic woman warrior), 178, 180

guerrilla war, 239

INDEX

Guibert, Jacques-Antoine-Hippolyte, comte de: on citizen armies, 54; on citizenship, 172; correspondence of, 61; on emotions, 135; and military reforms, 190, 196, 200; on military system, 23–24, 42–43, 45, 57–58, 135, 191

Guichard, Karl Theophilus (Quintus Icilius), 40

Guillotin, Joseph-Ignace, 144

Hague Conventions, 228, 236–37
Haitian Revolution, 215
happiness: Enlightenment associated with, 241n3; and Freemason lodges, 80; and *médecins philosophes*, 115, 120–21, 127, 130; and military psychology, 131, 134, 135, 136, 138, 205; and *théâtre de guerre*, 92–93, 94
Hapsburgs, 13, 14
Helvétius, Claude-Adrien, 31, 120
heroism: and class divisions, 70; and commoners, 157, 158–60, 165, 166–67, 169–71, 172, 173–74, 190, 196; contesting of, 157–58; culture of, 190–91; democratization of, 157, 160, 191, 215; and domesticity, 168–69; and dysfunction in French armed forces, 66; egalitarianism in, 235; of foreigners, 159, 184, 185, 194; and Freemason lodges, 63–64; and French Revolution, 200, 206; hierarchy of, 153, 155–56, 159, 160, 162; and humanity in war, 150; and king as original military hero, 152, 153, 156, 157; and Napoleon, 218, 219, 220, 221; and patriotism, 157, 162–66, 168, 170, 171, 172–73; *philosophes* on, 55; public debates on, 12, 16, 150, 156–63, 194; relationship to empire, 183–84; and Sergent's portraits of French military men, 25–26; and *théâtre de guerre*, 97; and women, 157, 174–83, 210, 227
historicism, 230, 231
Hobbes, Thomas, 5, 54, 57, 132
Homer, 37, 39, 46, 160
homme illustre, 161, 162, 165
honor: aristocratic code of, 66, 67–68, 70, 71, 245n35; bodily rhetoric of honor, 116; and heroism, 163; as motivator for military men, 133, 136, 137, 205–6; and Napoleon, 219–22; nationalization of, 16, 172; as noble value, 68, 70, 73, 133, 256n13; *philosophes* on, 55; physical semiotics of, 116; and social competition, 10
Hôtel des Invalides, 124, 125–26, 135, 140, 185, 267n59

Hugo, Victor, 192–93
humanitarian reforms, 35, 109, 115, 119, 132
humanity in war: and compassion, 117–18, 126; and cultural understanding, 115; and Dettingen cartel, 112, 113; and docile soldierly body, 116–17, 119; and emotions, 131–33, 134, 135, 137, 142; and French Revolution, 198, 205, 215; and global war, 145–49; and heroism, 150; and human heart, 118–19; and human rights, 138–45; and international law, 9, 229, 236–39, 240; meaning of humanity, 8, 112–13; and military medicine, 123–27; and military psychology, 131–38, 237; and Napoleon, 194–95, 221, 226–27, 238; new military humanism, 238; and patriotism, 166; and restraint of war, 7–8, 9, 26, 245n35; and *sensibilité*, 113, 115, 119–21, 123, 126, 127, 140, 150; and sensible bodies, 119–23; Sergent's portraits celebrating, 25, 26; and slavery, 148–49; and sociability, 12, 75, 83, 89, 137; and *soldats sensibles*, 115, 127–31, 190
human progress, 2, 241n3, 259n60
human rights, 115, 127, 138–45, 238–39, 271nn141, 142
Hume, David, 8, 119
Hundred Years' War (1337–1453), 13
Hyder Ali Khan, 46, 103, *104*, 147

India: British domination of, 19; French armed forces' fighting conditions in, 122; French interests in, 19, 21, 22, 23; and *militaires philosophes*, 46, 48, 147; relationship to empire, 99, 101–6, 109, 183; *sensibilité* discourses in, 147; and *société militaire*, 97
Indigènes (*Days of Glory*, 2006), 236
indigenous populations, 20–22, 23, 67, 115, 123, 184, 224–25
International Red Cross, 10, 236, 237, 239
Islam, 187, 225

Jacobin movement, 200–201, 205, 216
Jaucourt, Louis de, 55, 112, 127, 142, 161, 162, 163
Jeanne d'Arc, 128, 177, 178–79
Jesuits, 46, 102
Jomini, Antoine-Henri de, 230, 232
Julius Caesar, 37, 128
July Revolution (1830), 192
jus ad bellum, 55, 219, 245n35
just war theory, 7, 244n27
jus victoriae, 5–6

Kant, Immanuel, 4–5, 11, 240, 242n12
Kellerin, Madeleine, 178, 179–80

La Balle, Jeanne, 178–79
La Bruyère, Jean de, 53, 160
Lafayette, Gilbert de Motier, marquis de, 49, 63, 78, 108, 202, 204, 252–53n49
La Feuillade, Louis d'Aubusson, duc de, 69
Lally, Thomas Arthur, comte de, 105–6, 262n125
Lamée (army lieutenant), 82–85, 109, 259n72
Lameth, Alexandre-Théodore-Victor, comte de, 108, 205–6
Langlade, Charles-Michel de, 99, 148
Lannes, Jean, 221, 222
La Rochefoucauld, François de, 81–82, 160, 161
La Rochelambert, chevalier de, 135
La Roque, Antoine de, 44
Las Casas, Emmanuel-Augustin-Dieudonné-Joseph, comte de, 65, 228
Lauzun, Armand Louis de Gontaut, duc de, 49, 73, 108
Le Blanc, Claude, 29, 140
Le Blanc, Jean-Bernard, abbé, 163–64
Le Camus, Antoine, 92–93, 97, 115, 120, 128
Legion of the Americans, 212–14
L'Enfant, Pierre, "Battle of Fontenoy, May 11, 1745," 152, *155*, 156
Lenoir de Rouvray, Laurent-François, marquis de, 50, 106–7, 109, 147, 148, 188, 272n152
Léon, Pauline, 208–9
Lespinasse, Julie de, 42, 61
liberty, 207, 211, 223
literary works: on desertion, 142; on heroism, 150, 156, 158–61; on patriotism, 164, 180; on war, 28; on worldliness, 53, 71, 253n60
Locke, John, 8, 119
Louis, Antoine, 124, 144
Louisiana, 19, 22
Louis XIII (king of France), 6, 13, 14, 151
Louis XIV (king of France): aristocratic culture of war, 66, 67–68, 70, 71; artillery schools created by, 16–17; and Croix de Saint-Louis, 270n104; Voltaire and writing his history of, 29; and extraction of resources, 14; and Fénelon, 53, 253n58; and foreign troops, 185; and heroism, 165–66; military expenditures of, 13; military forces of, 6, 15, 25; and military intellectualism, 37; and military medicine, 125; and noble military officers, 67–68, 70, 71, 257n17; relations with soldiers, 65–68, 191; and Te Deum mass, 151–52, 156; and women's military service, 175, 178
Louis XV (king of France): and battle of Dettingen, 111; and battle of Fontenoy, 1, 151, 152–53, 156; colonial interests of, 19; and divine right of kings, 28; on military penal code, 143; and military reforms, 29, 35, 41, 263n3; and prestige of military action, 6; and Protestant military men, 185; and public opinion on war, 16; as reform absolutist, 29, 33; royal mistresses of, 29, 30, 31, 33; and smallpox, 126; and theater, 171, 173
Louis XVI (king of France): and American Revolutionary War, 60; and *cahiers de doléances*, 196; colonial interests of, 19; and divine right of kings, 28; and military penal code, 143; and military reforms, 29, 35, 190; and prestige of military action, 6; as reform absolutist, 29, 60
Louvois, François-Michel le Tellier, marquis de, 29, 37, 68
Lyautey, Louis Hubert, 232–33

Mably, Gabriel Bonnot de, 54, 163, 172
Maïzeroy, Paul-Gédéon Joly de, 39, 40, 41, 54
Malartic, Anne Joseph Hippolyte de Maurès, comte de, 48
Marathas, 98, 103, 104–5
Marchand, Jean-Henri, 157–58
Maria Leszcayńska (Queen of France), 29
Marmontel, Jean-François, 55–56
Martinique, 19, 122
Mascarene Islands, 19, 23, 48
masculine identity, 66, 67, 72–73, 109, 168, 218–21, 227
Maurepas, Jean-Frédéric Phélypeaux, comte de, 34–35, 186
médecins philosophes: on collective moral reform, 163; on human organism as "sensible body," 115, 119, 120–21, 123; on hygiene, 127–29, 267–68n73, 268n75; on military medicine, 56, 115, 121–22, 127–29
Medical Revolution, 123, 123–27
medical science: in *ancien régime*, 56, 126; development of, 17–18; and health as commodity, 121; and hygiene, 127–28, 267–68n73; philosophical medicine, 119; publications of, 24; and religious ideology, 126; and *sensibilité*, 117, 119–20, 123, 127, 128–29; and tropical medicine, 56. *See also* military medicine

Melfort, Louis Drummond, comte de, 88–89, 134, 137
Mercier, Louis-Sébastien, 73, 142, 168–70, 181, 214
Mesnil-Durand, François Jean de Graindorge d'Orgeville, baron de, 39, 40–41
"middle ground," 21, 98, 101, 104, 224–25, 248n78, 261–62n117
militaires philosophes: assertion of knowledge, 46–48; on citizenship, 172; on cultural matters, 42–45, 49, 50; on desertion, 142; on esprit de corps, 86–87, 194, 205; and ethnic "Others," 98–101; on Eurocentric stereotypes, 67; and French Revolution, 196; on heroism, 156, 161, 196; and humanity in war, 113, 146–47, 196; on martial matters, 39–42; on military penal code, 144; and military psychology, 131–38; and Napoleon, 218, 224–25; and rape, 150; relationship to empire, 20–21, 45–51, 98–99, 104, 107, 146–48; role of, 27–28, 36–45, 83; and *sensibilité*, 113, 131, 132, 146–47, 196; and sociability, 98, 101, 102–3, 104, 105, 109, 196, 202, 232–33; writings of, 38–47, 54
military academies, 16–17, 30, 185
military cafés, 62
military culture: and Freemason lodges, 63; and heroism, 157; of human rights, 127; and Napoleon, 218, 220, 222; *philosophes* on, 67, 115; public opinion of, 12, 18, 67, 115; and *sensibilité*, 113, 115, 117–18, 140, 198
military efficacy, 16–17, 27, 30, 39–40, 55, 76
military enlightenment: adaptations of continental frameworks of, 20; concept of, 2, 3, 11, 241n2; influence of science and mathematics on, 18; national versions of, 12; as transhistorical process, 4, 12, 22, 231
Military Enlightenment: and colonial power, 18–22, 23; continuity of, 230–32, 285n1; and definition of war, 7–8; eclecticism of, 22; and emotion and war, 138, 233; and *esprit philosophique*, 2, 4, 11, 18, 28, 39, 242–43n12; and forms of communication, 2–3, 57; and human progress, 2; legacy of, 24; military historians on, 3–4; reforms of, 16; and sociability, 67, 76, 109; successors of, 230; values of, 4, 8–9, 11, 26–27, 228–29, 231, 233–34, 235, 236–37, 239–40. See also French Military Enlightenment
military friendship: and *fraternité*, 194, 202–5; and Freemason lodges, 76–81; Napoleonic friendship, 66, 67, 194, 221–22

military humanism, of Renaissance, 7–8, 11
military intellectualism, 36–45
military journals, 58–60, 255nn81, 85
military medicine: and advances of Medical Revolution, 123–27; and ambulatory hospital service, 124–25; and autopsies, 124; and cosmopolitanism, 123, 266n51; and French armed forces' fighting conditions, 122–23; and French Revolution, 198–99; and hospital treatment, 121–22; and hygiene, 121, 126, 127–30, 131; improvements in treatment, 194; journals of, 60; *médecins philosophes* on, 56, 115, 121–22, 127–29; and medical academies, 60; and moral sentiments, 9; and reform efforts, 29, 34, 60, 123; and sanitation, 126; and state military hospital system, 125–26; and surgery, 124, 125, 237; and triage system, 125
military penal code (crime and punishment): for desertion, 18, 57, 115, 140, 141, 142–44, 150, 169–70, 202; and gendered humiliation, 208; and honor, 190, 199; and human rights, 138–45, 150, 271nn141, 142; justice and effectiveness of, 141, 149–50, 199, 271n127; for Nancy Affair, 216; and public opinion, 115, 141–43, 145
military psychology: and conditions of camp life, 133–38, 268n64; and emotions, 131–33, 134, 135, 137, 138, 142, 232, 233, 239, 269n86; and French Revolution, 199; and happiness, 131, 134, 135, 136, 138, 205; and *médecins philosophes*, 115, 119, 131
military romanticism, 11, 94, 231
military songs, 24, 94, 101, 164, 171, 205, 221, 227
mixed-race people (*gens de couleur*), 106, 149, 212, 214, 272n163, 283nn55, 57
le monde (social elite), 64, 71–73, 82, 90
Mons, siege of (1691), 67–68
Montaigne, Michel de, 92, 99, 160
Montaut, chevalier de, 87, 136, 232
Montcalm, Louis-Joseph de, 46, 101
Montecuccoli, Raimondo, count of, 39, 130
Montesquieu, Charles-Louis de Secondat, baron de, 31, 42, 54, 133, 163, 164
moral philosophy: and heroism, 156, 160; and *philosophes* on war, 54; of *sensibilité*, 8–9, 10, 112, 113, 141; of sociability, 67, 75, 76, 79–80, 109; and *société militaire*, 84

Napoleon Bonaparte (emperor of the French): on citizen-soldiers, 218–19; and

INDEX

conflicts of imperial conquest, 193; Egyptian campaign, 19, 223, 224–26; establishment of Consulate, 195; establishment of military education, 41; fall of, 11; and French Military Enlightenment, 217, 218, 221, 222; imperialism of, 219, 222–23, 225–26; militarizing process of, 194, 218–20, 222; and military culture, 218, 220, 222; military education of, 196, 217–18; and military identity, 194–95, 196, 220; as military intellectual, 37; and narrative of French Revolution, 207; nationalist and militarist propaganda system of, 66; overthrow of Directory, 195; and prestige of military action, 6; and Raynal, 19; and reconstruction of officer corps, 201; slash and burn philosophy of, 227–28; and slavery, 149, 226–27; and territorial gains for France, 20; and universal principles of war, 230; veterans' reflections on, 65–66

Napoleonic friendship, 66, 67, 194, 221–22
National Guard, 191, 202, 215–16
nationalism, 12, 16, 164, 190, 191, 219
natural law, 9, 10, 83, 84, 109, 142–43, 209
neo-Stoic doctrine, 7–8, 9, 132
Newton, Isaac, 17, 37, 42
Nine Years' War (1688–1697), 6, 13, 76
Noailles, Adrien Maurice, duc de, 110–11, 112
nobility and noblemen: and battle of Fontenoy, 153, 155; and epistolary communication, 61; and honor, 68, 70, 73, 133, 256nn11, 13, 257n27; and hygiene, 268n75; Napoleon's reestablishment of titles, 219, 222, 223; and *noblesse du coeur*, 8; transnational culture of, 12, 70
noble military officers: and absentee officers, 259n73; and Bourbon family politics, 91; and commodification of ennoblement, 14–15, 16, 71; corruption of, 71–72, 73, 200; cosmopolitanism of, 12, 108; creation of *noblesse militaire*, 30, 31, 33; degeneration of, 70–71; gentlemanly cartels of, 9–10; and heroism, 157, 158–59; and hygiene, 129, 268n75; and Louis XIV, 67–68, 70; mass emigration of 1791, 195, 200, 201, 217; military education of, 268n75; and military intellectualism, 37–38; and military reform, 33–34, 37, 38, 41, 136; mobility of, 12, 33, 50; refinement and civility of, 68, 69, 70, 256nn11, 13; and Ségur Law of 1781, 190; subaltern officers,

16, 33, 64, 71, 74, 75, 79, 81, 88, 91, 129, 134, 136, 166–67, 169, 171, 200, 201; and system of *privilèges*, 14, 196, 200, 217
noblesse d'épée (nobility of the sword), 3, 36, 71–72, 78, 113, 138, 156, 159, 257n17
noblesse du coeur (nobility of the heart), 8, 113, 115, 134
Noël, Joseph-Louis-Gabriel, 204
North American colonies: French armed forces' fighting conditions in, 122–23; French interests in, 19, 20, 21, 22, 23; and *militaires philosophes*, 147–48; *sensibilité* discourses in, 147–48; and sociability, 99–101, 105, 109; and *société militaire*, 97

offensive à outrance (all-out attack), 237–38
Opéra-Comique, Paris, 90, 170
opéra comique genre, 91–93, 142, 170
orientalism, 186–87, 225
"Others": Eurocentric stereotypes of, 20, 46, 47–48, 50, 67, 98, 105, 115, 147, 148, 234–35; and heroism, 157; martial alliances with, 10–11, 106–7, 261n111, 262n125; and *militaires philosophes*, 98–101; and orientalism, 186–87, 225; and sociability, 97–107, 109. See also race and racism
Ovid, 94, 128

Paris Commune (1870–1871), 193
Pâris de Meyzieu, Jean-Baptiste, 30, 31
Paris Hôtel-Dieu hospital, 121–22
Pascal, Blaise, 52–53
paternalism, 70, 88, 89
patriotism: colonial patriotism, 187–88; culture of, 163–64, 191; discourse of, 16; and French Revolution, 203, 205, 206; and heroism, 157, 162–66, 168, 170, 171, 172–73; and Napoleon, 219, 220; and race, 145–47, 184; and *sensibilité*, 150, 166, 181, 183, 208; in Seven Years' War, 57, 163; and women, 174, 180, 181, 182, 183, 209
Pawlet de Caumartin, chevalier de, 81
peace: and pacifism, 53, 54; perpetual peace, 5, 192–93, 229, 240; and phases of intensified conflict, 6; year of peace, 215
Petit, Émilien, 187–88
philosophes: on citizenship, 172; and Freemason lodges, 63; on heroism, 156, 158, 161, 196; on human rights, 139; on military culture, 67, 115; on military penal code, 142; on military subjects, 54–55; on patriotism, 164. See also *médecins philosophes*; *militaires philosophes*

INDEX

Pillai, Ananda Ranga, 103–4, 183, 262n123
Plutarch, 39, 56, 181
Poissonnier-Desperrières, Antoine, 56, 126–27
Polybius, 37, 39
Pompadour, marquise de (née Jeanne-Antoinette Poisson), 29, 30, 31, *32*, 35, 41, 105
Pondicherry, 102, 104, 105, 183
power, cultures of, 5, 21
Pragmatic Army, 110–11, 112
Prague, siege of (1742), 121
Protestants, 159, 185
Prussia, 14, 15, 36, 37, 113
public opinion: of military culture, 12, 18, 67, 115; of military penal code, 115, 141–43, 145; on military subjects, 56–57; and Napoleon, 220
public sphere/domestic sphere, 174–75, 180
Pufendorf, Samuel von, 83, 84, 109
Puységur, Jacques-François de Chastenet, marquis de, 39–40

Quarrel of the Ancients and Moderns, 2, 10
Quincy, Joseph Sevin, comte de, 68, 73

race and racism: and citizenship, 157; and heroism, 184, 194; and military service, 107, 207, 211–12, 224, 234–35; and mixed-race people (*gens de couleur*), 106, 149, 212, 214, 272n163; and Napoleon, 226–27; and racial egalitarianism, 147, 272n152; in Saint Domingue, 106, 109, 145–47, 187–88, 189; theories of race, 98, 106–8; and white *sensibilité*, 146. *See also* free people of color; "Others"
Raimond, Julien, 212, 214
rational scientific inquiry, 37, 39, 241n3
Raynal, Guillaume-Thomas, 18–19, 46, 214
régimes de vivre (regimes of life), 115, 128
religious ideology: and medical science, 126; and military penal code, 143, 144; and religious intolerance, 139, 159, 185; and Te Deum mass, 151–52, 153, 156
Renaissance, 7–8, 11
Revolutionary and Napoleonic Wars (1792–1815), 5, 12, 43, 193–95, 231. *See also* French Revolution (1789–1799)
Richelieu, Louis-François-Armand de Vignerot du Plessis, duc de, 13, 29, 100, 150
Roannais, Louis d'Aubusson de la Feuillade, duc de, 68, 70

Rochambeau, Jean-Baptiste Donatien de Vimeur, comte de, 49, 78, 108, 148–49
Rocoux, battle of, 93–94, 97, 221
romanticism, 230, 231
Rougé, Pierre-François, marquis de, 113, *114*
Rousseau, Jean-Baptiste, 160–61
Rousseau, Jean-Jacques: on desertion, 142; and Guibert, 42; on hygiene of nobles, 268n75; literary works of, 37, 113; and *militaires philosophes*, 47; and Napoleon, 218; on patriotism, 163, 172, 174; on *sensibilité*, 8, 80, 113, 264n13; Turpin de Crissé's correspondence with, 45; on war, 5, 54
Rozoi, Barnabé Farmin de, 181–82, 183, 208, 209, 227, 277n81
Russel, lieutenant colonel, 40, 103, 104, 105, 109, 147

Sade, Donatien Alphonse François, marquis de, 43–44
Saint-Domingue: and abolitionism, 149; Chasseurs volontaires d'Amérique of, 22, 106–7, 146–47, 149, 189; and Freemason lodges, 80; as French colony, 19, 22, 145; and French Revolution, 214; and heroism, 184, 187; and humanity in war, 145–46; and mixed-race people (*gens de couleur*), 212, 214; and Napoleon, 226–27; and patriotism, 189; *sensibilité* discourses in, 145–46; slave uprisings in, 214–15; social tensions in, 106–7, 109; and theater, 173; writings of French officers serving in, 22, 23
sainte travestie (cross-dressed saint), 178, 179, 180
Saint-Georges, chevalier de, 212, *213*, 214
Saint-Germain, Claude-Louis, comte de, *33*, 143, 144–45, 149–50, 193, 271n142
Saint-Pierre, Charles-Irénée Castel, abbé de, 4, 162, 165, 192, 240
Salic Law, 174, 182
salons: art salons, 165; as conversational military spaces, 11, 37, 38, 42, 57, 61–62, 63; and human progress, 259n60; ideology of, 82; and military friendship, 76; and reciprocal communication, 84; and sociability, 82, 84, 109, 259n60
Sand, George, 192–93
Sartine, Antoine de, 59–60
Saxe, Maurice de: and battle of Fontenoy, 152–53; campaigns of, 40; on citizen armies, 54; on compassion, 117–18; on

INDEX

conditions of camp life, 117–18, 138, 190; and Marc-Pierre d'Argenson, 30; on docile soldierly body and disciplinary power, 116–17, 119; and eloquence competition, 165; foreign troops of, 185, 186, 187; and Freemason lodges, 77; free people of color and slaves in regiment of, 185–87; on hope, 135, 136; on human heart, 42, 118–19, 129–31, 232, 233; and humanity in war, 113, 115, 130, 138, 150; military identity of, 220; on military system, 23–24, 37, 47, 116; on military tactics, 41, 57–58, 130–31, 240; portrait of, 96; and Scharnhorst, 231; and *sensibilité*, 113, 115, 117–18, 123, 127, 129–31, 205; in Sergent's portraits, 25; and sociability, 67, 109, 130; and term *pauvre*, 117–18; and *théâtre de guerre*, 90, 91, 92–94, 97, 109, 170, 227, 261nn103, 104; on universal military service, 135; and Villars, 61; and Volontaires de Saxe, 185–87; and War of Austrian Succession, 25, 90–91

Second Estate, 30, 71, 153, 242n9. *See also* nobility and noblemen; noble military officers

Second Franco-Mexican War (1861–1867), 193

Second Italian War of Independence, 193

Second Opium War in China (1856–1860), 193

secular humanism, 53

secular liberalism, 241n3

Ségur, Louis-Philippe, comte de, 78, 143–44, 200

Ségur, Philippe Henri, marquis de, 33, 60

Ségur Law of 1781, 190

Senegal, 20, 46

sensibilité (sensibility): cult of sentiment, 8–9, 10, 11, 37, 113, 229; and *fraternité*, 203; and French civilizing mission, 145; and French military men, 22, 169; Guibert on, 42; and humanitarian reforms, 109, 115, 119, 132; and humanity in war, 113, 115, 119–21, 123, 126, 127, 140, 150; and human organism as "sensible body," 115, 119–23; and human rights, 138, 139; and international law, 236; military culture of, 113, 115, 117–18, 140, 198; and military friendship, 194, 205; and military penal code, 142, 143, 145, 199; and military psychology, 131–38, 237; moral culture of, 109; moral philosophy of, 8–9, 10, 112, 113, 141; and Napoleon, 221, 222, 224, 227; in Saint-Domingue, 145–46; and sociability, 75; and *soldats sensibles*, 115, 127–31, 190; and women, 181, 209

Sergent, Antoine Louis François, 25–26, 27, 28, *104*

Servan de Gerbey, Joseph, 54, 142–43, 172

Service historique de la défense (SHD), 20, 22, 23, 60

Seven Years' War (1756–1764): and culture of war, 5; desertions during, 140; and humanity in war, 150; losses of, 15–16, 19–20, 164, 165, 170; and military medicine, 121, 122, 126; and newspapers, 58; opening battles of, 52; and patriotism, 57, 163; and sociability, 101, 105, 262n117; and Te Deum mass, 156

slavery: and American Revolutionary War, 148–49, 272n163; French interests in, 19, 22; French laws concerning, 186, 215, 226, 278n88; and humanity in war, 148–49; and *militaire philosophes*, 50, 145; and Napoleon, 149, 226–27; treatises against, 139

smallpox, 121, 123, 126

sociability: and American Revolutionary War, 107–9; and Amerindian tribes, 99–101, 261n111, 261–62n117; Diderot on, 75–76; and diplomacy, 98–108, 145; and epistolary communication, 61; and Freemason lodges, 63–64, 78; and French Revolution, 202, 203; and humanity, 12, 75; and *militaires philosophes*, 98, 101, 102–3, 104, 105, 109, 196, 202, 232–33; moral philosophy of, 67, 75, 76, 79–80, 109; and Napoleon, 221, 222, 223, 224; and nobility, 70, 73; and patriotism, 166; and relations between soldiers, 66, 67, 74, 205; relationship to empire, 98–108, 261–62n117, 262nn123, 125; and salons, 82, 84, 109, 259n60; unifying nature of, 10, 89–90

social class: in French army, 30, 41, 54, 66, 67–68, 70, 71, 74–75, 76, 90, 108, 109, 190, 200, 203–4, 257n17; and heroism, 156, 157; and hygiene, 128–29; and medical treatment in battle, 124–25; and *le monde*, 64, 71–73, 82, 90; and sociability, 80, 81, 90, 258n51. *See also* commoners (*roturiers*); noble military officers

Société des amis des noirs (Society of the Friends of Blacks), 149

300   INDEX

société militaire (military society or community): and collective culture, 67, 86–87, 260n83; and communication, 88–90; and equality, 84–85, 259n72; and functional utility of subordination, 84–85, 109, 259n72; and group solidarity, 66, 67, 76, 82, 87; and Napoleon, 218; and sociability, 82–84, 85, 86, 87, 97–109, 260n85; *théâtre de guerre*, 90, 91–94, 97, 261nn103, 104
Société royale de médecine, 124
Society of the Cincinnati, 108–9, 149
Socrates, 39, 160
Spain, 14, 19, 21, 192
Suffren, Pierre Andre de, *104*
Switzerland, 185, 260n83

taxation, in France, 13–14, 16, 30, 246n49
Tenon, Jacques, 121–22
theater: and desertion, 142–43; and gender norms, 175; and heroism, 150, 157, 166, 167–74, 176, 177, 182–83, 196; portrayals of women in, 174, 175–77, 180–82; and royal propaganda, 273n12; *théâtre de guerre*, 90, 91–94, 97, 170, 261nn103, 104; and war, 28
théâtre de la foire, 91–92
Théâtre du Maréchal de Saxe à Bruxelles, 93, *95*
Third Estate, 70, 157, 196, 242n9. *See also* commoners (*roturiers*)
Thirty Years' War (1618–1648), 8
Thomas, Antoine Léonard, 165–66, 174, 181
Tipu Sultan, 103, 147
Toussaint-Louverture, François-Dominique, 214–15
Treaty and Conventions of Brandebourg, 113, *114*
Treaty of Aix-la-Chapelle, 38
Treaty of Paris of 1763, 16, 19, 52
Treaty of Rastatt (1714), 71
Treaty of Tilsit (1807), 220
Treaty of Westphalia, 9
Trochu, Louis-Jules, 232, 233
Truguet, Laurent Jean-François, comte de, 149, 226–27
Turenne, Henri de la Tour d'Auvergne, vicomte de, 39, 128, 165
Turin, siege of (1640), 26
Turin, siege of (1706), 68
Turkey, 237
Turpin de Crissé et de Sanzay, Lancelot, comte, 37, 39–40, 45, 54, 63, 150, 161

United Nations, 139, 238
U.S. Army, 37, 235, 238

U.S. humanitarian interventions, 238
U.S. Marines, 286n9
unmanned combat aerial vehicles (UCAVs), 239

Valfons, Charles de Mattei, marquis de, 136–37
Vauban, Sébastien le Prestre, marquis de, 37, 40, 71
Vegetius, 37, 39, 268n75
Verger, Jean-Baptiste-Antoine de, 49, 50
Villars, Claude-Louis-Hector de, 61, 118, 140
virtue: civic virtues, 188, 189, 278n94; and heroism, 162, 163; imperial virtue, 219, 220, 227; as noble value, 68, 73, 256n13; and patriotism, 163
Voltaire: on battle of Fontenoy, 153, 155–56, 158, 159; and Marc-Pierre d'Argenson, 29, 153; René-Louis d'Argenson's correspondence with, 1–2; on France's military losses, 16; and Guibert, 42; on Jeanne d'Arc, 177, 178–79; on Lally, 106; on martial prowess, 54; on military penal code, 143, 144; as *philosophe*, 63; publications of, 58; as royal historiographer, 29; on Saint-Pierre's pacifism, 193; on *sensibilité*, 119; on siege of Prague, 121; on war, 2, 5, 51–52, 53, 56–57, 239
von Clausewitz, Carl, 68
von Closen, baron Ludwig, 49, 50, 149
von Haller, Albrecht, 120, 124

war: costs of, 240; cultural study of, 22, 249n80; cultures of, 4–6, 16, 21, 24, 37, 66, 67–68, 70, 71–72; debates on, 1–3, 12, 13, 16, 26, 27–28, 53–54, 56–57, 168; and *esprit philosophe*, 4, 45–51, 98, 242–43n12; and good war, 7–12; just war theory, 7, 244n27; and limited war, 15, 247n59; metadiscourse on, 3, 6, 9; and military humanism, 7–8, 11; "perfecting" of, 18; publications on art of war, 38–40; restraint in warfare, 7–8, 9, 245n35; and Sergent's portraits, 25, 26; stigmatization of, 273–74n15; total war, 193, 239, 279n4; universal principles of, 4, 7, 17, 39–41, 64, 230. *See also* humanity in war; *and specific wars*
War of Austrian Succession (1740–1748): and battle of Dettingen, 110–11, 112; and conscription, 134; and culture of war, 5, 16; desertions during, 140, 142; and d'Estaing, 20; and foreign troops, 185; and Freemason lodges, 77; and military agenda, 90; and

military medicine, 126; and military penal code, 141; military performance in, 15, 247n59; and military reforms, 30; and newspapers, 58; and Saxe, 25, 90–91
War of Spanish Succession (1701–1714): and aristocratic ethos, 68, 70; desertions during, 140; and heroism, 160; and military expenditures, 6; and military medicine, 123, 125; political aims of, 15; Watteau's paintings of, 53–54; and women's military service, 179
Wars of Religion (1562–1598), 8
wars on terrorism, 238–39
Washington, George, 49, 108, 170, 278n83
Watteau, Jean-Antoine, 53–54
West Africa, 19, 23
Westlake, John, 228–29
women: advocating abolishing death penalty for deserters, 18, 57, 144; and assumed male identity, 175, 178, 179, 182, 209–10; and citizenship, 174, 177, 180, 207–8, 209, 211; collective biographies of, 180; and corruption of white male colonists, 106; and epistolary communication, 61; and heroinism, 157, 174, 180–81, 182, 183, 194, 210, 227; and hygiene of noble women, 268n75; of Iroquois Confederacy, 101; Laclos on education of, 43; military agency of, 174–76, 181–82, 183; military service of, 22, 175, 178–80, 186, 207, 208–11, 233, 235, 277n73, 286n9; and novels of worldliness, 53, 71; and patriotism, 174, 180, 181, 182, 183, 209; and rape, 150, 194, 227, 285n94; and salons, 18, 57, 82, 259n60; and *sensibilité*, 181, 209; at siege of Mons, 68; worldliness associated with, 72–73, 109
worldliness, 53, 64, 71, 72–73, 109, 253n60
World War I, 237, 238
World War II, 139, 235, 237, 239

Xenophon, 39

www.ingramcontent.com/pod-product-compliance
Lightning Source LLC
Chambersburg PA
CBHW030812230426
43667CB00008B/1182